Boarding School Juliet

vol. 2

YOUSUKE KANEDA

To LOVE, or not to LOVE

To LOVE, or not to LOVE

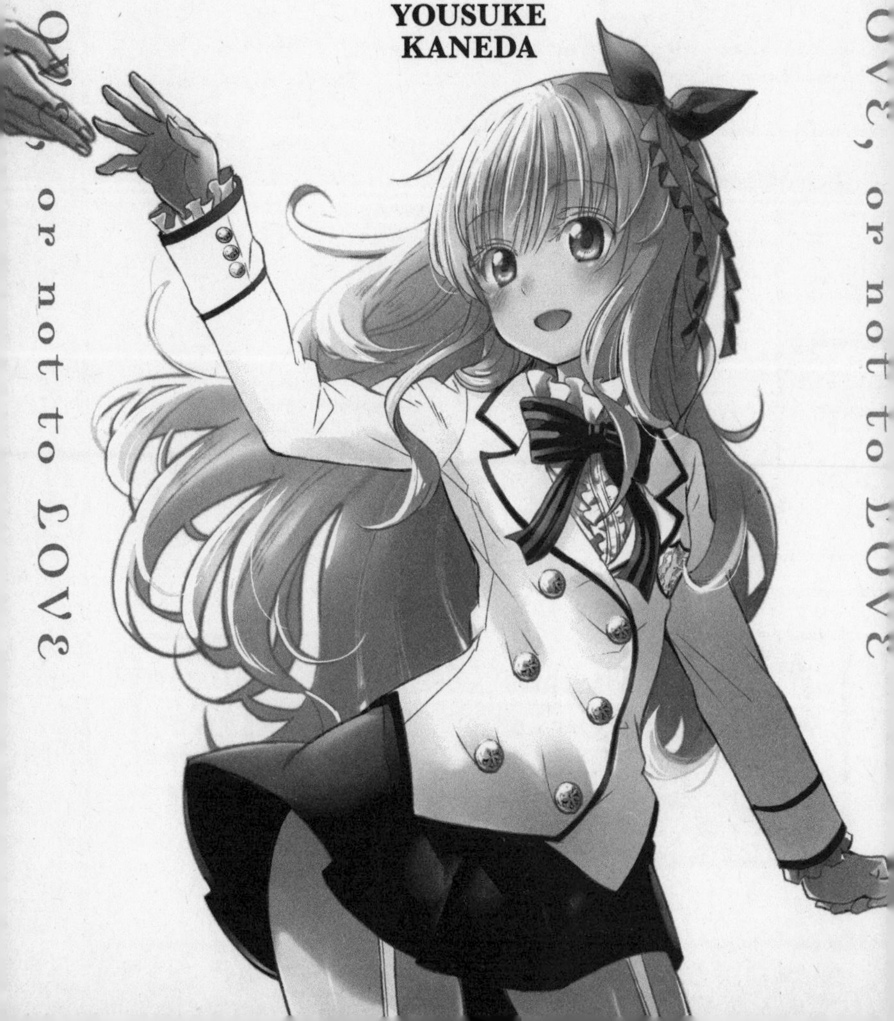

JULIET: THE PLAYERS

character

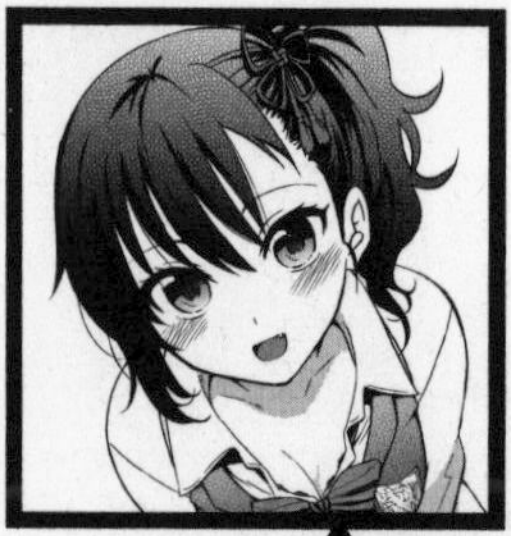

HASUKI

Inuzuka's best bud since they were little. She suspects Inuzuka might be batting for the other team.

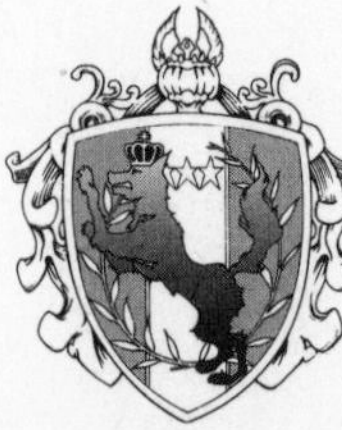

BLACK DOGGY HOUSE

(NATION OF TOUWA DORM)

BEST BUDS

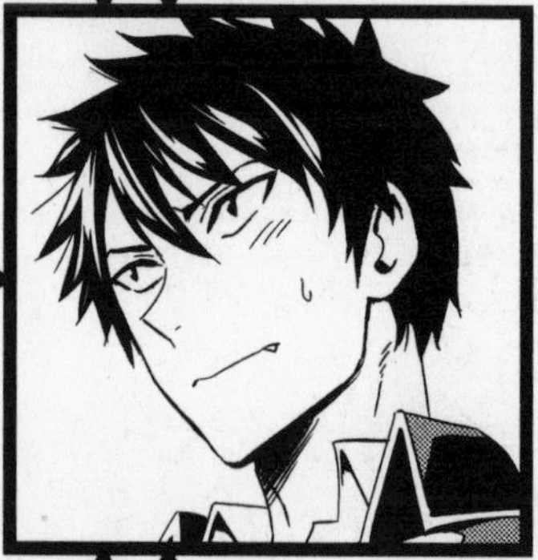

ROMIO INUZUKA

Leader of the Black Doggy first-years. All brawn and no brains. Has had one-sided feelings for Persia since forever.

ECRETLY ATING

WANTS TO KILL

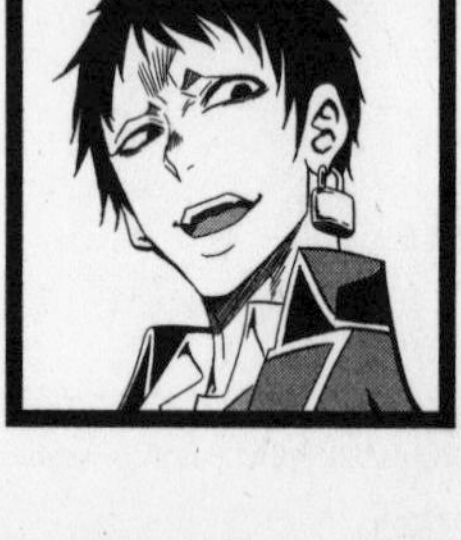

MARU

A Black Doggy outlaw. Has seen Inuzuka as an enemy ever since Inuzuka foiled his plan to defeat Persia.

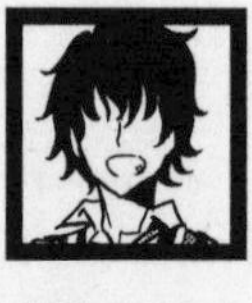

KOHITSUJI

Idiot.

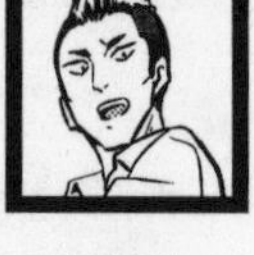

TOSA

Idiot.

BOARDING SCHOO

To LOVE, or not to LOVE

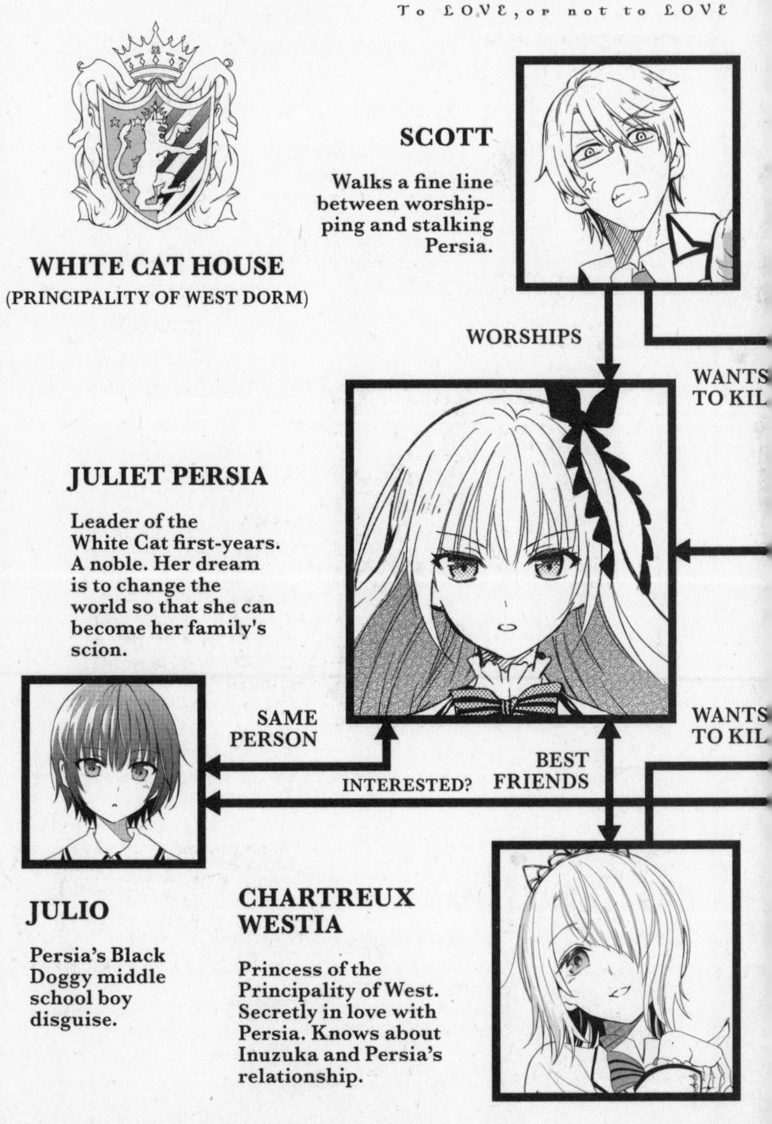

WHITE CAT HOUSE
(PRINCIPALITY OF WEST DORM)
SCOTT
Walks a fine line between worshipping and stalking Persia.
WORSHIPS
WANTS TO KIL
JULIET PERSIA
Leader of the White Cat first-years. A noble. Her dream is to change the world so that she can become her family's scion.
SAME PERSON
WANTS TO KIL
BEST FRIENDS
INTERESTED?
JULIO
Persia's Black Doggy middle school boy disguise.
CHARTREUX WESTIA
Princess of the Principality of West. Secretly in love with Persia. Knows about Inuzuka and Persia's relationship.

contents

story

At boarding school Dahlia Academy, attended by
students from two feuding countries, one first-year longs for a forbidden love.
His name: Romio Inuzuka, leader of the Black Doggy House first-years.
The apple of his eye: Juliet Persia,
leader of the White Cat House first-years.
It all begins when Inuzuka confesses his feelings to her.
This is Inuzuka and Persia's secret, star-cross'd love story...

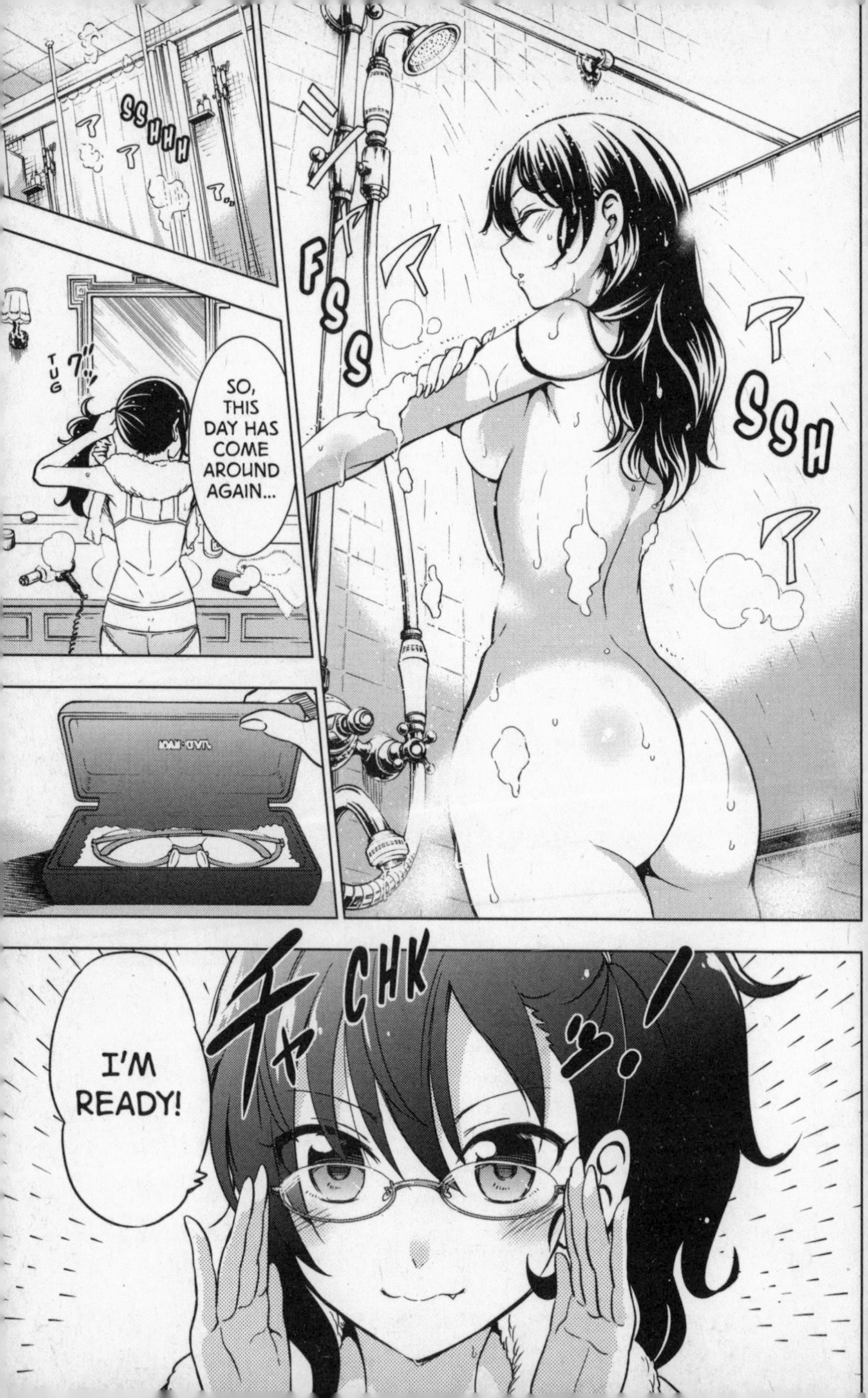
FSSS
SSH
SSHHH
TUG
SO, THIS DAY HAS COME AROUND AGAIN...
CHK
I'M READY!

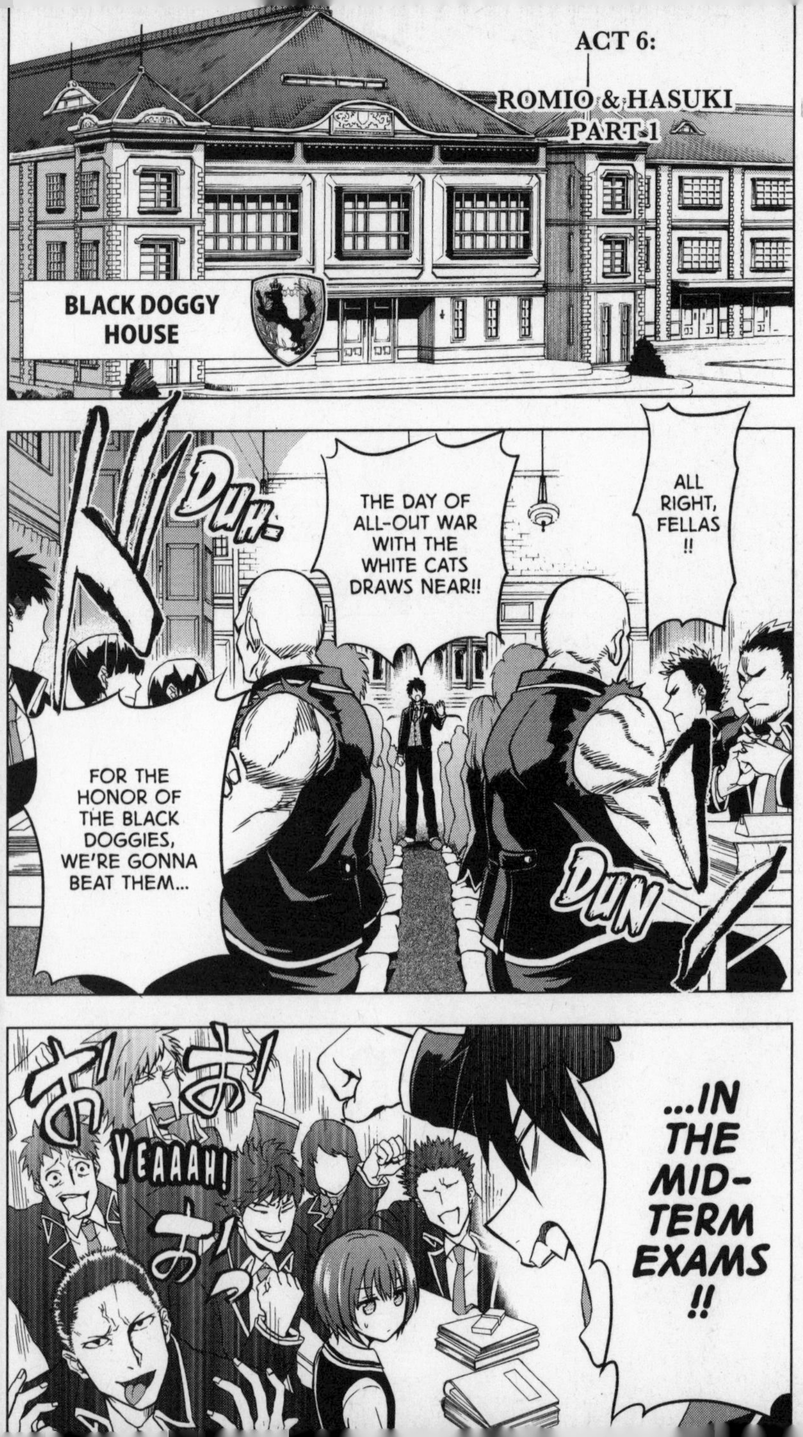

ACT 6:
ROMIO & HASUKI PART 1
BLACK DOGGY HOUSE
ALL RIGHT, FELLAS!!
THE DAY OF ALL-OUT WAR WITH THE WHITE CATS DRAWS NEAR!!
DUH-
DUN
FOR THE HONOR OF THE BLACK DOGGIES, WE'RE GONNA BEAT THEM...
...IN THE MID-TERM EXAMS!!
YEAAAH!

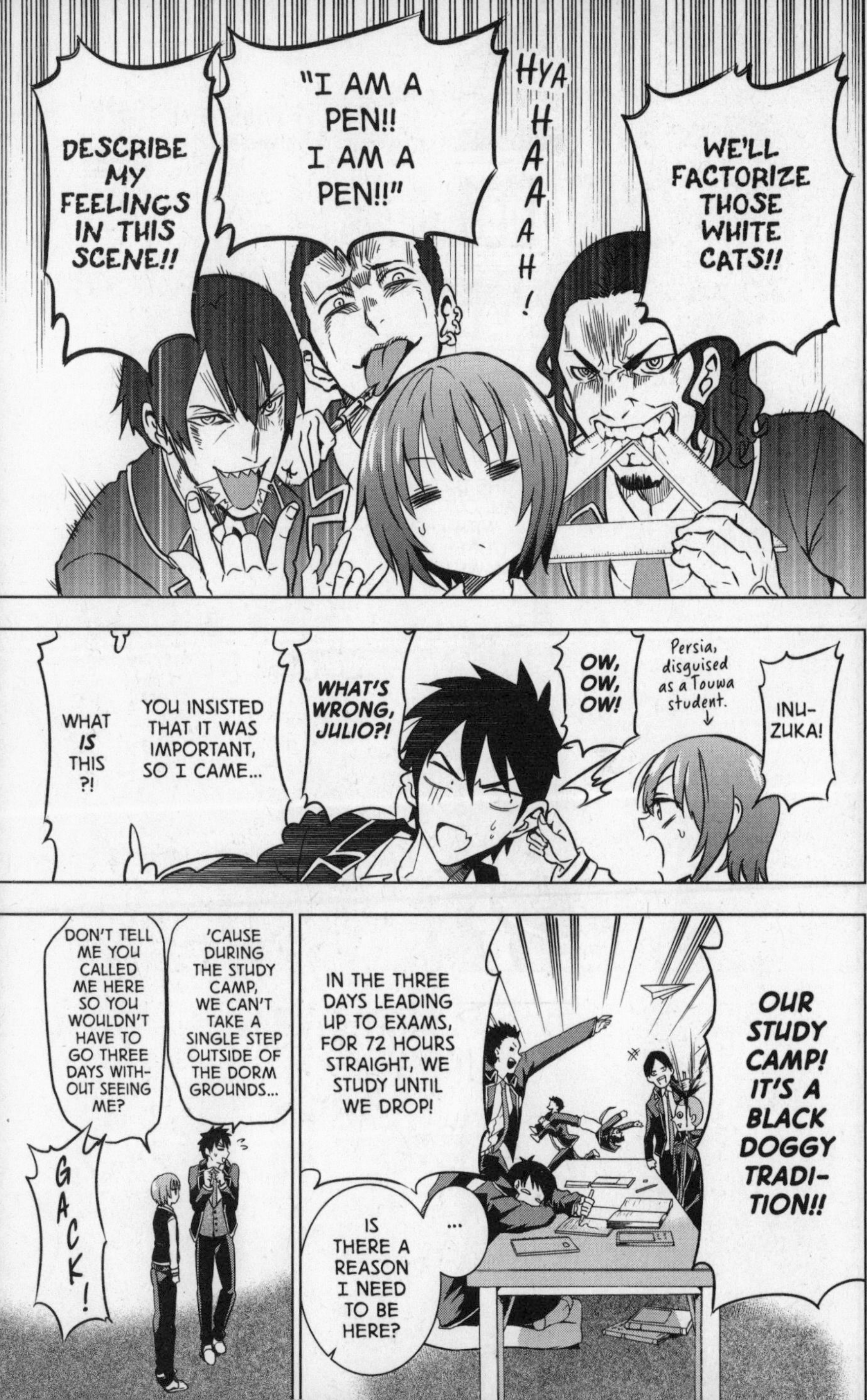
WE'LL FACTORIZE THOSE WHITE CATS!!
HYAHAAAH!
"I AM A PEN!! I AM A PEN!!"
DESCRIBE MY FEELINGS IN THIS SCENE!!
INU-ZUKA!
Persia, disguised as a Touwa student.
OW, OW, OW!
WHAT'S WRONG, JULIO?!
YOU INSISTED THAT IT WAS IMPORTANT, SO I CAME...
WHAT *IS* THIS ?!
OUR STUDY CAMP! IT'S A BLACK DOGGY TRADITION!!
IN THE THREE DAYS LEADING UP TO EXAMS, FOR 72 HOURS STRAIGHT, WE STUDY UNTIL WE DROP!
...
IS THERE A REASON I NEED TO BE HERE?
'CAUSE DURING THE STUDY CAMP, WE CAN'T TAKE A SINGLE STEP OUTSIDE OF THE DORM GROUNDS...
DON'T TELL ME YOU CALLED ME HERE SO YOU WOULDN'T HAVE TO GO THREE DAYS WITHOUT SEEING ME?
GACK!

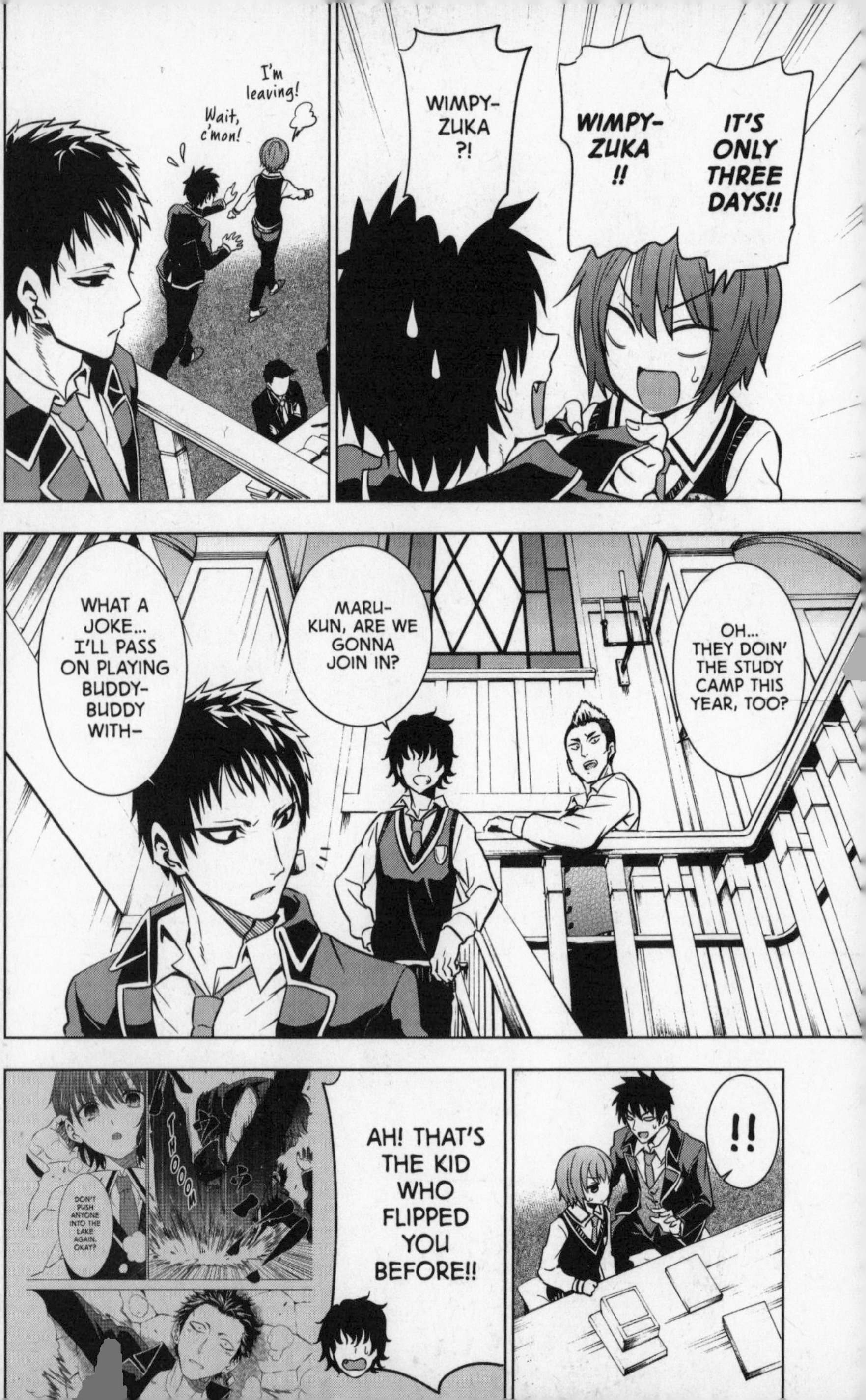
WIMPY-ZUKA!! IT'S ONLY THREE DAYS!!
WIMPY-ZUKA?!
I'm leaving!
Wait, c'mon!
OH... THEY DOIN' THE STUDY CAMP THIS YEAR, TOO?
MARU-KUN, ARE WE GONNA JOIN IN?
WHAT A JOKE... I'LL PASS ON PLAYING BUDDY-BUDDY WITH–
!!
AH! THAT'S THE KID WHO FLIPPED YOU BEFORE!!
DON'T PUSH ANYONE INTO THE LAKE AGAIN, OKAY?

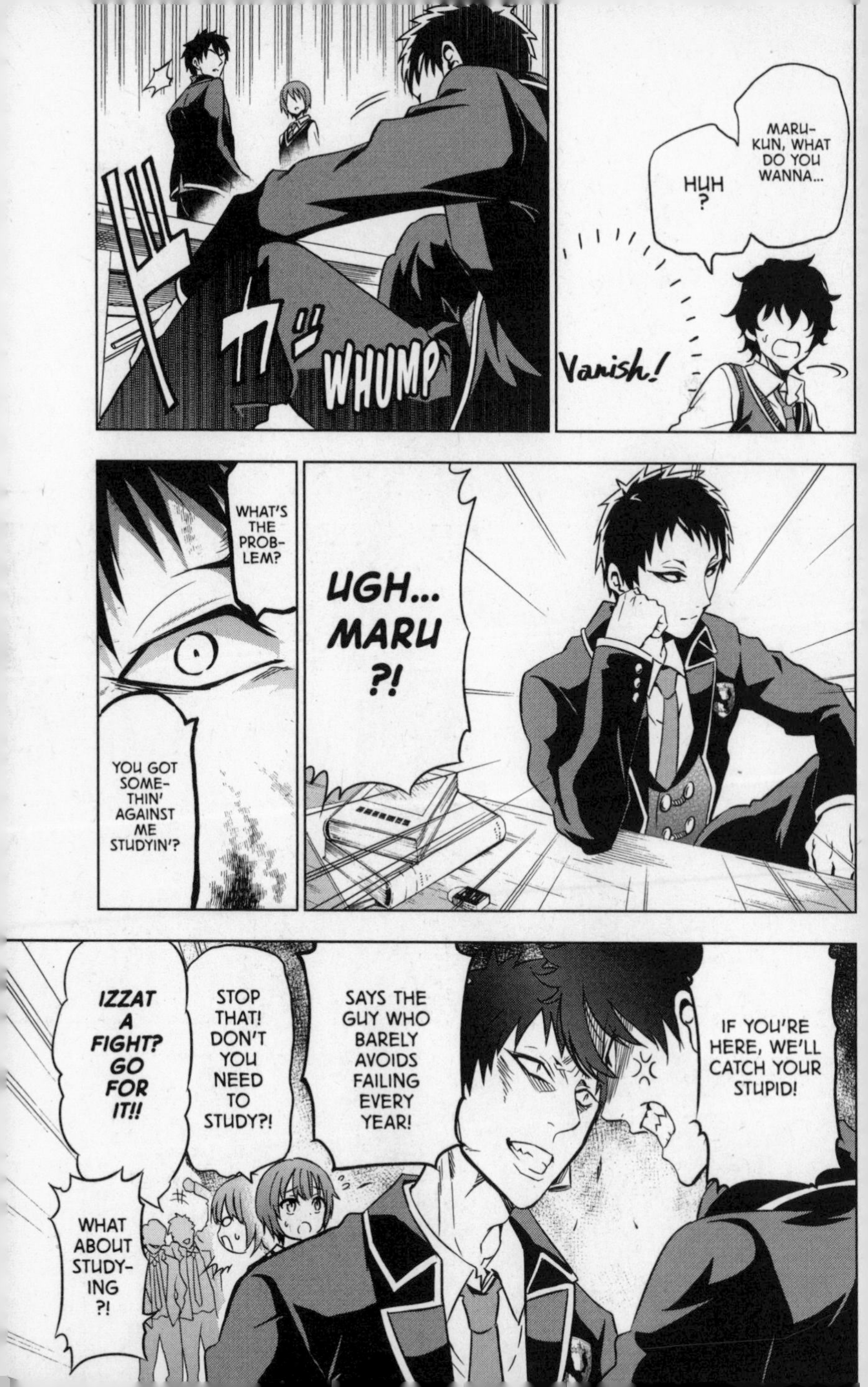
MARU-KUN, WHAT DO YOU WANNA...
HUH?
Vanish!
WHUMP
UGH... MARU?!
WHAT'S THE PROBLEM?
YOU GOT SOMETHIN' AGAINST ME STUDYIN'?
IF YOU'RE HERE, WE'LL CATCH YOUR STUPID!
SAYS THE GUY WHO BARELY AVOIDS FAILING EVERY YEAR!
STOP THAT! DON'T YOU NEED TO STUDY?!
IZZAT A FIGHT? GO FOR IT!!
WHAT ABOUT STUDYING?!

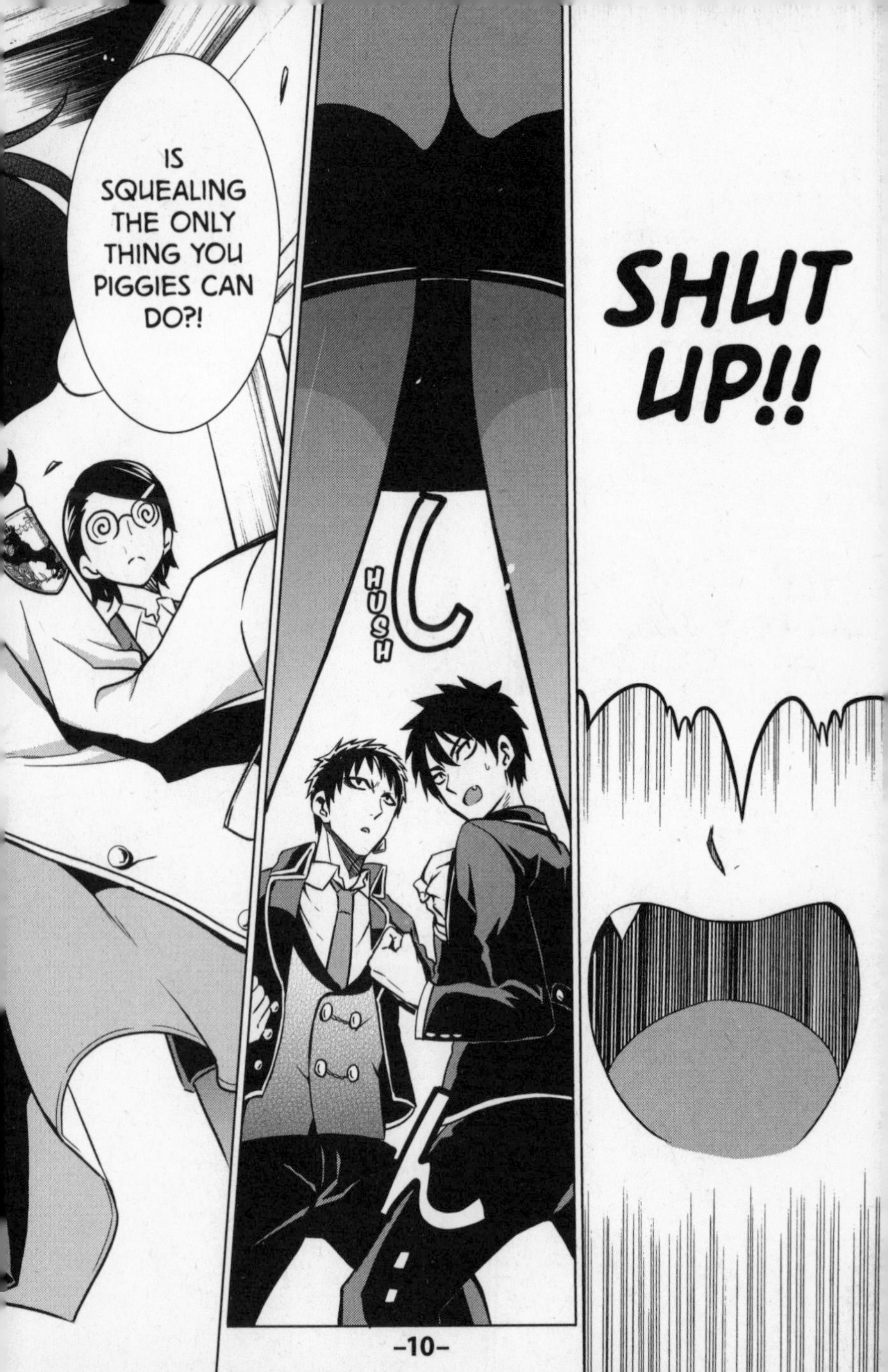
SHUT UP!!
HUSH
IS SQUEALING THE ONLY THING YOU PIGGIES CAN DO?!

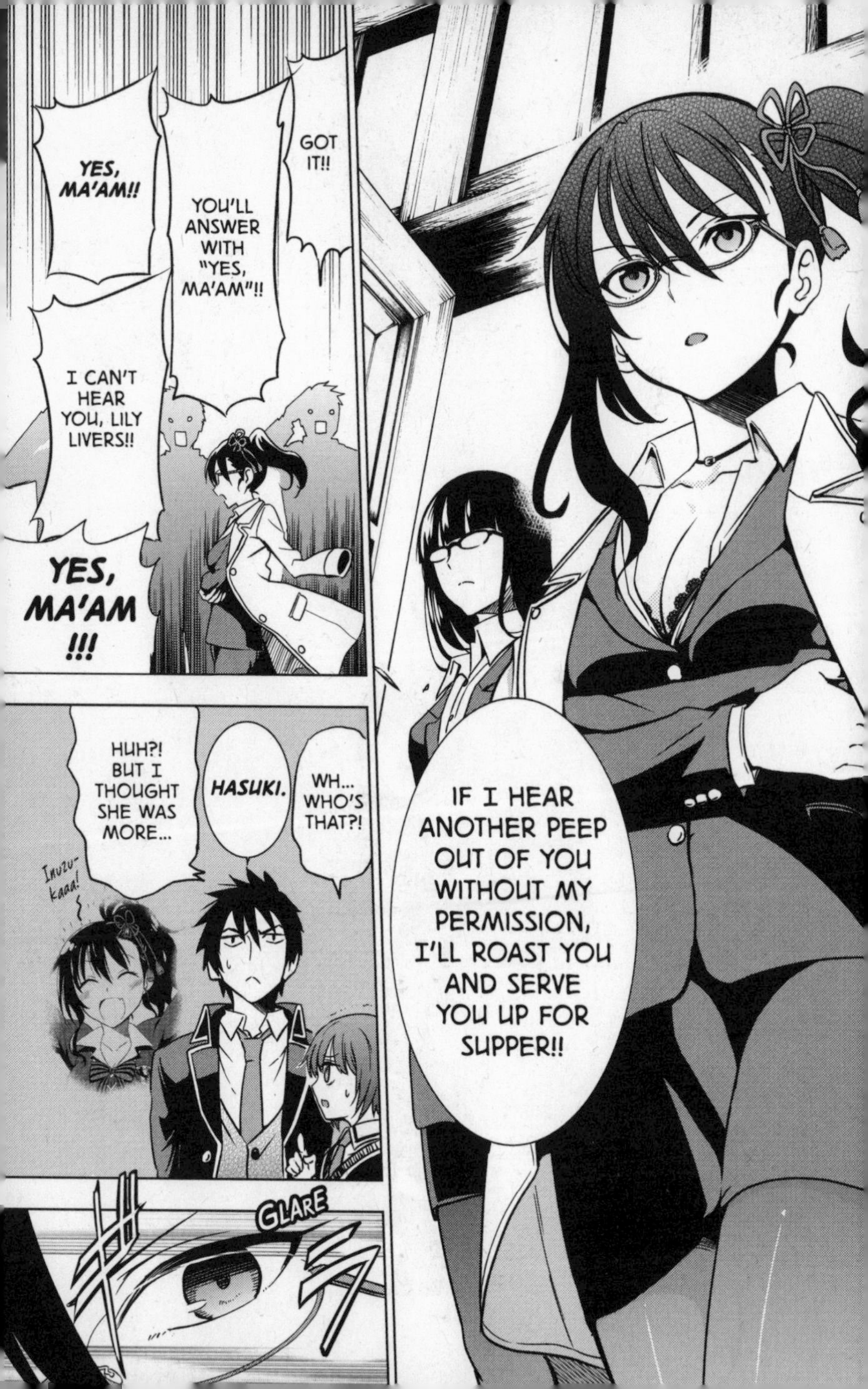
IF I HEAR ANOTHER PEEP OUT OF YOU WITHOUT MY PERMISSION, I'LL ROAST YOU AND SERVE YOU UP FOR SUPPER!!
GOT IT!!
YOU'LL ANSWER WITH "YES, MA'AM"!!
YES, MA'AM!!
I CAN'T HEAR YOU, LILY LIVERS!!
YES, MA'AM!!!
WH... WHO'S THAT?!
HASUKI.
HUH?! BUT I THOUGHT SHE WAS MORE...
Inuzu-kaaa!
GLARE

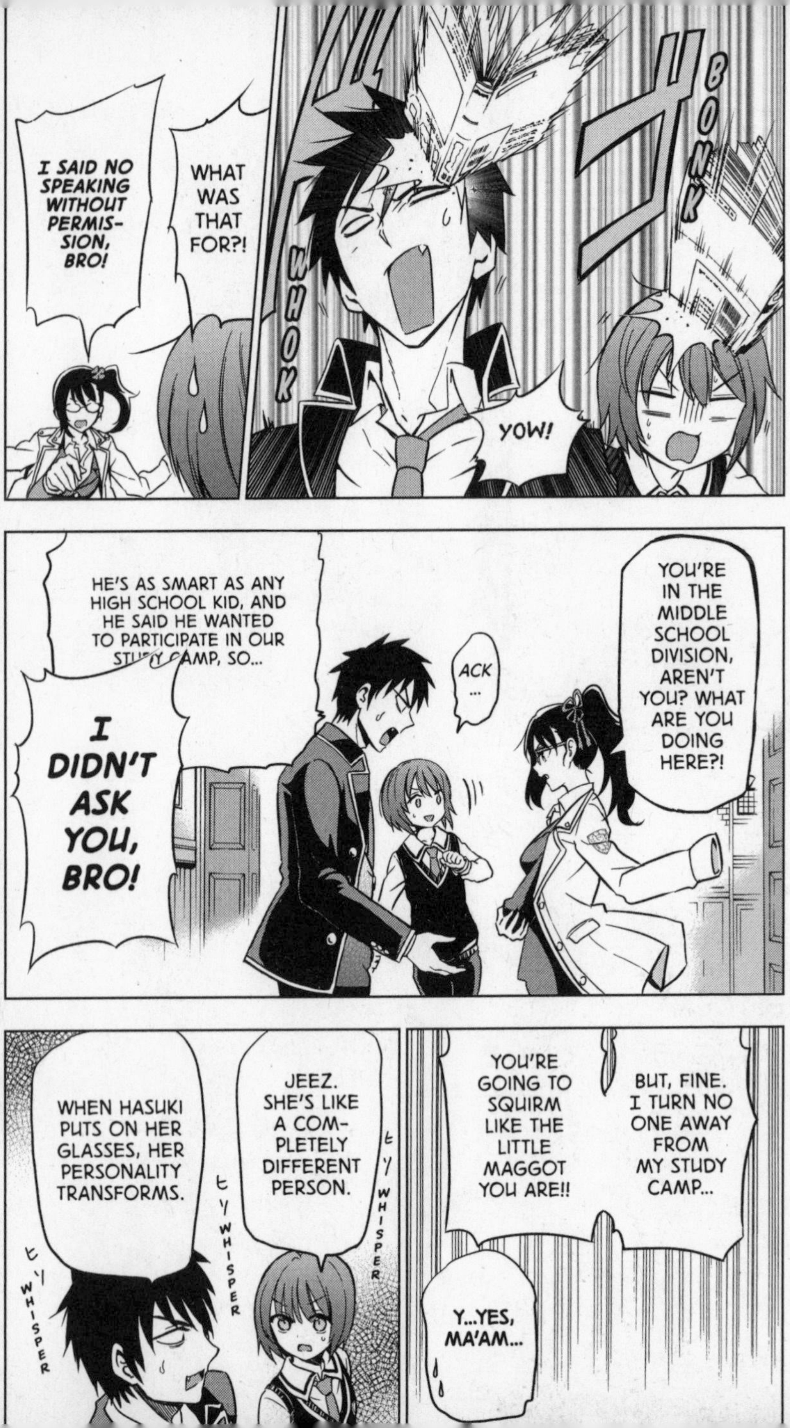
BONK
WHOK
YOW!
WHAT WAS THAT FOR?!
I SAID NO SPEAKING WITHOUT PERMIS-SION, BRO!
YOU'RE IN THE MIDDLE SCHOOL DIVISION, AREN'T YOU? WHAT ARE YOU DOING HERE?!
ACK ...
HE'S AS SMART AS ANY HIGH SCHOOL KID, AND HE SAID HE WANTED TO PARTICIPATE IN OUR STUDY CAMP, SO...
I DIDN'T ASK YOU, BRO!
BUT, FINE. I TURN NO ONE AWAY FROM MY STUDY CAMP...
YOU'RE GOING TO SQUIRM LIKE THE LITTLE MAGGOT YOU ARE!!
Y...YES, MA'AM...
ヒソ WHISPER
JEEZ. SHE'S LIKE A COM-PLETELY DIFFERENT PERSON.
ヒソ WHISPER
WHEN HASUKI PUTS ON HER GLASSES, HER PERSONALITY TRANSFORMS.
ヒソ WHISPER

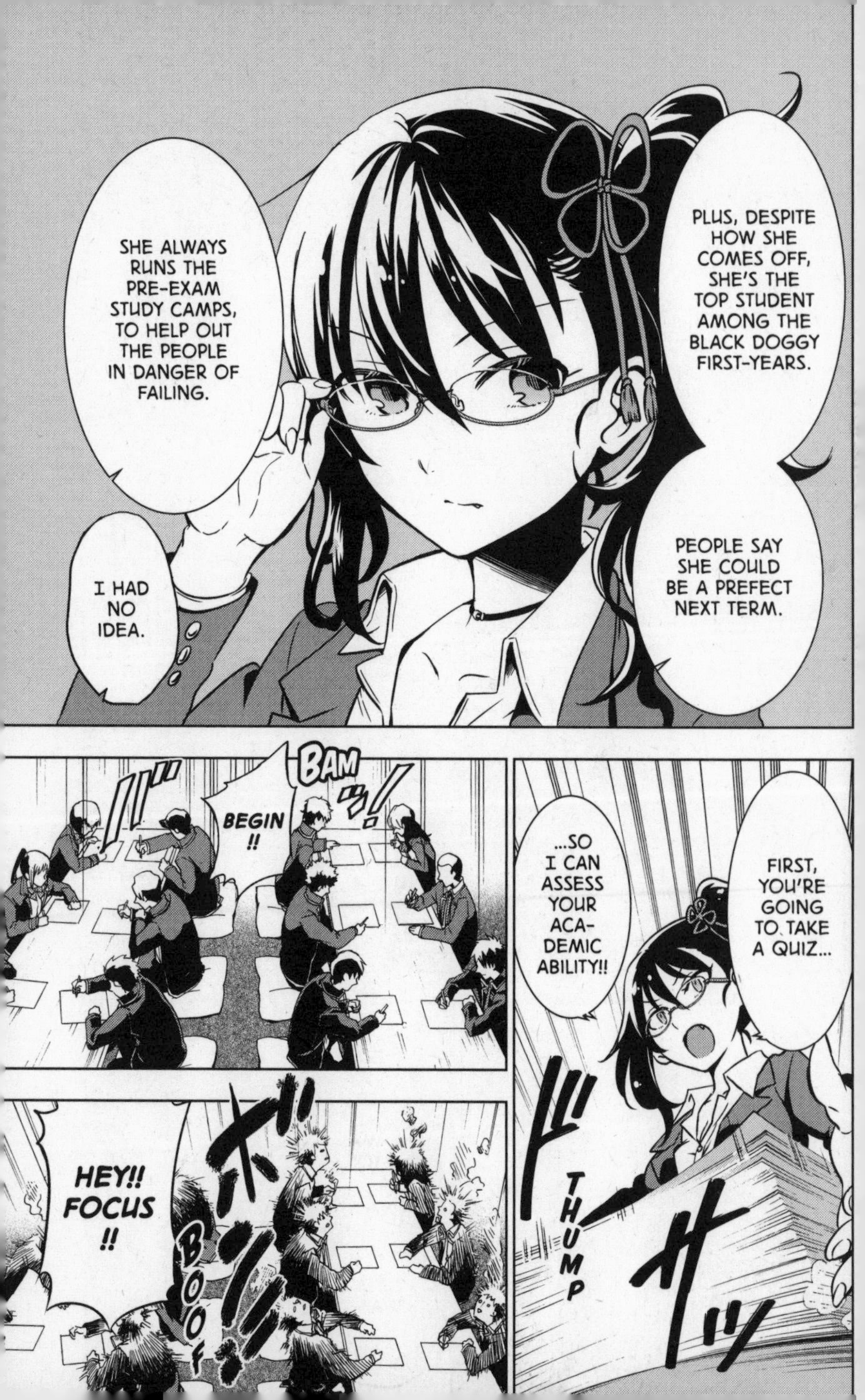
PLUS, DESPITE HOW SHE COMES OFF, SHE'S THE TOP STUDENT AMONG THE BLACK DOGGY FIRST-YEARS.
SHE ALWAYS RUNS THE PRE-EXAM STUDY CAMPS, TO HELP OUT THE PEOPLE IN DANGER OF FAILING.
PEOPLE SAY SHE COULD BE A PREFECT NEXT TERM.
I HAD NO IDEA.
FIRST, YOU'RE GOING TO TAKE A QUIZ...
...SO I CAN ASSESS YOUR ACA-DEMIC ABILITY!!
THUMP
BAM
BEGIN!!
HEY!! FOCUS!!
BOOF

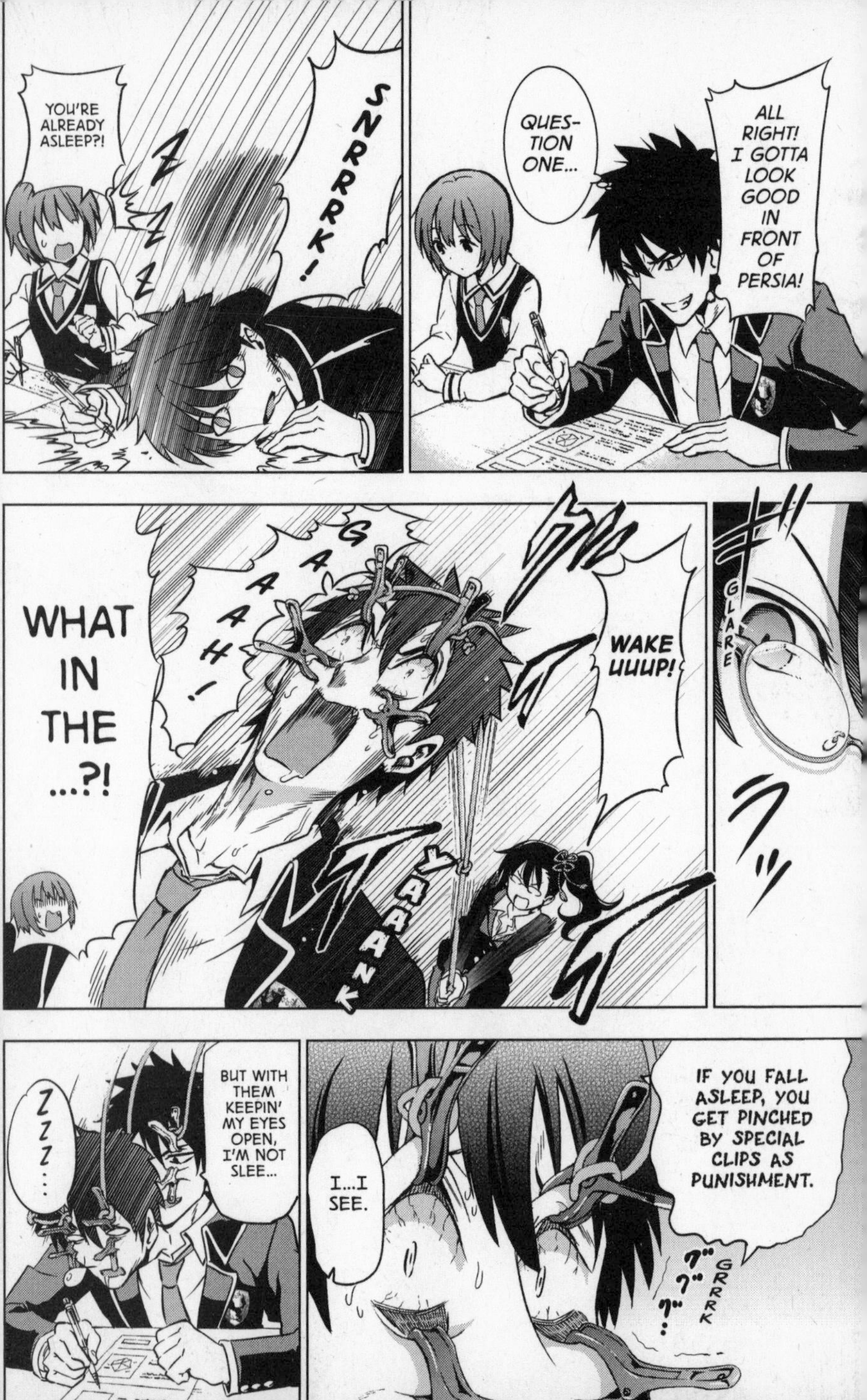
ALL RIGHT! I GOTTA LOOK GOOD IN FRONT OF PERSIA!
QUES-TION ONE...
SNRRRK!
ZZZZ
YOU'RE ALREADY ASLEEP?!
GLARE
WAKE UUUP!
GAAAAH!
YAAAANK
WHAT IN THE ...?!
IF YOU FALL ASLEEP, YOU GET PINCHED BY SPECIAL CLIPS AS PUNISHMENT.
GRRRK
I...I SEE.
BUT WITH THEM KEEPIN' MY EYES OPEN, I'M NOT SLEE...
ZZZ...

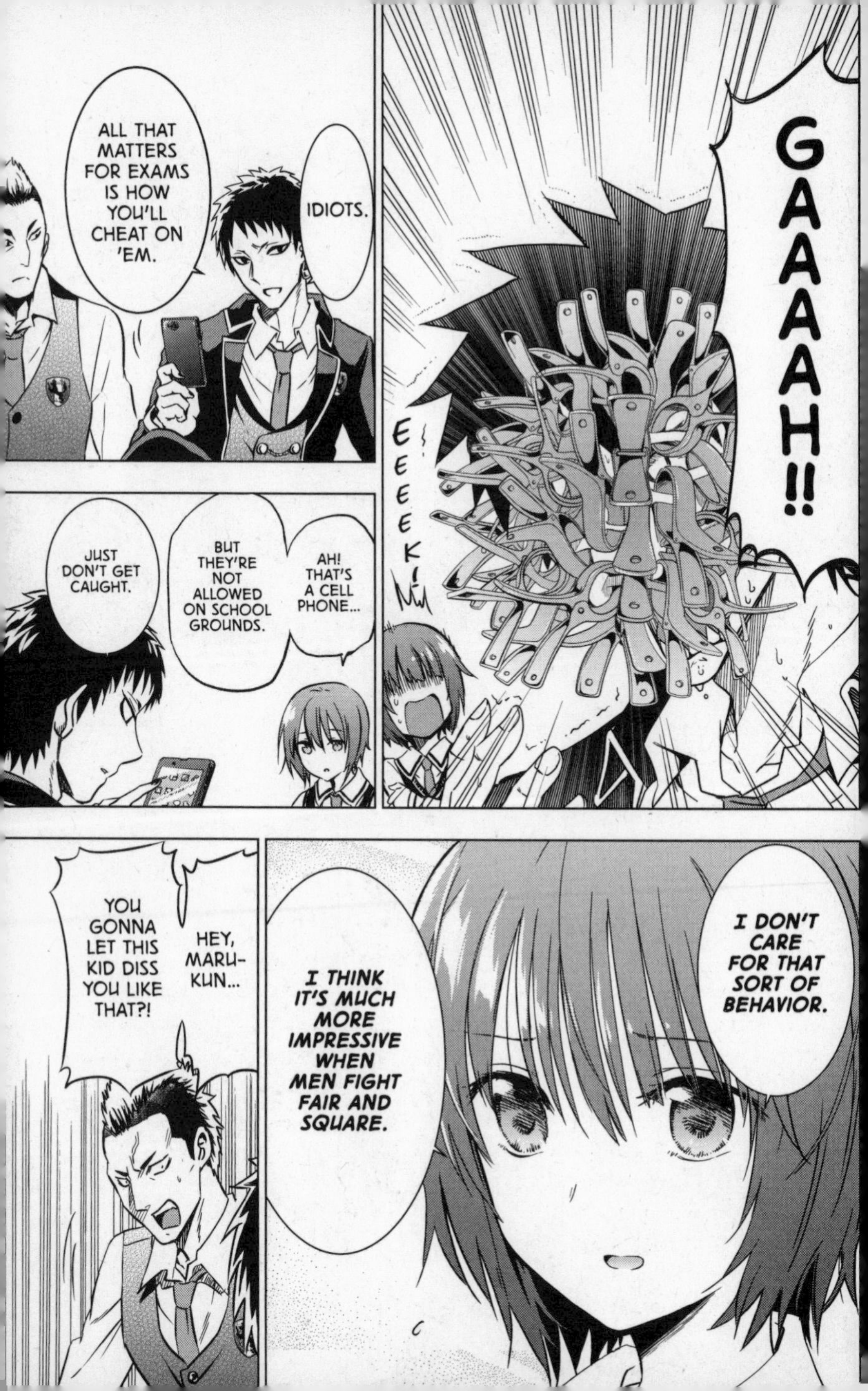
GAAAAH!!
EEEEK!
IDIOTS.
ALL THAT MATTERS FOR EXAMS IS HOW YOU'LL CHEAT ON 'EM.
AH! THAT'S A CELL PHONE...
BUT THEY'RE NOT ALLOWED ON SCHOOL GROUNDS.
JUST DON'T GET CAUGHT.
I DON'T CARE FOR THAT SORT OF BEHAVIOR.
I THINK IT'S MUCH MORE IMPRESSIVE WHEN MEN FIGHT FAIR AND SQUARE.
HEY, MARU-KUN...
YOU GONNA LET THIS KID DISS YOU LIKE THAT?!

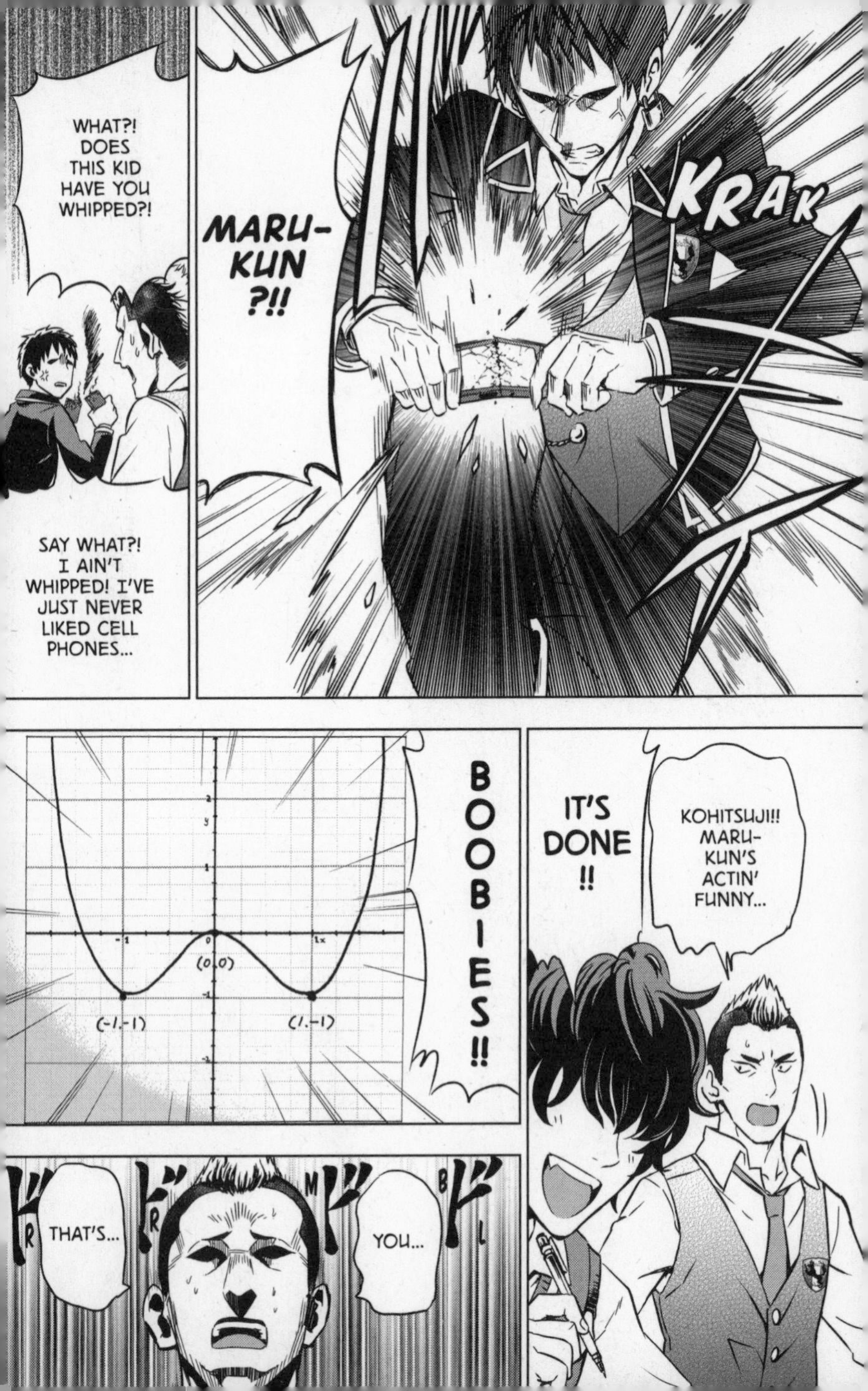
KRAK
MARU-KUN ?!!
WHAT?! DOES THIS KID HAVE YOU WHIPPED?!
SAY WHAT?! I AIN'T WHIPPED! I'VE JUST NEVER LIKED CELL PHONES...
KOHITSUJI!! MARU-KUN'S ACTIN' FUNNY...
IT'S DONE !!
BOOBIES!!
(0,0)
(-1,-1)
(1,-1)
YOU...
THAT'S...

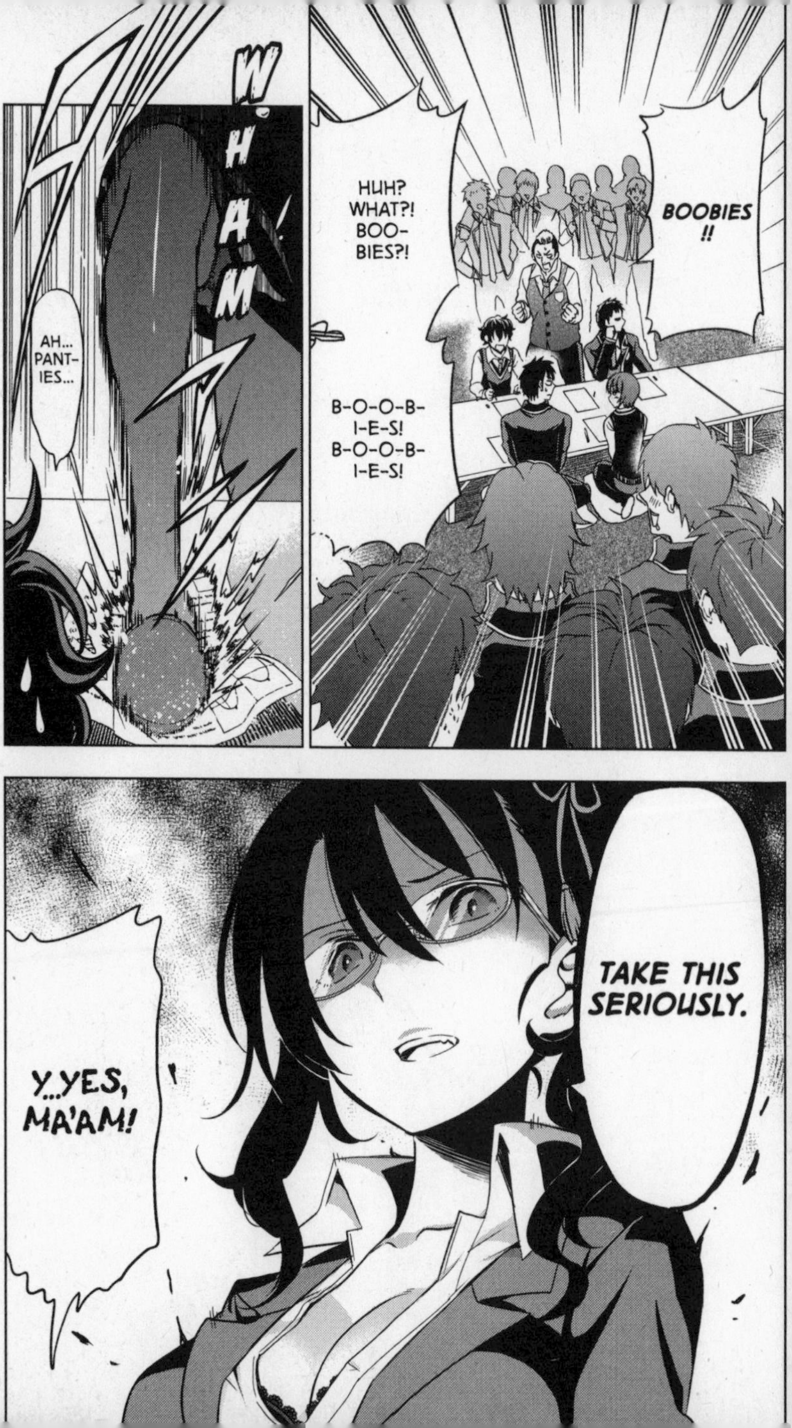
BOOBIES !!
HUH? WHAT?! BOO-BIES?!
B-O-O-B-I-E-S! B-O-O-B-I-E-S!
WHAM
AH... PANT-IES...
TAKE THIS SERIOUSLY.
Y...YES, MA'AM!

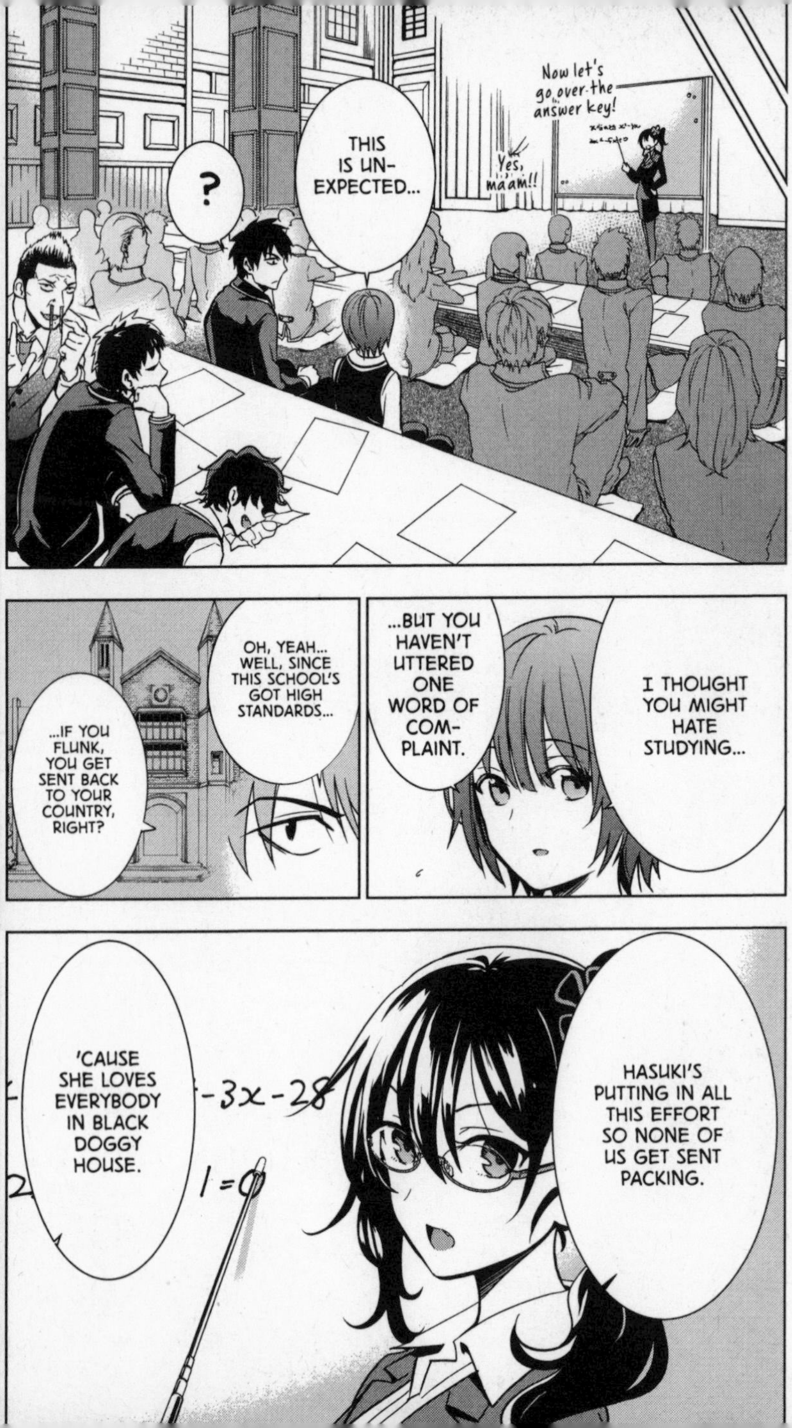
Now let's go over the answer key!
Yes, ma'am!!
THIS IS UN-EXPECTED...
?
I THOUGHT YOU MIGHT HATE STUDYING...
...BUT YOU HAVEN'T UTTERED ONE WORD OF COM-PLAINT.
OH, YEAH... WELL, SINCE THIS SCHOOL'S GOT HIGH STANDARDS...
...IF YOU FLUNK, YOU GET SENT BACK TO YOUR COUNTRY, RIGHT?
HASUKI'S PUTTING IN ALL THIS EFFORT SO NONE OF US GET SENT PACKING.
'CAUSE SHE LOVES EVERYBODY IN BLACK DOGGY HOUSE.

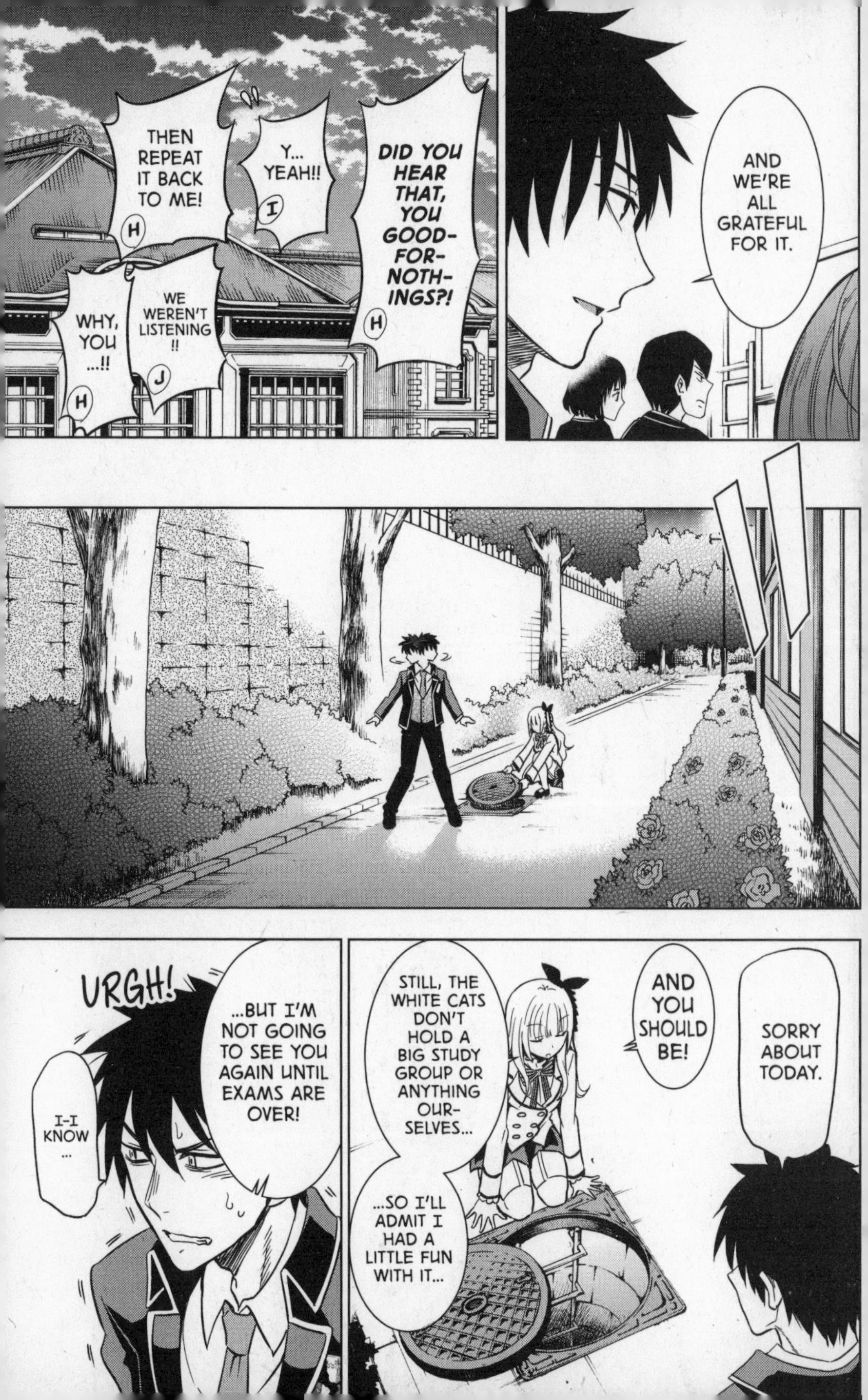
AND WE'RE ALL GRATEFUL FOR IT.
DID YOU HEAR THAT, YOU GOOD-FOR-NOTHINGS?!
H
Y... YEAH!!
I
THEN REPEAT IT BACK TO ME!
H
WE WEREN'T LISTENING!!
J
WHY, YOU ...!!
H
SORRY ABOUT TODAY.
AND YOU SHOULD BE!
STILL, THE WHITE CATS DON'T HOLD A BIG STUDY GROUP OR ANYTHING OURSELVES...
...SO I'LL ADMIT I HAD A LITTLE FUN WITH IT...
...BUT I'M NOT GOING TO SEE YOU AGAIN UNTIL EXAMS ARE OVER!
URGH!
I-I KNOW ...

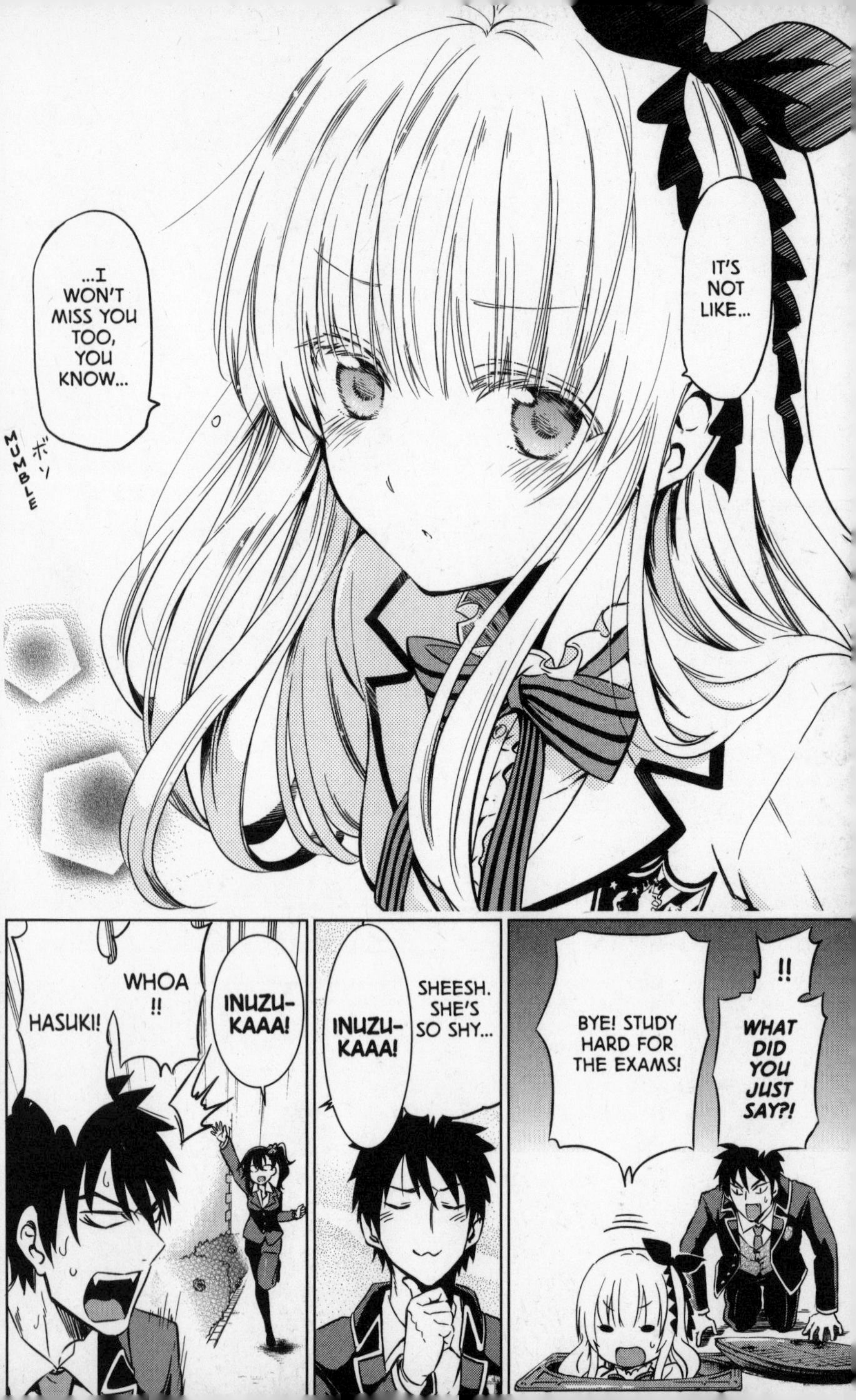
IT'S NOT LIKE...
...I WON'T MISS YOU TOO, YOU KNOW...
ボソ
MUMBLE
!! WHAT DID YOU JUST SAY?!
BYE! STUDY HARD FOR THE EXAMS!
SHEESH. SHE'S SO SHY...
INUZU-KAAA!
INUZU-KAAA!
WHOA !!
HASUKI!

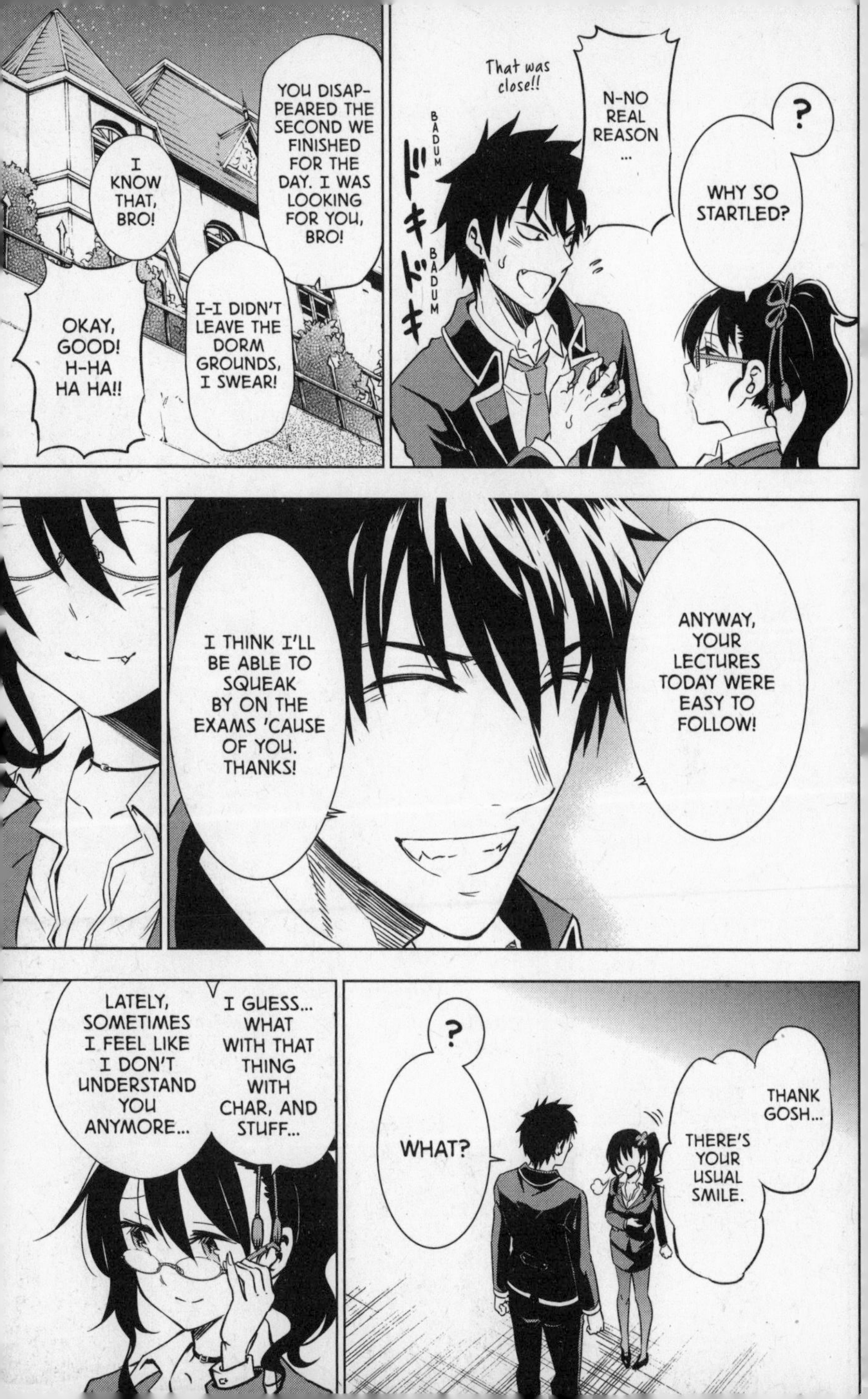
?
WHY SO STARTLED?
N-NO REAL REASON ...
That was close!!
ドキドキ
BADUM BADUM
YOU DISAP-PEARED THE SECOND WE FINISHED FOR THE DAY. I WAS LOOKING FOR YOU, BRO!
I-I DIDN'T LEAVE THE DORM GROUNDS, I SWEAR!
I KNOW THAT, BRO!
OKAY, GOOD! H-HA HA HA!!
ANYWAY, YOUR LECTURES TODAY WERE EASY TO FOLLOW!
I THINK I'LL BE ABLE TO SQUEAK BY ON THE EXAMS 'CAUSE OF YOU. THANKS!
THANK GOSH...
THERE'S YOUR USUAL SMILE.
?
WHAT?
I GUESS... WHAT WITH THAT THING WITH CHAR, AND STUFF...
LATELY, SOMETIMES I FEEL LIKE I DON'T UNDERSTAND YOU ANYMORE...

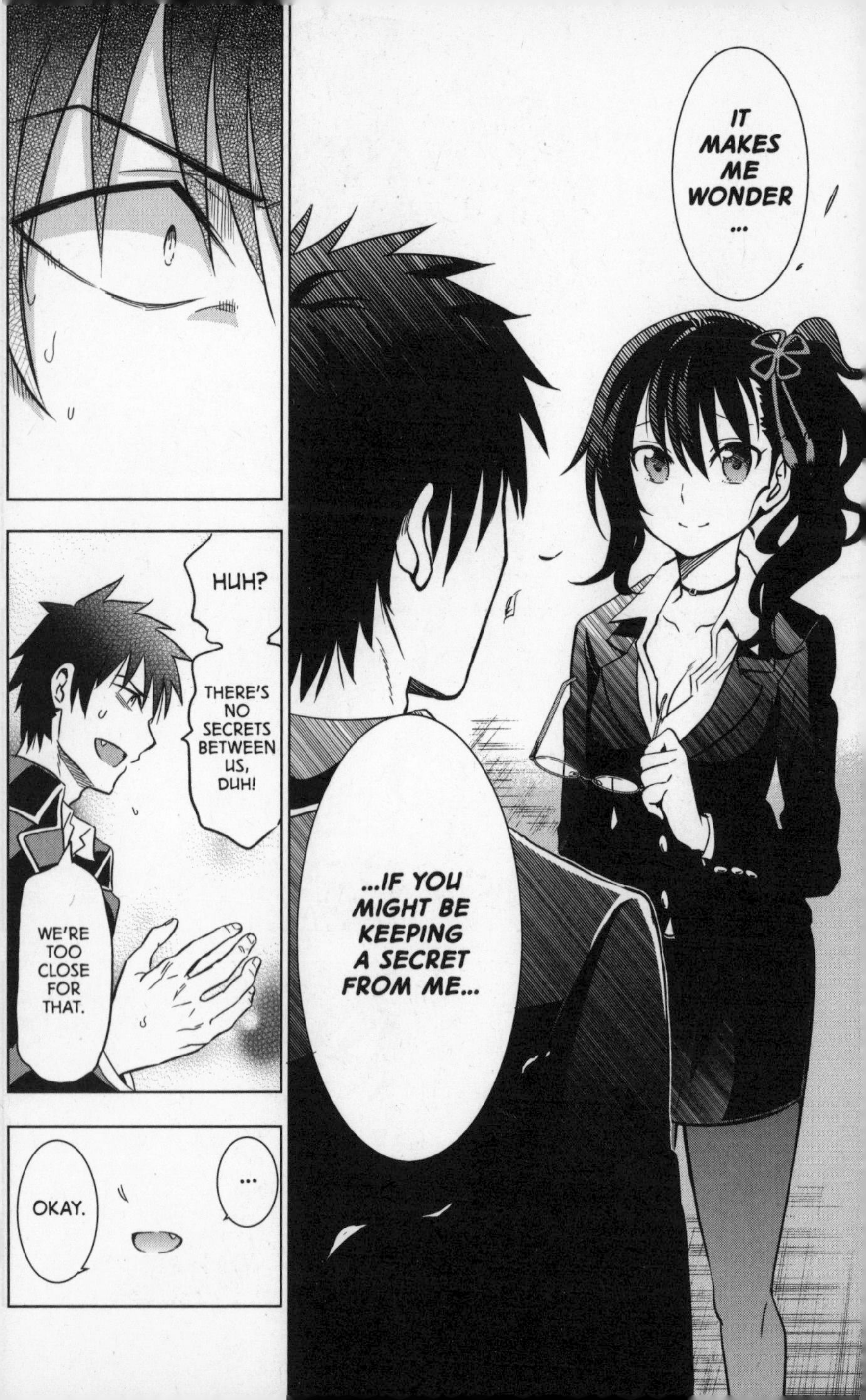
IT MAKES ME WONDER...
...IF YOU MIGHT BE KEEPING A SECRET FROM ME...
HUH?
THERE'S NO SECRETS BETWEEN US, DUH!
WE'RE TOO CLOSE FOR THAT.
...
OKAY.

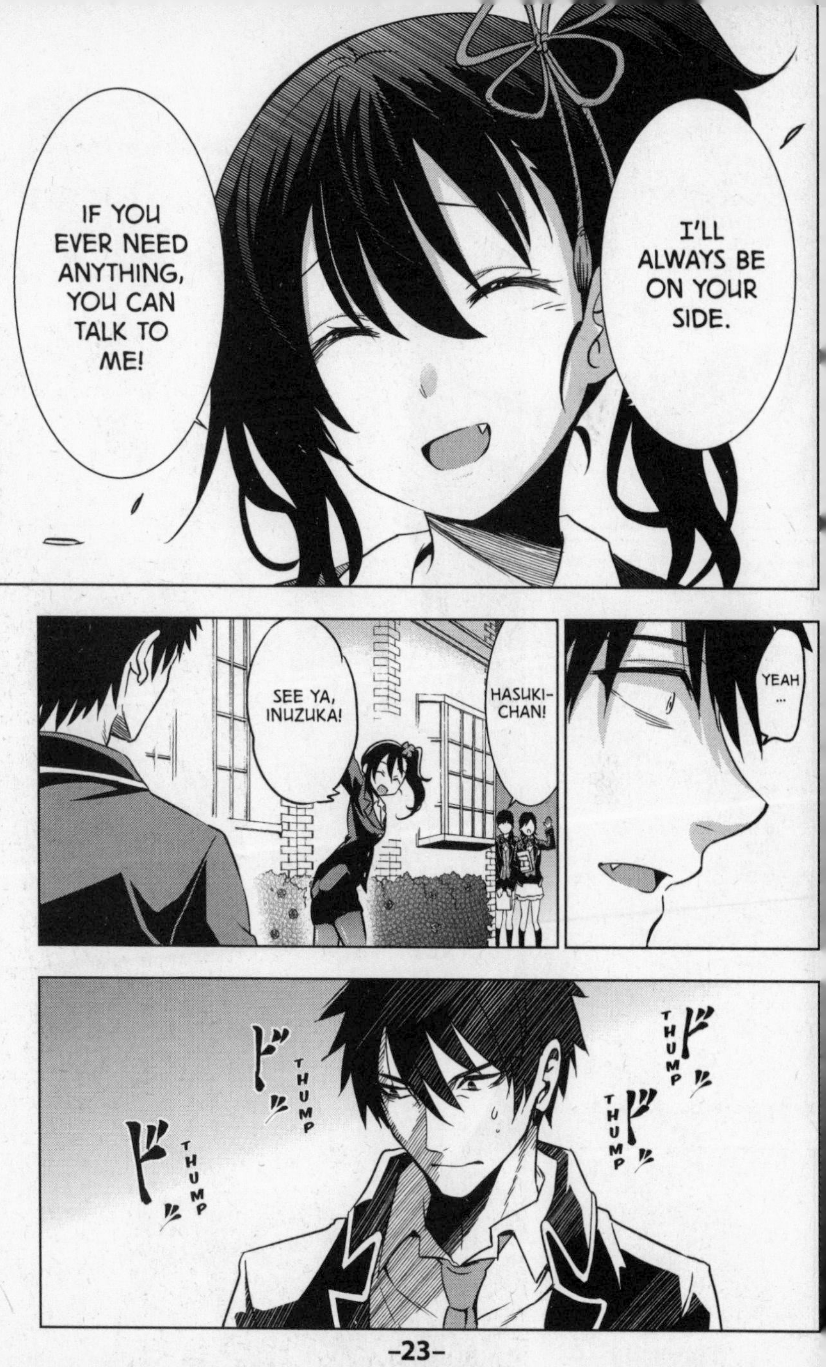
I'LL ALWAYS BE ON YOUR SIDE.
IF YOU EVER NEED ANYTHING, YOU CAN TALK TO ME!
YEAH ...
HASUKI-CHAN!
SEE YA, INUZUKA!
ド THUMP
ド THUMP
ド THUMP
ド THUMP

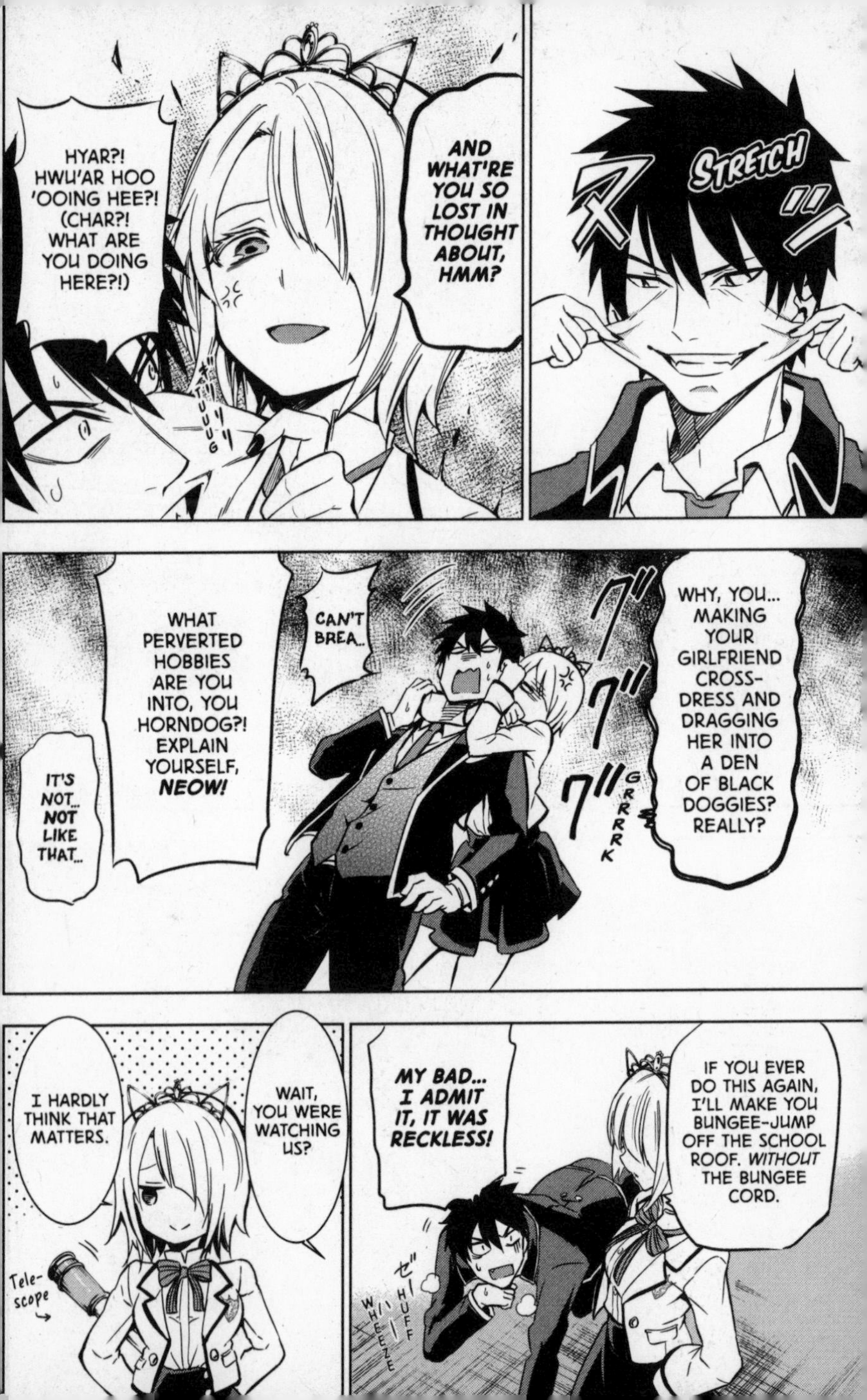
STRETCH
AND WHAT'RE YOU SO LOST IN THOUGHT ABOUT, HMM?
HYAR?! HWU'AR HOO 'OOING HEE?! (CHAR?! WHAT ARE YOU DOING HERE?!)
TUUUG
WHY, YOU... MAKING YOUR GIRLFRIEND CROSS-DRESS AND DRAGGING HER INTO A DEN OF BLACK DOGGIES? REALLY?
GRRRRK
CAN'T BREA..
WHAT PERVERTED HOBBIES ARE YOU INTO, YOU HORNDOG?! EXPLAIN YOURSELF, NEOW!
IT'S NOT... NOT LIKE THAT...
IF YOU EVER DO THIS AGAIN, I'LL MAKE YOU BUNGEE-JUMP OFF THE SCHOOL ROOF. WITHOUT THE BUNGEE CORD.
MY BAD... I ADMIT IT, IT WAS RECKLESS!
HUFF
WHEEZE
WAIT, YOU WERE WATCHING US?
I HARDLY THINK THAT MATTERS.
Tele-scope

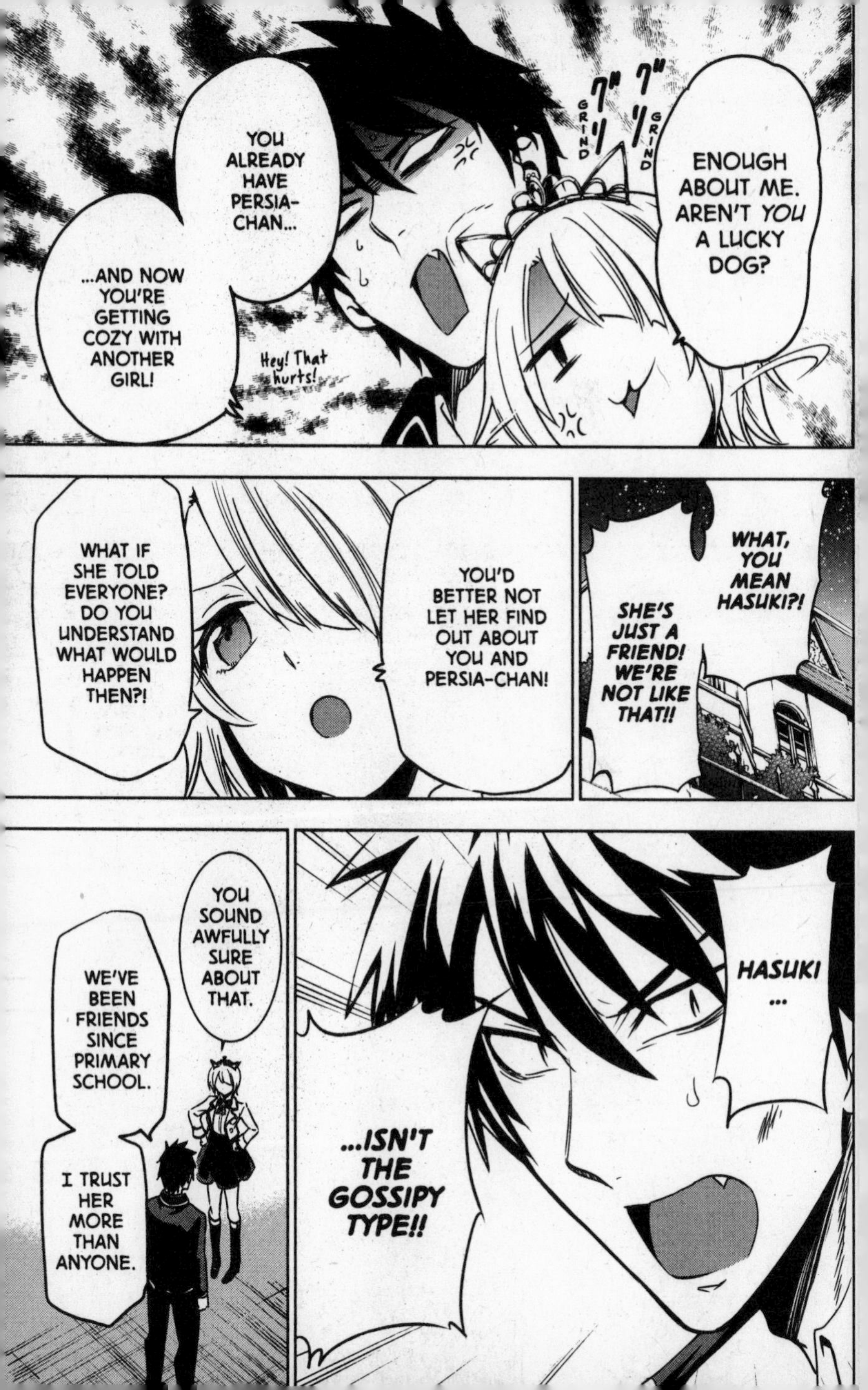
ENOUGH ABOUT ME. AREN'T *YOU* A LUCKY DOG?
GRIND GRIND
YOU ALREADY HAVE PERSIA-CHAN...
...AND NOW YOU'RE GETTING COZY WITH ANOTHER GIRL!
Hey! That hurts!
WHAT, YOU MEAN HASUKI?!
SHE'S JUST A FRIEND! WE'RE NOT LIKE THAT!!
YOU'D BETTER NOT LET HER FIND OUT ABOUT YOU AND PERSIA-CHAN!
WHAT IF SHE TOLD EVERYONE? DO YOU UNDERSTAND WHAT WOULD HAPPEN THEN?!
HASUKI ...
...ISN'T THE GOSSIPY TYPE!!
YOU SOUND AWFULLY SURE ABOUT THAT.
WE'VE BEEN FRIENDS SINCE PRIMARY SCHOOL.
I TRUST HER MORE THAN ANYONE.

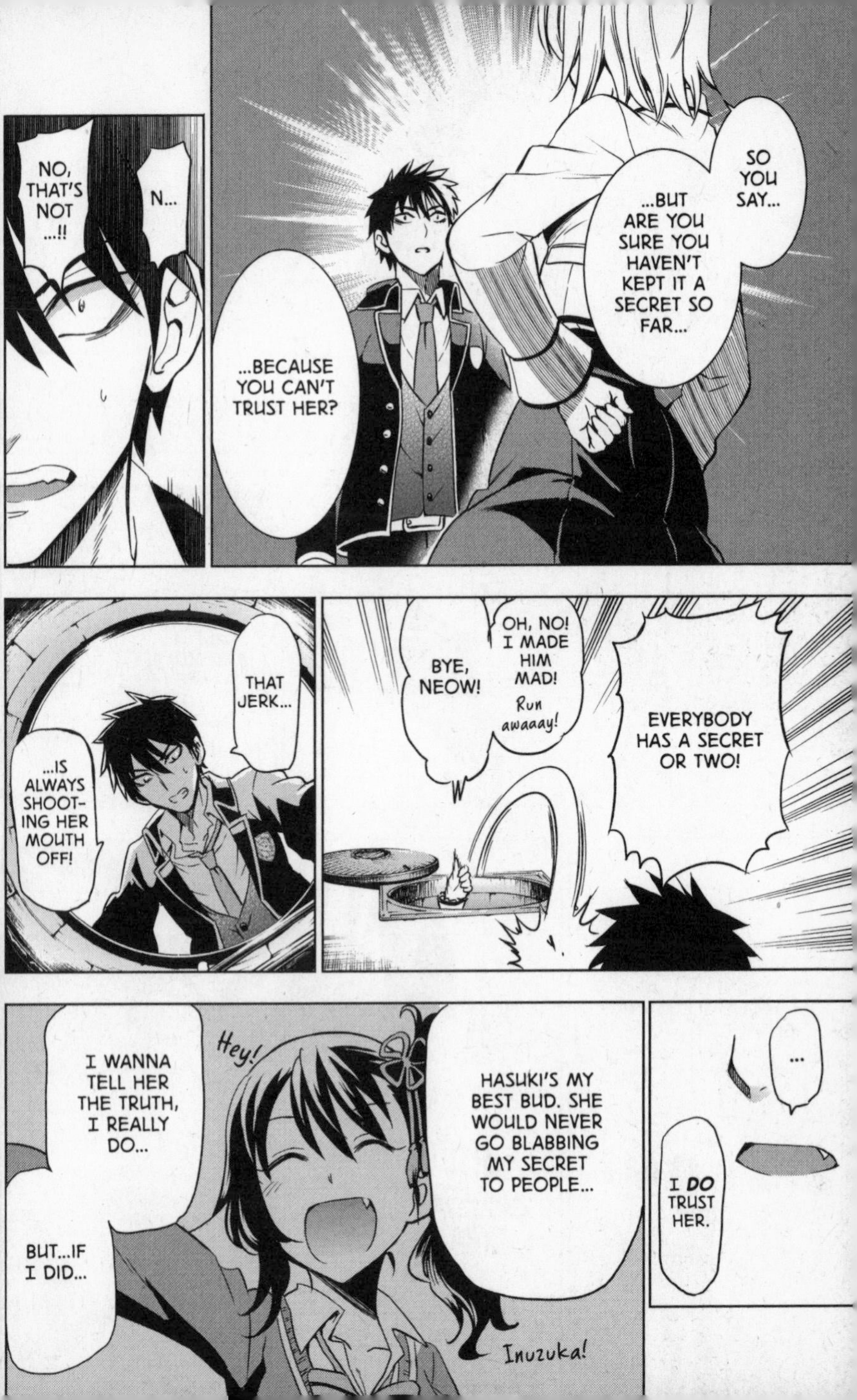
SO YOU SAY...
...BUT ARE YOU SURE YOU HAVEN'T KEPT IT A SECRET SO FAR...
...BECAUSE YOU CAN'T TRUST HER?
N...
NO, THAT'S NOT ...!!
EVERYBODY HAS A SECRET OR TWO!
OH, NO! I MADE HIM MAD!
Run awaaay!
BYE, NEOW!
THAT JERK...
...IS ALWAYS SHOOTING HER MOUTH OFF!
...
I *DO* TRUST HER.
HASUKI'S MY BEST BUD. SHE WOULD NEVER GO BLABBING MY SECRET TO PEOPLE...
Hey!
Inuzuka!
I WANNA TELL HER THE TRUTH, I REALLY DO...
BUT...IF I DID...

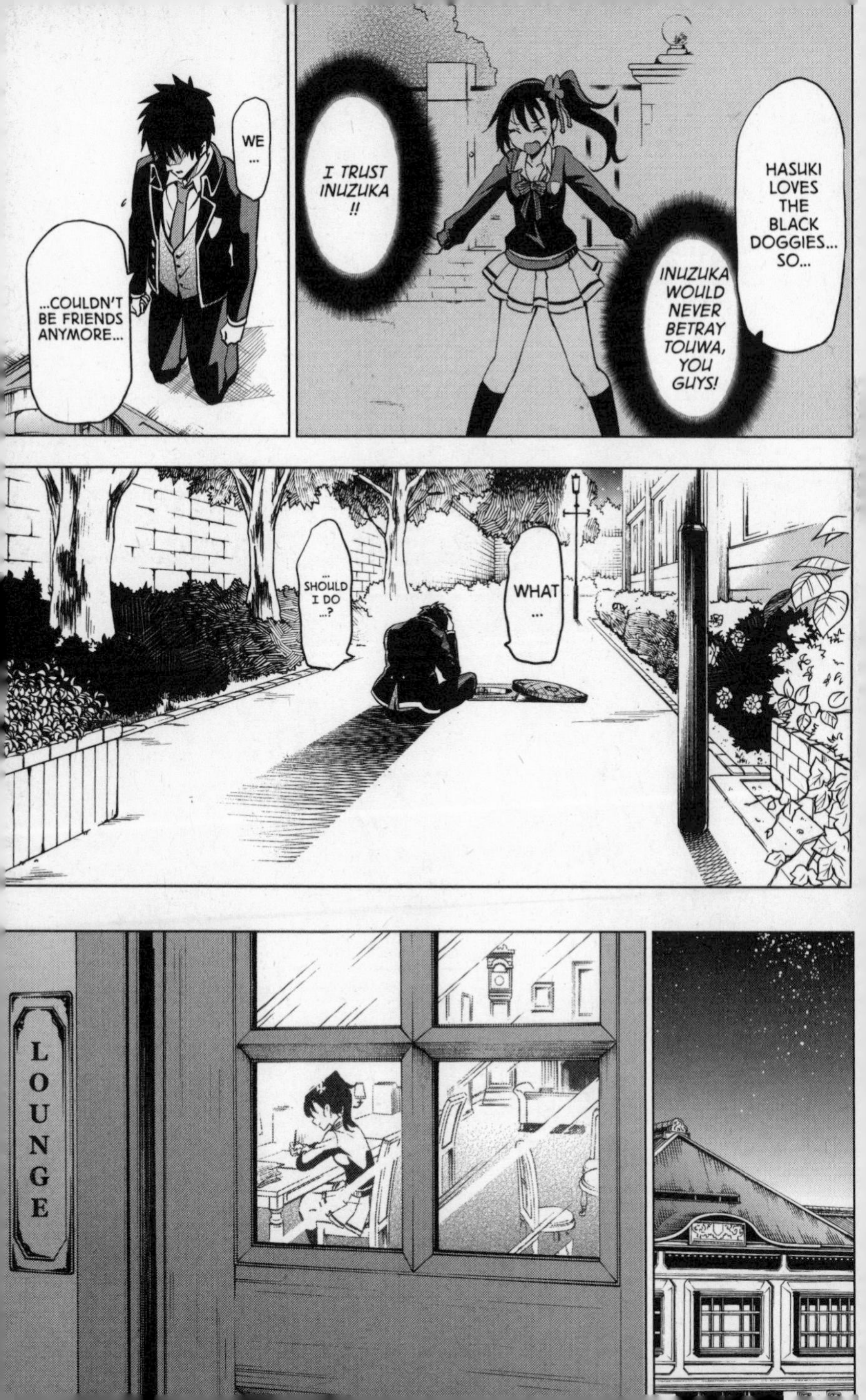
HASUKI LOVES THE BLACK DOGGIES... SO...
INUZUKA WOULD NEVER BETRAY TOUWA, YOU GUYS!
I TRUST INUZUKA !!
WE ...
...COULDN'T BE FRIENDS ANYMORE...
WHAT ...
... SHOULD I DO ...?
LOUNGE

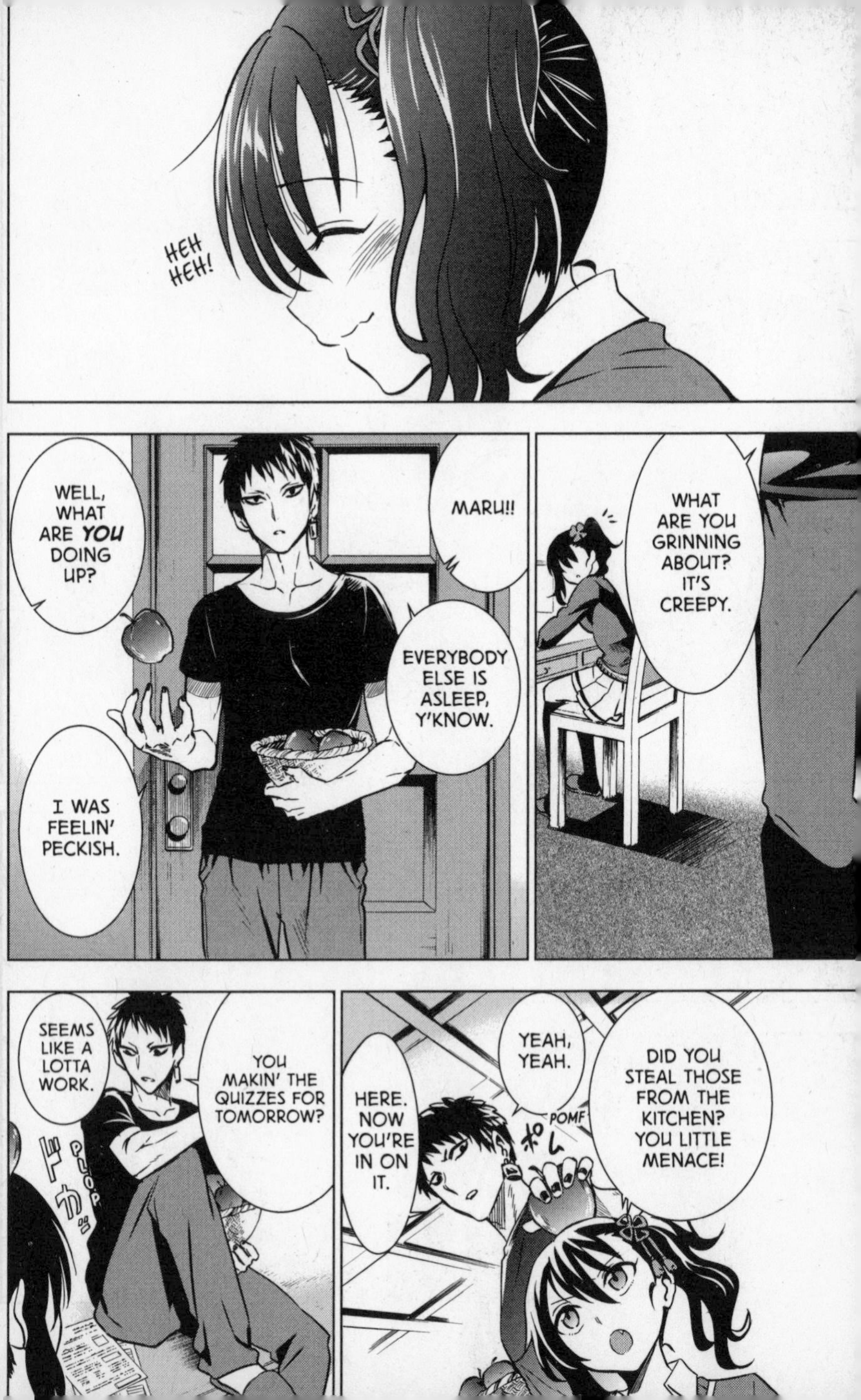
HEH HEH!
WHAT ARE YOU GRINNING ABOUT? IT'S CREEPY.
MARU!!
EVERYBODY ELSE IS ASLEEP, Y'KNOW.
WELL, WHAT ARE *YOU* DOING UP?
I WAS FEELIN' PECKISH.
DID YOU STEAL THOSE FROM THE KITCHEN? YOU LITTLE MENACE!
YEAH, YEAH.
POMF
HERE. NOW YOU'RE IN ON IT.
YOU MAKIN' THE QUIZZES FOR TOMORROW?
SEEMS LIKE A LOTTA WORK.
PLOP

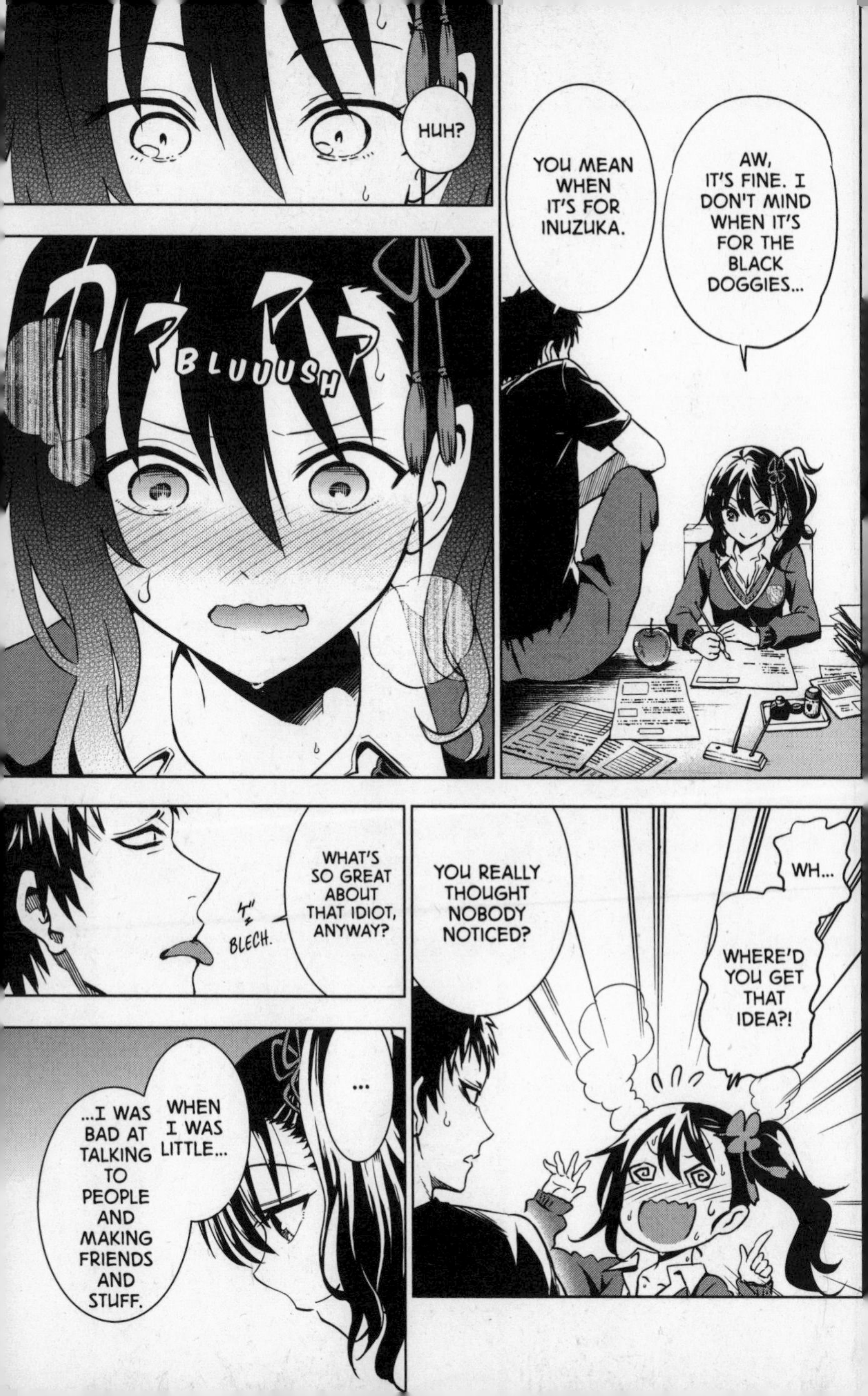
AW, IT'S FINE. I DON'T MIND WHEN IT'S FOR THE BLACK DOGGIES...
YOU MEAN WHEN IT'S FOR INUZUKA.
HUH?
BLUUUSH
YOU REALLY THOUGHT NOBODY NOTICED?
WH...
WHERE'D YOU GET THAT IDEA?!
WHAT'S SO GREAT ABOUT THAT IDIOT, ANYWAY?
BLECH.
...
WHEN I WAS LITTLE...
...I WAS BAD AT TALKING TO PEOPLE AND MAKING FRIENDS AND STUFF.

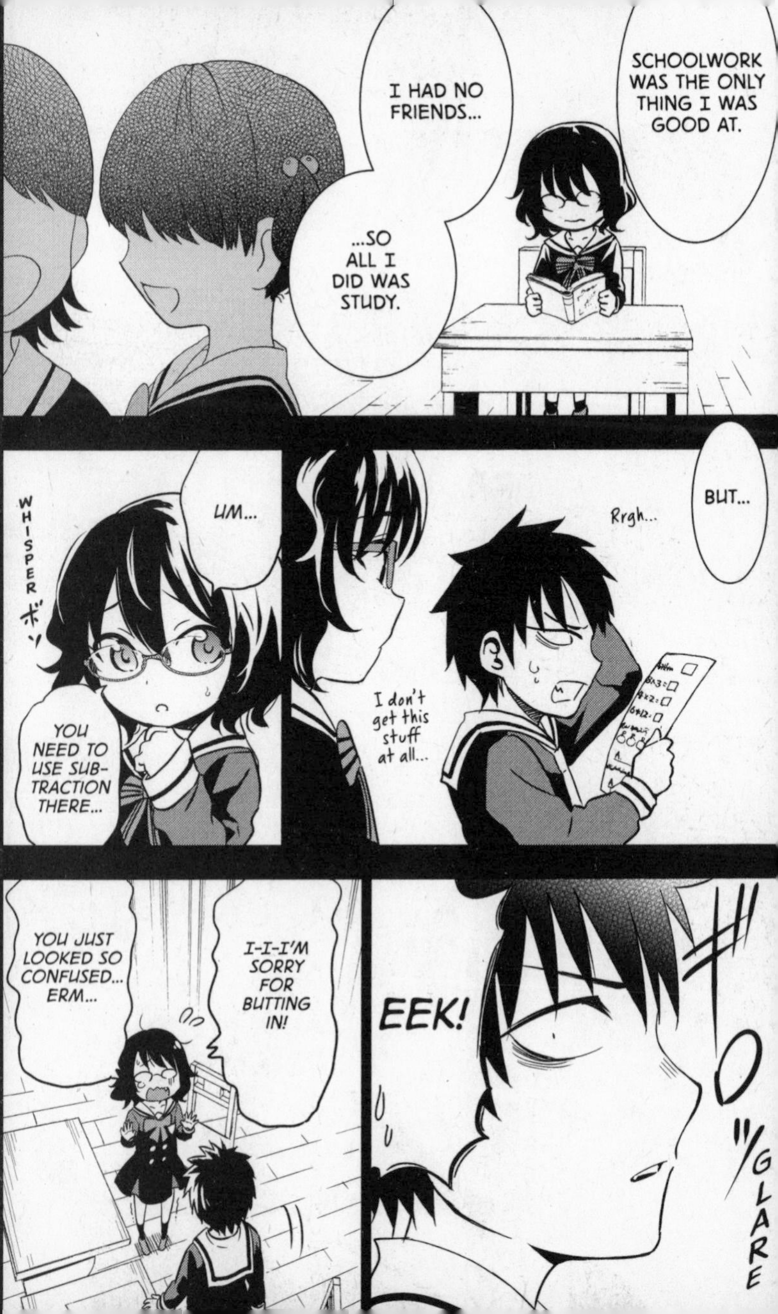
SCHOOLWORK WAS THE ONLY THING I WAS GOOD AT.
I HAD NO FRIENDS...
...SO ALL I DID WAS STUDY.
BUT...
Rrgh...
I don't get this stuff at all...
UM...
WHISPER ボソ
YOU NEED TO USE SUB-TRACTION THERE...
GLARE
EEK!
I-I-I'M SORRY FOR BUTTING IN!
YOU JUST LOOKED SO CONFUSED... ERM...

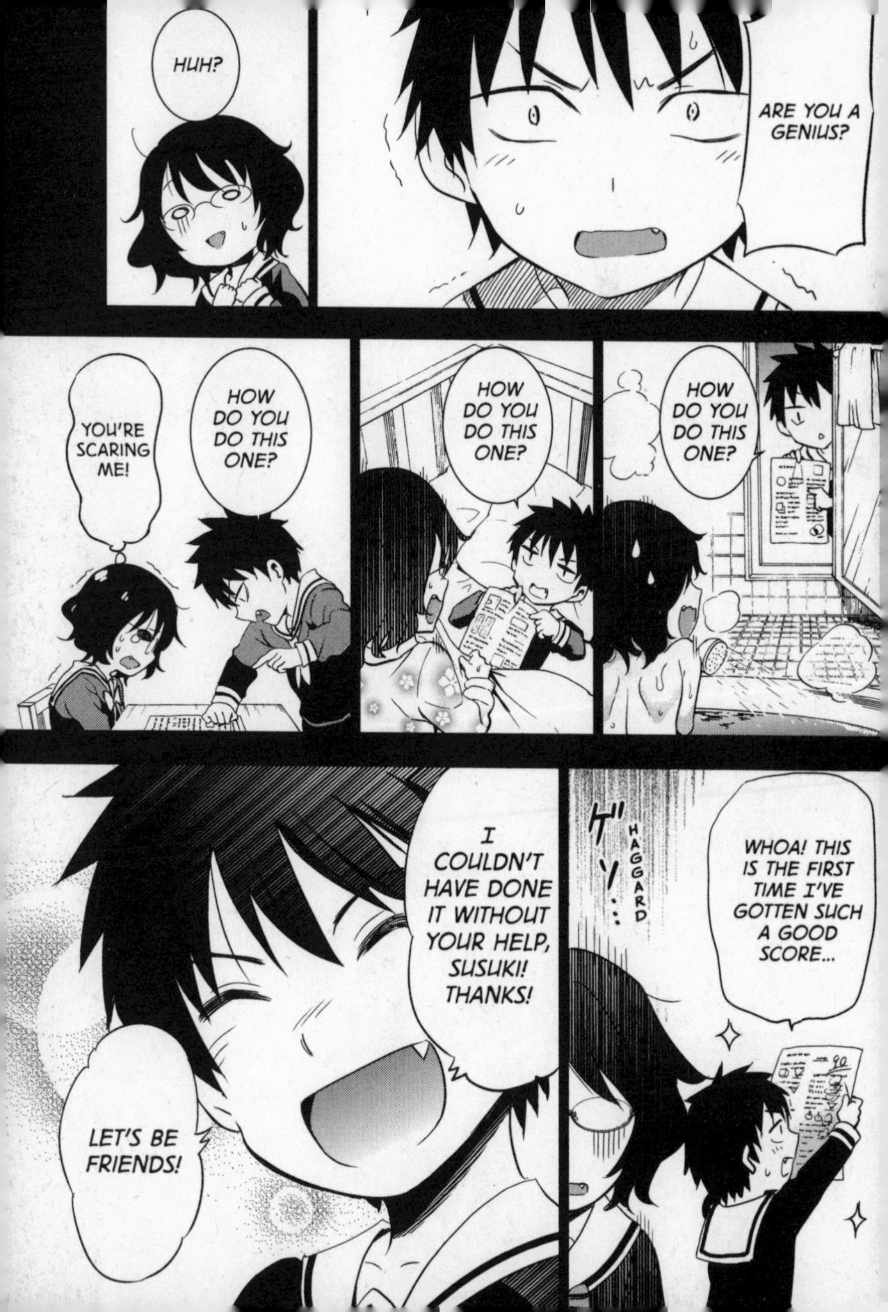
ARE YOU A GENIUS?
HUH?
HOW DO YOU DO THIS ONE?
HOW DO YOU DO THIS ONE?
HOW DO YOU DO THIS ONE?
YOU'RE SCARING ME!
WHOA! THIS IS THE FIRST TIME I'VE GOTTEN SUCH A GOOD SCORE...
HAGGARD
I COULDN'T HAVE DONE IT WITHOUT YOUR HELP, SUSUKI! THANKS!
LET'S BE FRIENDS!

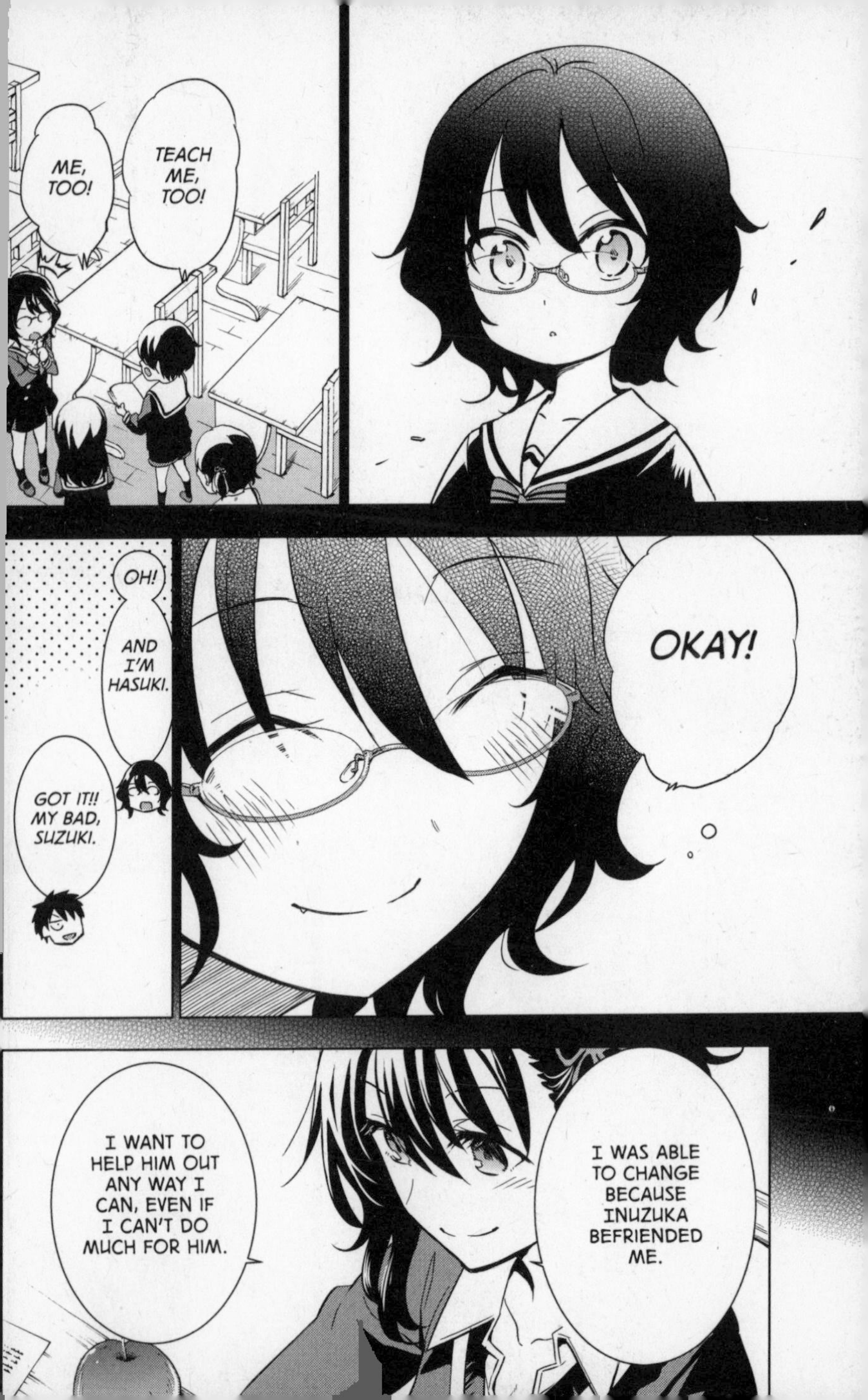
TEACH ME, TOO!
ME, TOO!
OKAY!
OH! AND I'M HASUKI.
GOT IT!! MY BAD, SUZUKI.
I WAS ABLE TO CHANGE BECAUSE INUZUKA BEFRIENDED ME.
I WANT TO HELP HIM OUT ANY WAY I CAN, EVEN IF I CAN'T DO MUCH FOR HIM.

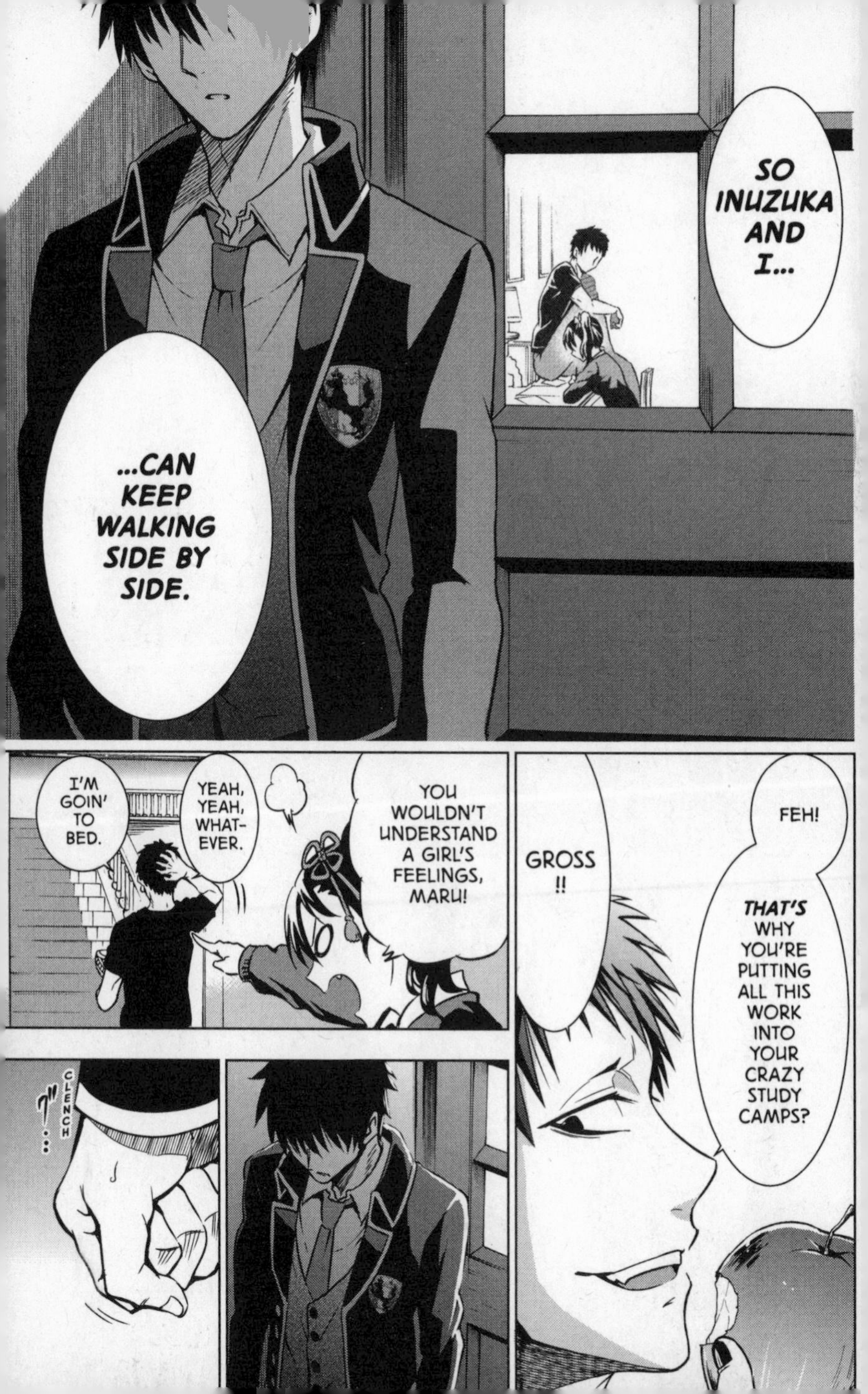
SO INUZUKA AND I...
...CAN KEEP WALKING SIDE BY SIDE.
FEH!
THAT'S WHY YOU'RE PUTTING ALL THIS WORK INTO YOUR CRAZY STUDY CAMPS?
GROSS!!
YOU WOULDN'T UNDERSTAND A GIRL'S FEELINGS, MARU!
YEAH, YEAH, WHATEVER.
I'M GOIN' TO BED.
CLENCH

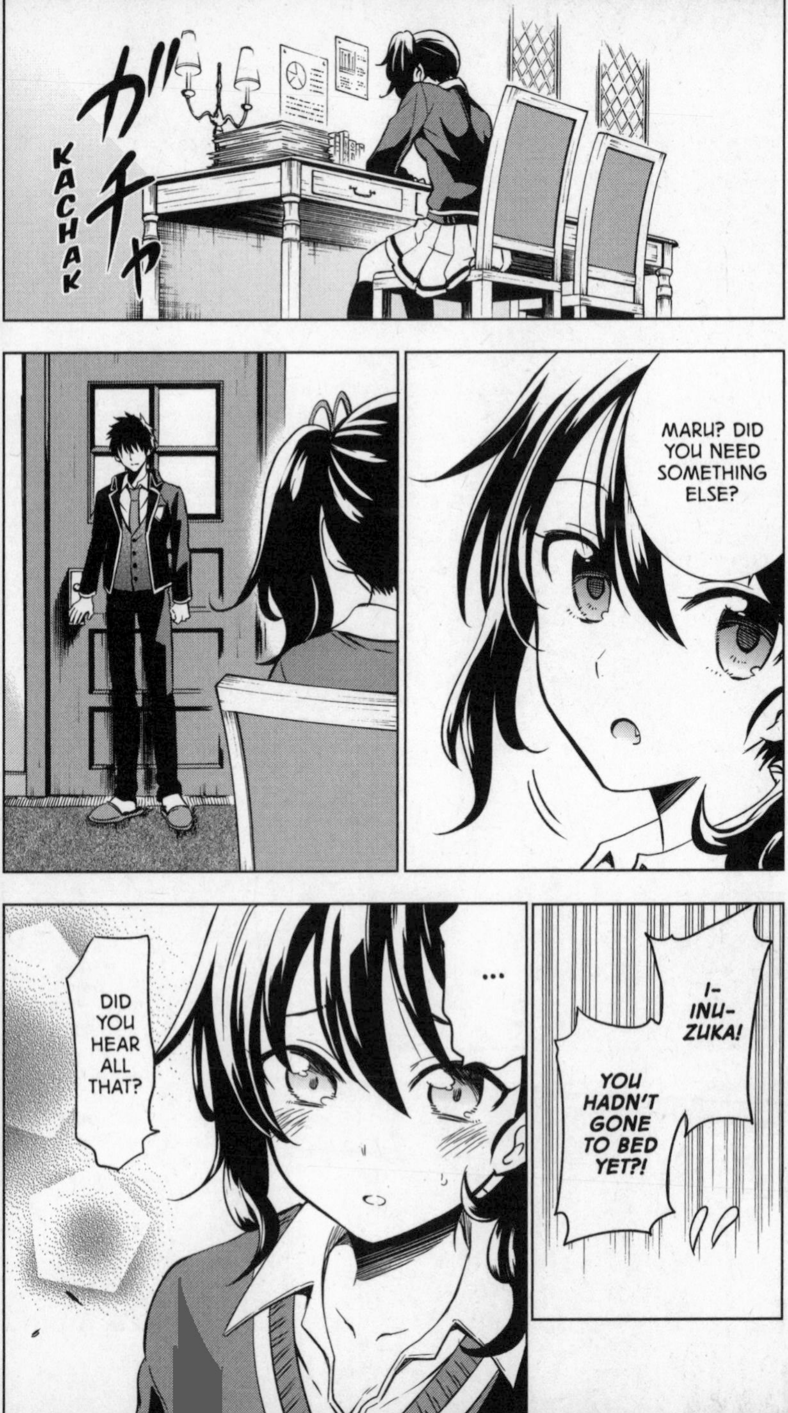
ガチャ
KACHAK
MARU? DID YOU NEED SOMETHING ELSE?
I- INUZUKA!
YOU HADN'T GONE TO BED YET?!
...
DID YOU HEAR ALL THAT?

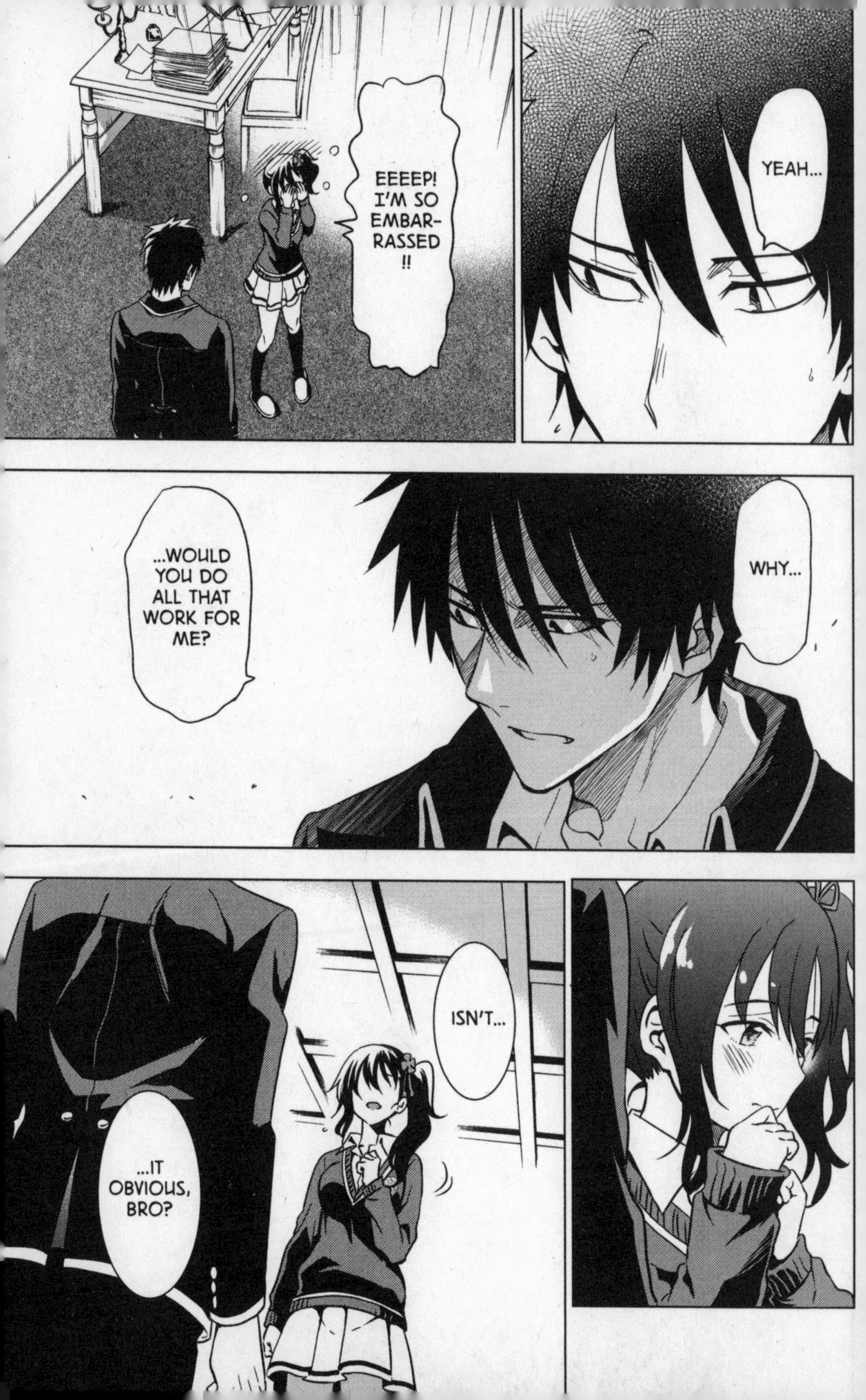
YEAH...
EEEEP! I'M SO EMBAR-RASSED!!
WHY...
...WOULD YOU DO ALL THAT WORK FOR ME?
ISN'T...
...IT OBVIOUS, BRO?

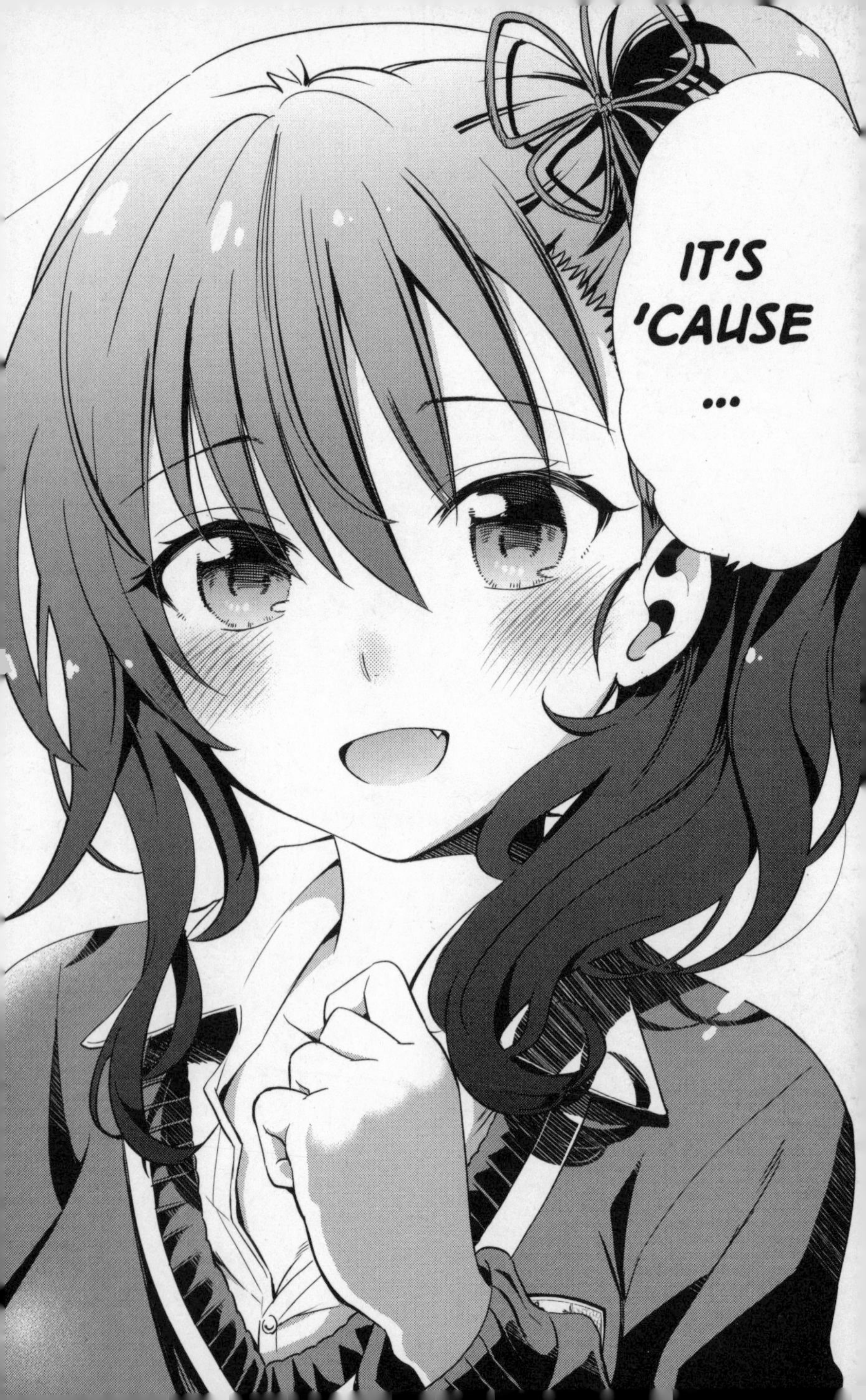
IT'S 'CAUSE ...

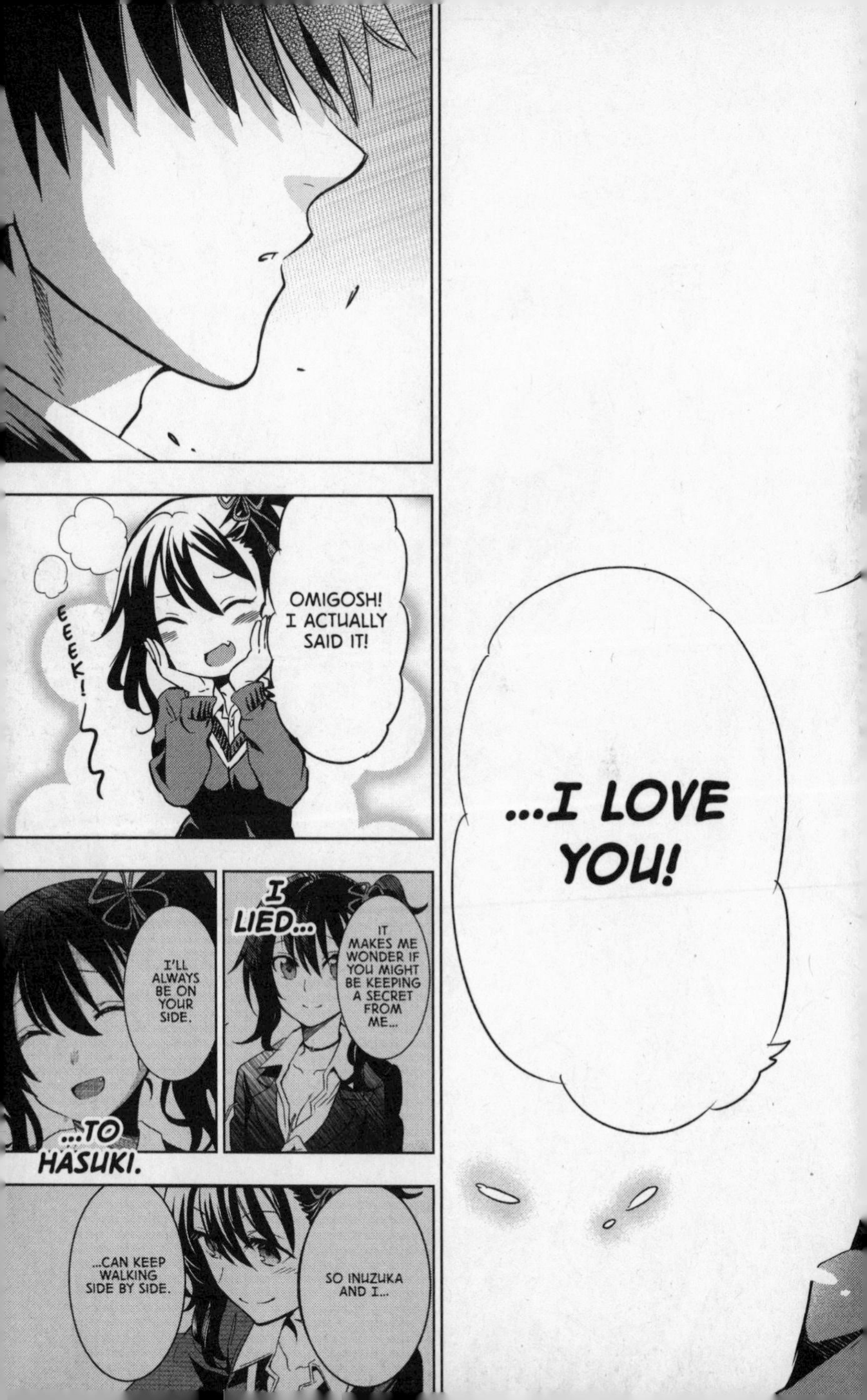
...I LOVE YOU!
OMIGOSH! I ACTUALLY SAID IT!
EEEK!
IT MAKES ME WONDER IF YOU MIGHT BE KEEPING A SECRET FROM ME...
I LIED...
I'LL ALWAYS BE ON YOUR SIDE.
...TO HASUKI.
SO INUZUKA AND I...
...CAN KEEP WALKING SIDE BY SIDE.

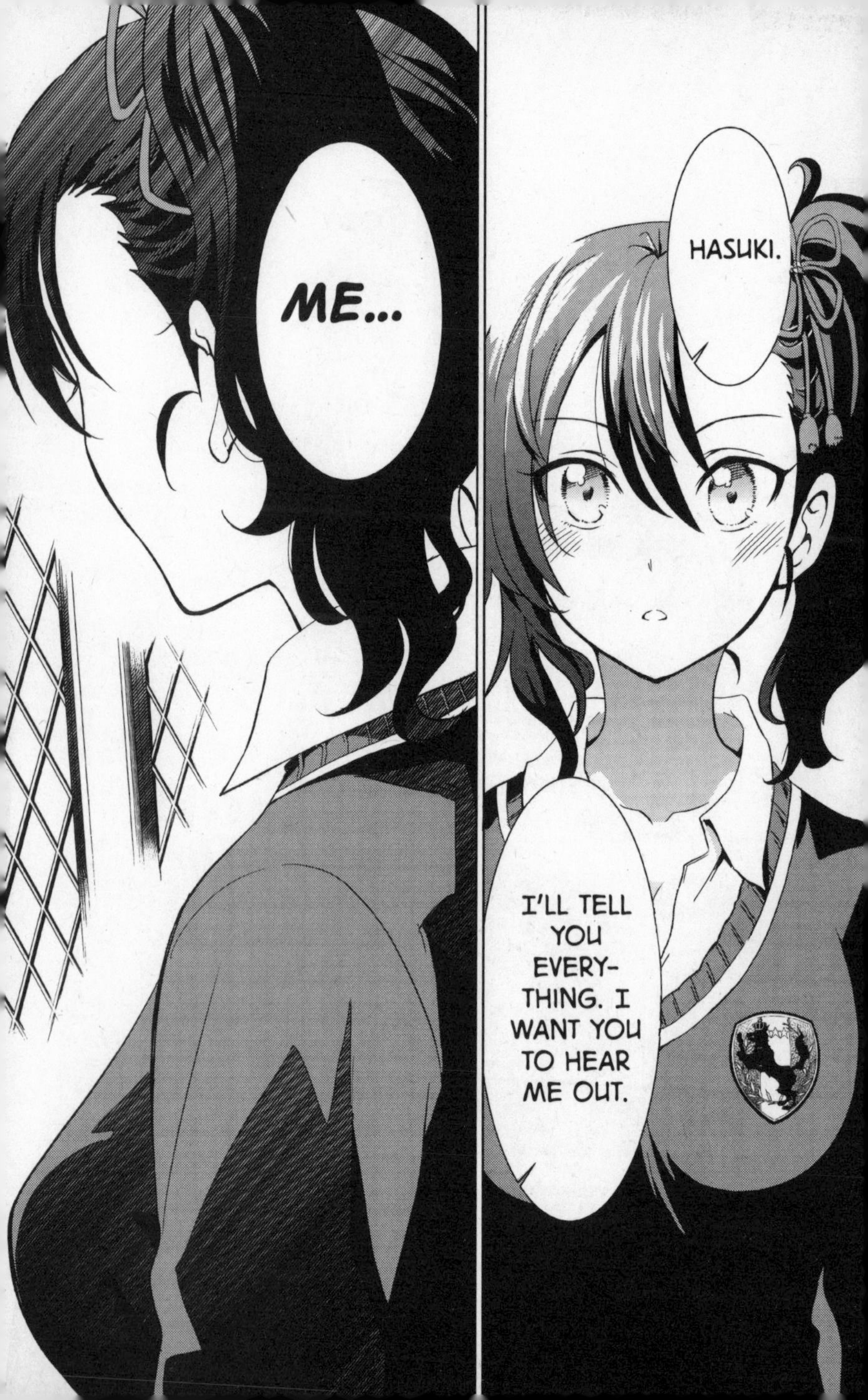
HASUKI.
I'LL TELL YOU EVERY-THING. I WANT YOU TO HEAR ME OUT.
ME...

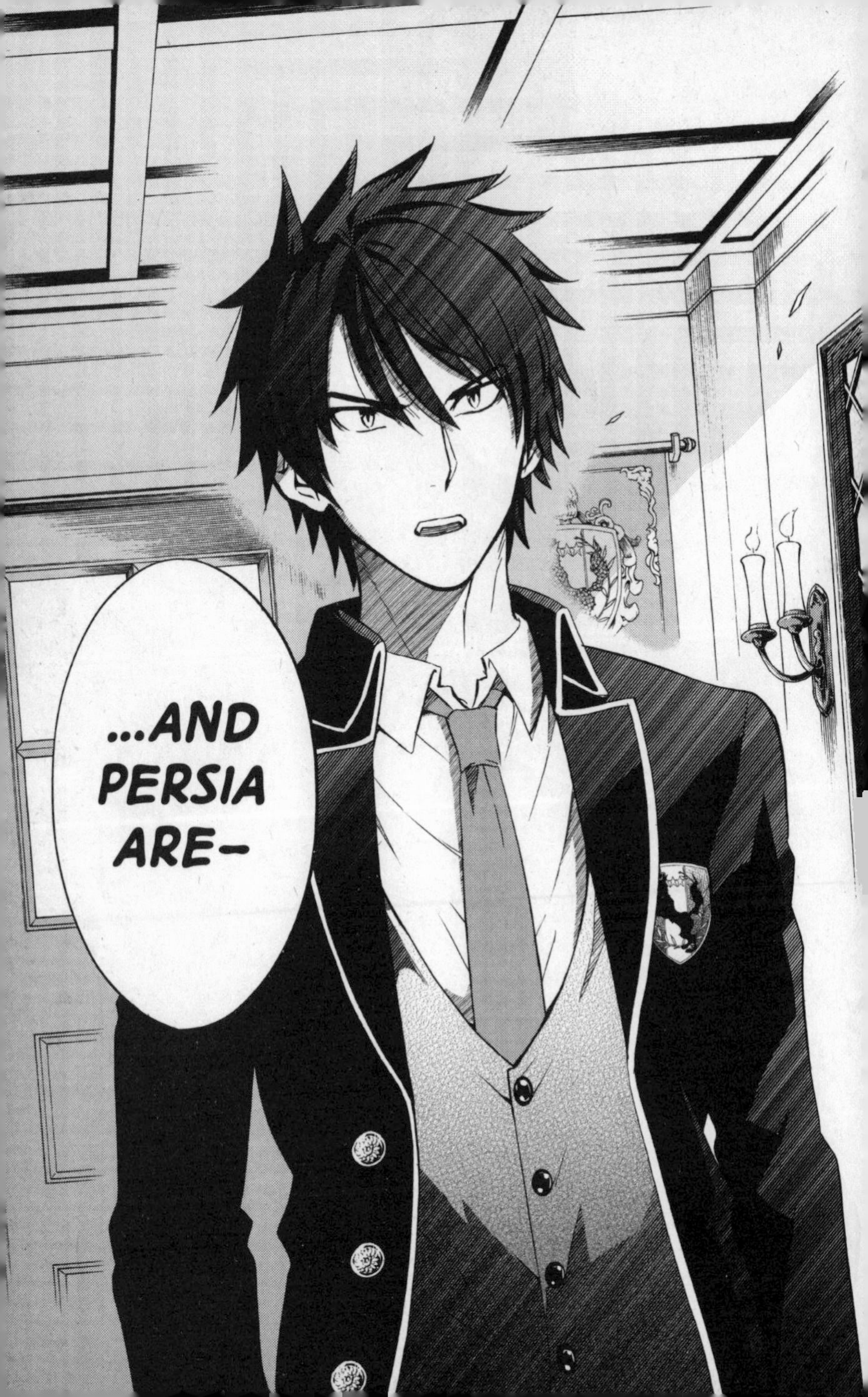
...AND PERSIA ARE-

INSIDE JULIET
~THE SECRETS BEHIND BLACK DOGGY OUTLAW MARU~

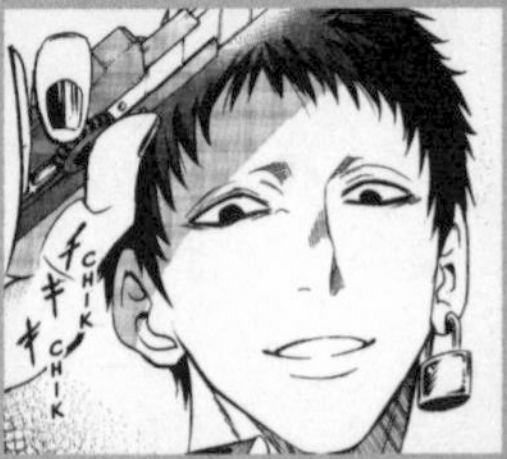

CHIK
CHIK

Black Doggy's sneaky, slimy, subservient guy, Maru. When he appeared in Act 1, he had a rough-looking style—no eyebrows and a short crop.

← As of Volume 1, he had no eyebrows at all, only the shadows of his features...

Perhaps some of you noticed? When he appeared in Act 6, there was something unusual on his face... →

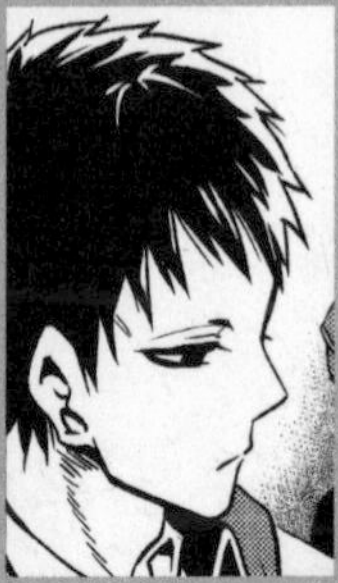

MYSTERIOUS BLACK OBJECTS HAD APPEARED ABOVE HIS EYES...
SNOT?
NO...EYEBROWS!

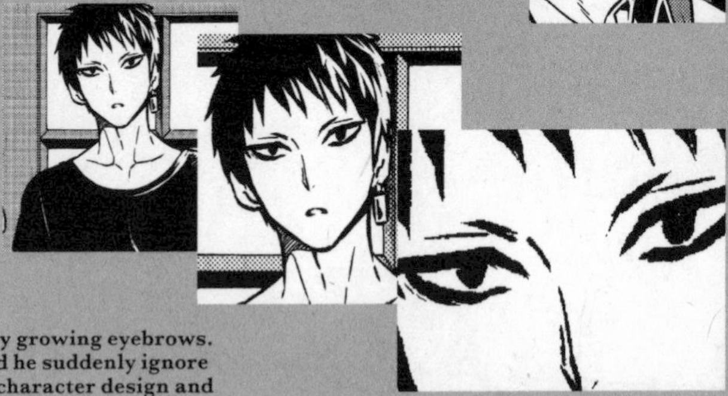

He's clearly growing eyebrows. So, why did he suddenly ignore his initial character design and start growing out eyebrows?

According to his close friends...

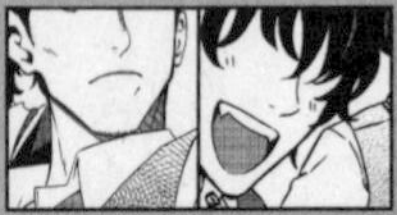

Mr. T: "Lately, he's been mumbling stuff like, 'Maybe it would be better to have eyebrows' and, 'Maybe I'll grow out my hair.' We're at that age where we care about looking good, so maybe it's just natural?"Mr. K: "It's a sexual awakening! Dunno who, but I bet he has the hots for somebody! Whee-Whoo!!"

Interesting. Even though he projects an outlaw-type persona, on the inside, he's still a high school boy at the height of puberty. This confirms it—it's definitely not that the author forgot his design, accidentally drew eyebrows on him, and went, "Oh, crap." Meanwhile, we'll keep chasing the inside stories, the mysteries, and the mistakes!

ACT 7:

ROMIO & HASUKI PART 2

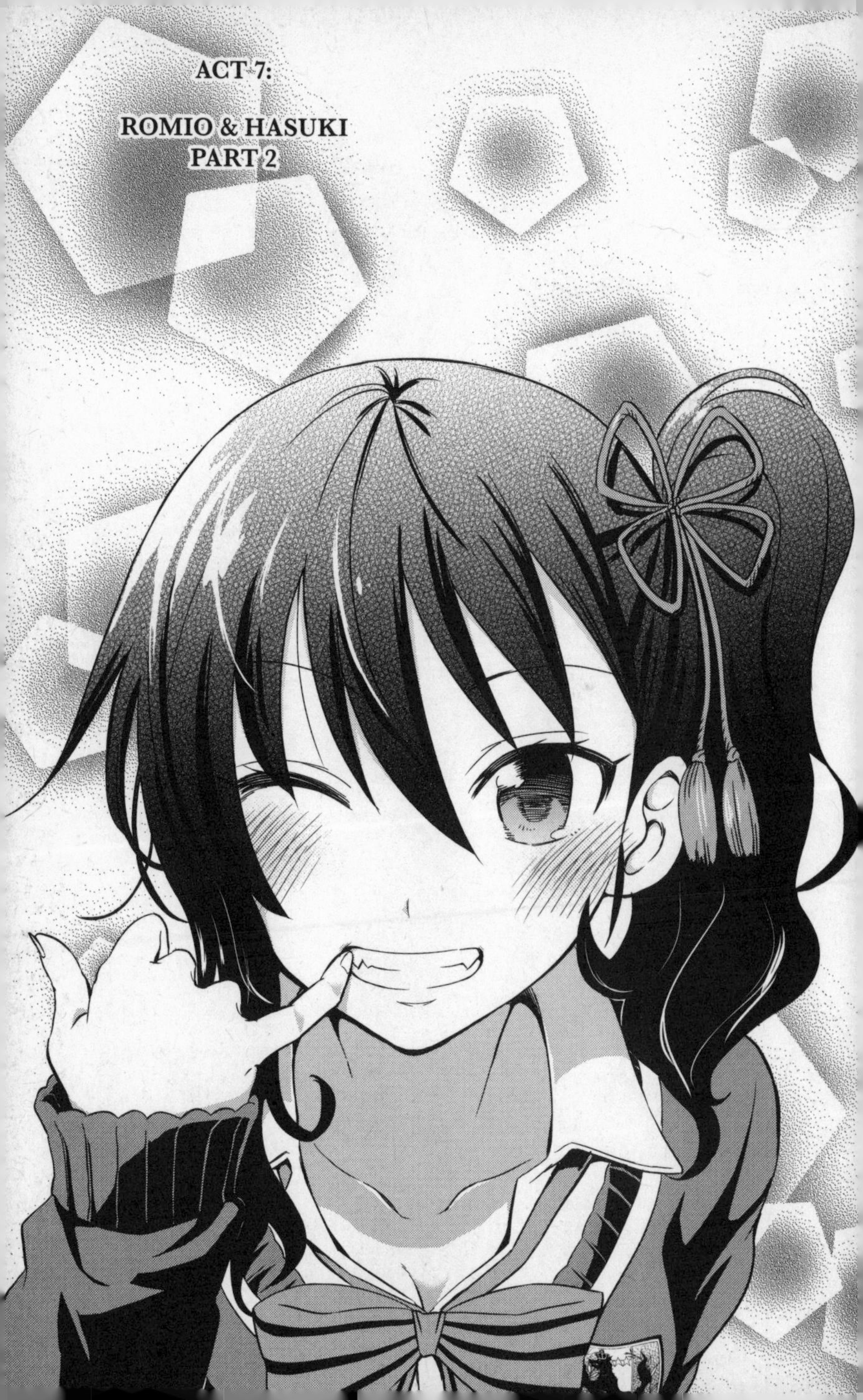

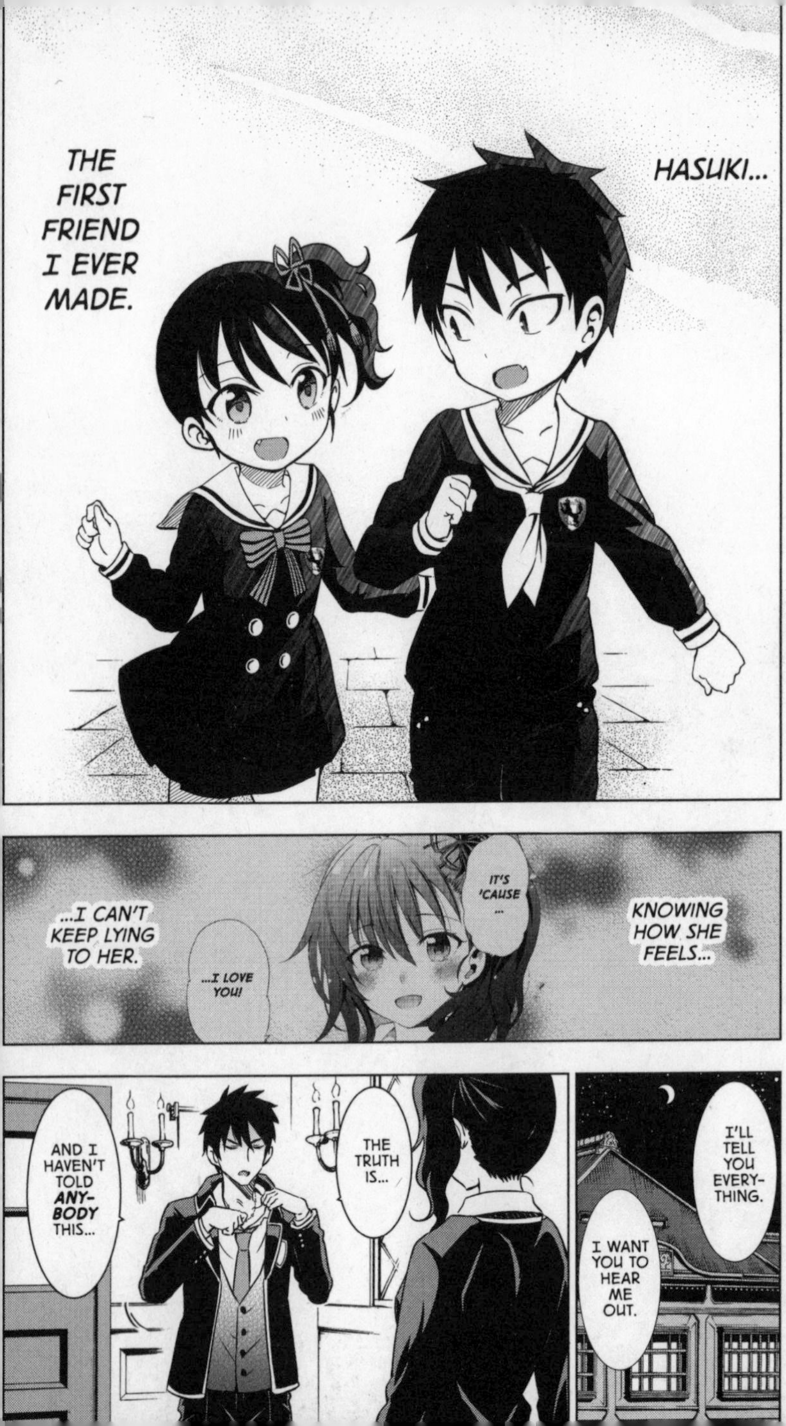
HASUKI...
THE FIRST FRIEND I EVER MADE.
KNOWING HOW SHE FEELS...
IT'S 'CAUSE ...
...I LOVE YOU!
...I CAN'T KEEP LYING TO HER.
I'LL TELL YOU EVERYTHING.
I WANT YOU TO HEAR ME OUT.
THE TRUTH IS...
AND I HAVEN'T TOLD ANYBODY THIS...

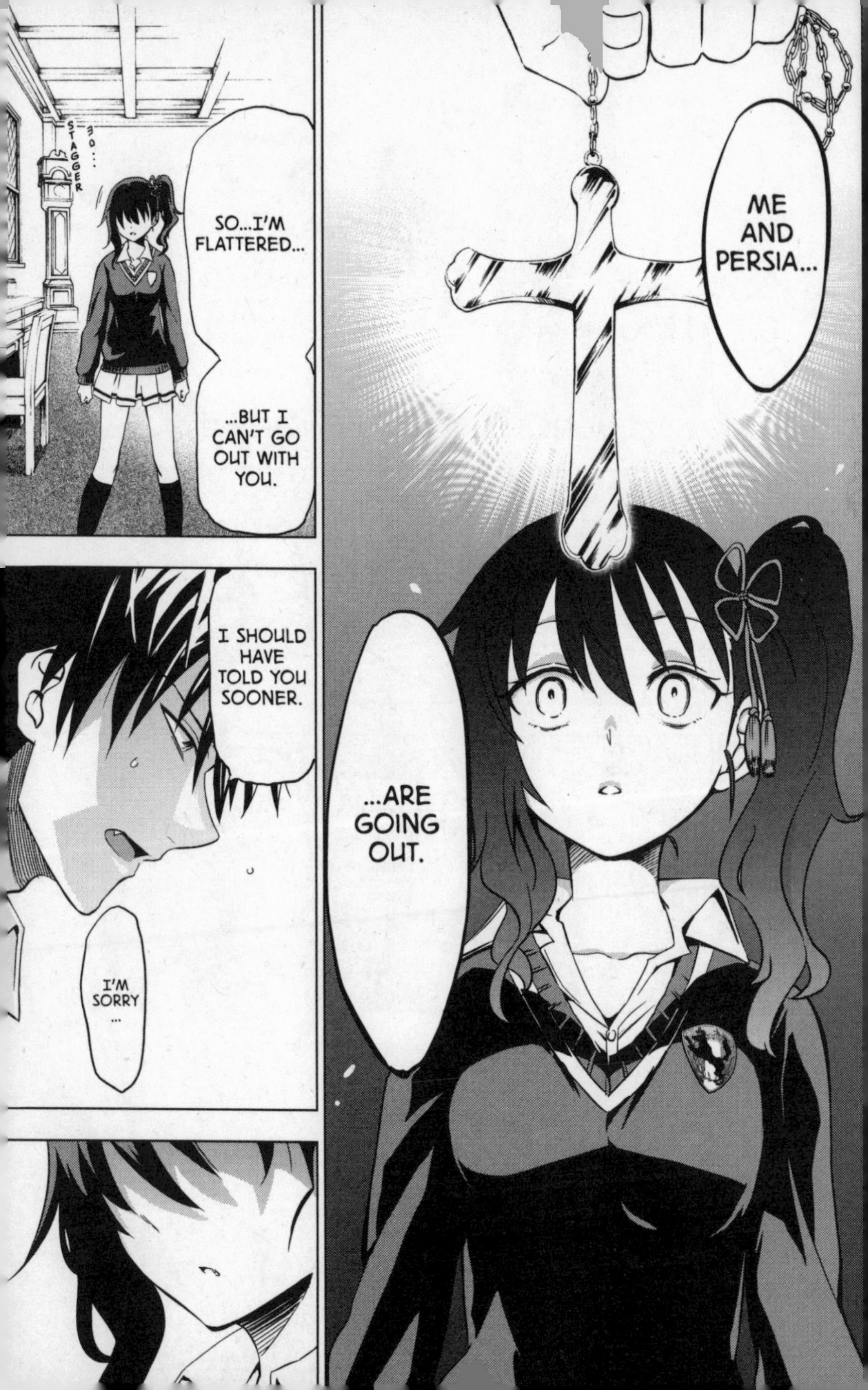
ME AND PERSIA...
...ARE GOING OUT.
STAGGER
SO...I'M FLATTERED...
...BUT I CAN'T GO OUT WITH YOU.
I SHOULD HAVE TOLD YOU SOONER.
I'M SORRY...

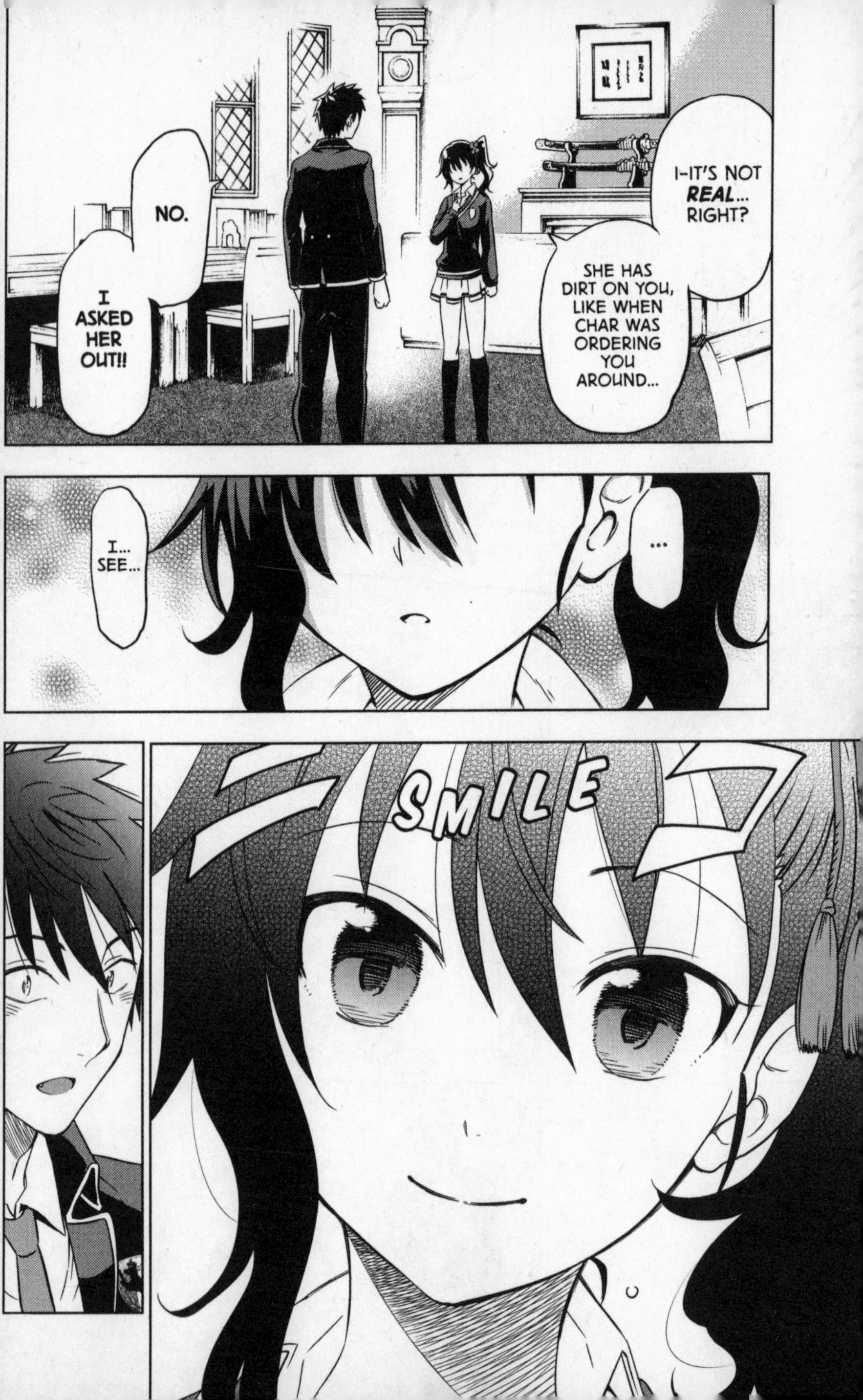
I-IT'S NOT ***REAL***... RIGHT?
SHE HAS DIRT ON YOU, LIKE WHEN CHAR WAS ORDERING YOU AROUND...
NO.
I ASKED HER OUT!!
...
I... SEE...
SMILE

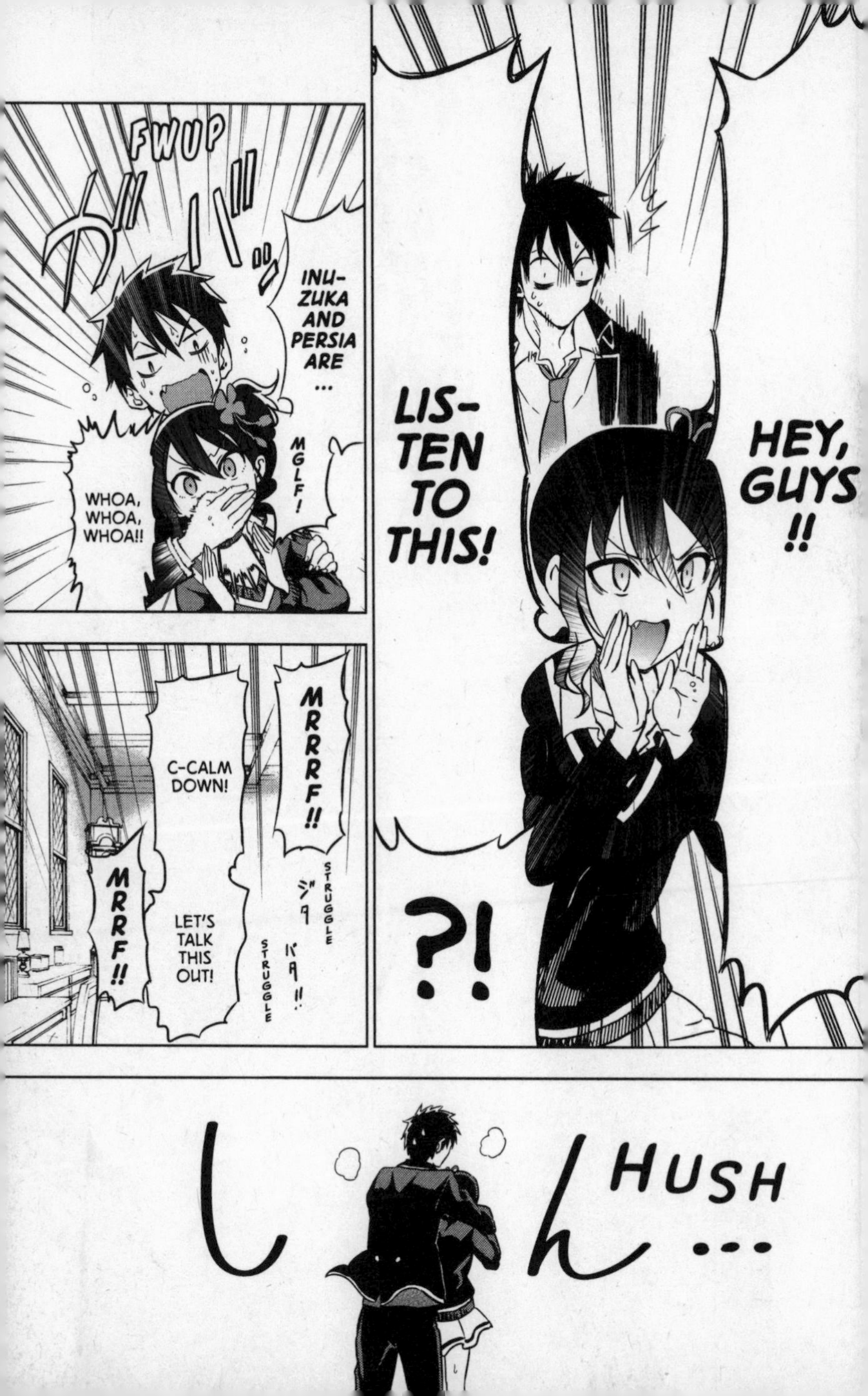
HEY, GUYS!!
LIS-TEN TO THIS!
?!
FWUP
INU-ZUKA AND PERSIA ARE ...
MGLF!
WHOA, WHOA, WHOA!!
MRRRF!!
STRUGGLE
ジタ バタ!!
STRUGGLE
C-CALM DOWN!
LET'S TALK THIS OUT!
MRRF!!
しん...
HUSH

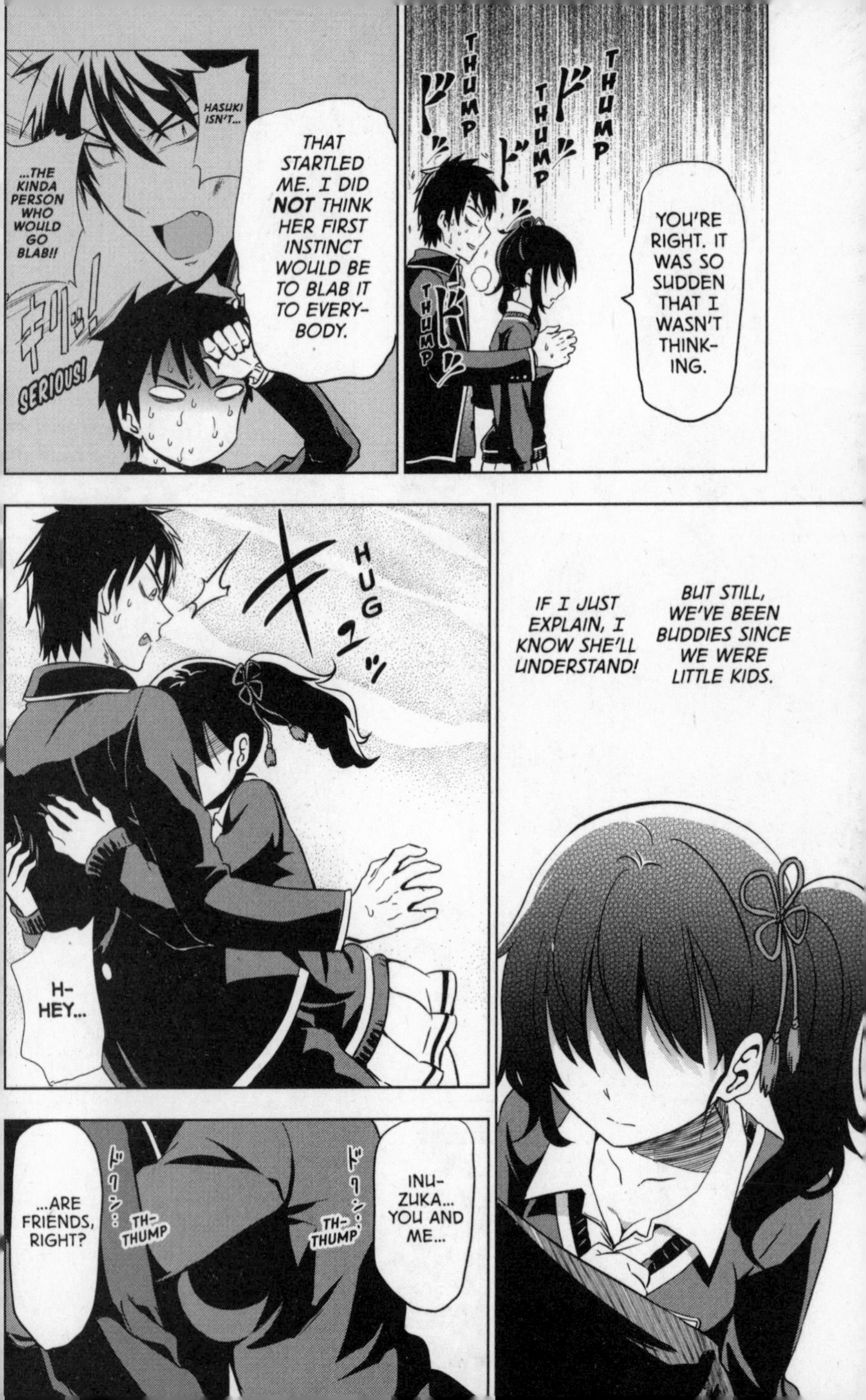
THUMP
THUMP
THUMP
THUMP
THUMP
YOU'RE RIGHT. IT WAS SO SUDDEN THAT I WASN'T THINKING.
THAT STARTLED ME. I DID **NOT** THINK HER FIRST INSTINCT WOULD BE TO BLAB IT TO EVERYBODY.
HASUKI ISN'T...
...THE KINDA PERSON WHO WOULD GO BLAB!!
SERIOUS!
BUT STILL, WE'VE BEEN BUDDIES SINCE WE WERE LITTLE KIDS.
IF I JUST EXPLAIN, I KNOW SHE'LL UNDERSTAND!
HUG
H-HEY...
INU-ZUKA... YOU AND ME...
TH-THUMP
TH-THUMP
...ARE FRIENDS, RIGHT?

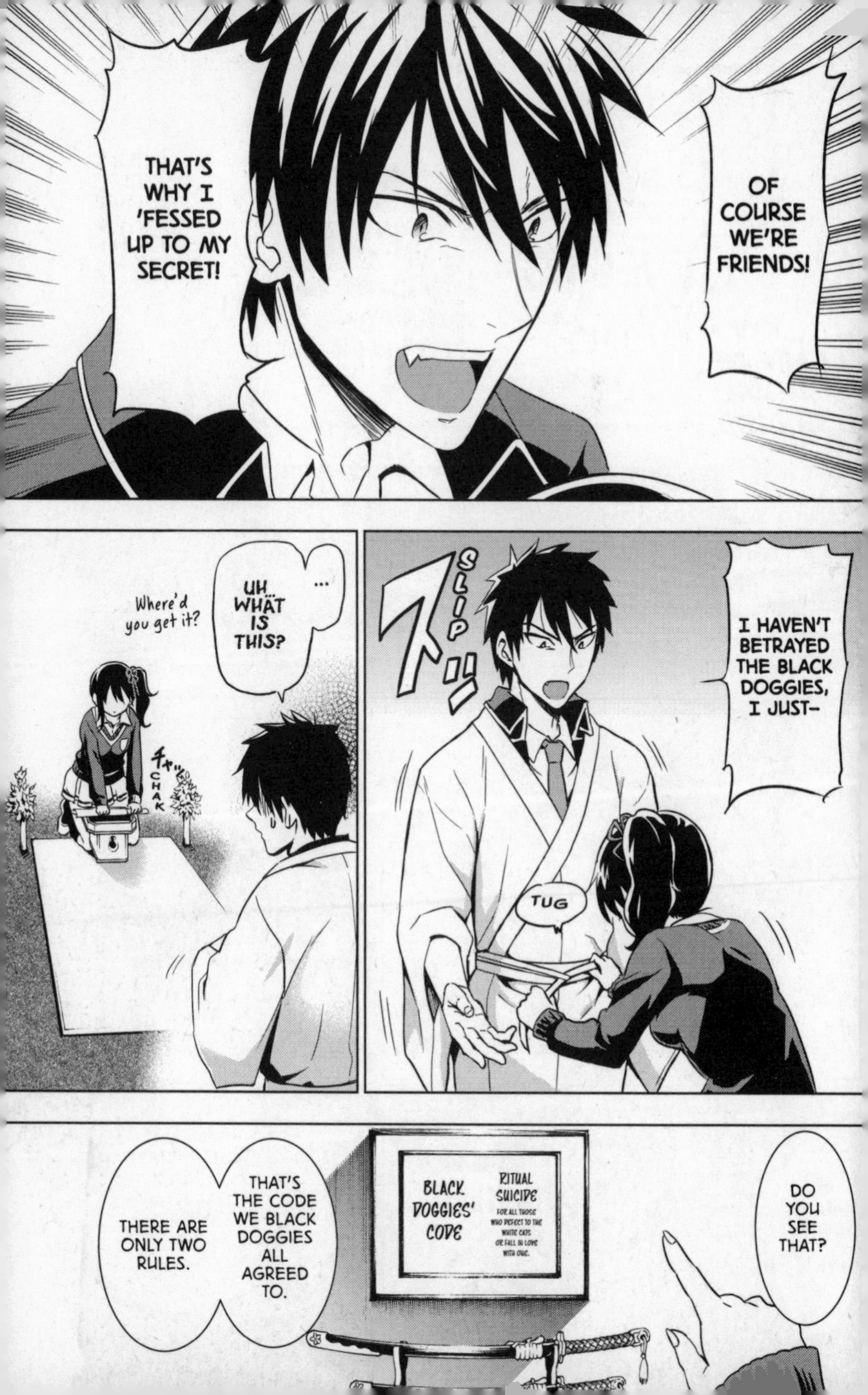
OF COURSE WE'RE FRIENDS!
THAT'S WHY I 'FESSED UP TO MY SECRET!
I HAVEN'T BETRAYED THE BLACK DOGGIES, I JUST–
SLIP
TUG
...
UH... WHAT IS THIS?
Where'd you get it?
CHAK
DO YOU SEE THAT?
BLACK DOGGIES' CODE
RITUAL SUICIDE
FOR ALL THOSE WHO DEFECT TO THE WHITE CATS OR FALL IN LOVE WITH ONE.
THAT'S THE CODE WE BLACK DOGGIES ALL AGREED TO.
THERE ARE ONLY TWO RULES.

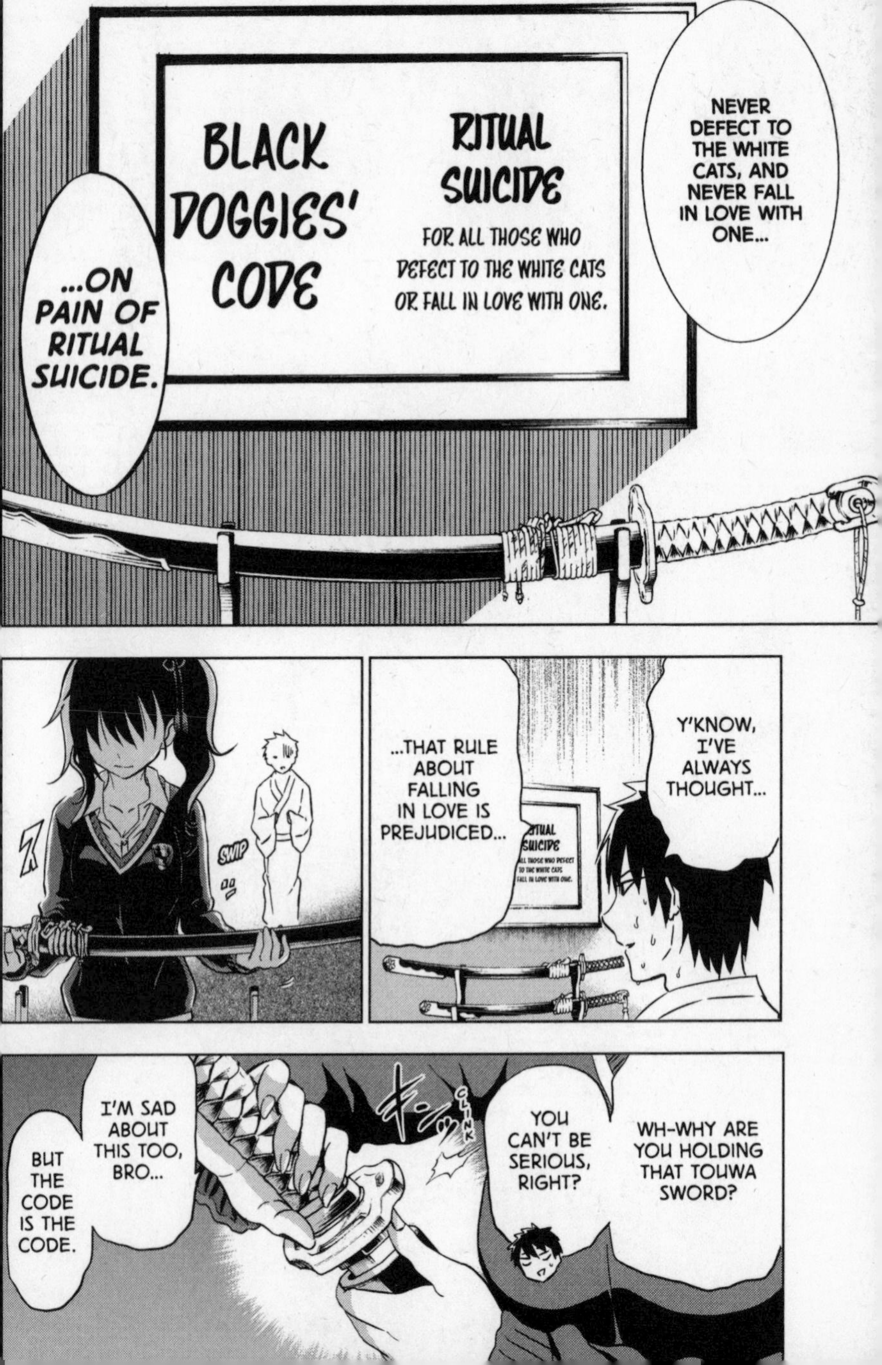
NEVER DEFECT TO THE WHITE CATS, AND NEVER FALL IN LOVE WITH ONE...
BLACK DOGGIES' CODE
RITUAL SUICIDE
FOR ALL THOSE WHO DEFECT TO THE WHITE CATS OR FALL IN LOVE WITH ONE.
...ON PAIN OF RITUAL SUICIDE.
Y'KNOW, I'VE ALWAYS THOUGHT...
...THAT RULE ABOUT FALLING IN LOVE IS PREJUDICED...
SWIP
WH-WHY ARE YOU HOLDING THAT TOUWA SWORD?
YOU CAN'T BE SERIOUS, RIGHT?
CLINK
I'M SAD ABOUT THIS TOO, BRO...
BUT THE CODE IS THE CODE.

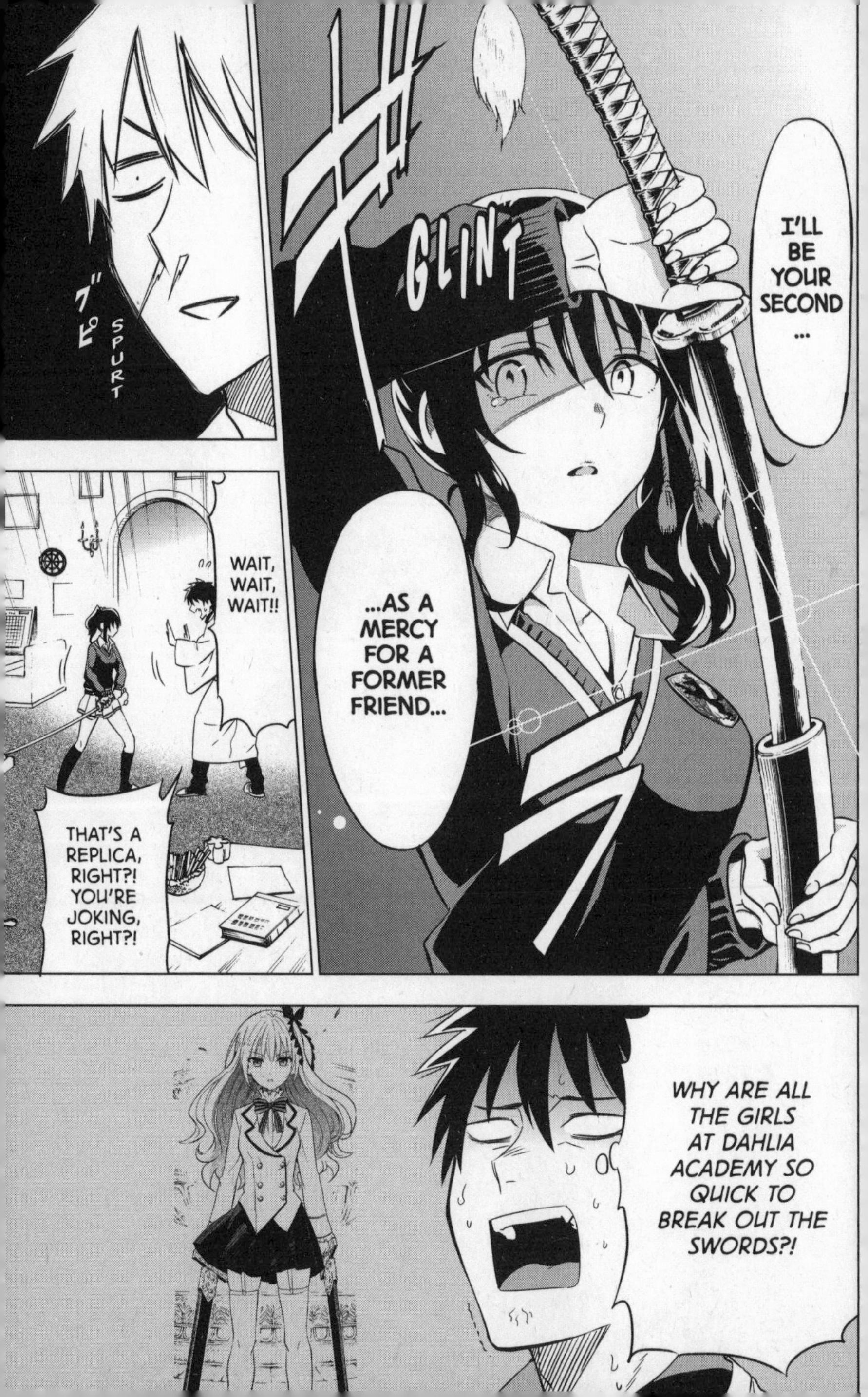
I'LL BE YOUR SECOND ...
GLINT
...AS A MERCY FOR A FORMER FRIEND...
SPURT
WAIT, WAIT, WAIT!!
THAT'S A REPLICA, RIGHT?! YOU'RE JOKING, RIGHT?!
WHY ARE ALL THE GIRLS AT DAHLIA ACADEMY SO QUICK TO BREAK OUT THE SWORDS?!

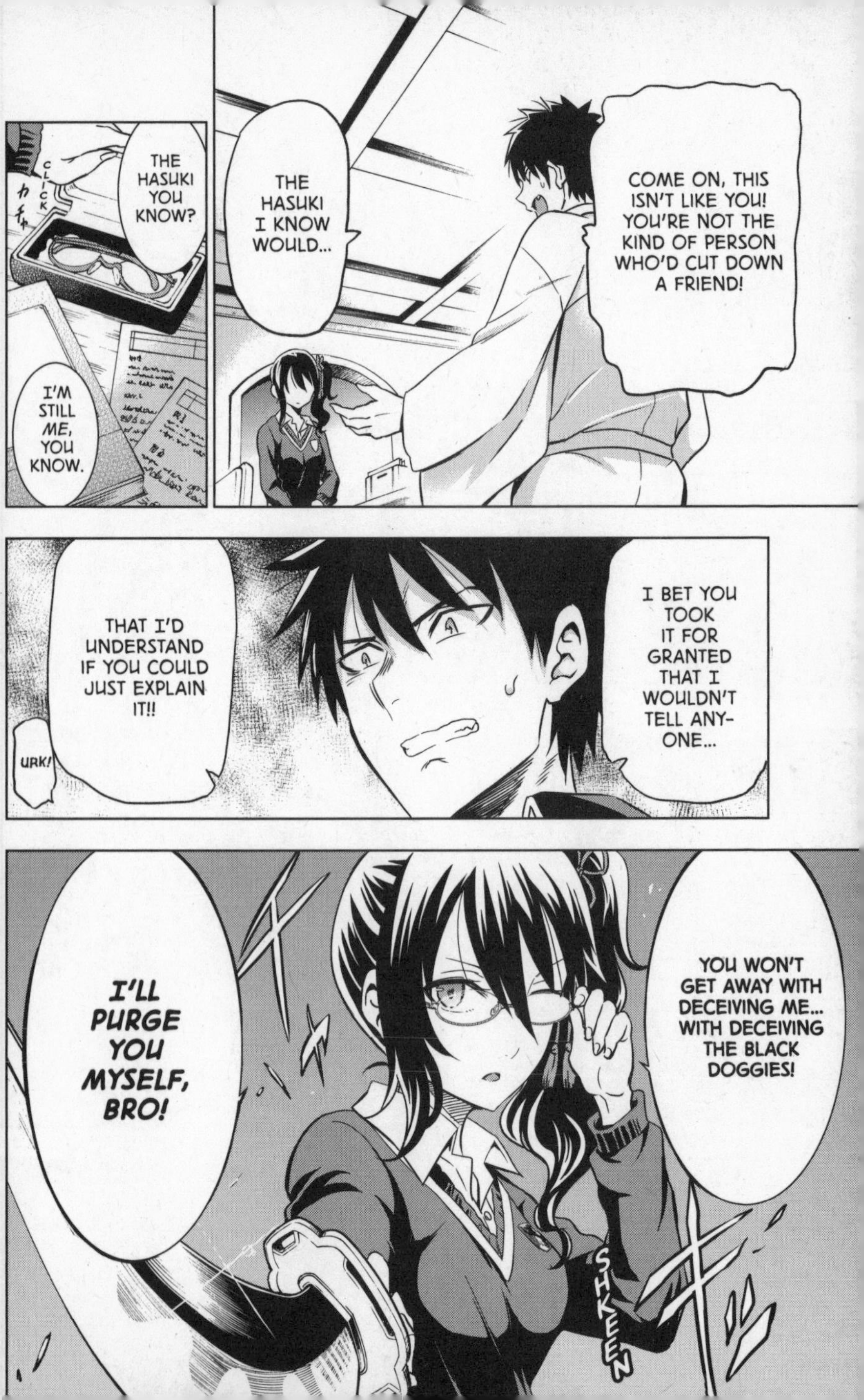
COME ON, THIS ISN'T LIKE YOU! YOU'RE NOT THE KIND OF PERSON WHO'D CUT DOWN A FRIEND!
THE HASUKI I KNOW WOULD...
THE HASUKI YOU KNOW?
CLICK
カチャ
I'M STILL *ME*, YOU KNOW.
I BET YOU TOOK IT FOR GRANTED THAT I WOULDN'T TELL ANY-ONE...
THAT I'D UNDERSTAND IF YOU COULD JUST EXPLAIN IT!!
URK!
YOU WON'T GET AWAY WITH DECEIVING ME... WITH DECEIVING THE BLACK DOGGIES!
SHKEEN
I'LL PURGE YOU MYSELF, BRO!

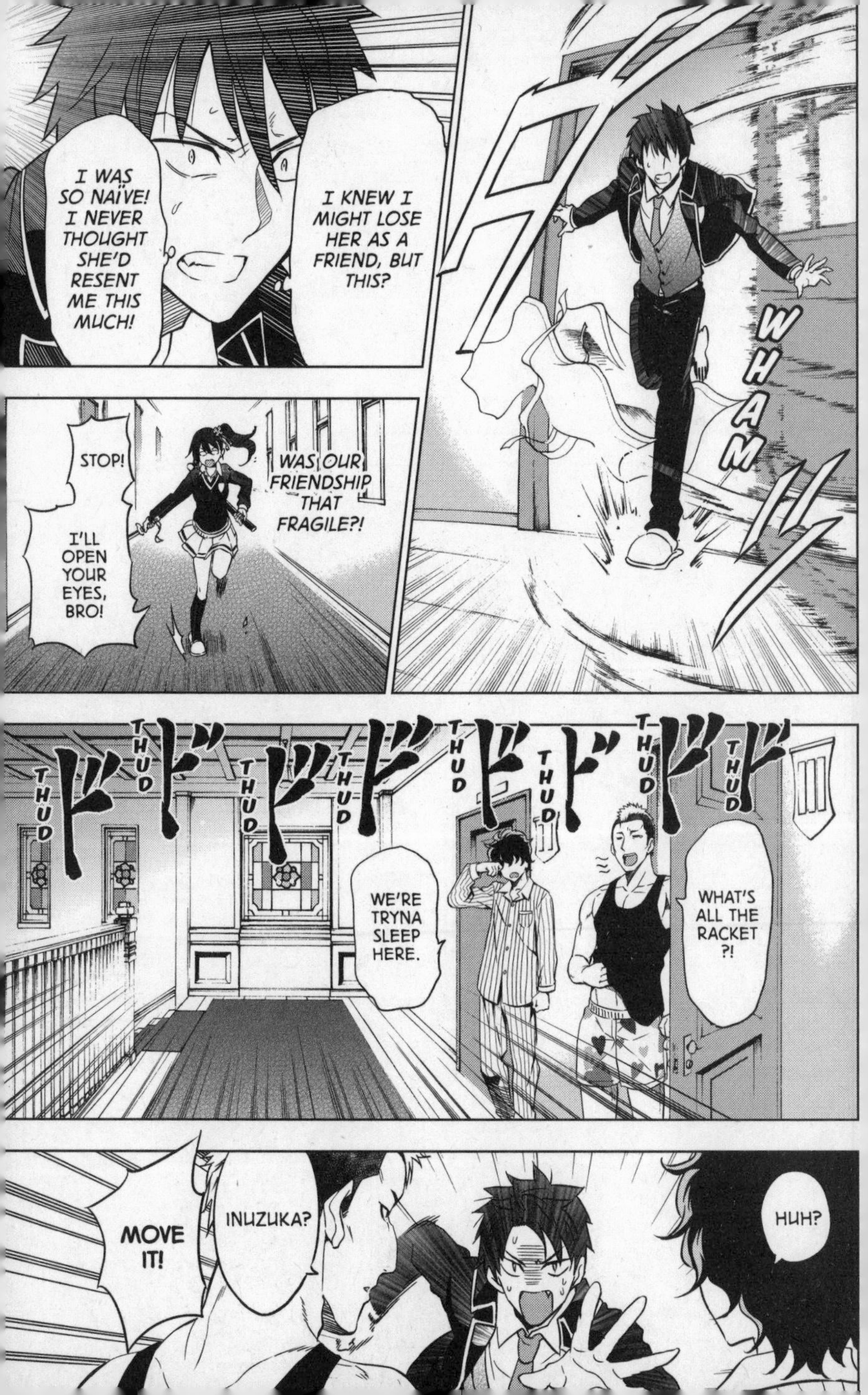
WHAM
I KNEW I MIGHT LOSE HER AS A FRIEND, BUT THIS?
I WAS SO NAÏVE! I NEVER THOUGHT SHE'D RESENT ME THIS MUCH!
WAS OUR FRIENDSHIP THAT FRAGILE?!
STOP!
I'LL OPEN YOUR EYES, BRO!
THUD THUD THUD THUD THUD THUD THUD THUD
WHAT'S ALL THE RACKET?!
WE'RE TRYNA SLEEP HERE.
HUH?
INUZUKA?
MOVE IT!

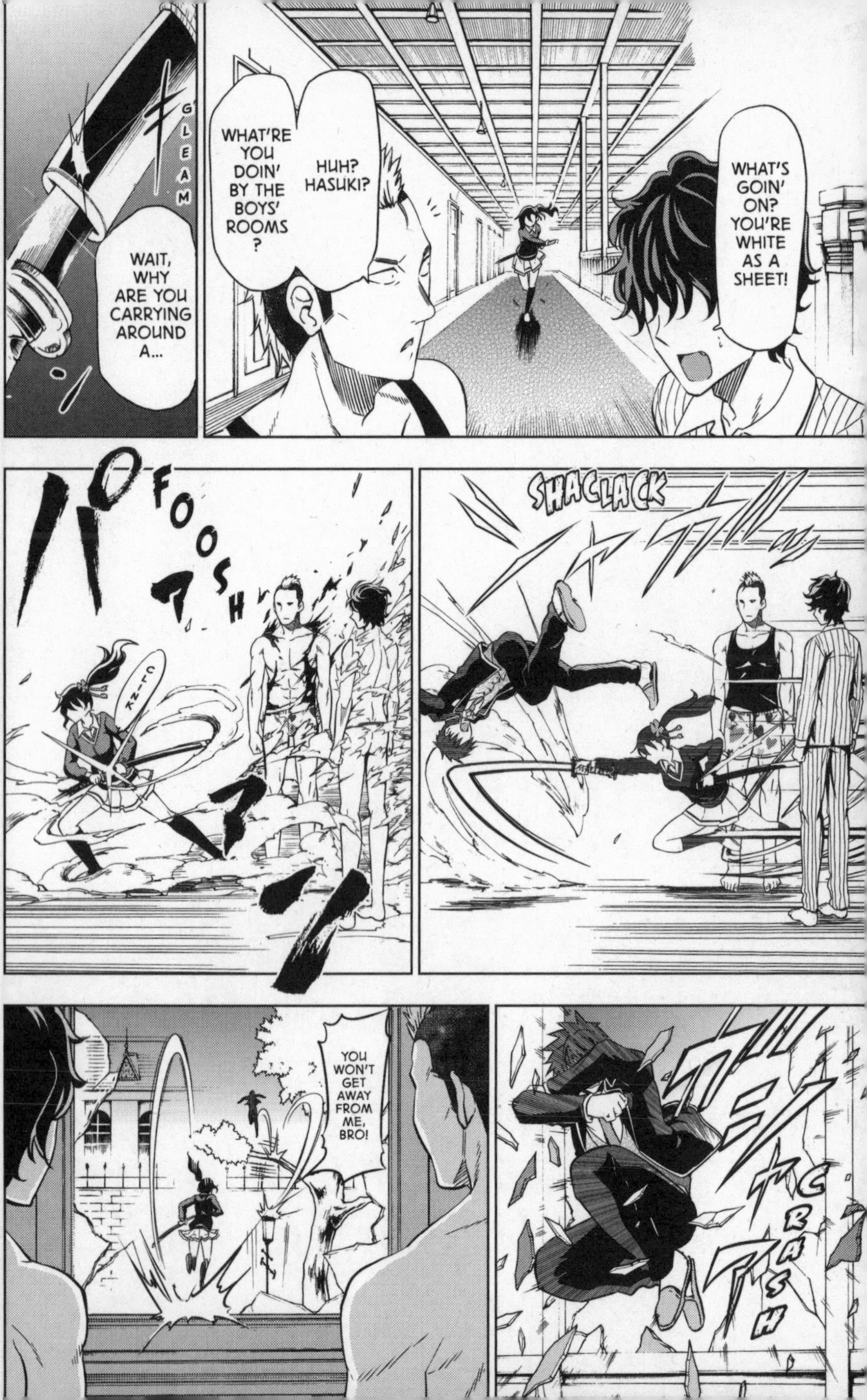
WHAT'S GOIN' ON? YOU'RE WHITE AS A SHEET!
HUH? HASUKI?
WHAT'RE YOU DOIN' BY THE BOYS' ROOMS?
GLEAM
WAIT, WHY ARE YOU CARRYING AROUND A...
SHACLACK
FOOSH
CLINK
CRASH
YOU WON'T GET AWAY FROM ME, BRO!

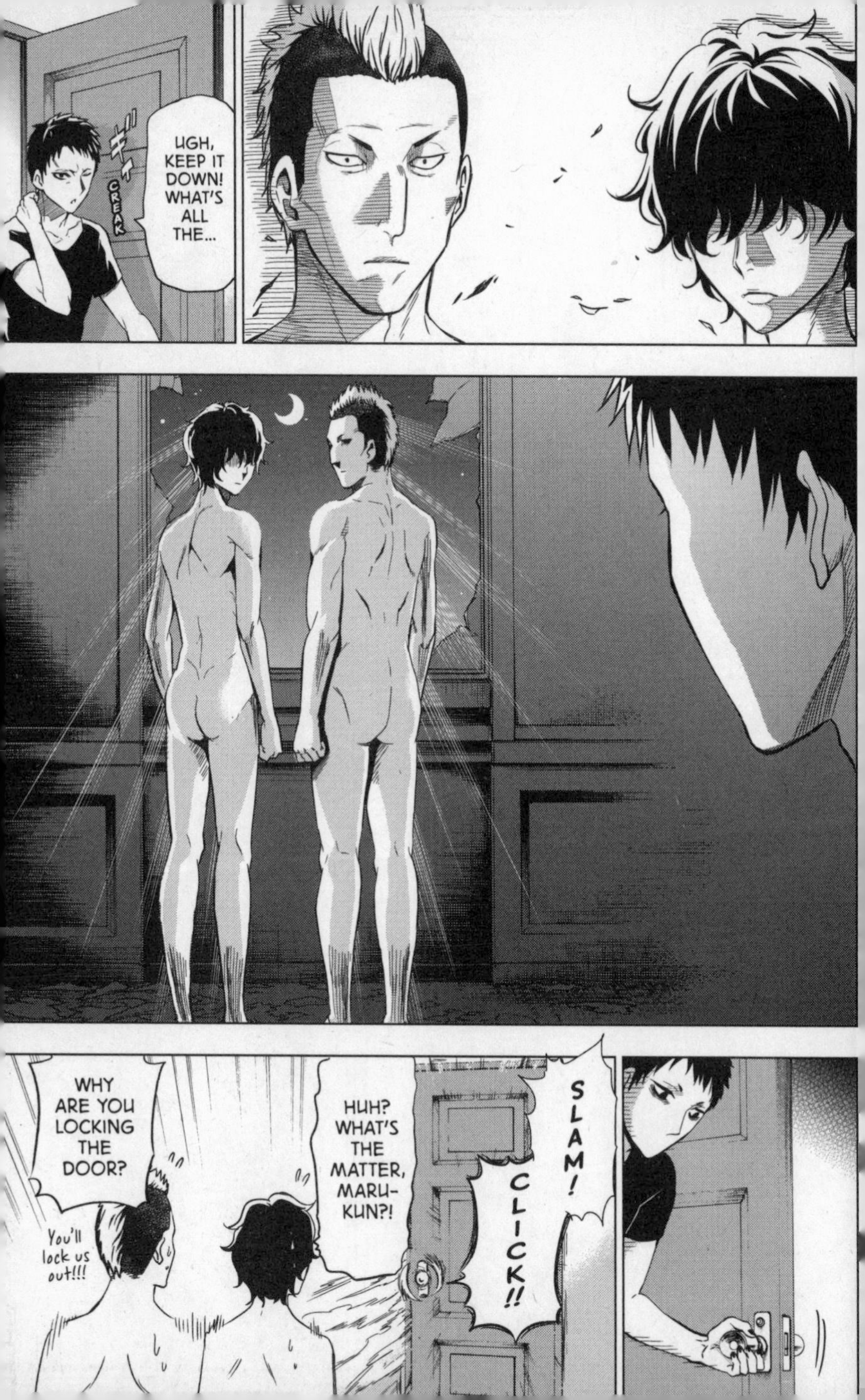
CREAK
UGH, KEEP IT DOWN! WHAT'S ALL THE...
SLAM!
CLICK!!
HUH? WHAT'S THE MATTER, MARU-KUN?!
WHY ARE YOU LOCKING THE DOOR?
You'll lock us out!!!

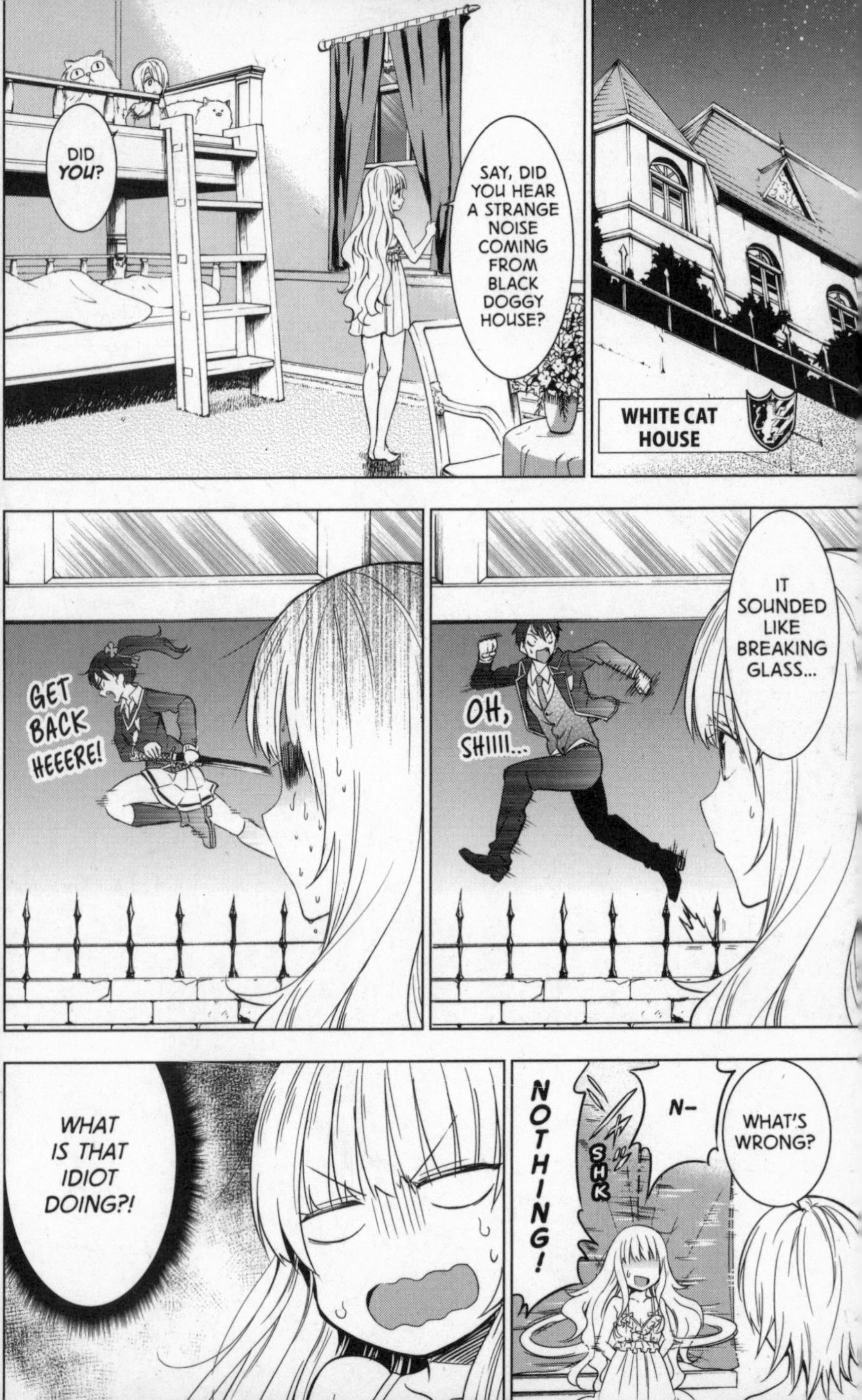
WHITE CAT HOUSE
SAY, DID YOU HEAR A STRANGE NOISE COMING FROM BLACK DOGGY HOUSE?
DID YOU?
IT SOUNDED LIKE BREAKING GLASS...
OH, SHIIII...
GET BACK HEEERE!
WHAT'S WRONG?
N-
NOTHING!
SHK
WHAT IS THAT IDIOT DOING?!

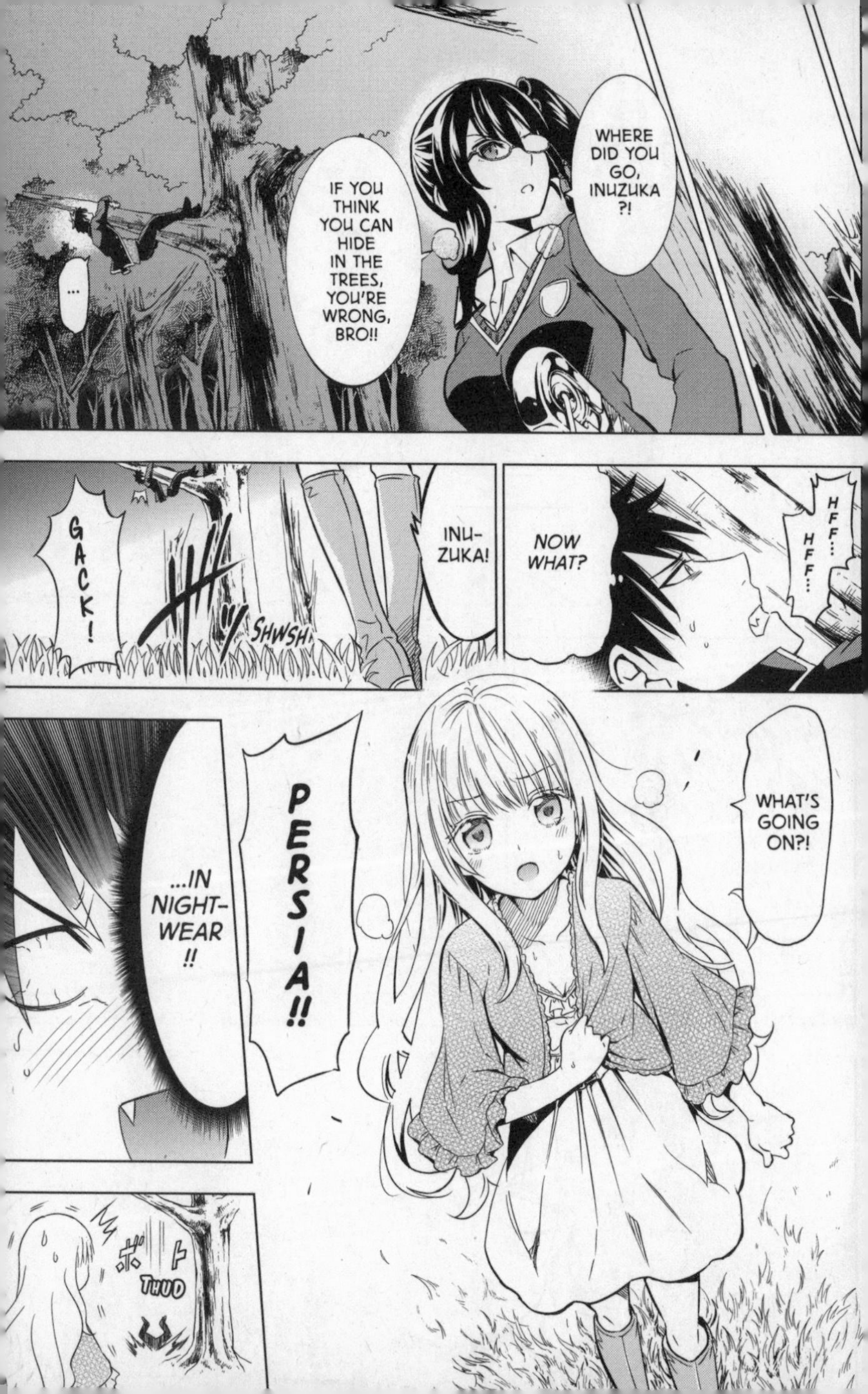

WHERE DID YOU GO, INUZUKA?!
IF YOU THINK YOU CAN HIDE IN THE TREES, YOU'RE WRONG, BRO!!
...
HFF... HFF...
NOW WHAT?
INUZUKA!
SHWSH
GACK!
WHAT'S GOING ON?!
PERSIA!!
...IN NIGHT-WEAR!!
ボト
THUD

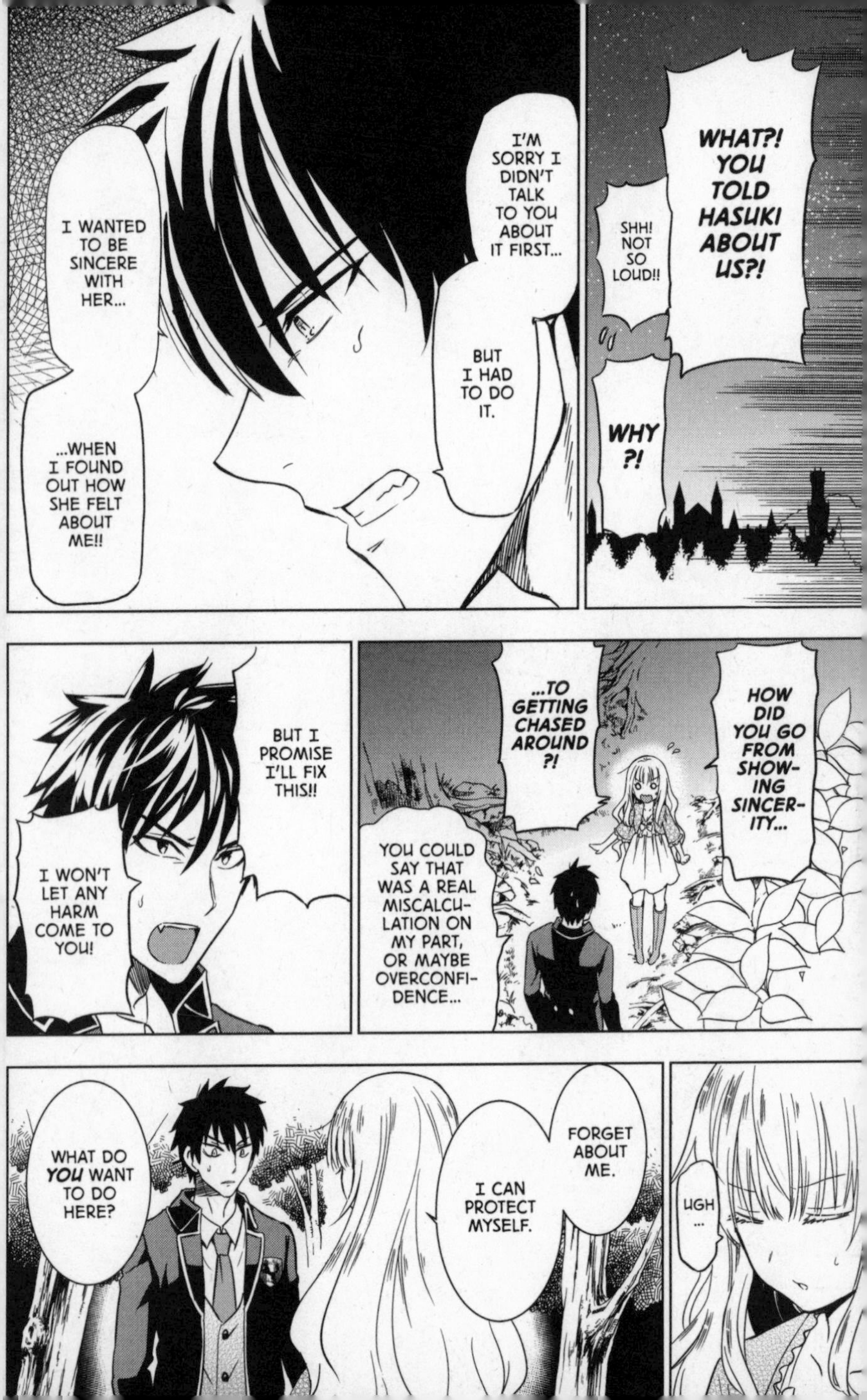
WHAT?! YOU TOLD HASUKI ABOUT US?!
SHH! NOT SO LOUD!!
WHY?!
I'M SORRY I DIDN'T TALK TO YOU ABOUT IT FIRST...
BUT I HAD TO DO IT.
I WANTED TO BE SINCERE WITH HER...
...WHEN I FOUND OUT HOW SHE FELT ABOUT ME!!
HOW DID YOU GO FROM SHOWING SINCERITY...
...TO GETTING CHASED AROUND?!
YOU COULD SAY THAT WAS A REAL MISCALCULATION ON MY PART, OR MAYBE OVERCONFIDENCE...
BUT I PROMISE I'LL FIX THIS!!
I WON'T LET ANY HARM COME TO YOU!
UGH...
FORGET ABOUT ME.
I CAN PROTECT MYSELF.
WHAT DO *YOU* WANT TO DO HERE?

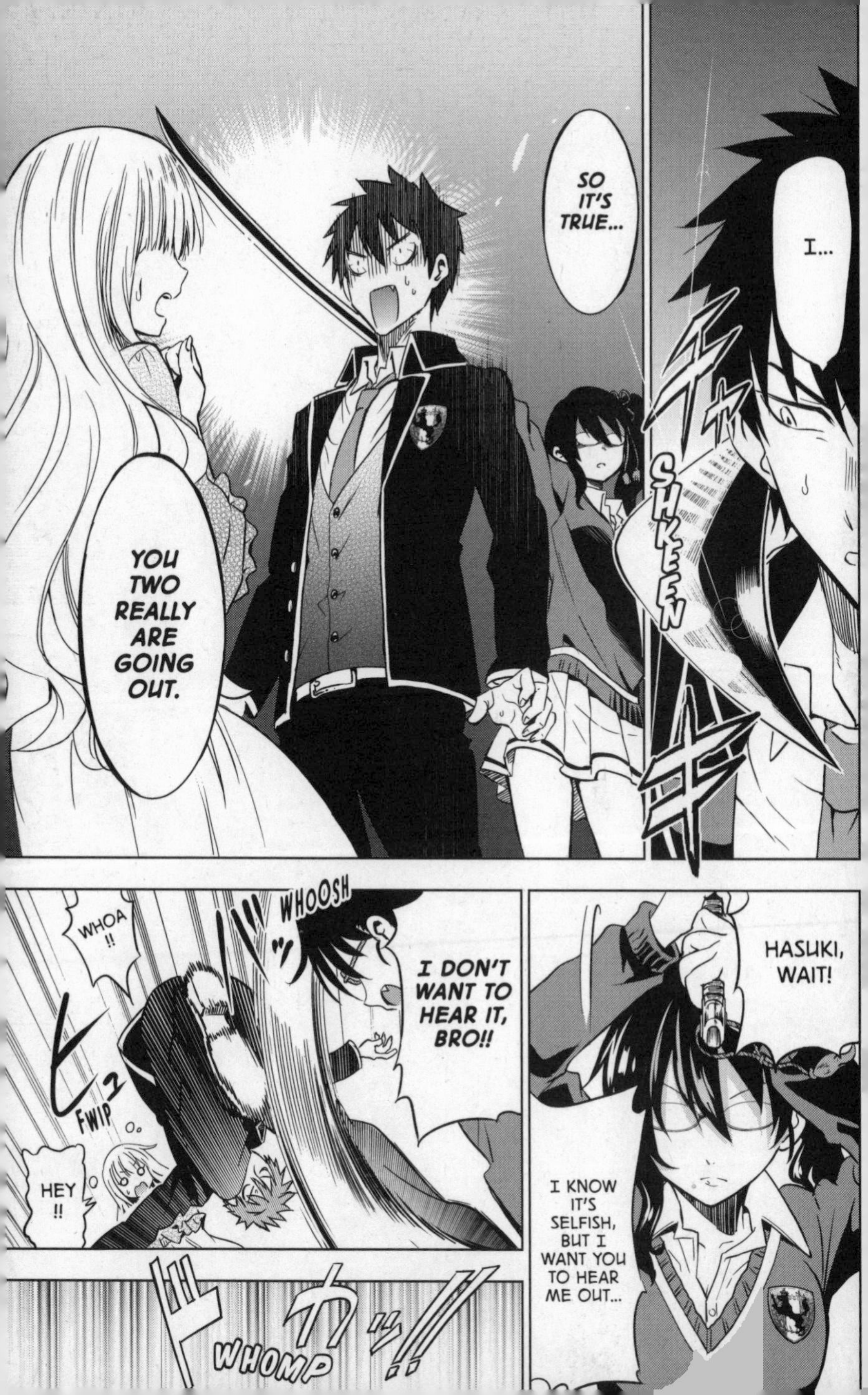
I...
SHKEEN
SO IT'S TRUE...
YOU TWO REALLY ARE GOING OUT.
HASUKI, WAIT!
I KNOW IT'S SELFISH, BUT I WANT YOU TO HEAR ME OUT...
WHOOSH
I DON'T WANT TO HEAR IT, BRO!!
WHOA !!
FWIP
HEY !!
WHOMP

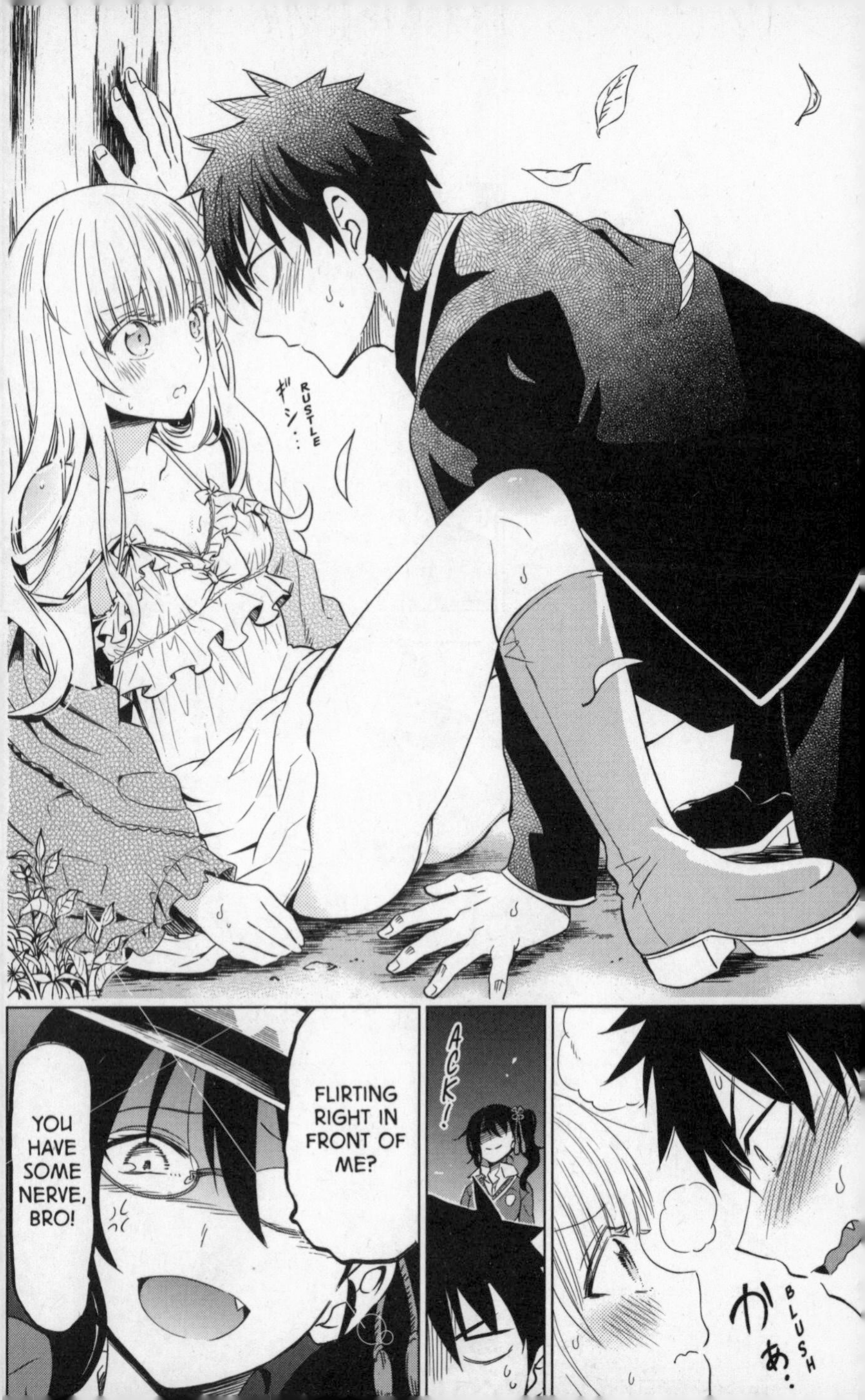
ガシ…
RUSTLE
かあ…
BLUSH
ACK!
FLIRTING RIGHT IN FRONT OF ME?
YOU HAVE SOME NERVE, BRO!

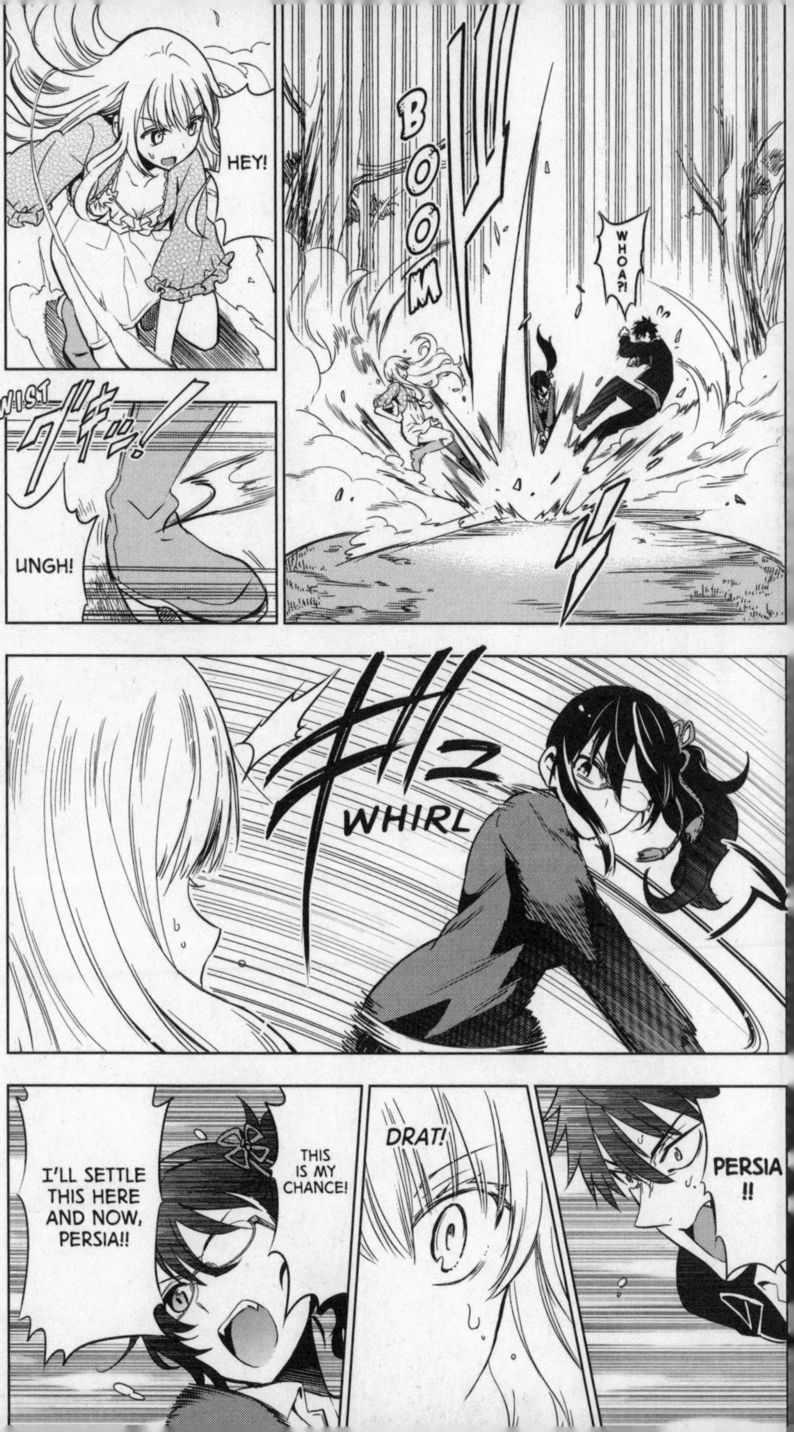
BOOM
WHOA?!
HEY!
TWIST
UNGH!
WHIRL
PERSIA!!
DRAT!
THIS IS MY CHANCE!
I'LL SETTLE THIS HERE AND NOW, PERSIA!!

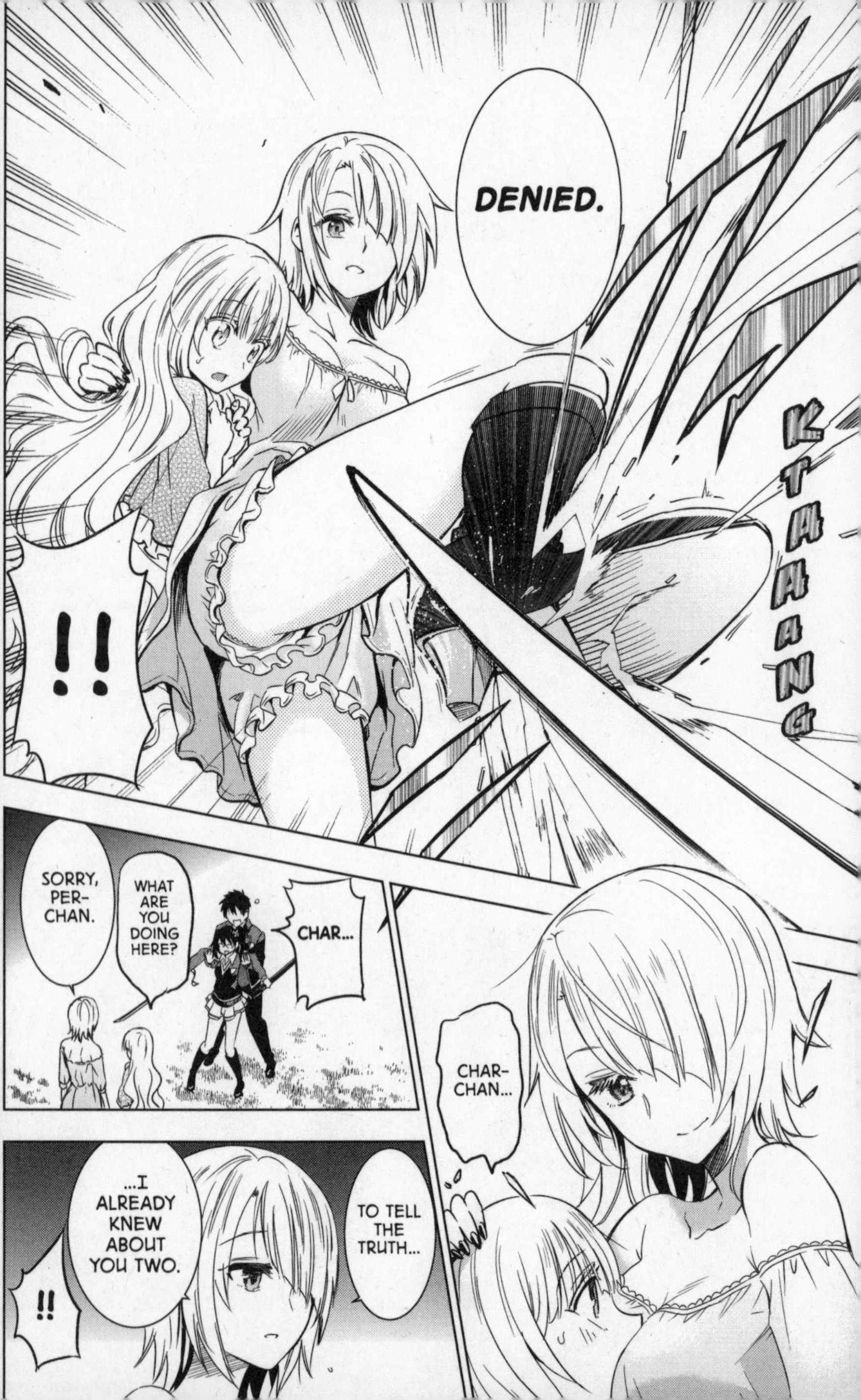
DENIED.
KTAAAANG
!!
CHAR-CHAN...
CHAR...
WHAT ARE YOU DOING HERE?
SORRY, PER-CHAN.
TO TELL THE TRUTH...
...I ALREADY KNEW ABOUT YOU TWO.
!!

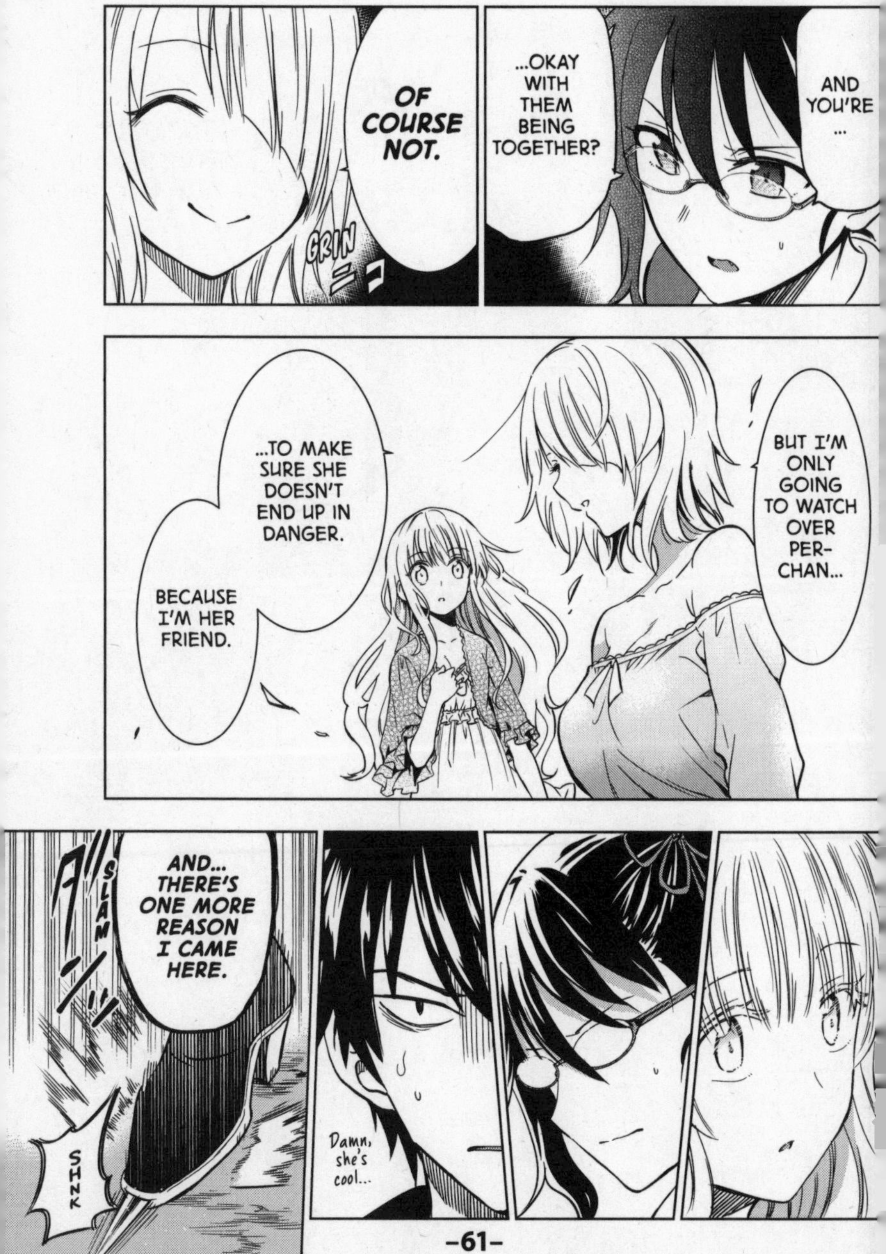
AND YOU'RE ...
...OKAY WITH THEM BEING TOGETHER?
OF COURSE NOT.
GRIN
BUT I'M ONLY GOING TO WATCH OVER PER-CHAN...
...TO MAKE SURE SHE DOESN'T END UP IN DANGER.
BECAUSE I'M HER FRIEND.
Damn, she's cool...
AND... THERE'S ONE MORE REASON I CAME HERE.
SLAM
SHNK

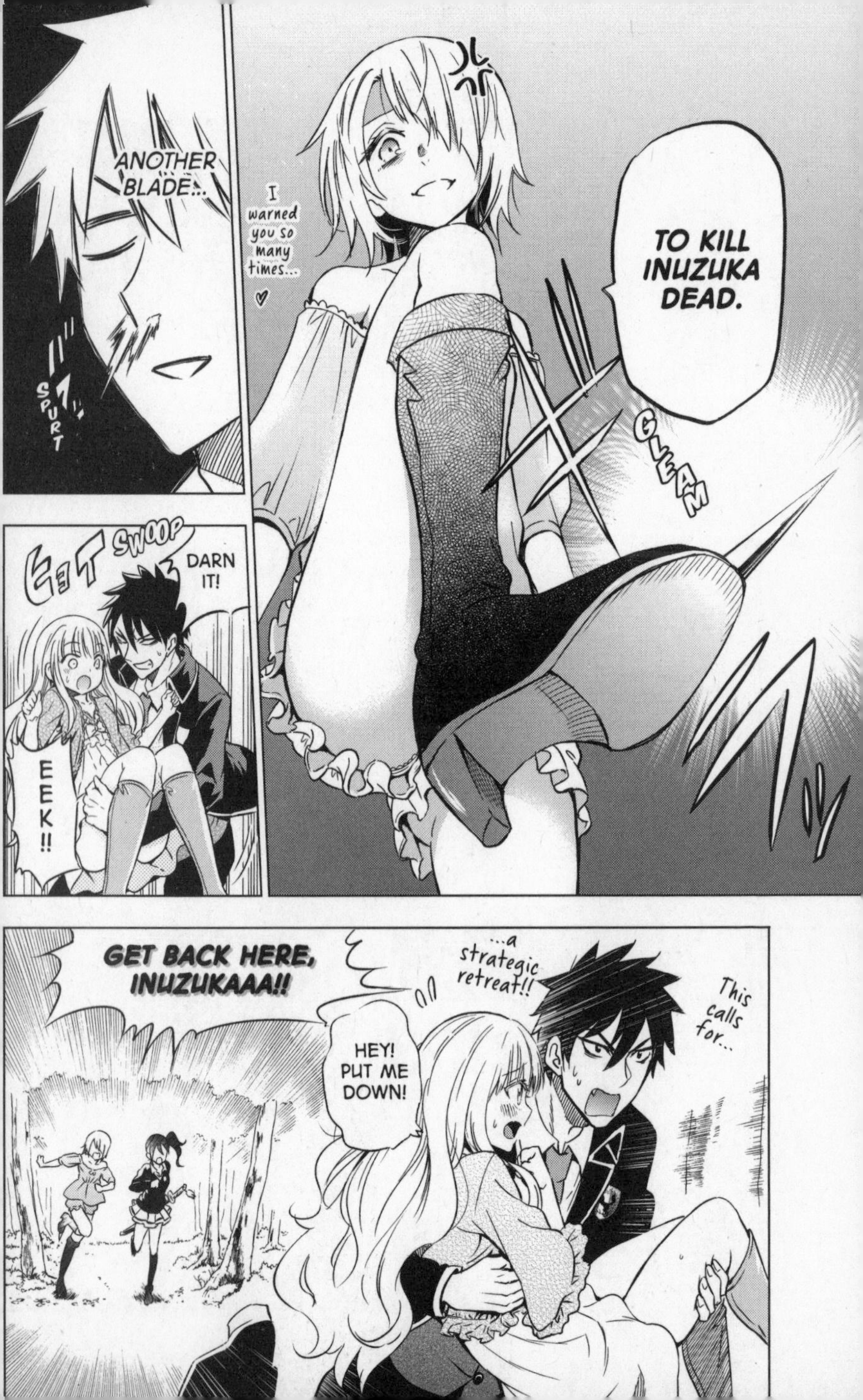
TO KILL INUZUKA DEAD.
I warned you so many times... ♥
GLEAM
ANOTHER BLADE...
SPURT
ヒョイ SWOOP
DARN IT!
EEK!!
This calls for...
...a strategic retreat!!
HEY! PUT ME DOWN!
GET BACK HERE, INUZUKAAA!!

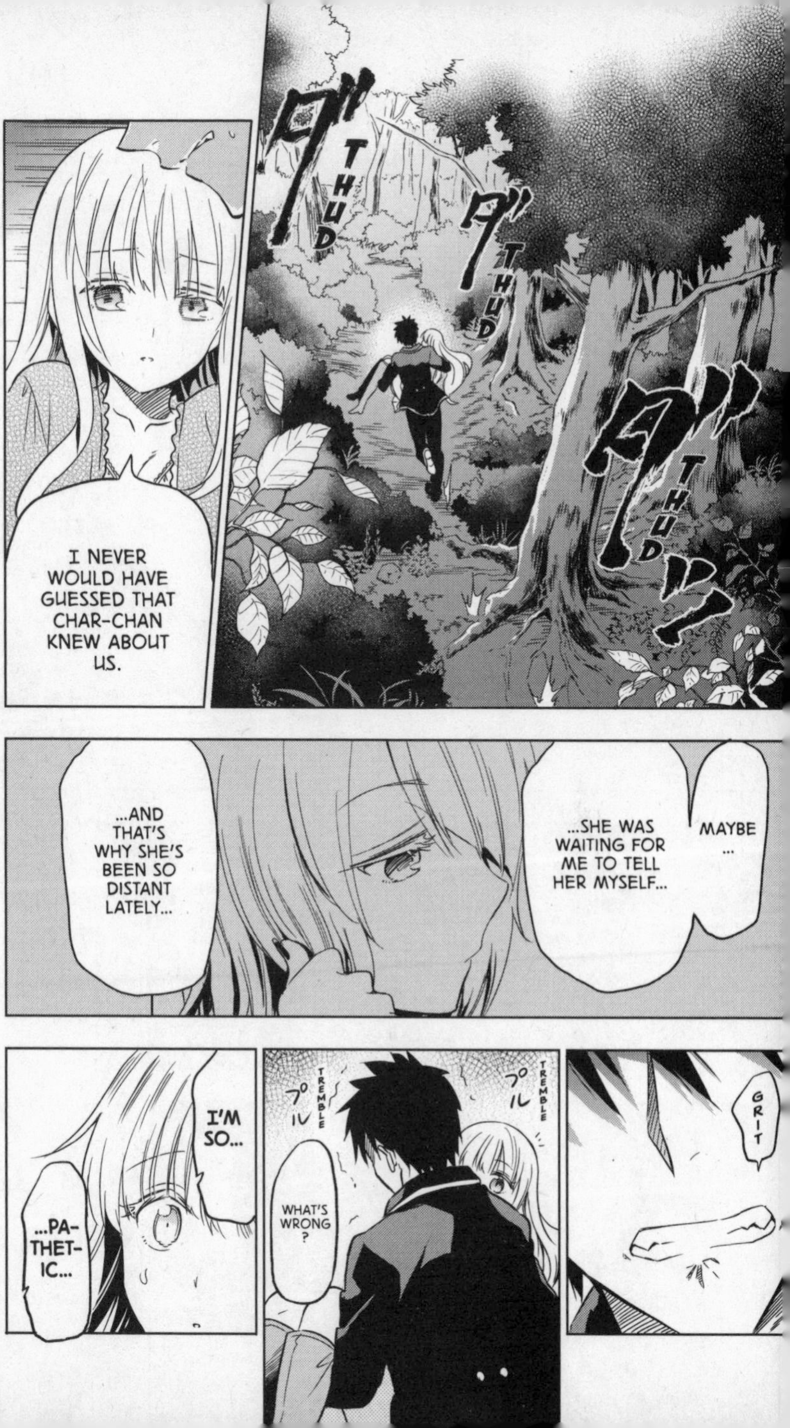
THUD
THUD
THUD
I NEVER WOULD HAVE GUESSED THAT CHAR-CHAN KNEW ABOUT US.
MAYBE ...
...SHE WAS WAITING FOR ME TO TELL HER MYSELF...
...AND THAT'S WHY SHE'S BEEN SO DISTANT LATELY...
GRIT
TREMBLE
TREMBLE
WHAT'S WRONG?
I'M SO...
...PA-THET-IC...

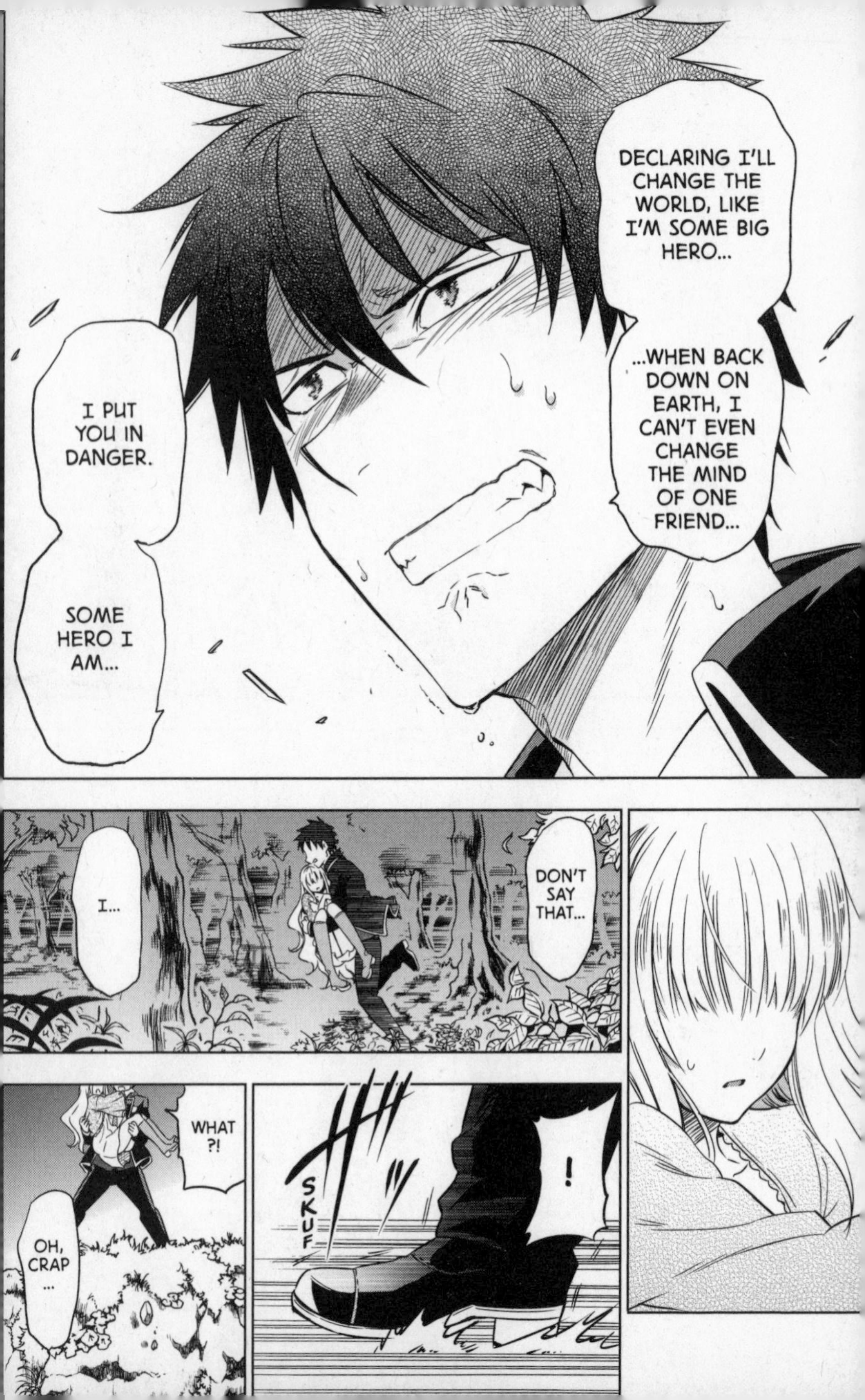
DECLARING I'LL CHANGE THE WORLD, LIKE I'M SOME BIG HERO...
...WHEN BACK DOWN ON EARTH, I CAN'T EVEN CHANGE THE MIND OF ONE FRIEND...
I PUT YOU IN DANGER.
SOME HERO I AM...
DON'T SAY THAT...
I...
!
SKUF
WHAT ?!
OH, CRAP ...

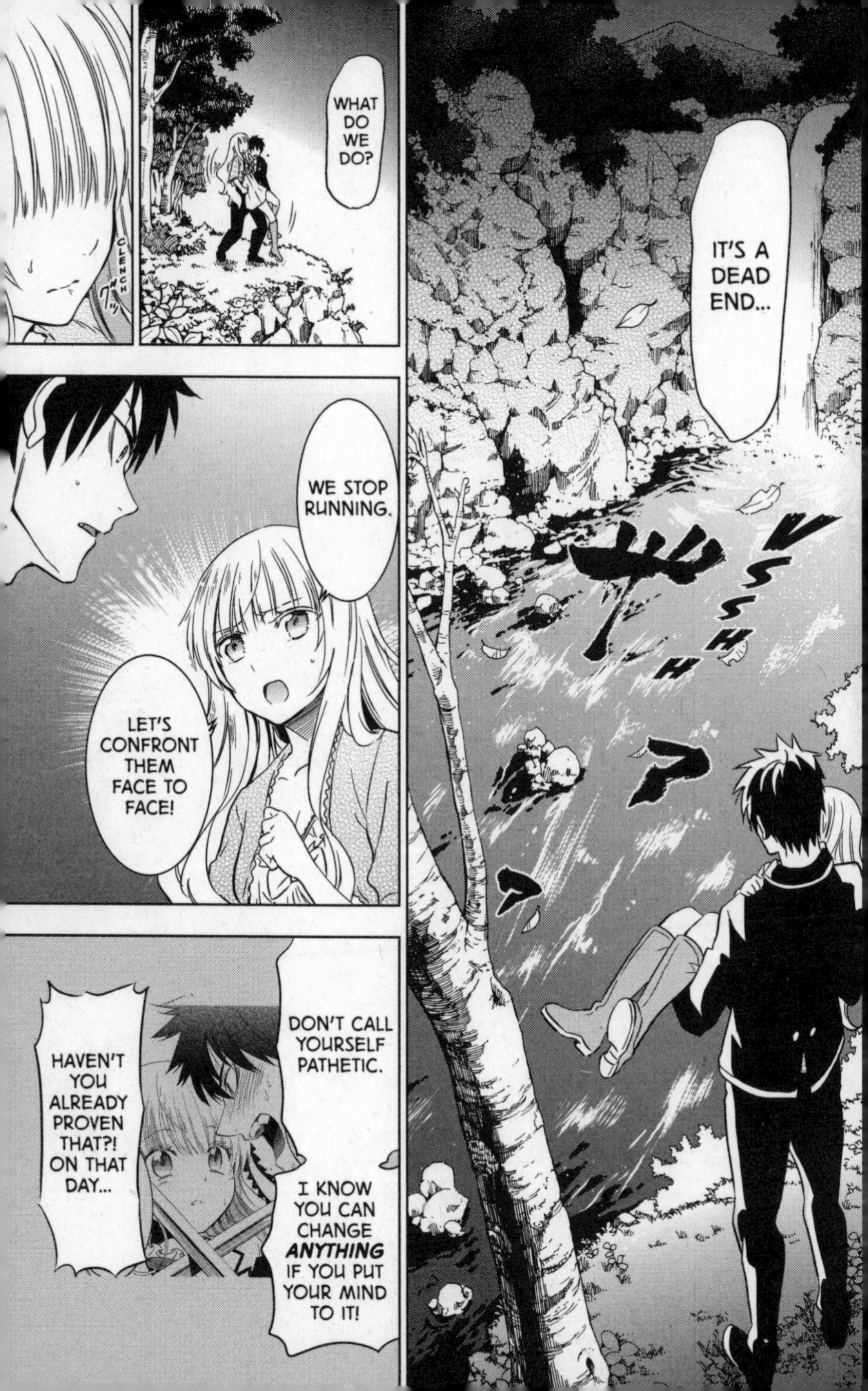
IT'S A DEAD END...
VSSHH
WHAT DO WE DO?
CLENCH
WE STOP RUNNING.
LET'S CONFRONT THEM FACE TO FACE!
DON'T CALL YOURSELF PATHETIC.
I KNOW YOU CAN CHANGE ***ANYTHING*** IF YOU PUT YOUR MIND TO IT!
HAVEN'T YOU ALREADY PROVEN THAT?! ON THAT DAY...

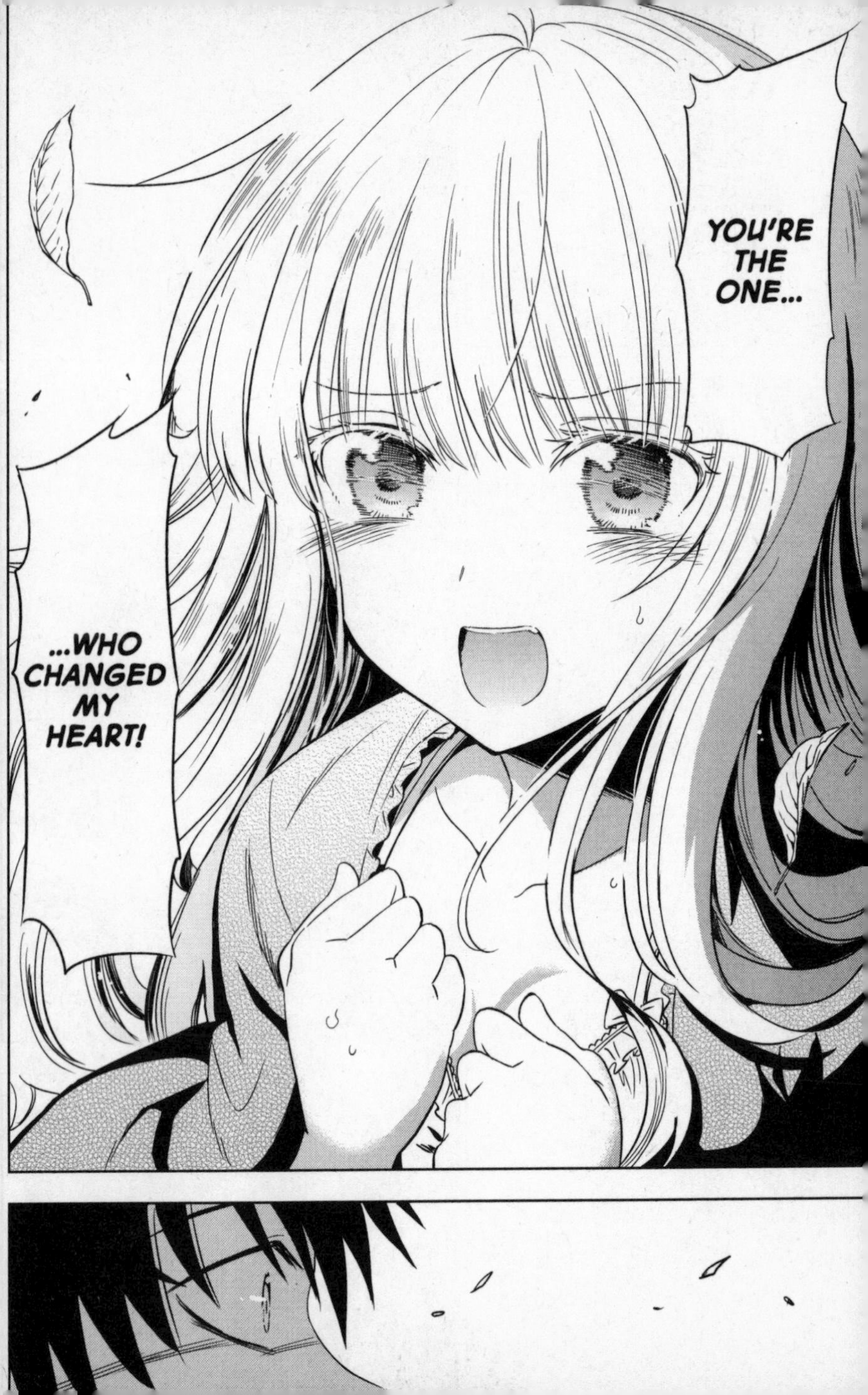
YOU'RE THE ONE...
...WHO CHANGED MY HEART!

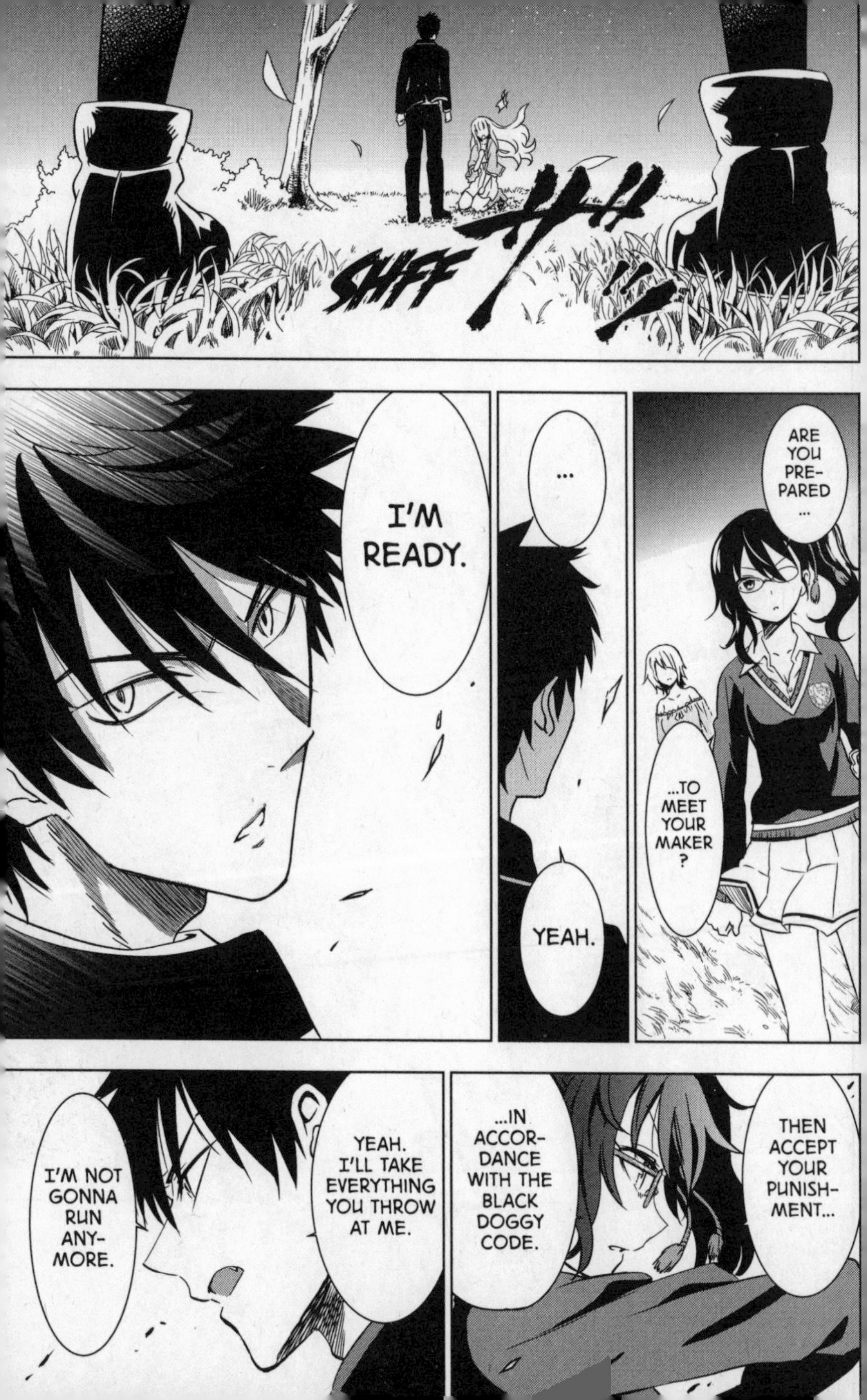
SHFF
ARE YOU PREPARED...
...TO MEET YOUR MAKER?
...
YEAH.
I'M READY.
THEN ACCEPT YOUR PUNISHMENT...
...IN ACCORDANCE WITH THE BLACK DOGGY CODE.
YEAH. I'LL TAKE EVERYTHING YOU THROW AT ME.
I'M NOT GONNA RUN ANYMORE.

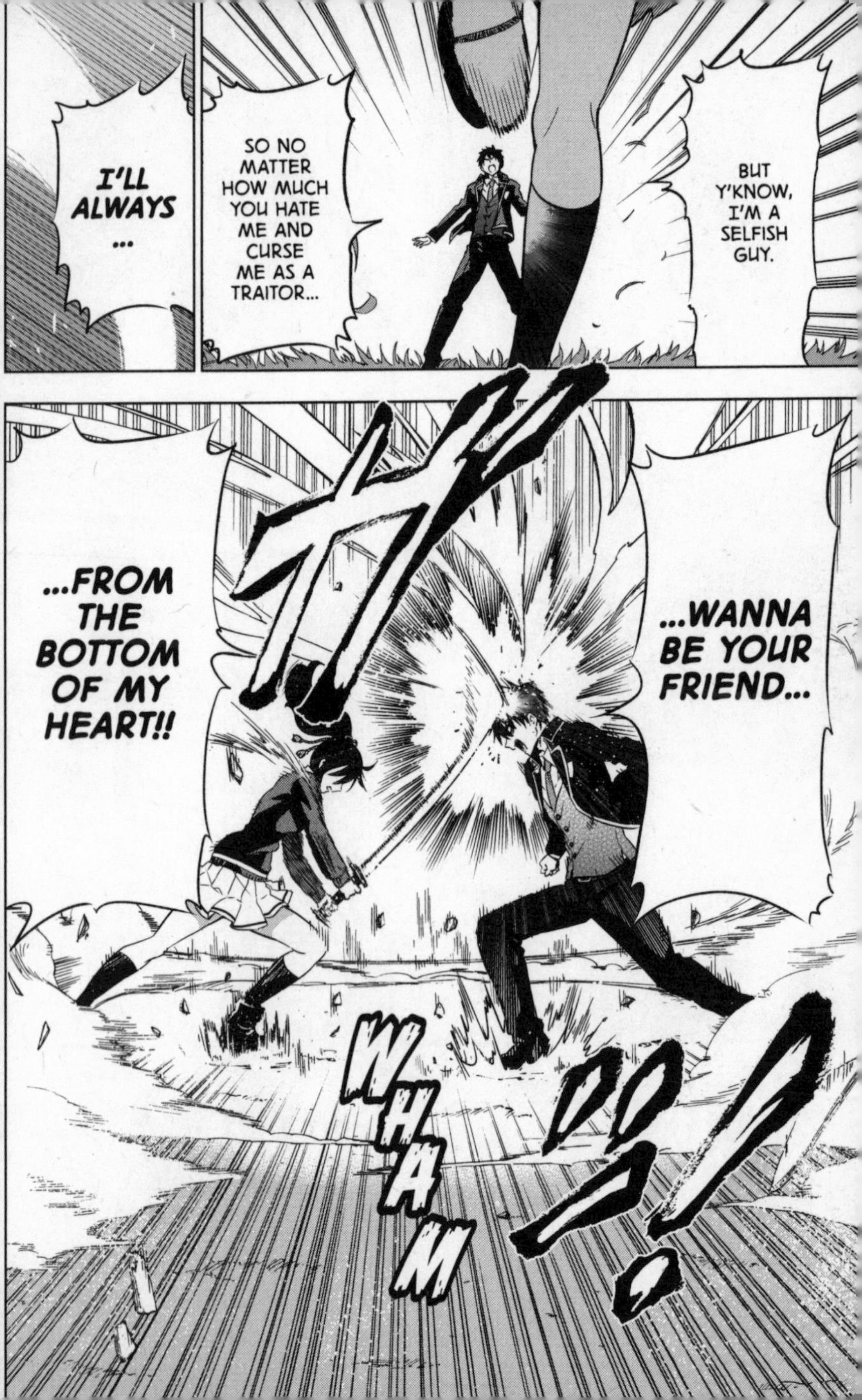
BUT Y'KNOW, I'M A SELFISH GUY.
SO NO MATTER HOW MUCH YOU HATE ME AND CURSE ME AS A TRAITOR...
I'LL ALWAYS ...
...WANNA BE YOUR FRIEND...
...FROM THE BOTTOM OF MY HEART!!
WHAM

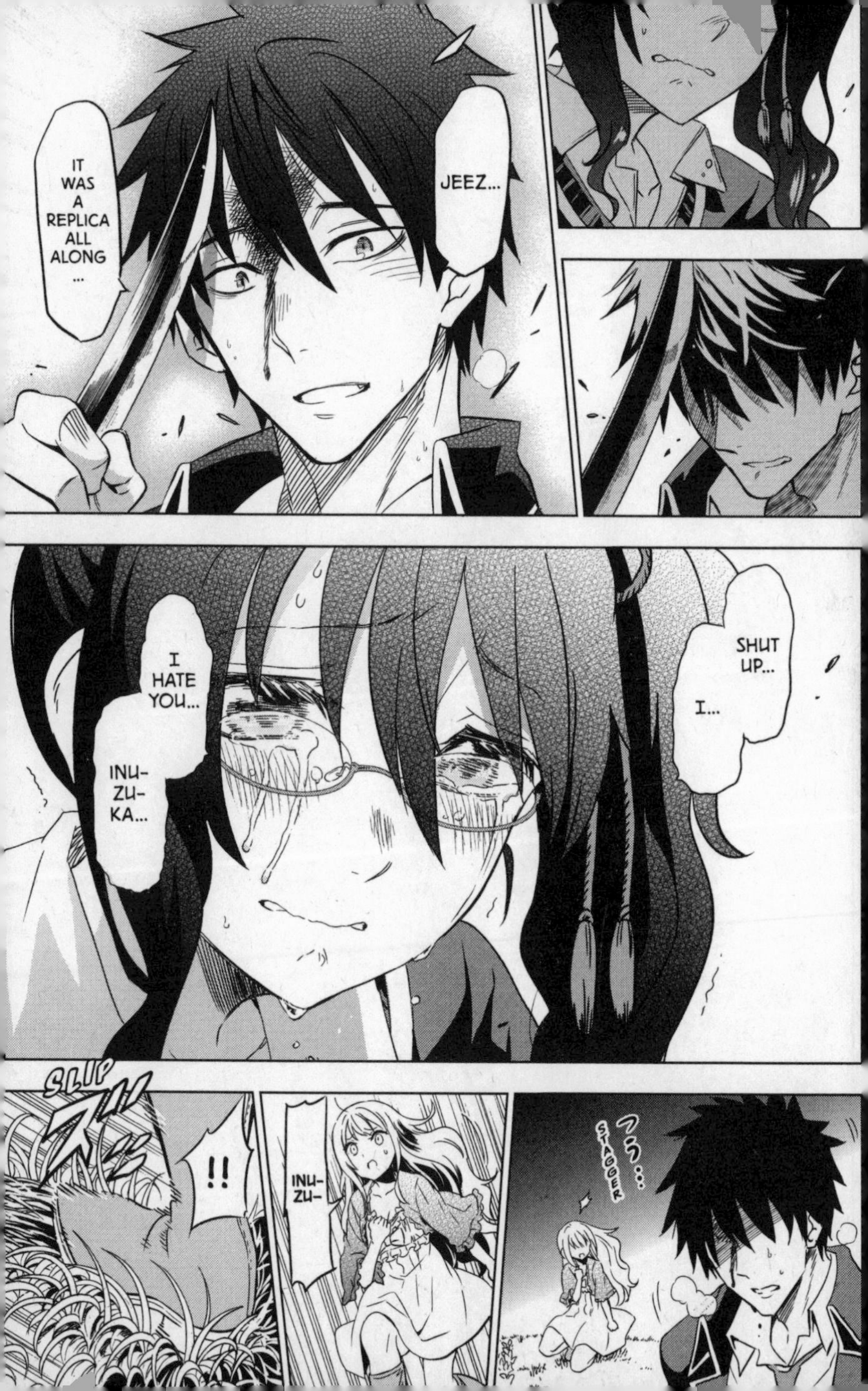
JEEZ...
IT WAS A REPLICA ALL ALONG ...
SHUT UP... I...
I HATE YOU... INUZUKA...
フラ…
STAGGER
INU-ZU-
!!
SLIP

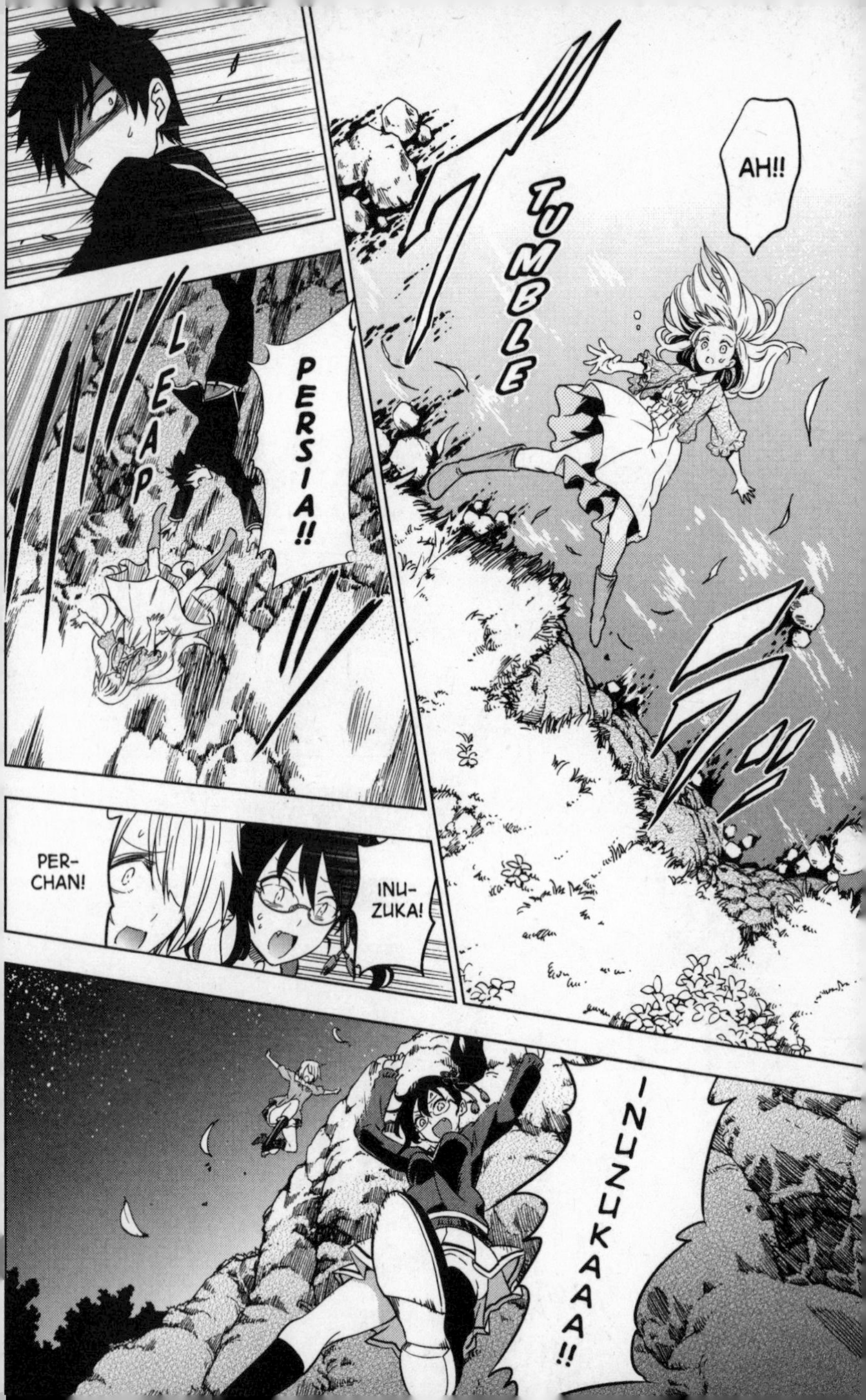
AH!!
TUMBLE
PERSIA!!
LEAP
INUZUKA!
PER-CHAN!
INUZUKAAA!!

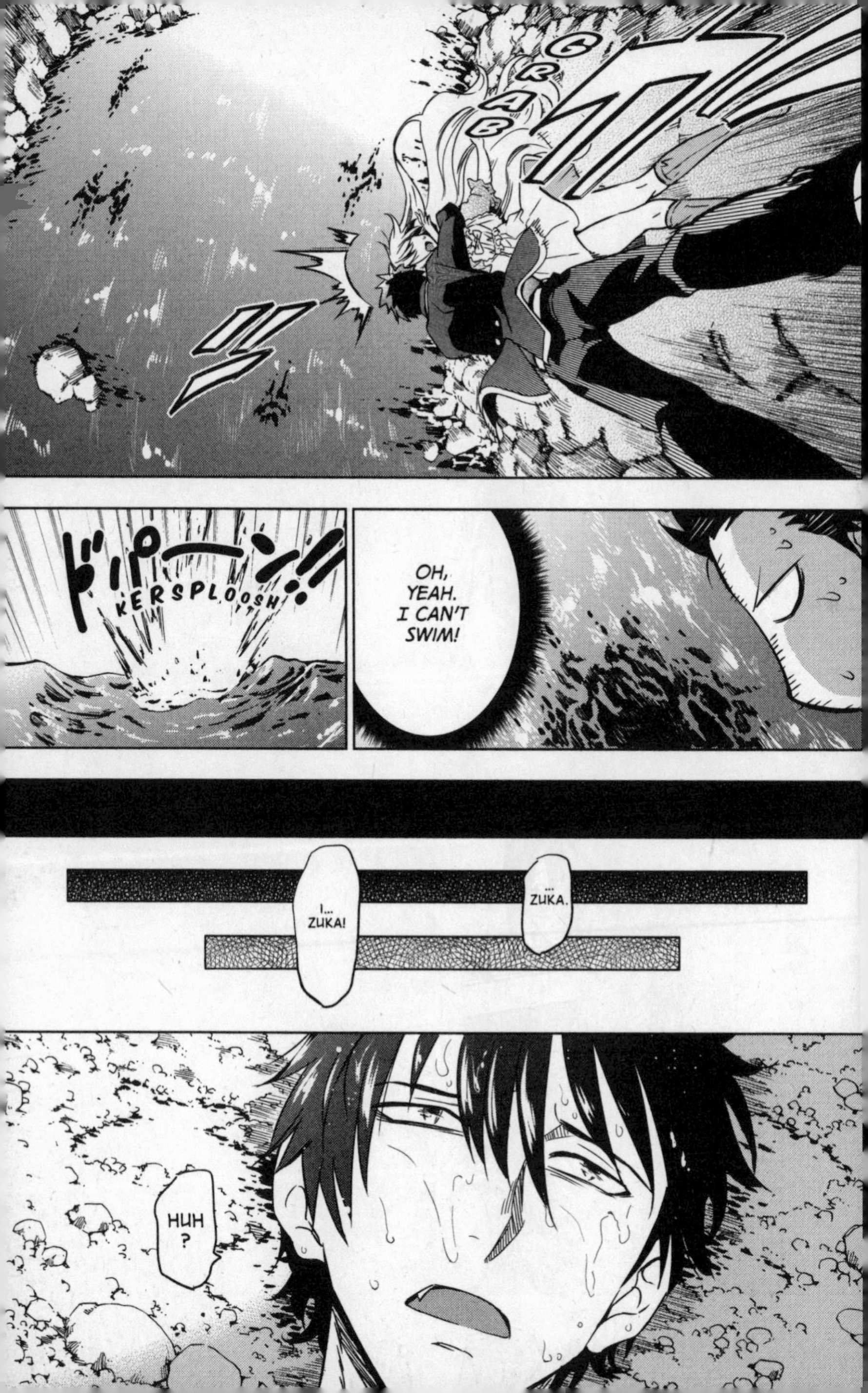
GRAB
OH, YEAH. I CAN'T SWIM!
ドパーン!!
KERSPLOOSH
...ZUKA.
I... ZUKA!
HUH?

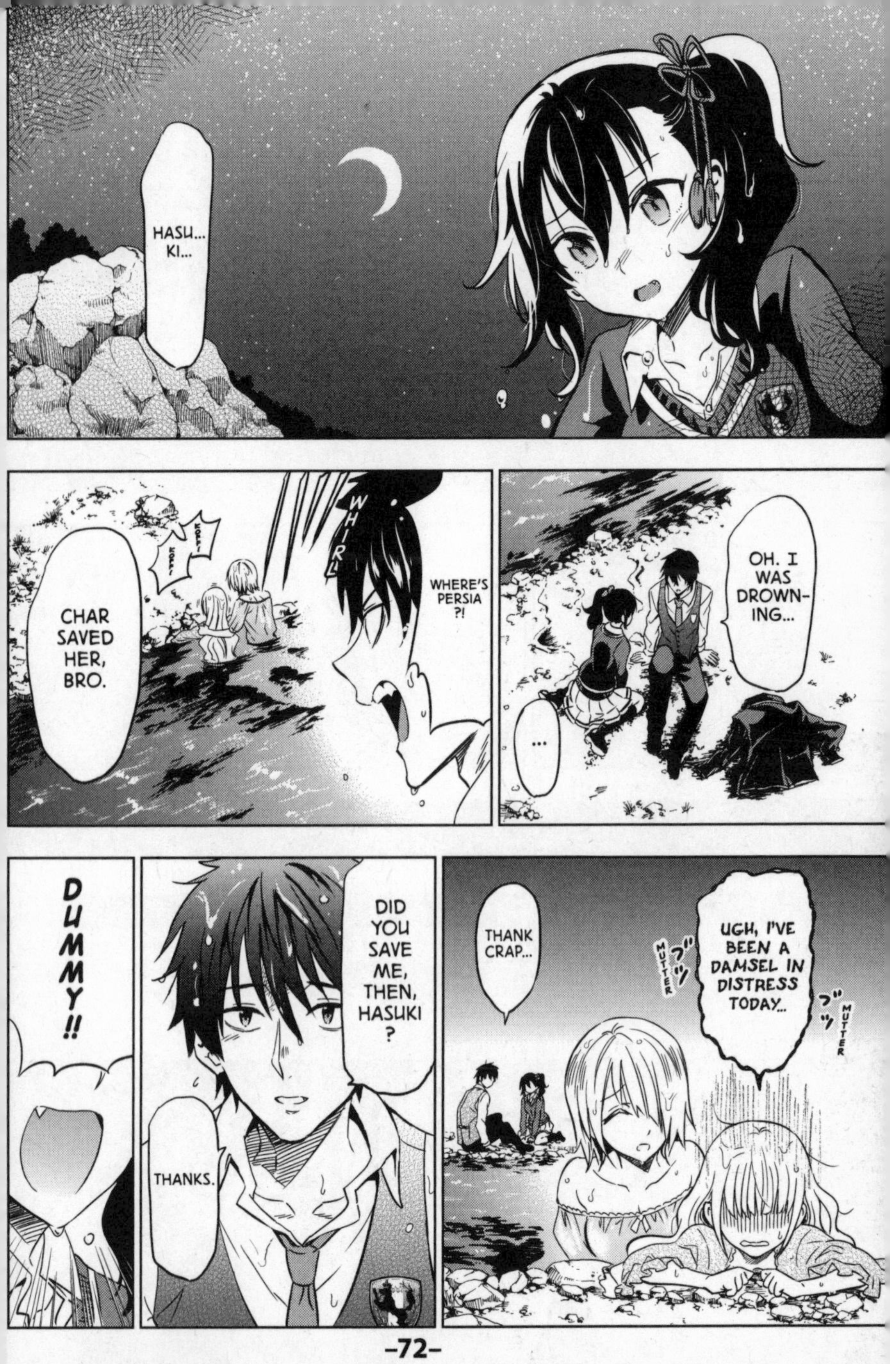
HASU... KI...
OH. I WAS DROWN-ING...
...
WHIRL
WHERE'S PERSIA ?!
KOFF KOFF
CHAR SAVED HER, BRO.
MUTTER
UGH, I'VE BEEN A DAMSEL IN DISTRESS TODAY...
MUTTER
THANK CRAP...
DID YOU SAVE ME, THEN, HASUKI ?
THANKS.
DUMMY!!

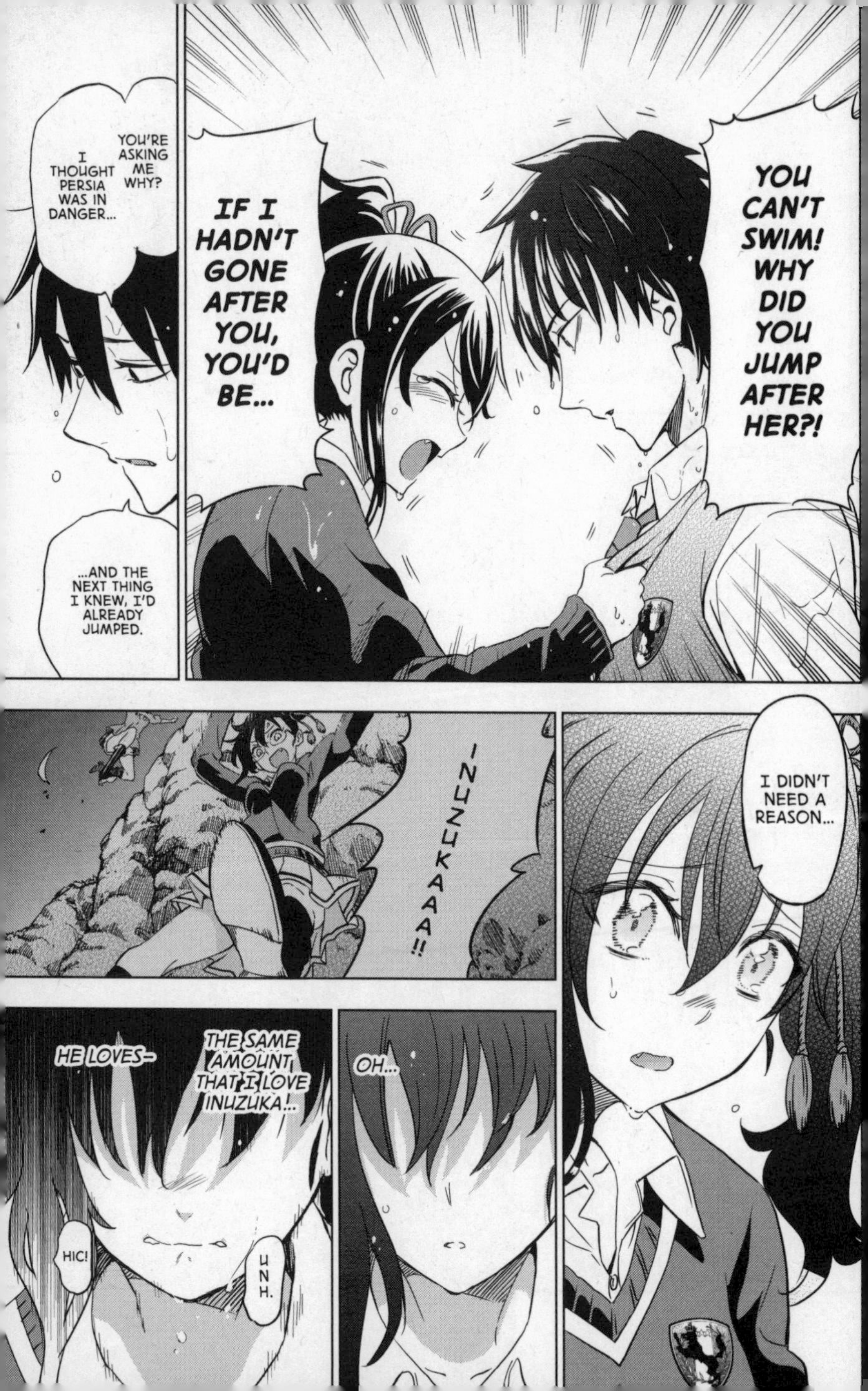
YOU CAN'T SWIM! WHY DID YOU JUMP AFTER HER?!
IF I HADN'T GONE AFTER YOU, YOU'D BE...
YOU'RE ASKING ME WHY?
I THOUGHT PERSIA WAS IN DANGER...
...AND THE NEXT THING I KNEW, I'D ALREADY JUMPED.
I DIDN'T NEED A REASON...
INUZUKAAAA!!
OH...
UNH.
THE SAME AMOUNT THAT I LOVE INUZUKA!..
HE LOVES–
HIC!

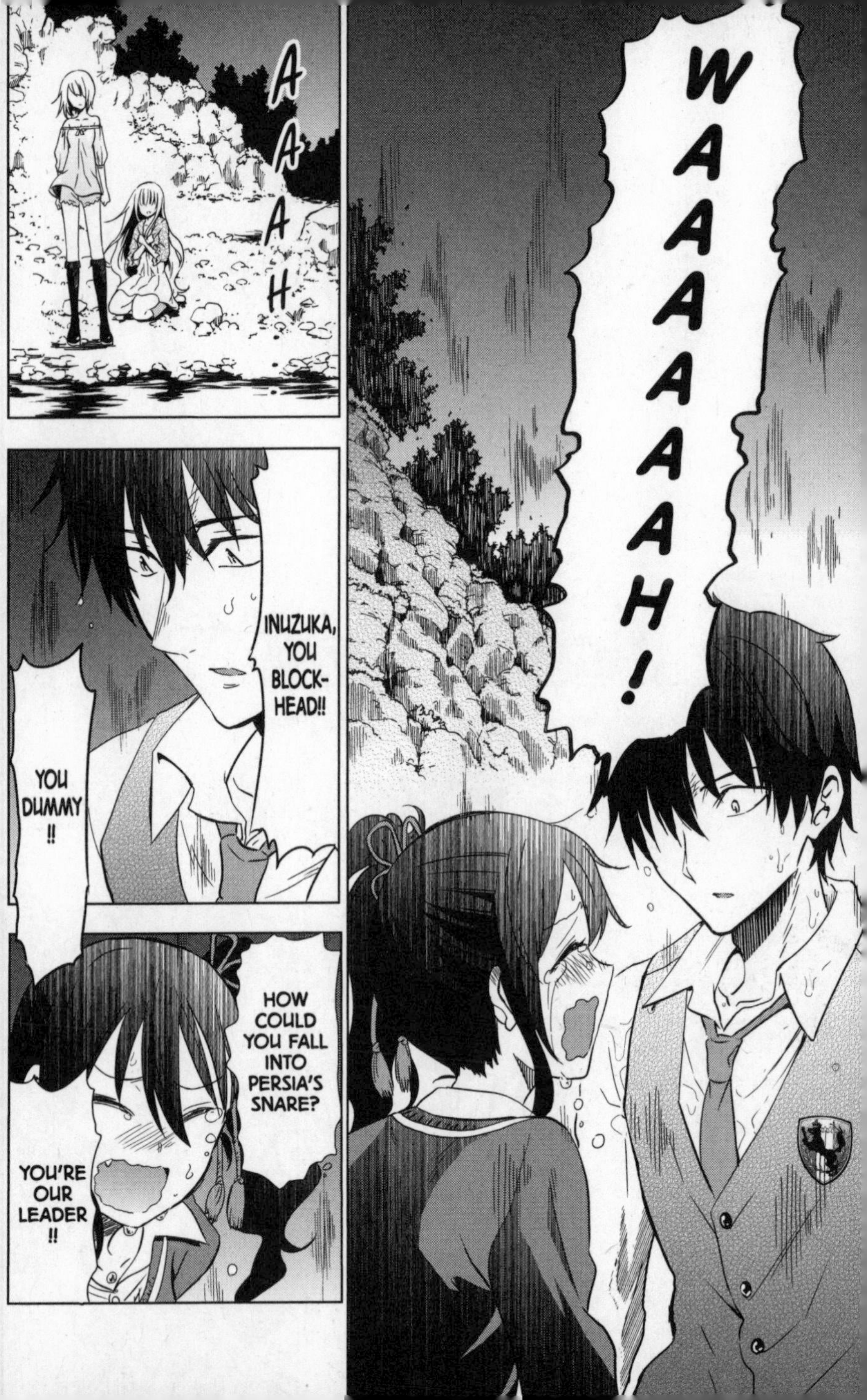
WAAAAAAAH!
AAAH
INUZUKA, YOU BLOCK-HEAD!!
YOU DUMMY!!
HOW COULD YOU FALL INTO PERSIA'S SNARE?
YOU'RE OUR LEADER!!

HEY!!

CLOSET PERV!

POSER!

NIN-COM-POOP!

TRAITOR!

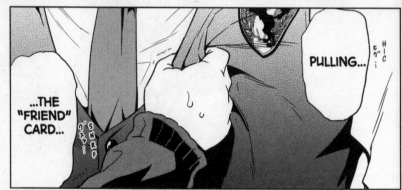

...THE "FRIEND" CARD...

PULLING...

HIC

SNRF

I HATE YOU!

YEAH...

I HATE YOU!!

I KNOW...

I CAN'T JUST ACT...

...LIKE NOTHING'S CHANGED, BRO!

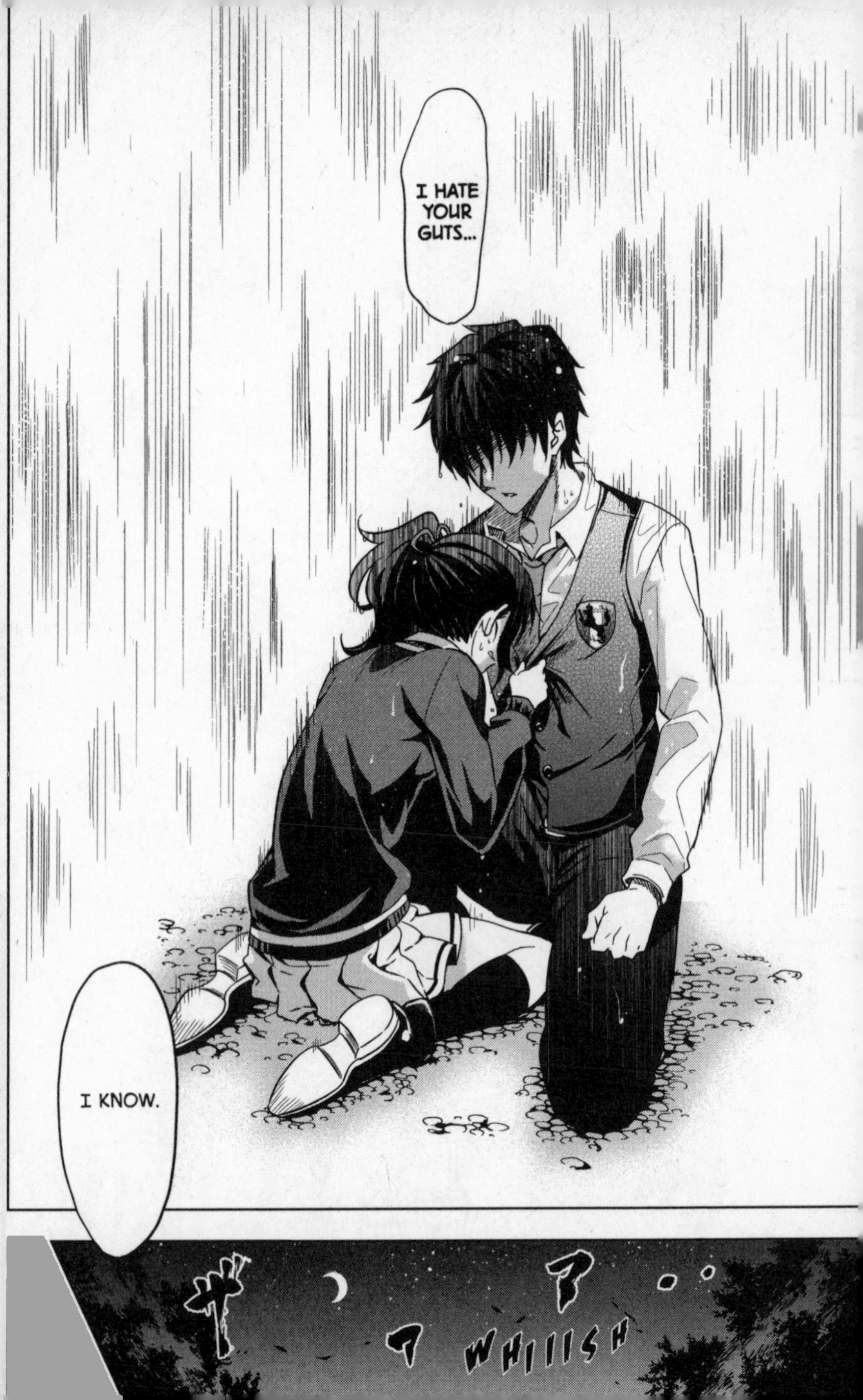
I HATE YOUR GUTS...
I KNOW.
WHIIISH

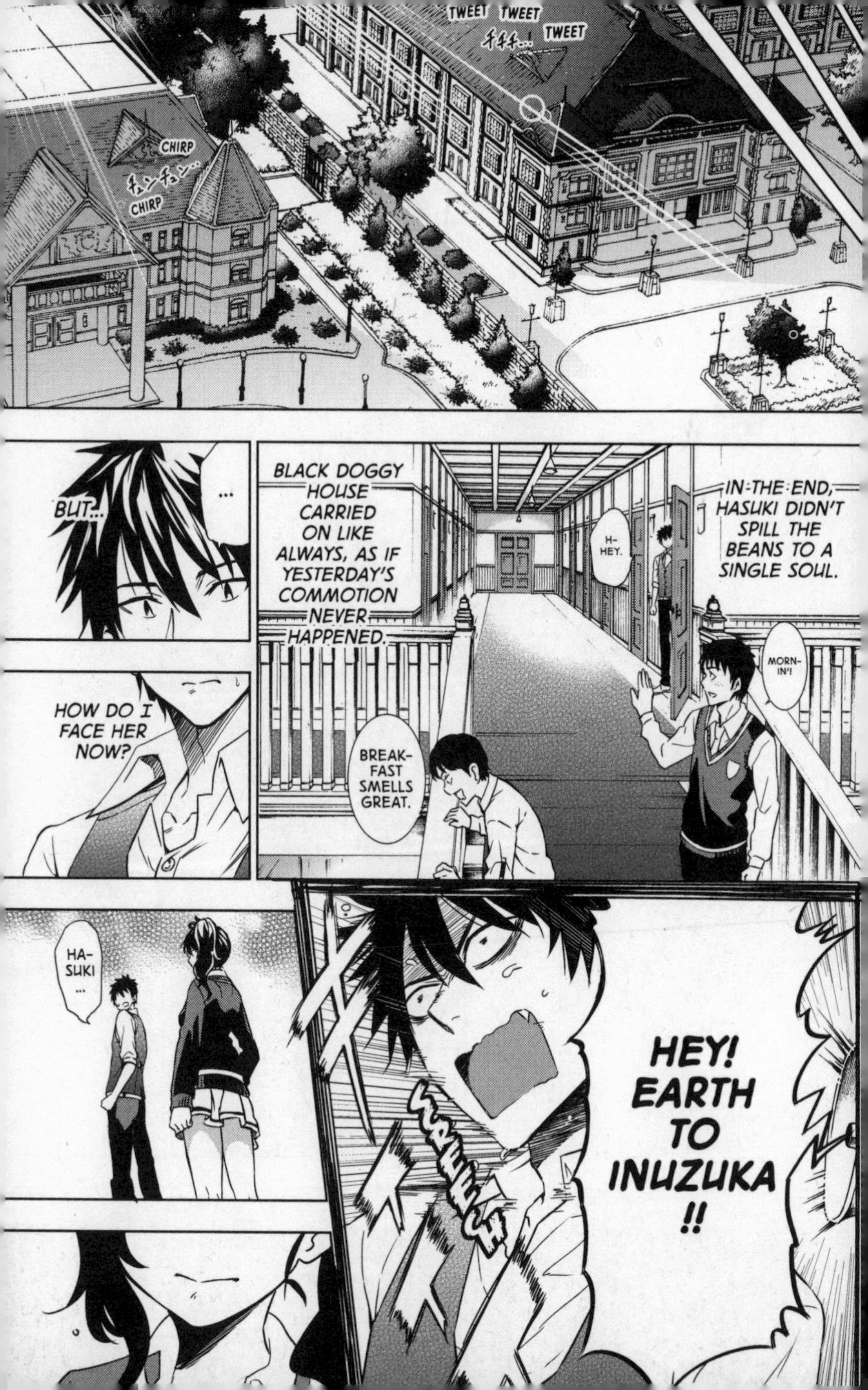
TWEET TWEET
チチチ…
TWEET
CHIRP
チュンチュン…
CHIRP
IN THE END, HASUKI DIDN'T SPILL THE BEANS TO A SINGLE SOUL.
MORN-IN'!
H-HEY.
BLACK DOGGY HOUSE CARRIED ON LIKE ALWAYS, AS IF YESTERDAY'S COMMOTION NEVER HAPPENED.
BREAK-FAST SMELLS GREAT.
...
BUT...
HOW DO I FACE HER NOW?
HEY! EARTH TO INUZUKA !!
HA-SUKI ...

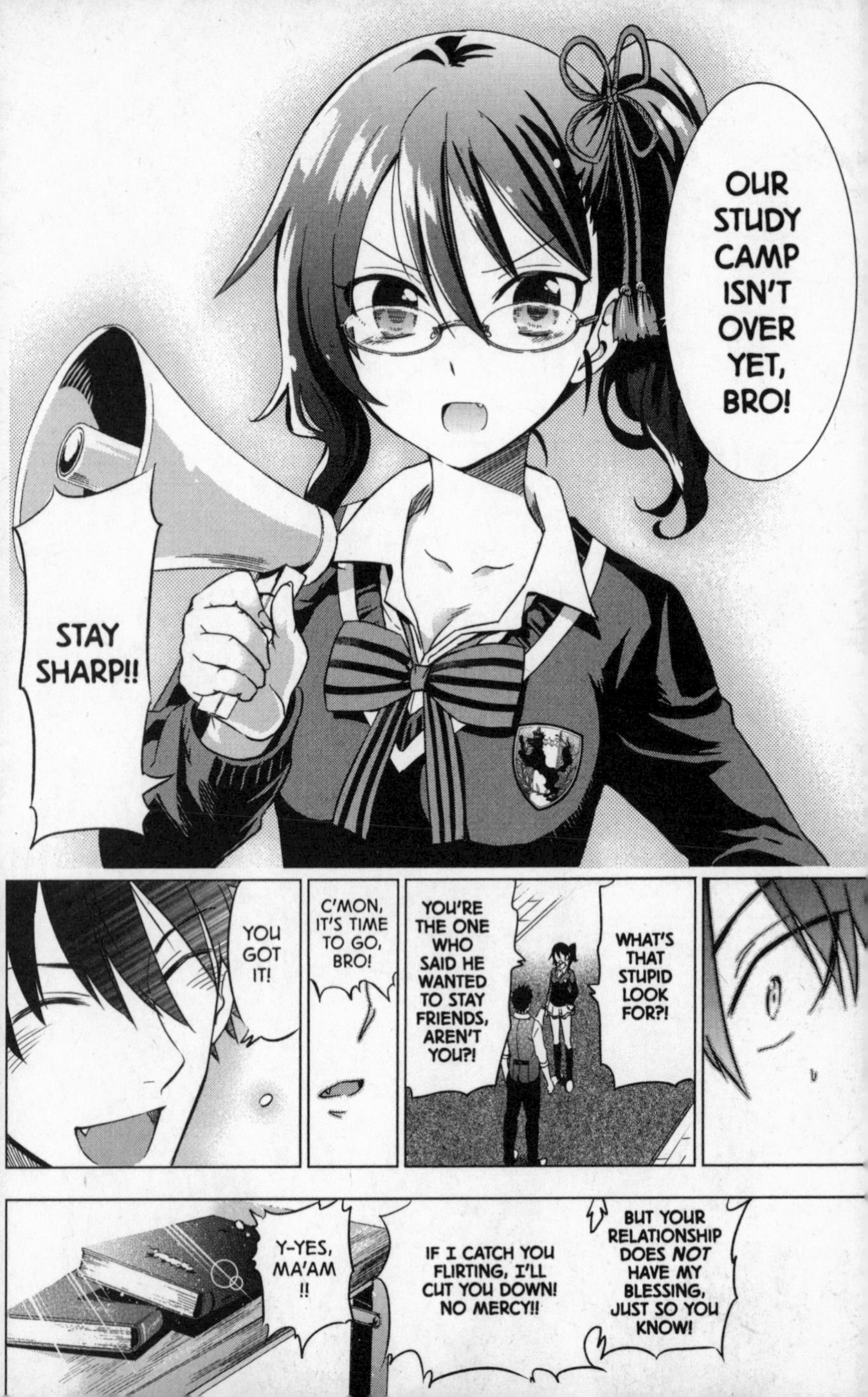
OUR STUDY CAMP ISN'T OVER YET, BRO!
STAY SHARP!!
WHAT'S THAT STUPID LOOK FOR?!
YOU'RE THE ONE WHO SAID HE WANTED TO STAY FRIENDS, AREN'T YOU?!
C'MON, IT'S TIME TO GO, BRO!
YOU GOT IT!
BUT YOUR RELATIONSHIP DOES *NOT* HAVE MY BLESSING, JUST SO YOU KNOW!
IF I CATCH YOU FLIRTING, I'LL CUT YOU DOWN! NO MERCY!!
Y-YES, MA'AM !!

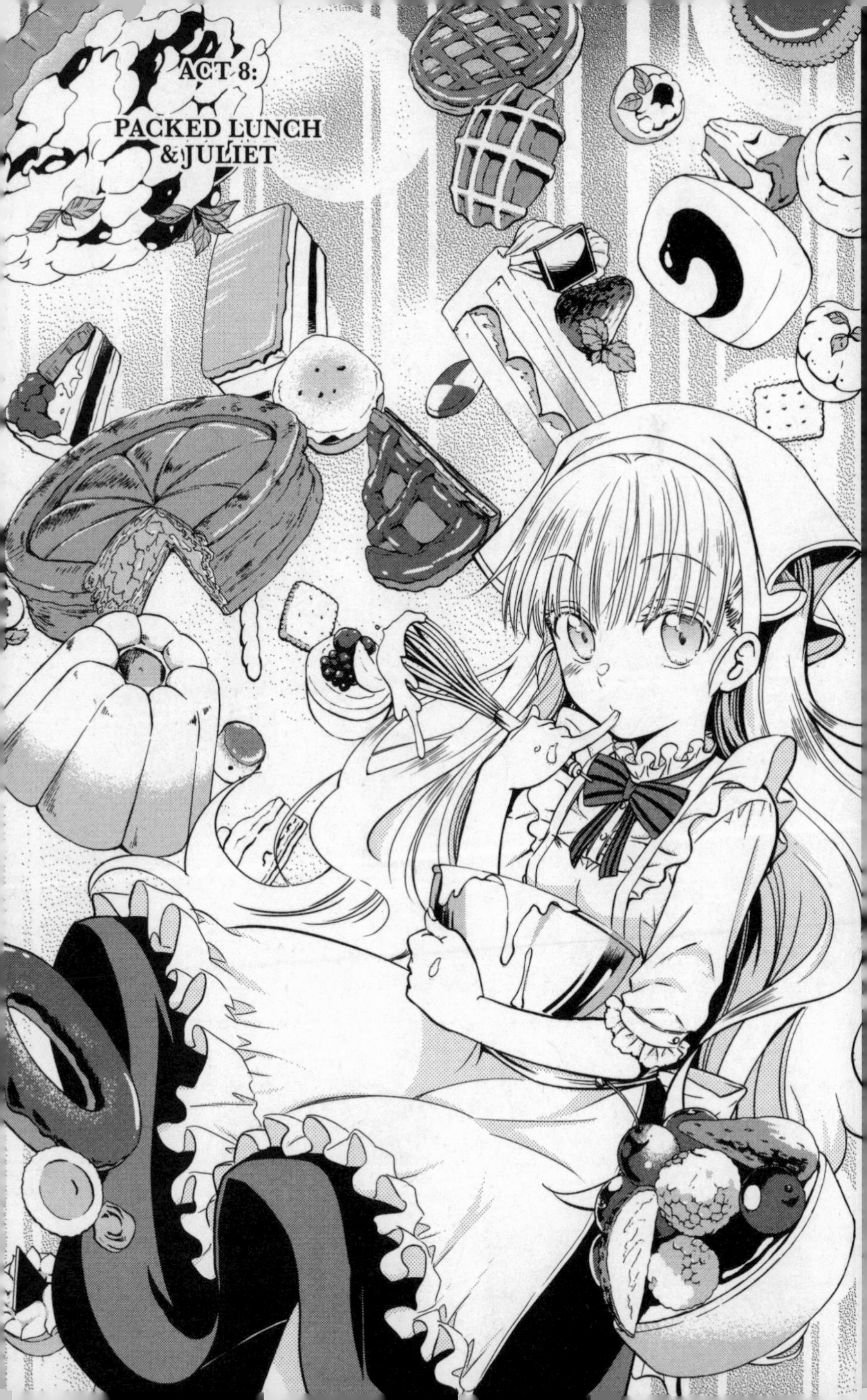
ACT 8:
PACKED LUNCH
& JULIET

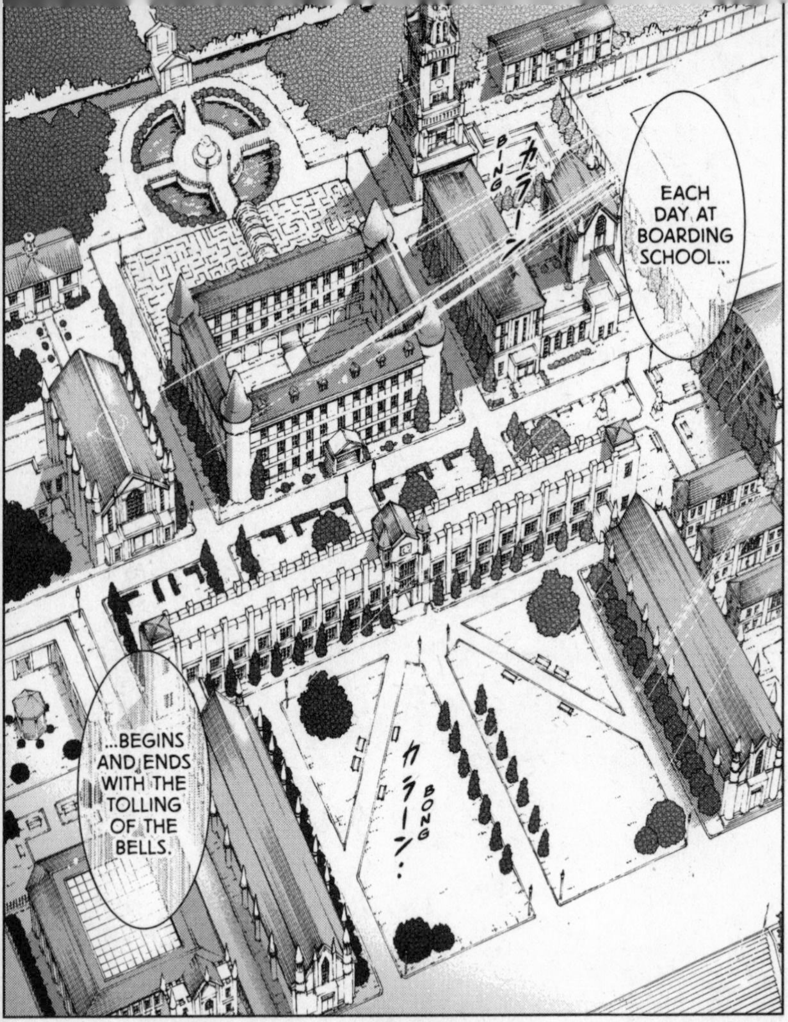
EACH DAY AT BOARDING SCHOOL...
カラーン
BING
...BEGINS AND ENDS WITH THE TOLLING OF THE BELLS.
カラーン…
BONG

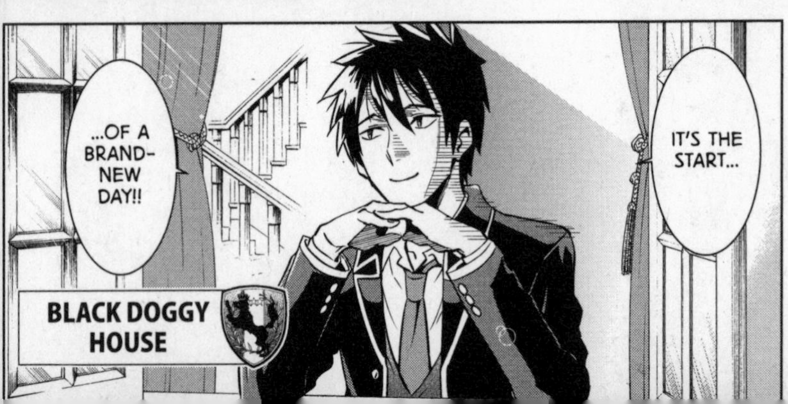
IT'S THE START...
...OF A BRAND-NEW DAY!!
BLACK DOGGY HOUSE

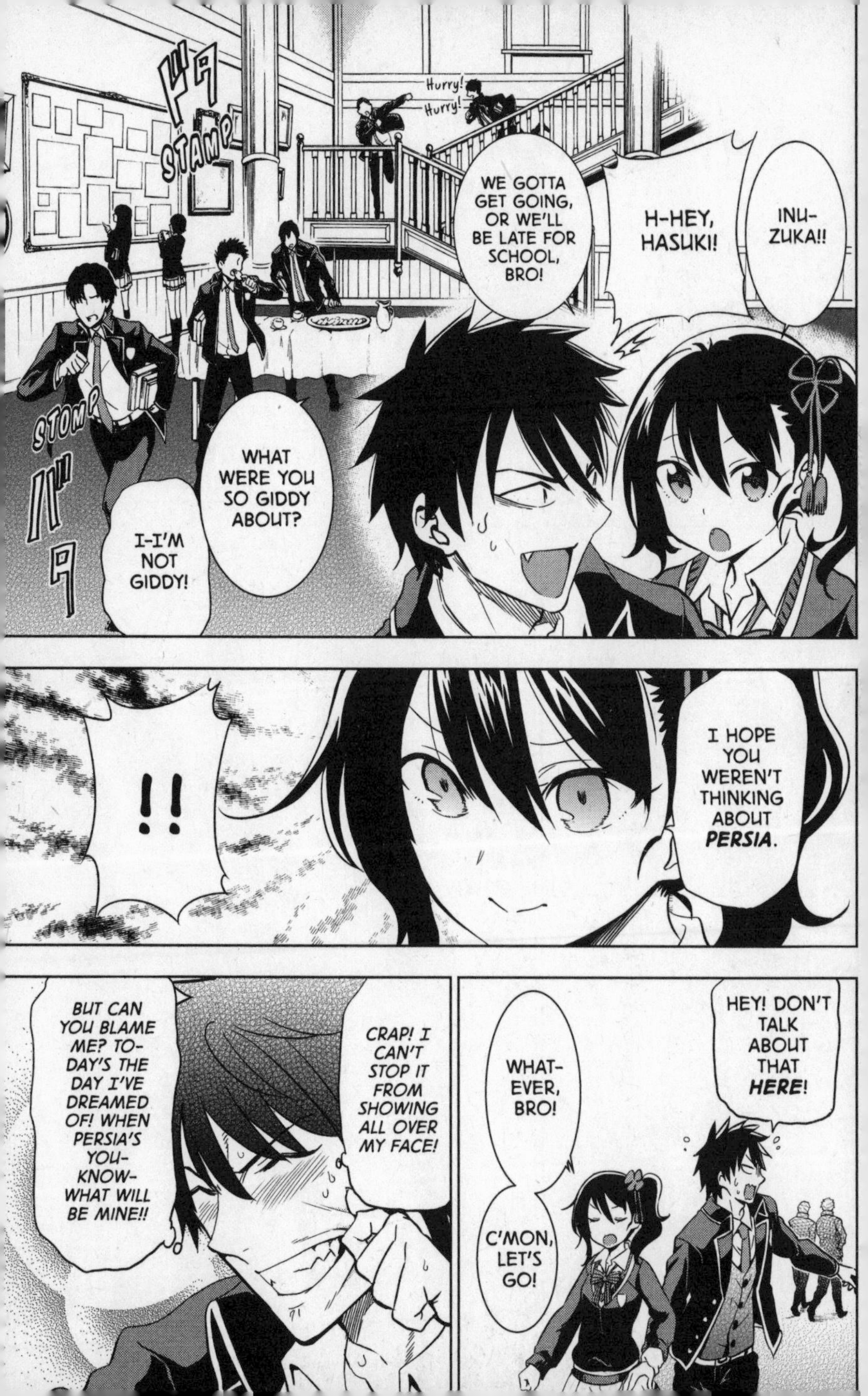

Hurry!
Hurry!
ドタ
STAMP
INU-ZUKA!!
H-HEY, HASUKI!
WE GOTTA GET GOING, OR WE'LL BE LATE FOR SCHOOL, BRO!
WHAT WERE YOU SO GIDDY ABOUT?
I-I'M NOT GIDDY!
STOMP
バタ
I HOPE YOU WEREN'T THINKING ABOUT **PERSIA**.
!!
HEY! DON'T TALK ABOUT THAT ***HERE***!
WHAT-EVER, BRO!
C'MON, LET'S GO!
CRAP! I CAN'T STOP IT FROM SHOWING ALL OVER MY FACE!
BUT CAN YOU BLAME ME? TO-DAY'S THE DAY I'VE DREAMED OF! WHEN PERSIA'S YOU-KNOW-WHAT WILL BE MINE!!

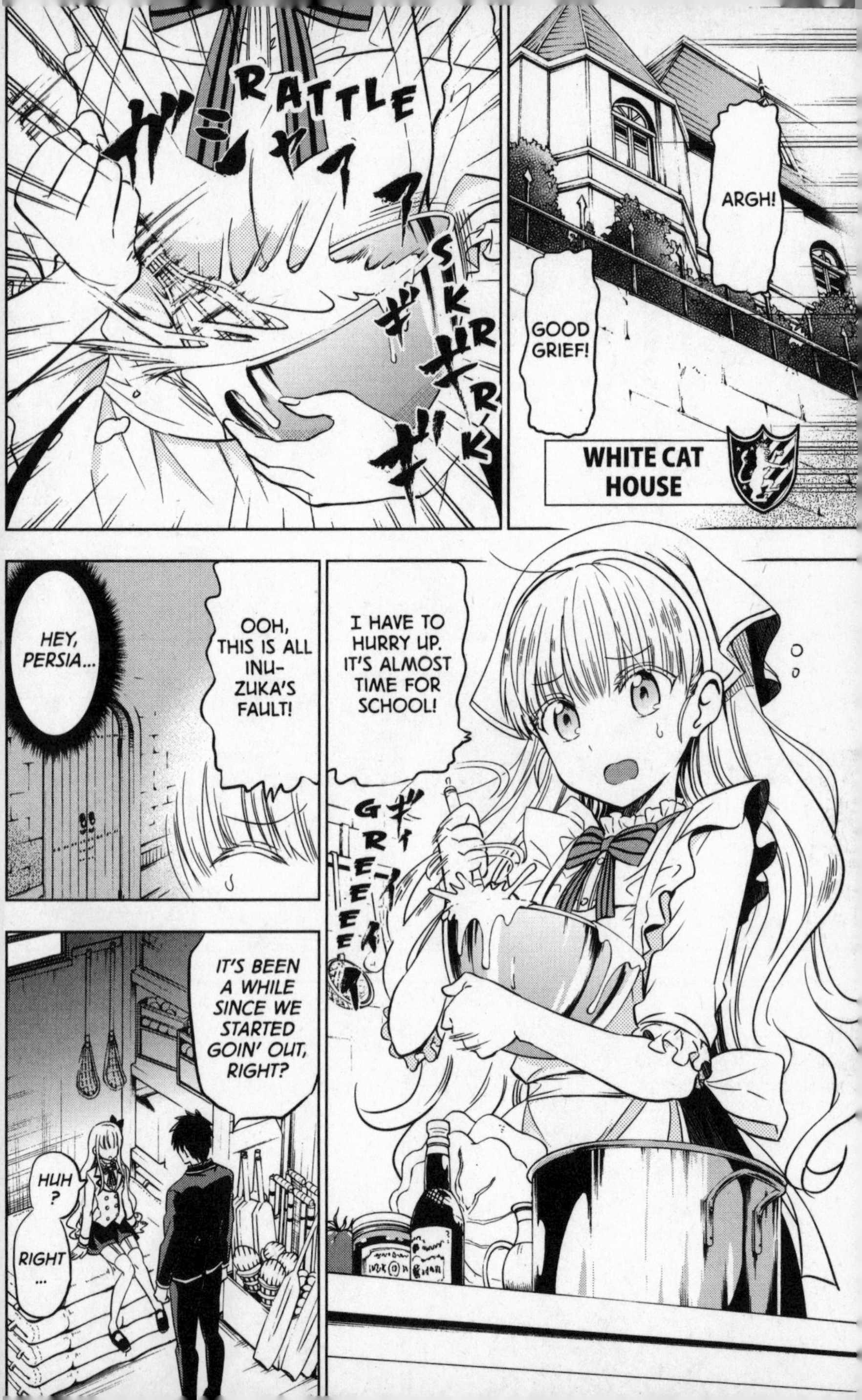

ARGH!
GOOD GRIEF!
WHITE CAT HOUSE
RATTLE
SKRRK
I HAVE TO HURRY UP. IT'S ALMOST TIME FOR SCHOOL!
GREEEEE
OOH, THIS IS ALL INU-ZUKA'S FAULT!
HEY, PERSIA...
IT'S BEEN A WHILE SINCE WE STARTED GOIN' OUT, RIGHT?
HUH?
RIGHT...

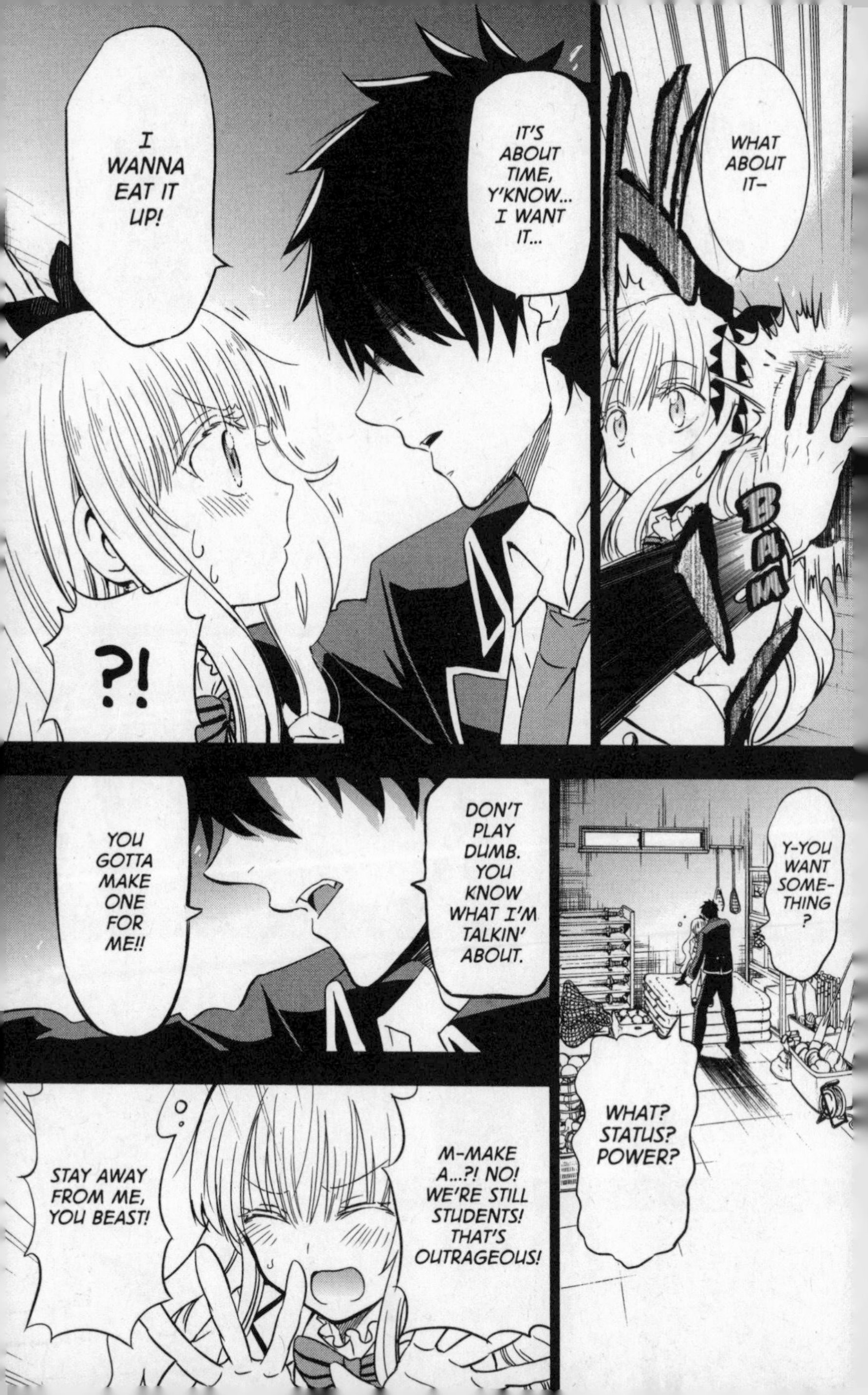
WHAT ABOUT IT–
BAM
IT'S ABOUT TIME, Y'KNOW... I WANT IT...
I WANNA EAT IT UP!
?!
Y-YOU WANT SOMETHING?
WHAT? STATUS? POWER?
DON'T PLAY DUMB. YOU KNOW WHAT I'M TALKIN' ABOUT.
YOU GOTTA MAKE ONE FOR ME!!
M-MAKE A...?! NO! WE'RE STILL STUDENTS! THAT'S OUTRAGEOUS!
STAY AWAY FROM ME, YOU BEAST!

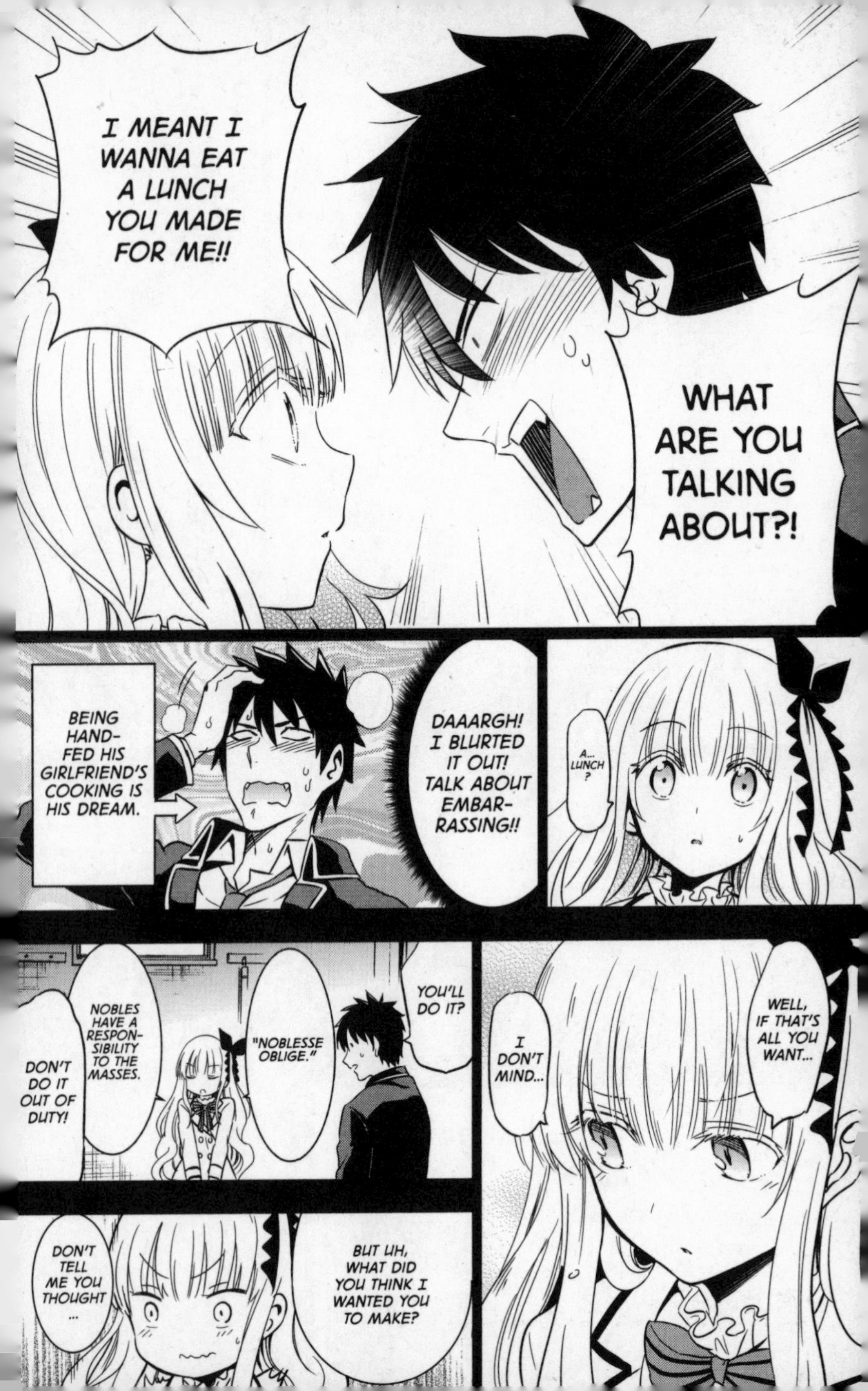
WHAT ARE YOU TALKING ABOUT?!
I MEANT I WANNA EAT A LUNCH YOU MADE FOR ME!!
A... LUNCH ?
DAAARGH! I BLURTED IT OUT! TALK ABOUT EMBAR-RASSING!!
BEING HAND-FED HIS GIRLFRIEND'S COOKING IS HIS DREAM.
WELL, IF THAT'S ALL YOU WANT...
I DON'T MIND...
YOU'LL DO IT?
"NOBLESSE OBLIGE."
NOBLES HAVE A RESPON-SIBILITY TO THE MASSES.
DON'T DO IT OUT OF DUTY!
BUT UH, WHAT DID YOU THINK I WANTED YOU TO MAKE?
DON'T TELL ME YOU THOUGHT ...

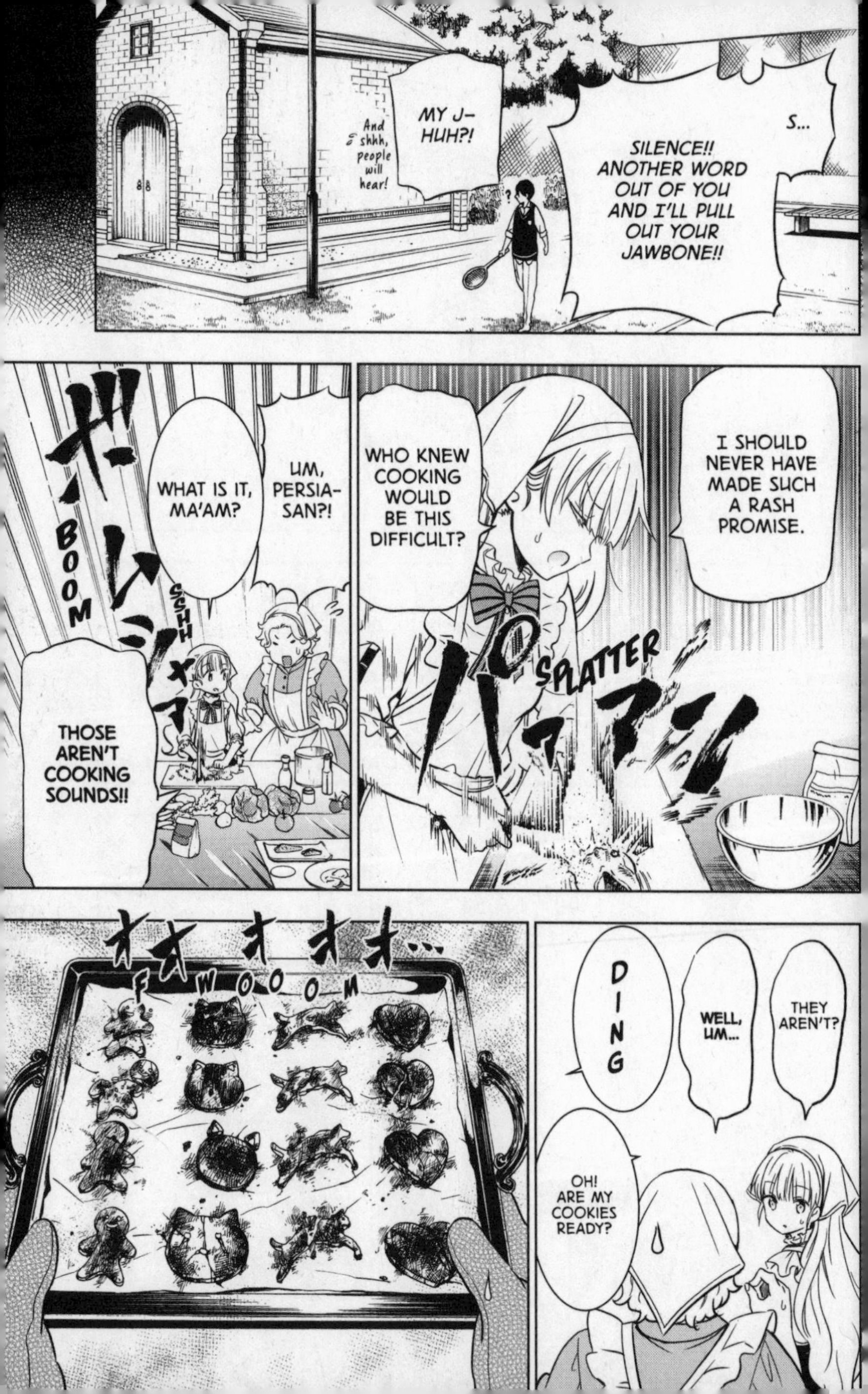
S...
SILENCE!! ANOTHER WORD OUT OF YOU AND I'LL PULL OUT YOUR JAWBONE!!
MY J— HUH?!
And shhh, people will hear!
I SHOULD NEVER HAVE MADE SUCH A RASH PROMISE.
WHO KNEW COOKING WOULD BE THIS DIFFICULT?
SPLATTER
UM, PERSIA-SAN?!
WHAT IS IT, MA'AM?
BOOM
SSHH
THOSE AREN'T COOKING SOUNDS!!
THEY AREN'T?
WELL, UM...
DING
OH! ARE MY COOKIES READY?
FWOOOM

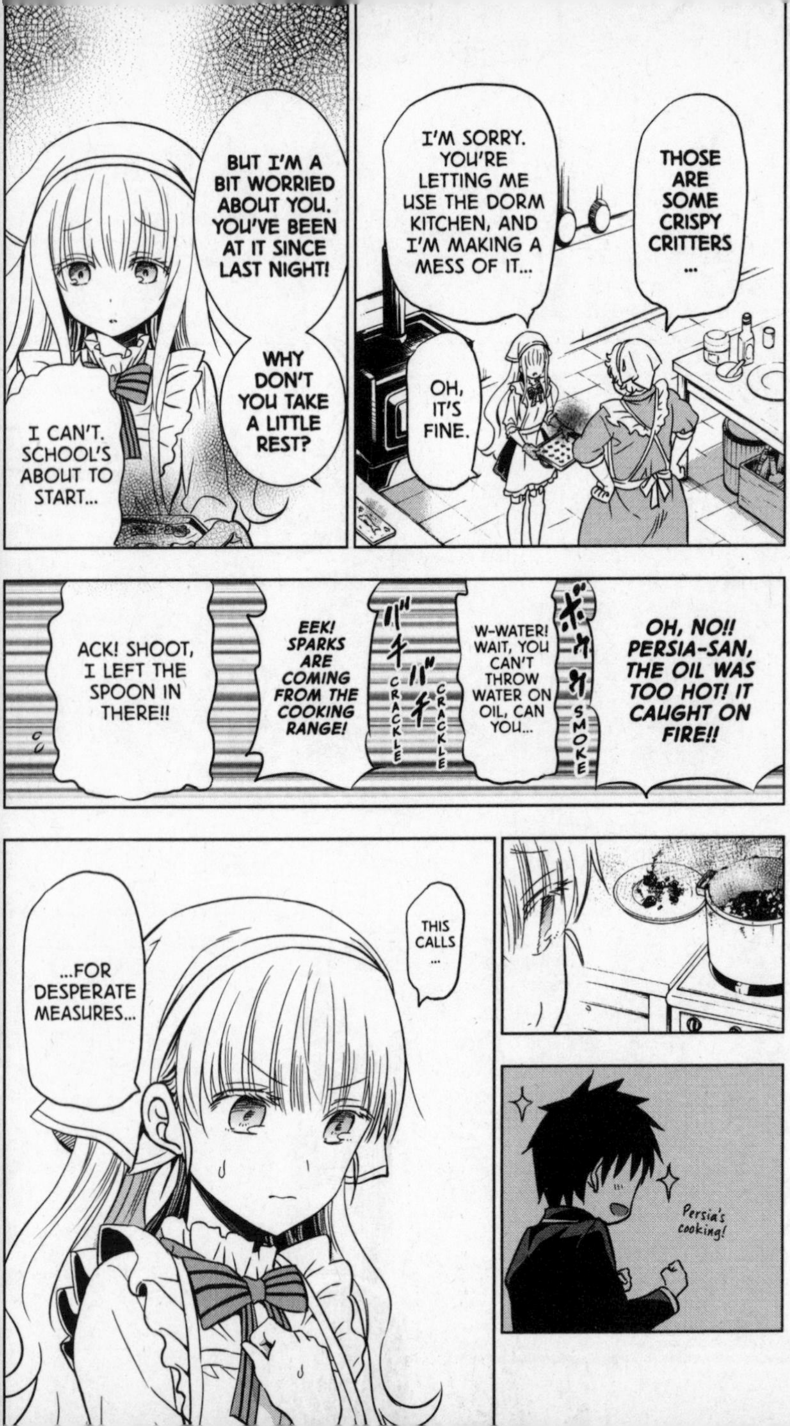
THOSE ARE SOME CRISPY CRITTERS...
I'M SORRY. YOU'RE LETTING ME USE THE DORM KITCHEN, AND I'M MAKING A MESS OF IT...
OH, IT'S FINE.
BUT I'M A BIT WORRIED ABOUT YOU. YOU'VE BEEN AT IT SINCE LAST NIGHT!
WHY DON'T YOU TAKE A LITTLE REST?
I CAN'T. SCHOOL'S ABOUT TO START...
OH, NO!! PERSIA-SAN, THE OIL WAS TOO HOT! IT CAUGHT ON FIRE!!
SMOKE
W-WATER! WAIT, YOU CAN'T THROW WATER ON OIL, CAN YOU...
CRACKLE
CRACKLE
EEK! SPARKS ARE COMING FROM THE COOKING RANGE!
ACK! SHOOT, I LEFT THE SPOON IN THERE!!
Persia's cooking!
THIS CALLS...
...FOR DESPERATE MEASURES...

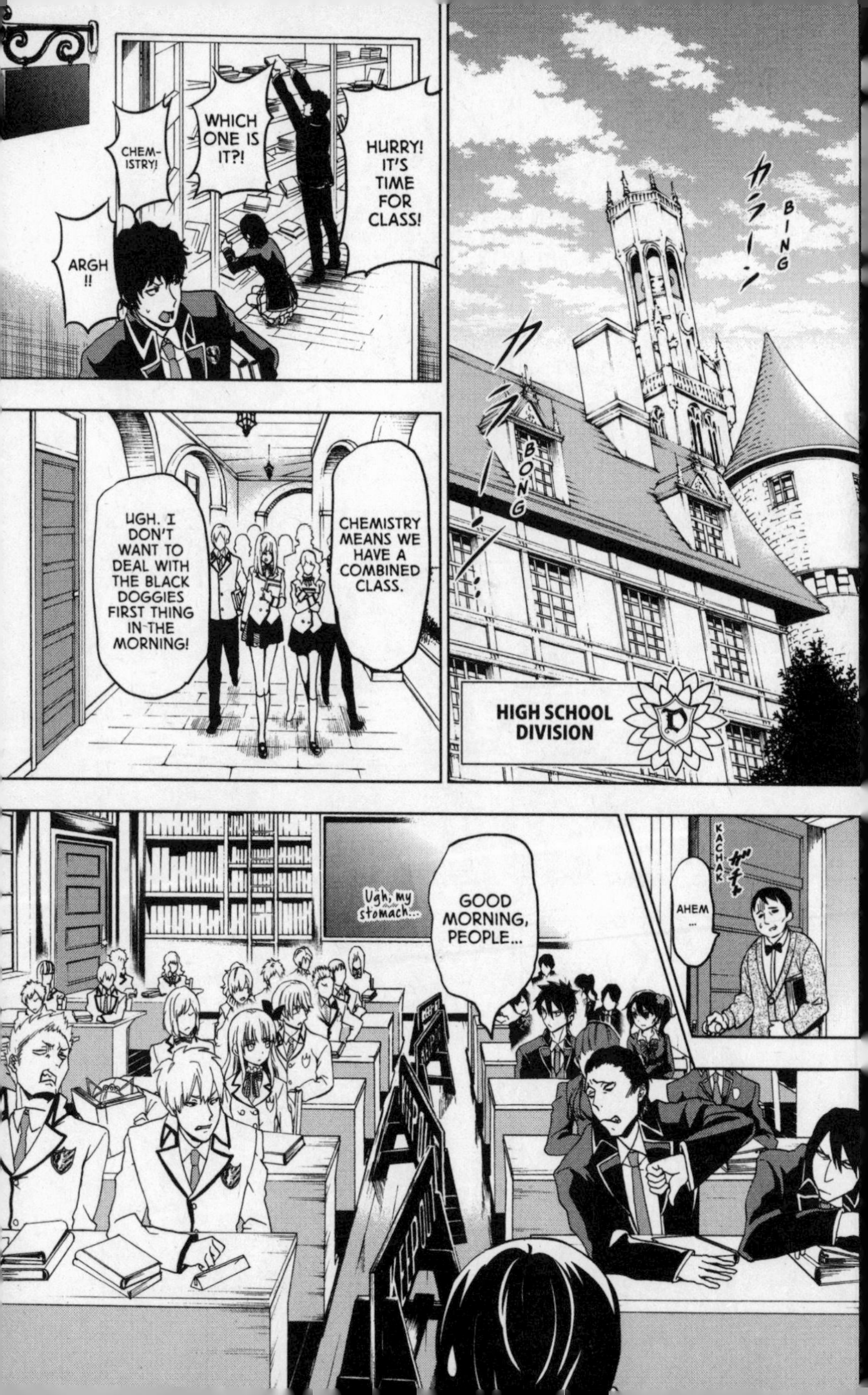
BING
BONG
HIGH SCHOOL DIVISION
HURRY! IT'S TIME FOR CLASS!
WHICH ONE IS IT?!
CHEM-ISTRY!
ARGH!!
CHEMISTRY MEANS WE HAVE A COMBINED CLASS.
UGH. I DON'T WANT TO DEAL WITH THE BLACK DOGGIES FIRST THING IN THE MORNING!
KACHAK
AHEM ...
GOOD MORNING, PEOPLE...
Ugh, my stomach...

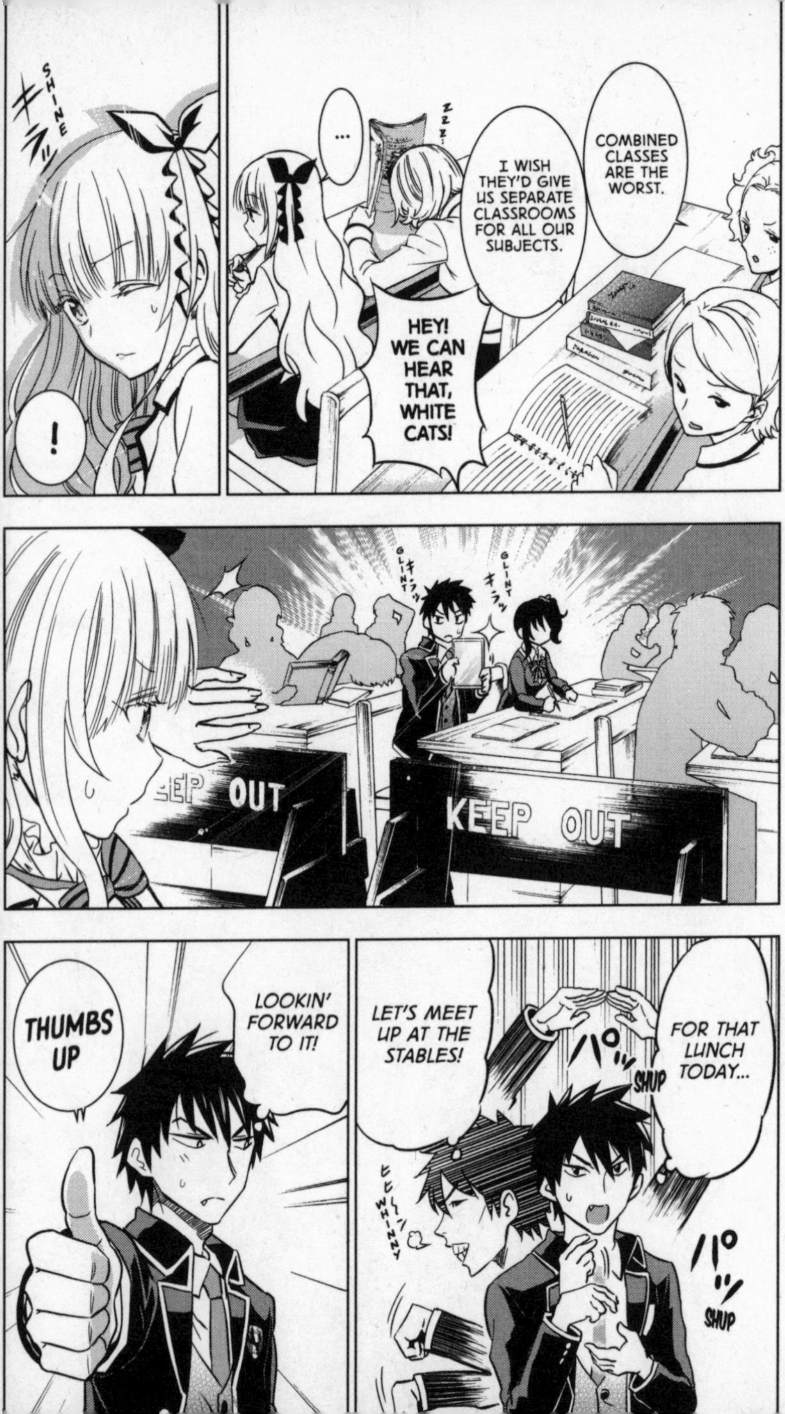
COMBINED CLASSES ARE THE WORST.
I WISH THEY'D GIVE US SEPARATE CLASSROOMS FOR ALL OUR SUBJECTS.
Z Z Z
...
HEY! WE CAN HEAR THAT, WHITE CATS!
SHINE
!
GLINT
GLINT
KEEP OUT
EEP OUT
FOR THAT LUNCH TODAY...
SHUP
LET'S MEET UP AT THE STABLES!
WHINNY
SHUP
LOOKIN' FORWARD TO IT!
THUMBS UP

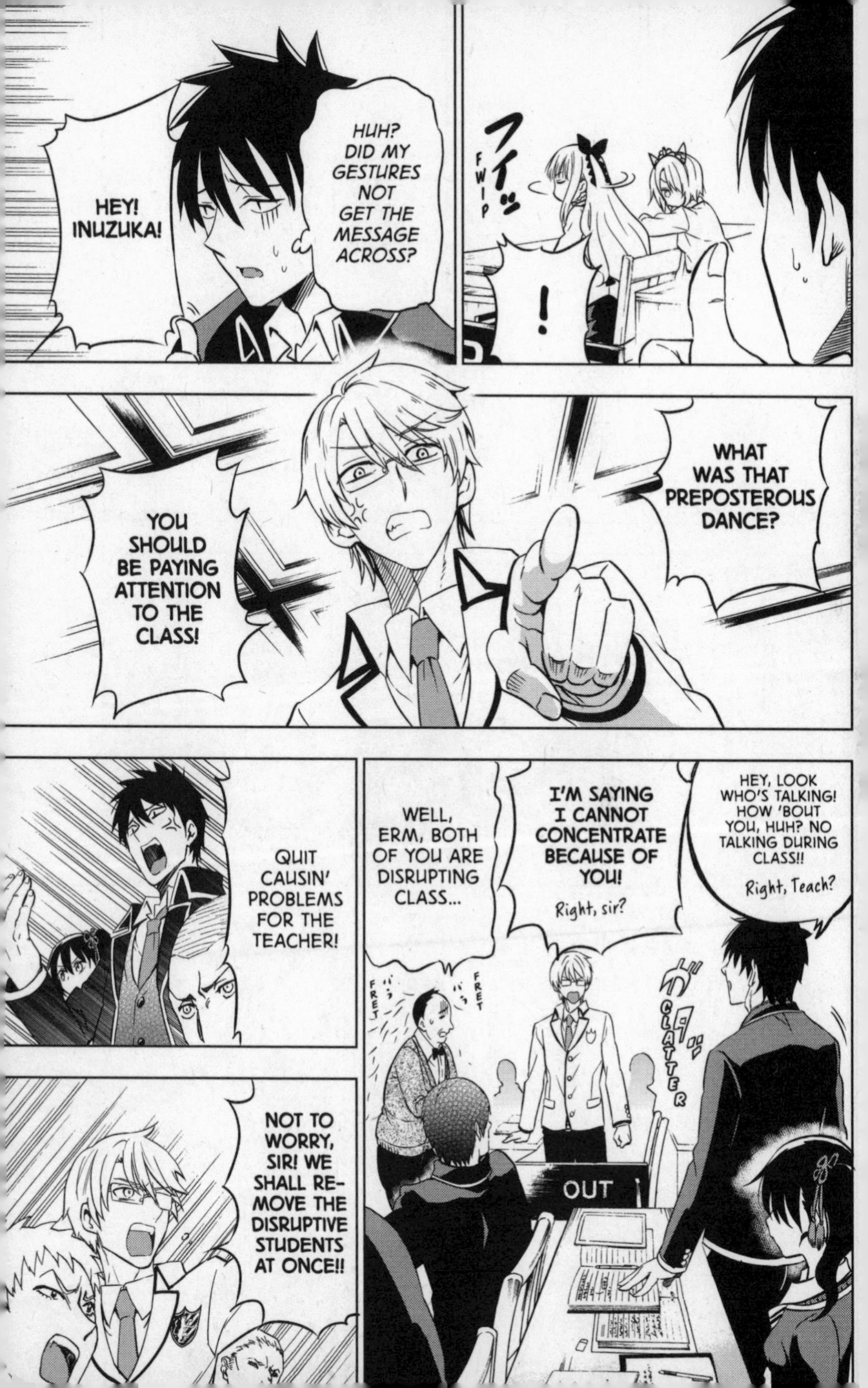
FWIP
!
HUH? DID MY GESTURES NOT GET THE MESSAGE ACROSS?
HEY! INUZUKA!
WHAT WAS THAT PREPOSTEROUS DANCE?
YOU SHOULD BE PAYING ATTENTION TO THE CLASS!
HEY, LOOK WHO'S TALKING! HOW 'BOUT YOU, HUH? NO TALKING DURING CLASS!!
Right, Teach?
I'M SAYING I CANNOT CONCENTRATE BECAUSE OF YOU!
Right, sir?
WELL, ERM, BOTH OF YOU ARE DISRUPTING CLASS...
FRET
FRET
CLATTER
OUT
QUIT CAUSIN' PROBLEMS FOR THE TEACHER!
NOT TO WORRY, SIR! WE SHALL RE-MOVE THE DISRUPTIVE STUDENTS AT ONCE!!

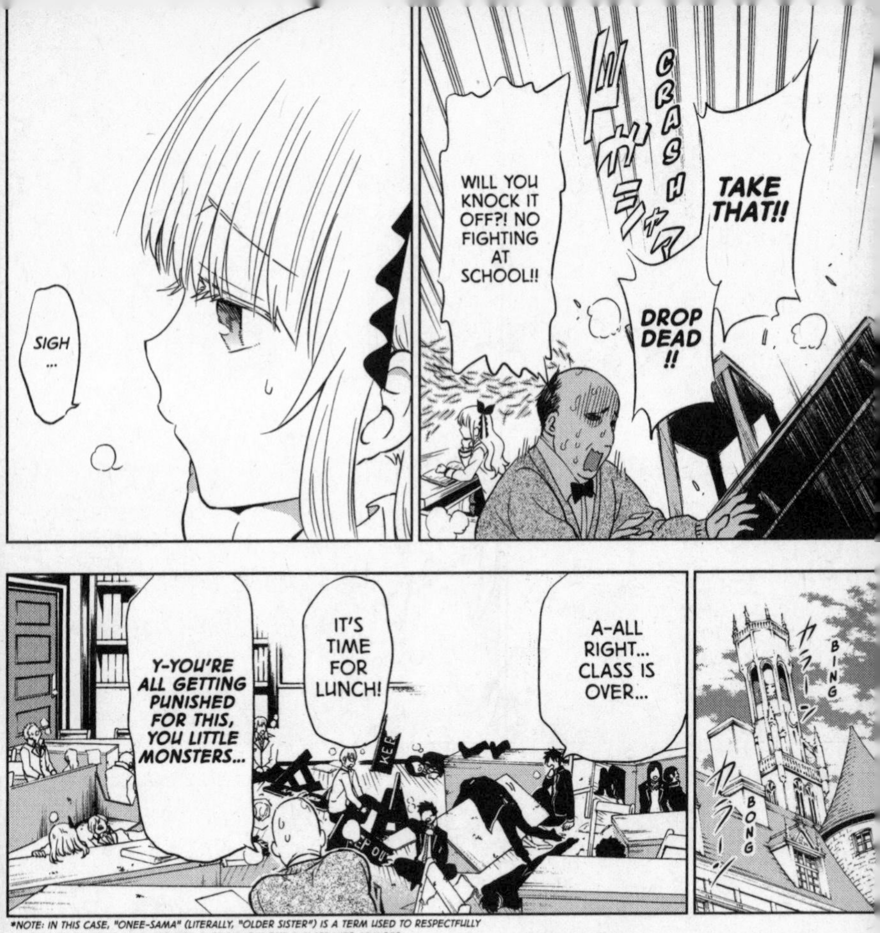
TAKE THAT!!
CRASH
DROP DEAD!!
WILL YOU KNOCK IT OFF?! NO FIGHTING AT SCHOOL!!
SIGH...
BING
BONG
A-ALL RIGHT... CLASS IS OVER...
IT'S TIME FOR LUNCH!
Y-YOU'RE ALL GETTING PUNISHED FOR THIS, YOU LITTLE MONSTERS...

*NOTE: IN THIS CASE, "ONEE-SAMA" (LITERALLY, "OLDER SISTER") IS A TERM USED TO RESPECTFULLY ADDRESS OR REFER TO AN OLDER GIRL, PARTICULARLY ONE THE SPEAKER ADMIRES.

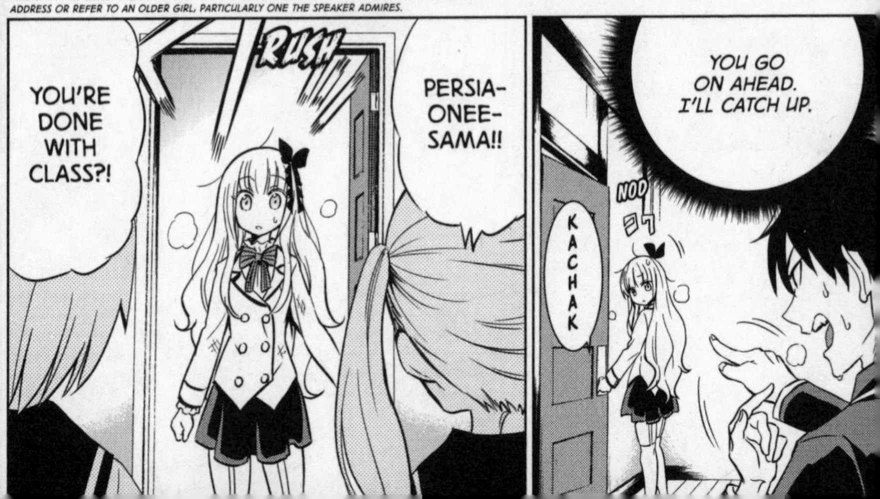
YOU GO ON AHEAD. I'LL CATCH UP.
NOD
KACHAK
PERSIA-ONEE-SAMA!!
RUSH
YOU'RE DONE WITH CLASS?!

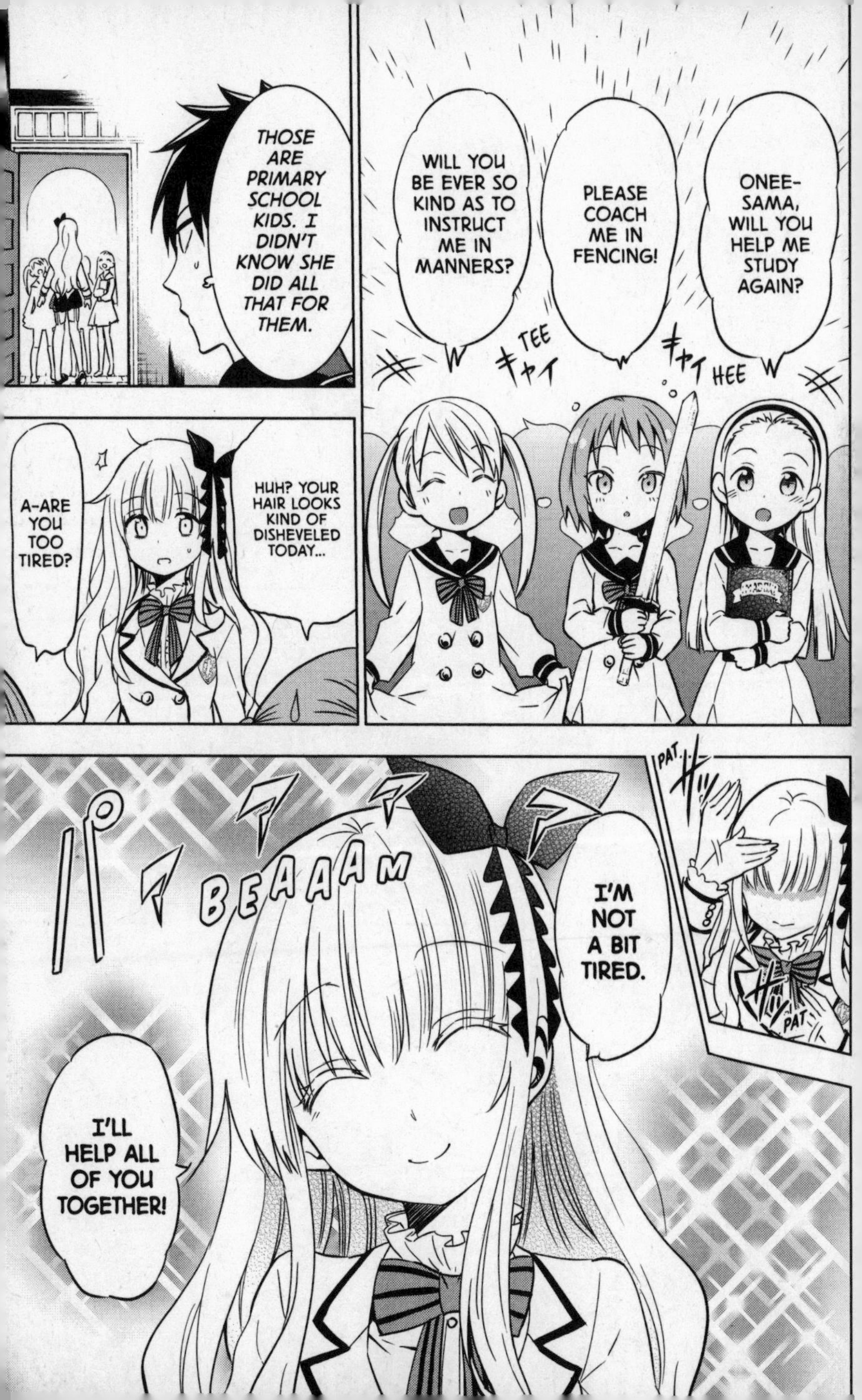
ONEE-SAMA, WILL YOU HELP ME STUDY AGAIN?
PLEASE COACH ME IN FENCING!
WILL YOU BE EVER SO KIND AS TO INSTRUCT ME IN MANNERS?
キャイ
キャイ
TEE HEE
THOSE ARE PRIMARY SCHOOL KIDS. I DIDN'T KNOW SHE DID ALL THAT FOR THEM.
HUH? YOUR HAIR LOOKS KIND OF DISHEVELED TODAY...
A-ARE YOU TOO TIRED?
PAT
PAT
I'M NOT A BIT TIRED.
パァァァ
BEAAAAM
I'LL HELP ALL OF YOU TOGETHER!

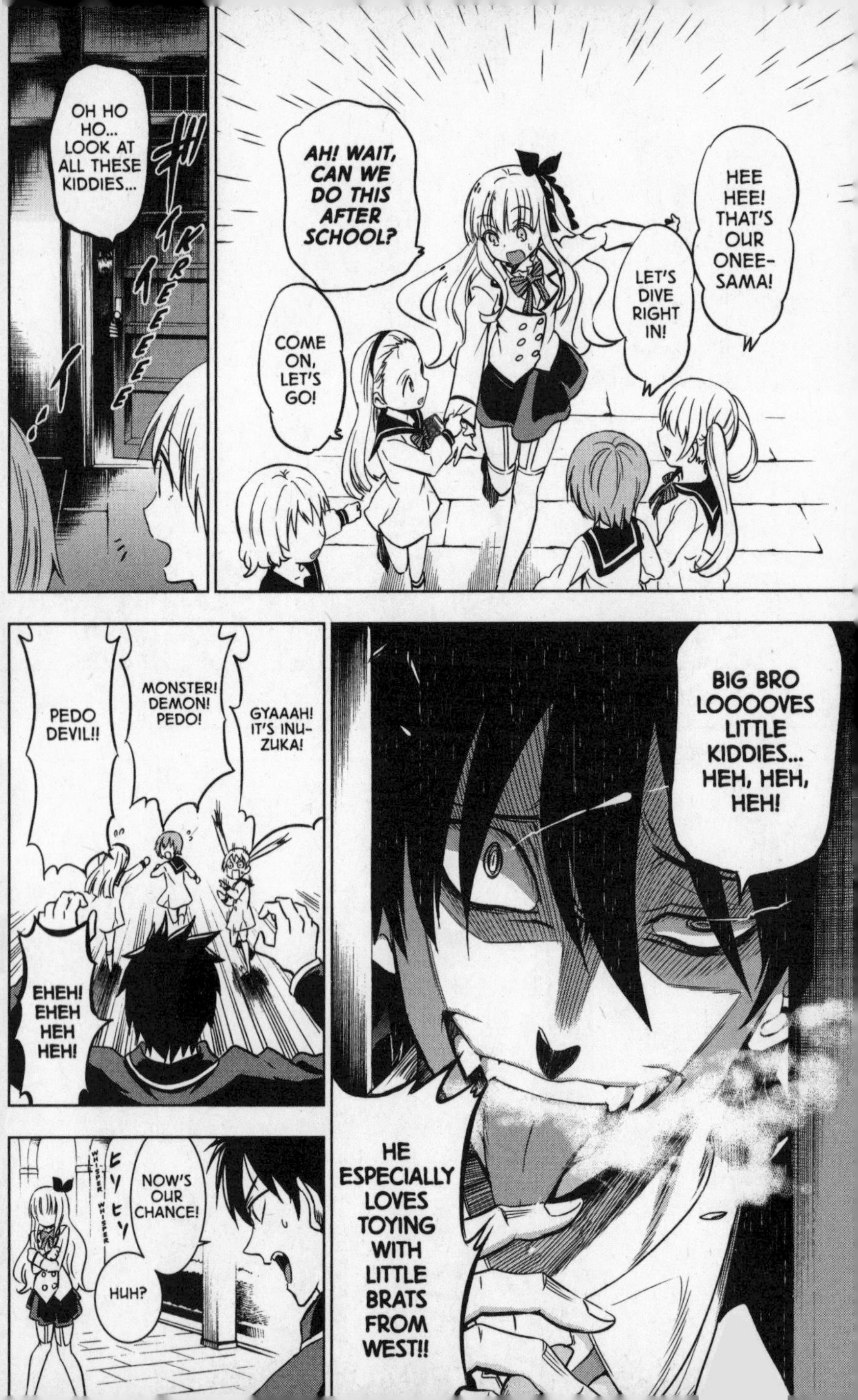
HEE HEE! THAT'S OUR ONEE-SAMA!
LET'S DIVE RIGHT IN!
AH! WAIT, CAN WE DO THIS AFTER SCHOOL?
COME ON, LET'S GO!
OH HO HO... LOOK AT ALL THESE KIDDIES...
KREEEEEEE
BIG BRO LOOOOVES LITTLE KIDDIES... HEH, HEH, HEH!
HE ESPECIALLY LOVES TOYING WITH LITTLE BRATS FROM WEST!!
GYAAAH! IT'S INU-ZUKA!
MONSTER! DEMON! PEDO!
PEDO DEVIL!!
EHEH! EHEH HEH HEH!
NOW'S OUR CHANCE!
WHISPER WHISPER
HUH?

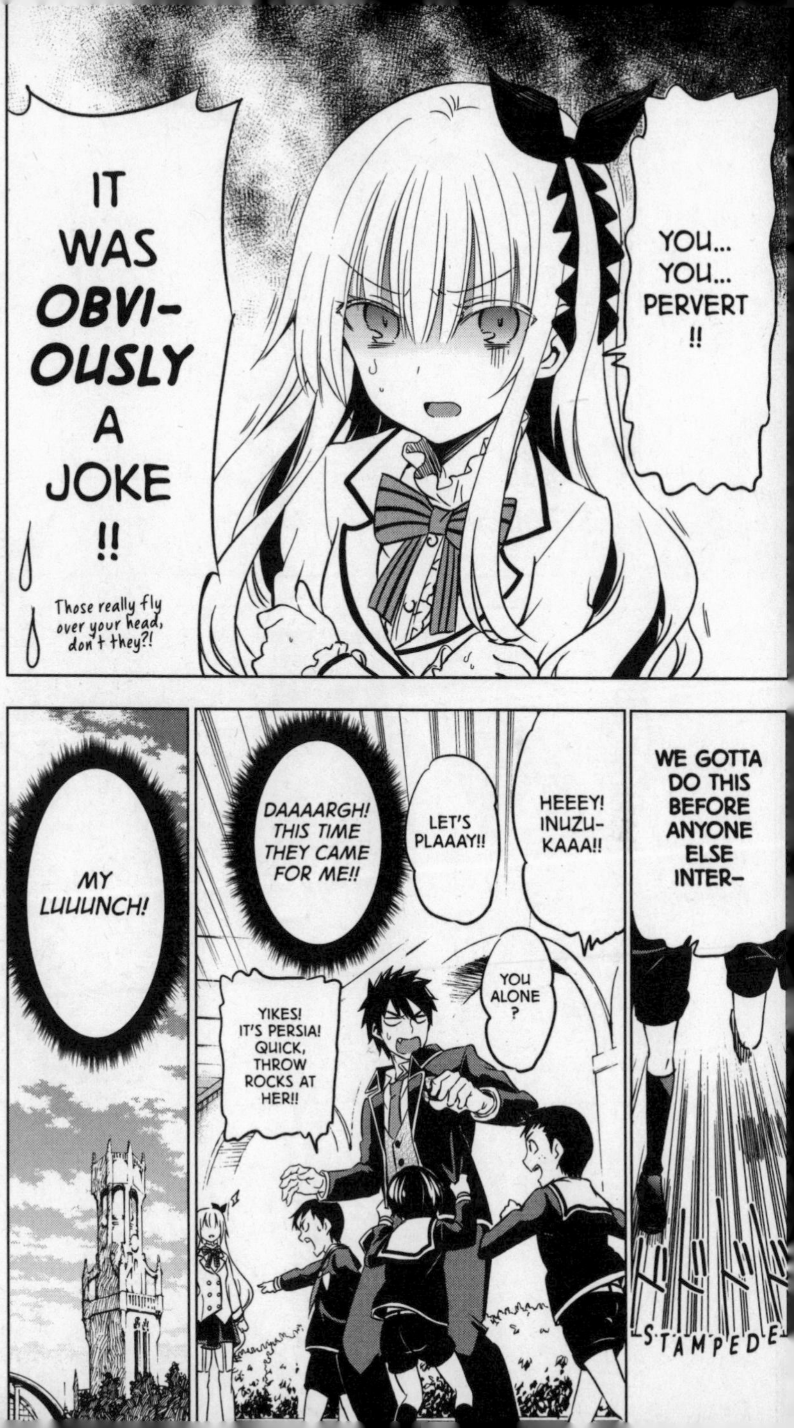
YOU... YOU... PERVERT!!
IT WAS OBVIOUSLY A JOKE!!
Those really fly over your head, don't they?!
WE GOTTA DO THIS BEFORE ANYONE ELSE INTER—
STAMPEDE
HEEEY! INUZUKAAA!!
LET'S PLAAAY!!
YOU ALONE?
DAAAARGH! THIS TIME THEY CAME FOR ME!!
YIKES! IT'S PERSIA! QUICK, THROW ROCKS AT HER!!
MY LUUUNCH!

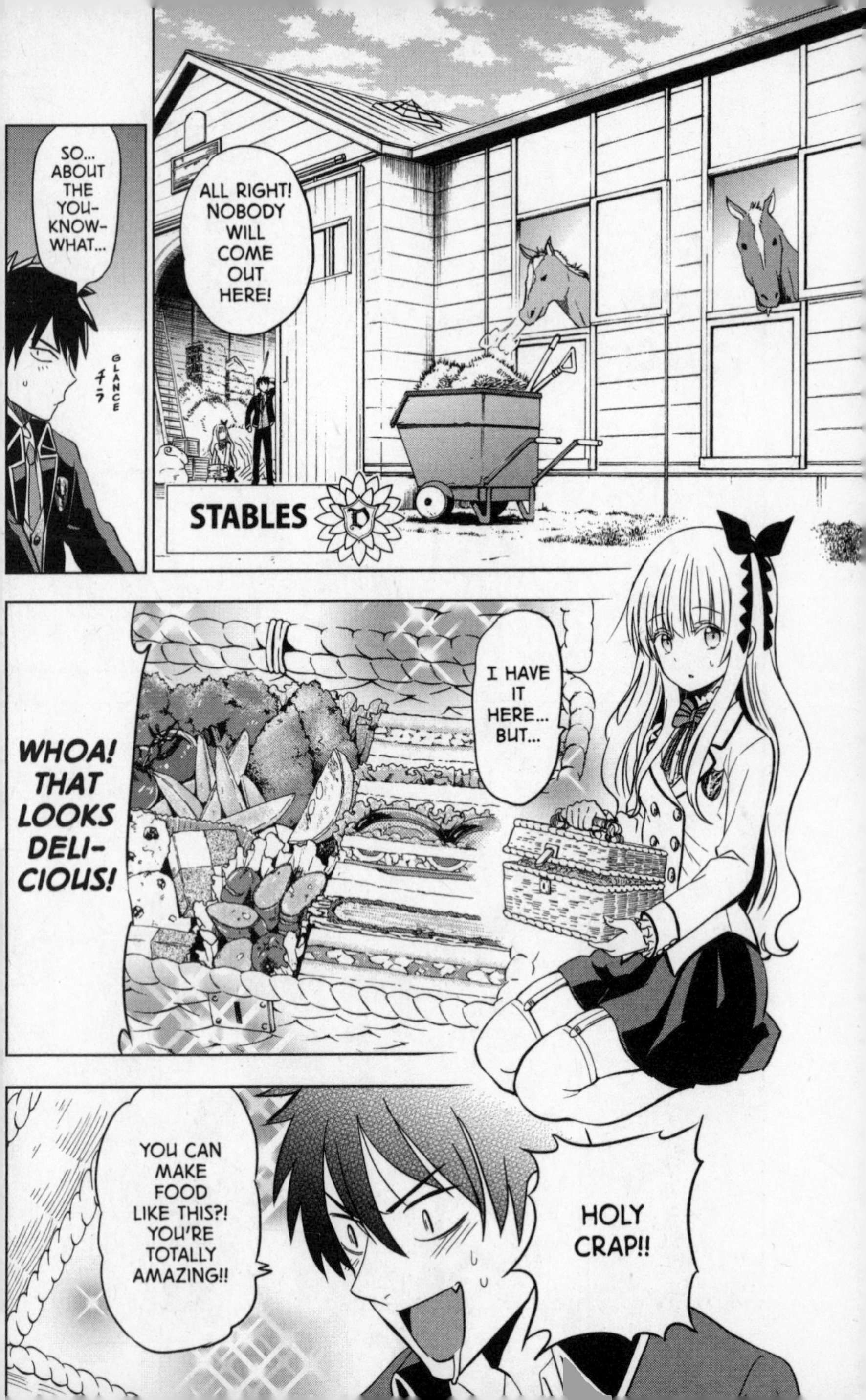
ALL RIGHT! NOBODY WILL COME OUT HERE!
STABLES
SO... ABOUT THE YOU-KNOW-WHAT...
チラ
GLANCE
I HAVE IT HERE... BUT...
WHOA! THAT LOOKS DELICIOUS!
HOLY CRAP!!
YOU CAN MAKE FOOD LIKE THIS?! YOU'RE TOTALLY AMAZING!!

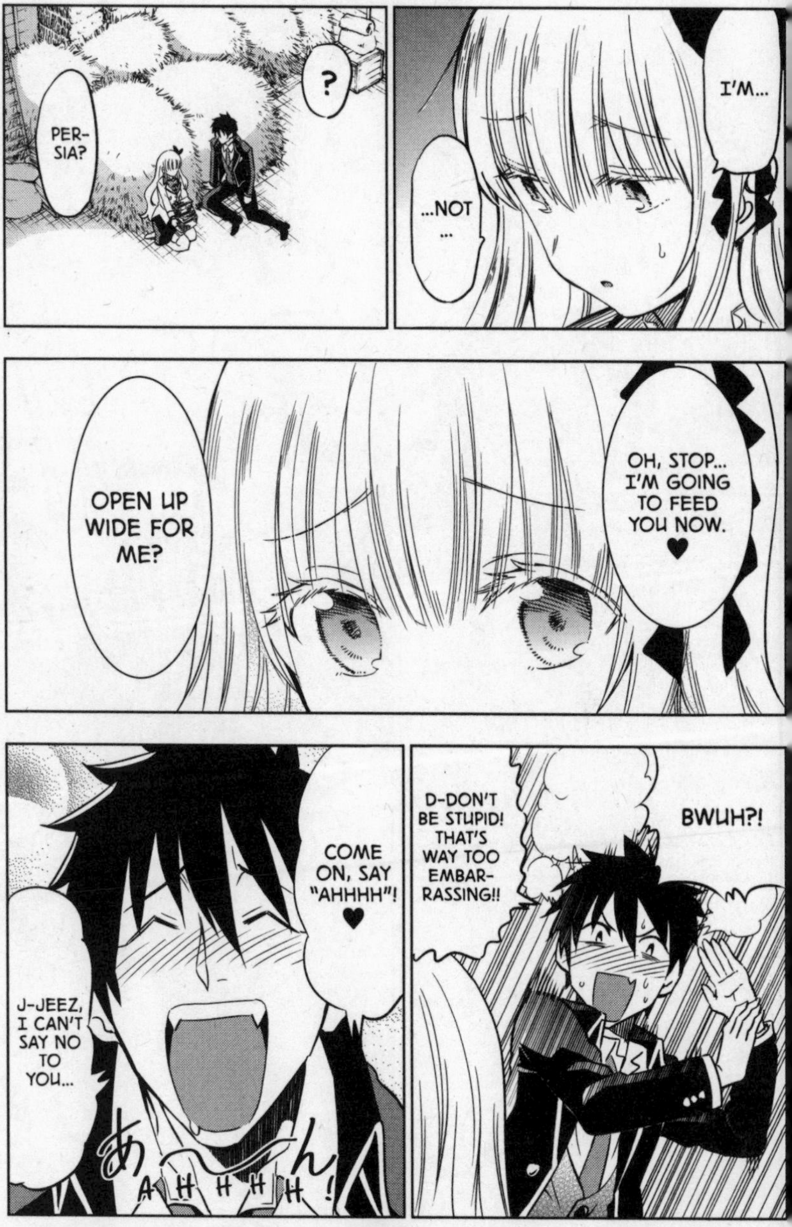
I'M...
...NOT ...
?
PER-SIA?
OH, STOP... I'M GOING TO FEED YOU NOW. ♥
OPEN UP WIDE FOR ME?
BWUH?!
D-DON'T BE STUPID! THAT'S WAY TOO EMBAR-RASSING!!
COME ON, SAY "AHHHH"! ♥
J-JEEZ, I CAN'T SAY NO TO YOU...
あ～ん
AHHHHH!

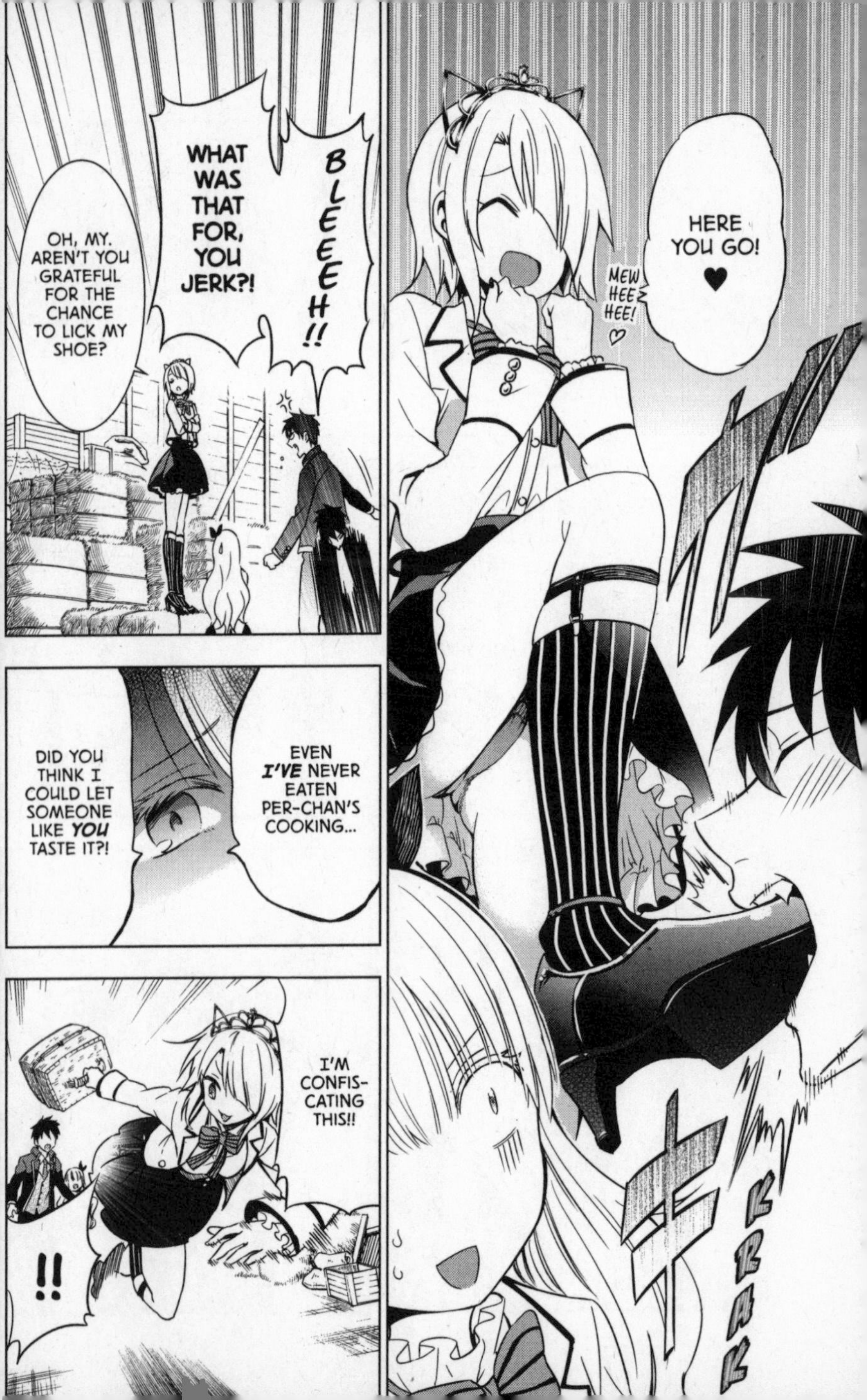
HERE YOU GO! ♥
MEW HEE HEE! ♡
KRAK
BLEEEH!!
WHAT WAS THAT FOR, YOU JERK?!
OH, MY. AREN'T YOU GRATEFUL FOR THE CHANCE TO LICK MY SHOE?
EVEN *I'VE* NEVER EATEN PER-CHAN'S COOKING...
DID YOU THINK I COULD LET SOMEONE LIKE *YOU* TASTE IT?!
I'M CONFIS-CATING THIS!!
!!

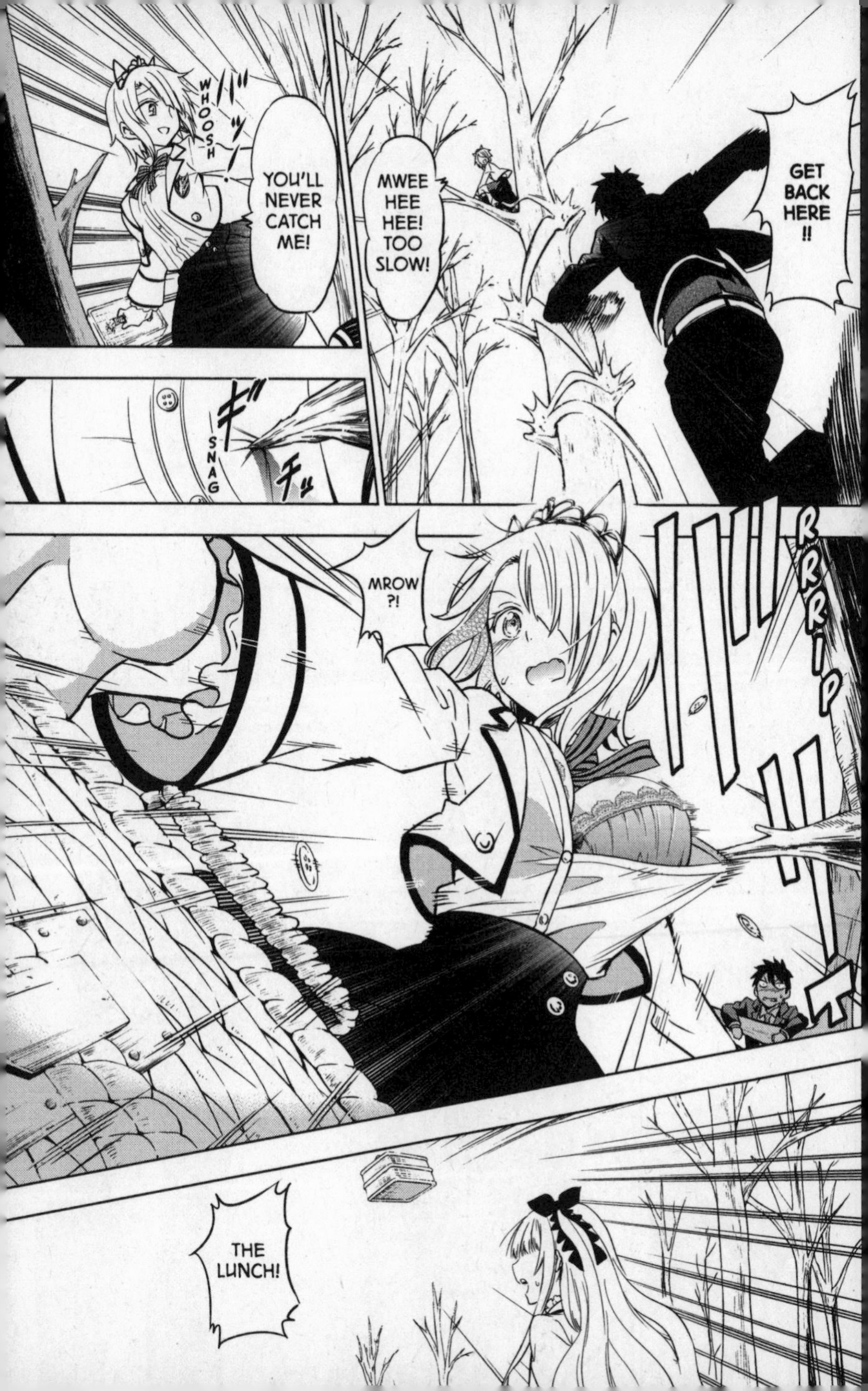
GET BACK HERE !!
MWEE HEE HEE! TOO SLOW!
WHOOSH
YOU'LL NEVER CATCH ME!
SNAG
RRRIP
MROW ?!
THE LUNCH!

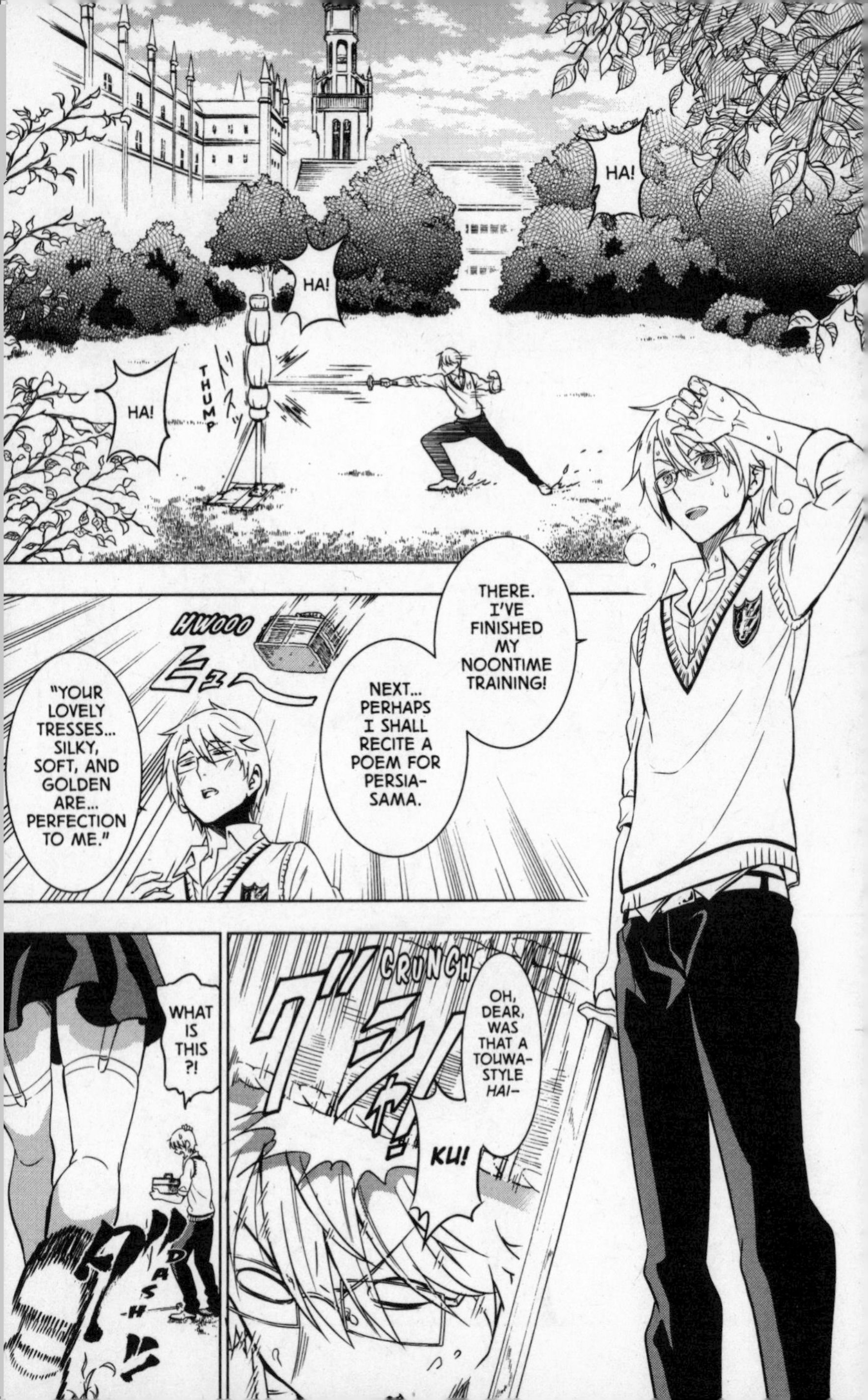
HA!
HA!
THUMP
HA!
THERE. I'VE FINISHED MY NOONTIME TRAINING!
NEXT... PERHAPS I SHALL RECITE A POEM FOR PERSIA-SAMA.
HWOOO
"YOUR LOVELY TRESSES... SILKY, SOFT, AND GOLDEN ARE... PERFECTION TO ME."
CRUNCH
OH, DEAR, WAS THAT A TOUWA-STYLE *HAI*–
KU!
WHAT IS THIS ?!
DASH-H

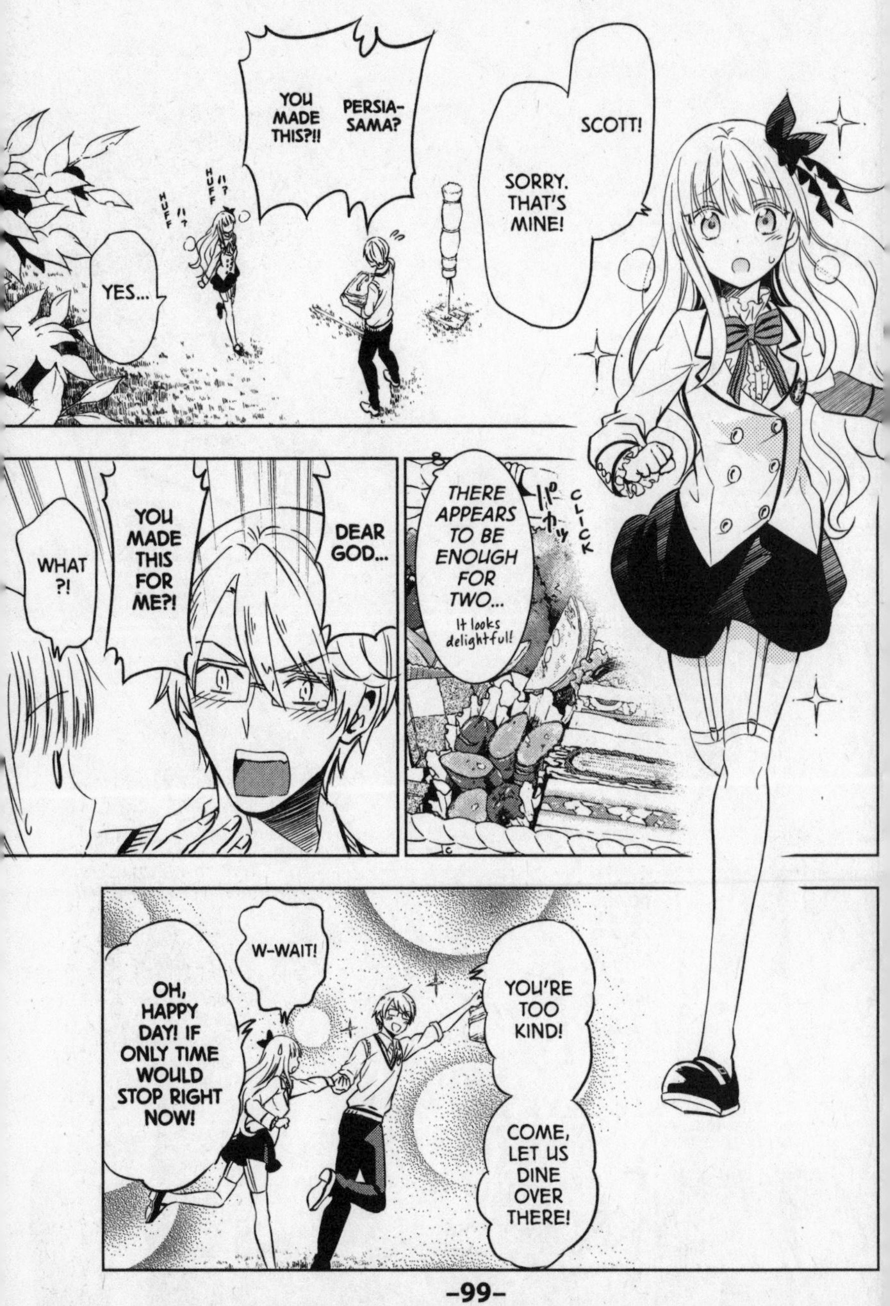
SCOTT!
SORRY. THAT'S MINE!
PERSIA-SAMA?
YOU MADE THIS?!!
HUFF HUFF
YES...
CLICK
THERE APPEARS TO BE ENOUGH FOR TWO... It looks delightful!
DEAR GOD...
YOU MADE THIS FOR ME?!
WHAT?!
YOU'RE TOO KIND!
COME, LET US DINE OVER THERE!
W-WAIT!
OH, HAPPY DAY! IF ONLY TIME WOULD STOP RIGHT NOW!

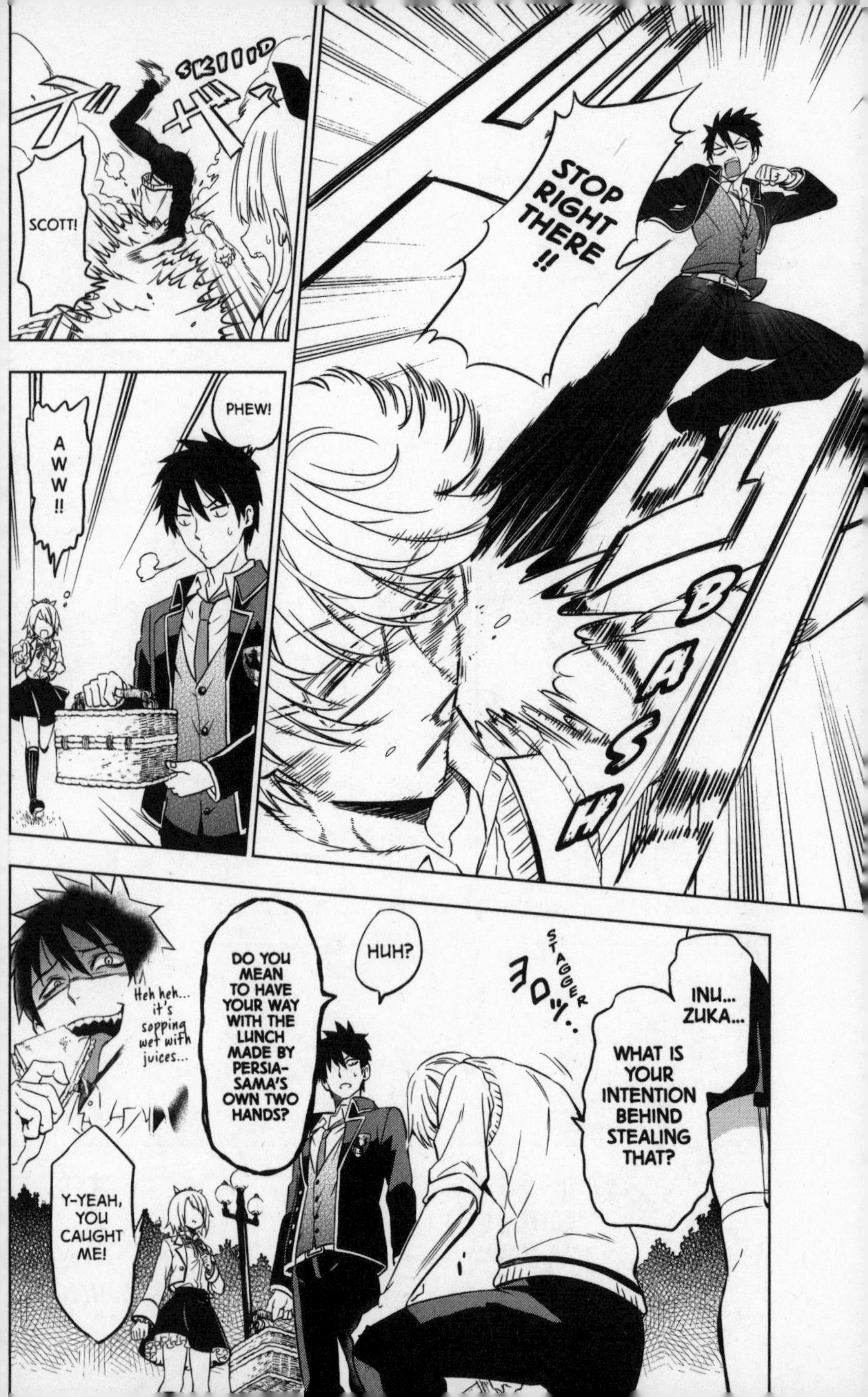
STOP RIGHT THERE!!
BASH
SKIIID
SCOTT!
PHEW!
AWW!!
STAGGER
INU... ZUKA...
WHAT IS YOUR INTENTION BEHIND STEALING THAT?
HUH?
DO YOU MEAN TO HAVE YOUR WAY WITH THE LUNCH MADE BY PERSIA-SAMA'S OWN TWO HANDS?
Heh heh... it's sopping wet with juices...
Y-YEAH, YOU CAUGHT ME!

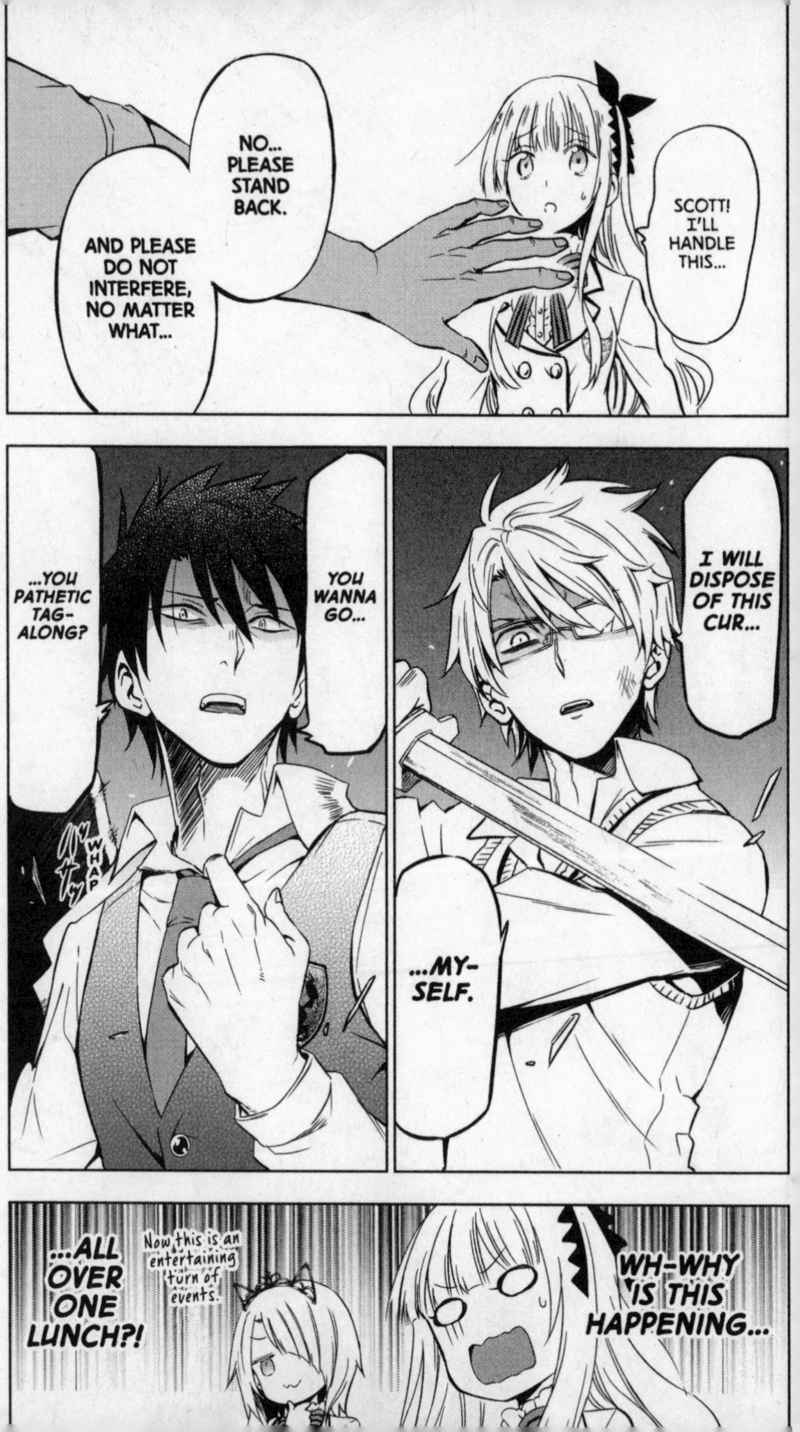
SCOTT! I'LL HANDLE THIS...
NO... PLEASE STAND BACK.
AND PLEASE DO NOT INTERFERE, NO MATTER WHAT...
I WILL DISPOSE OF THIS CUR...
...MY-SELF.
YOU WANNA GO...
...YOU PATHETIC TAG-ALONG?
WHAP
WH-WHY IS THIS HAPPENING...
Now this is an entertaining turn of events.
...ALL OVER ONE LUNCH?!

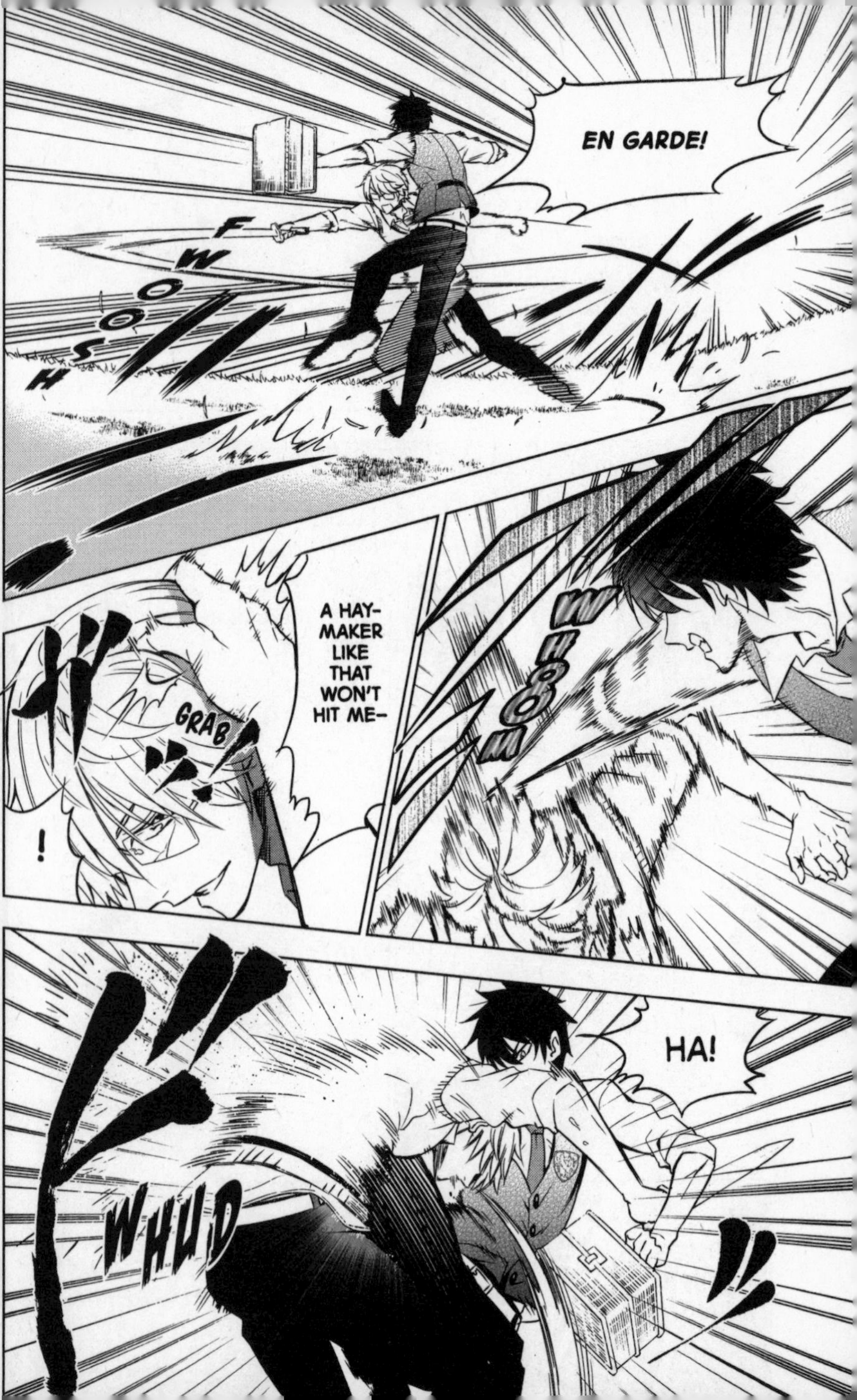
EN GARDE!
FWOOSH
WHOOM
A HAY-MAKER LIKE THAT WON'T HIT ME—
GRAB
!
HA!
WHUD

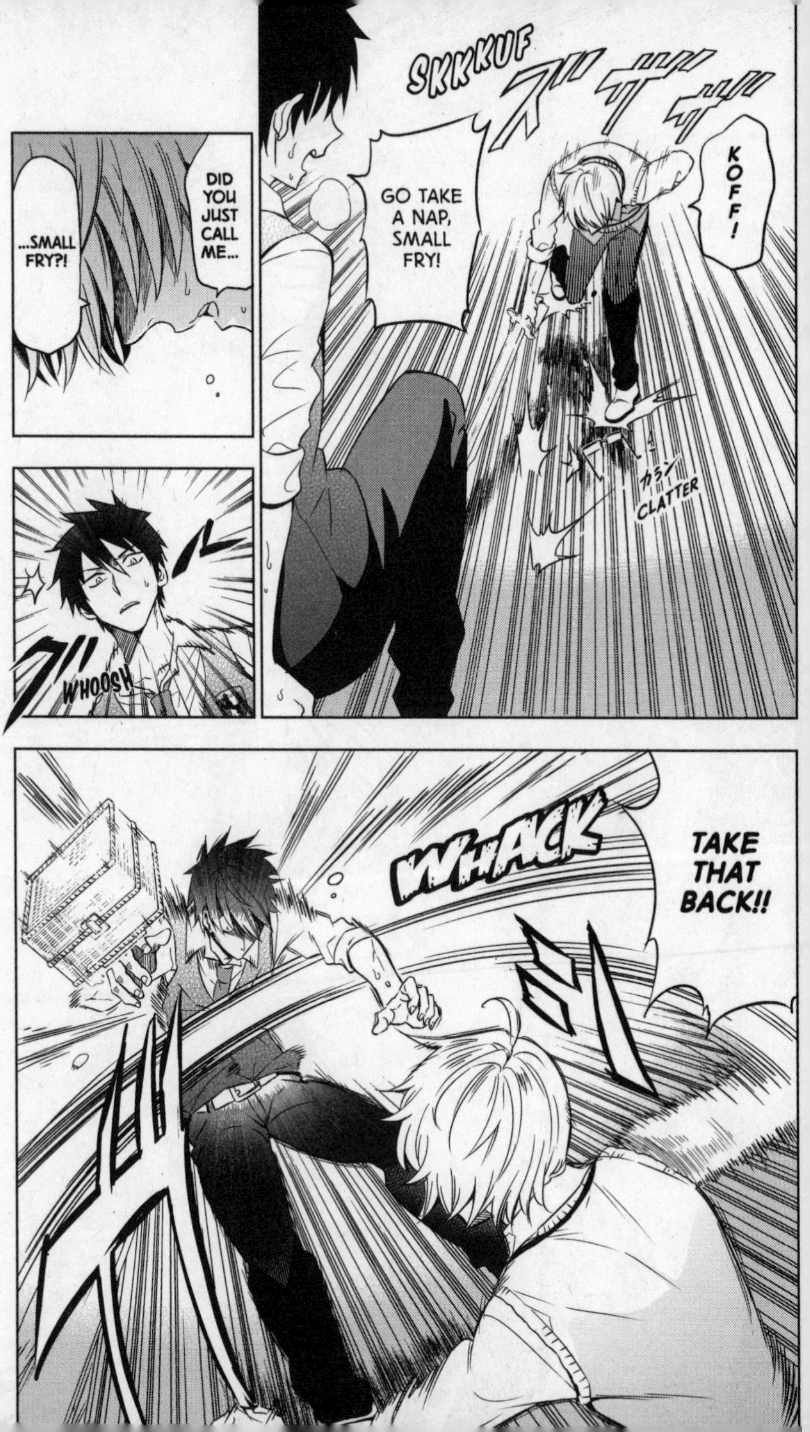
SKKUF
KOFF!
GO TAKE A NAP, SMALL FRY!
カラン
CLATTER
DID YOU JUST CALL ME...
...SMALL FRY?!
WHOOSH
TAKE THAT BACK!!
WHACK

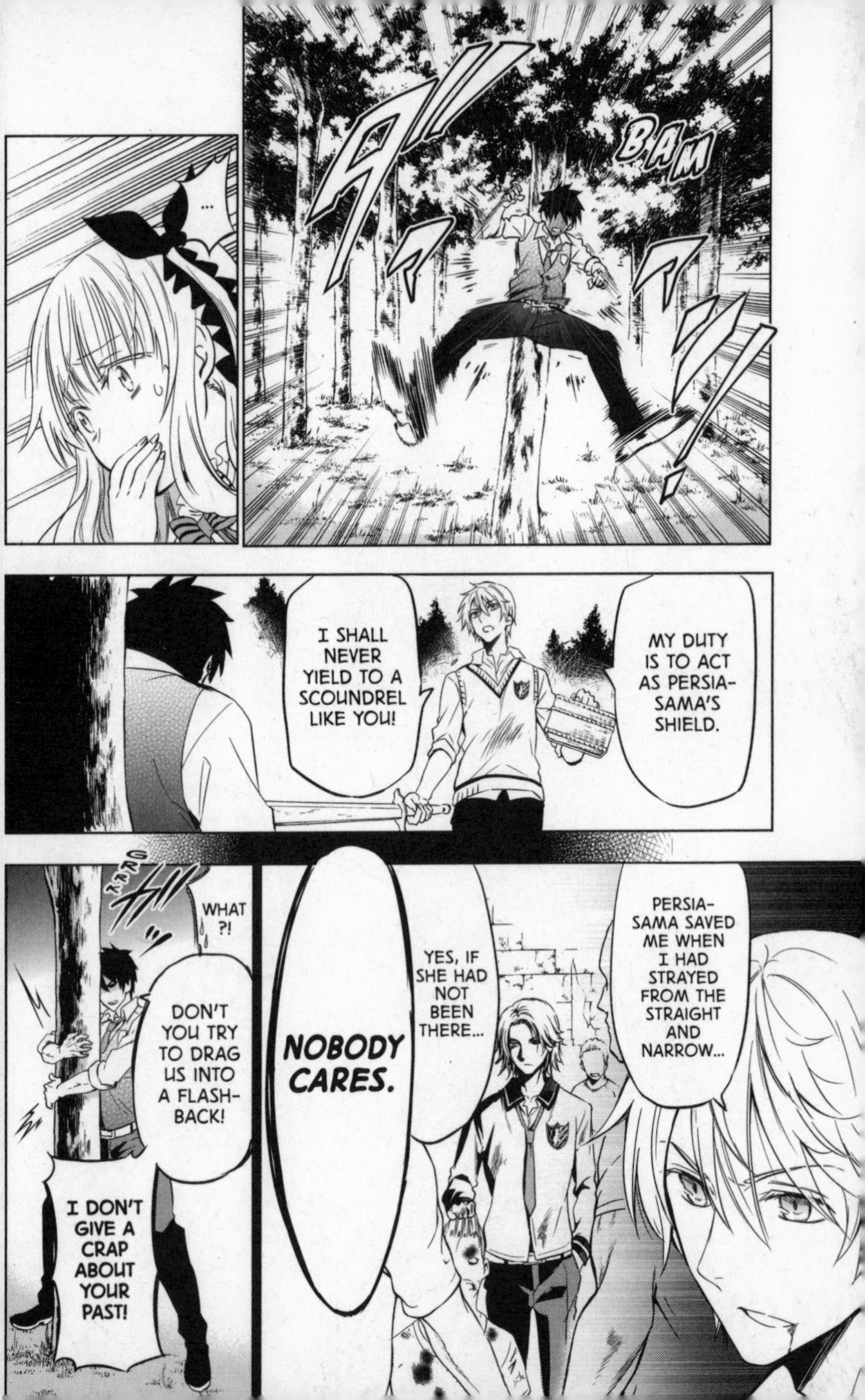
BAM
...
MY DUTY IS TO ACT AS PERSIA-SAMA'S SHIELD.
I SHALL NEVER YIELD TO A SCOUNDREL LIKE YOU!
PERSIA-SAMA SAVED ME WHEN I HAD STRAYED FROM THE STRAIGHT AND NARROW...
YES, IF SHE HAD NOT BEEN THERE...
NOBODY CARES.
WHAT?!
DON'T YOU TRY TO DRAG US INTO A FLASH-BACK!
I DON'T GIVE A CRAP ABOUT YOUR PAST!

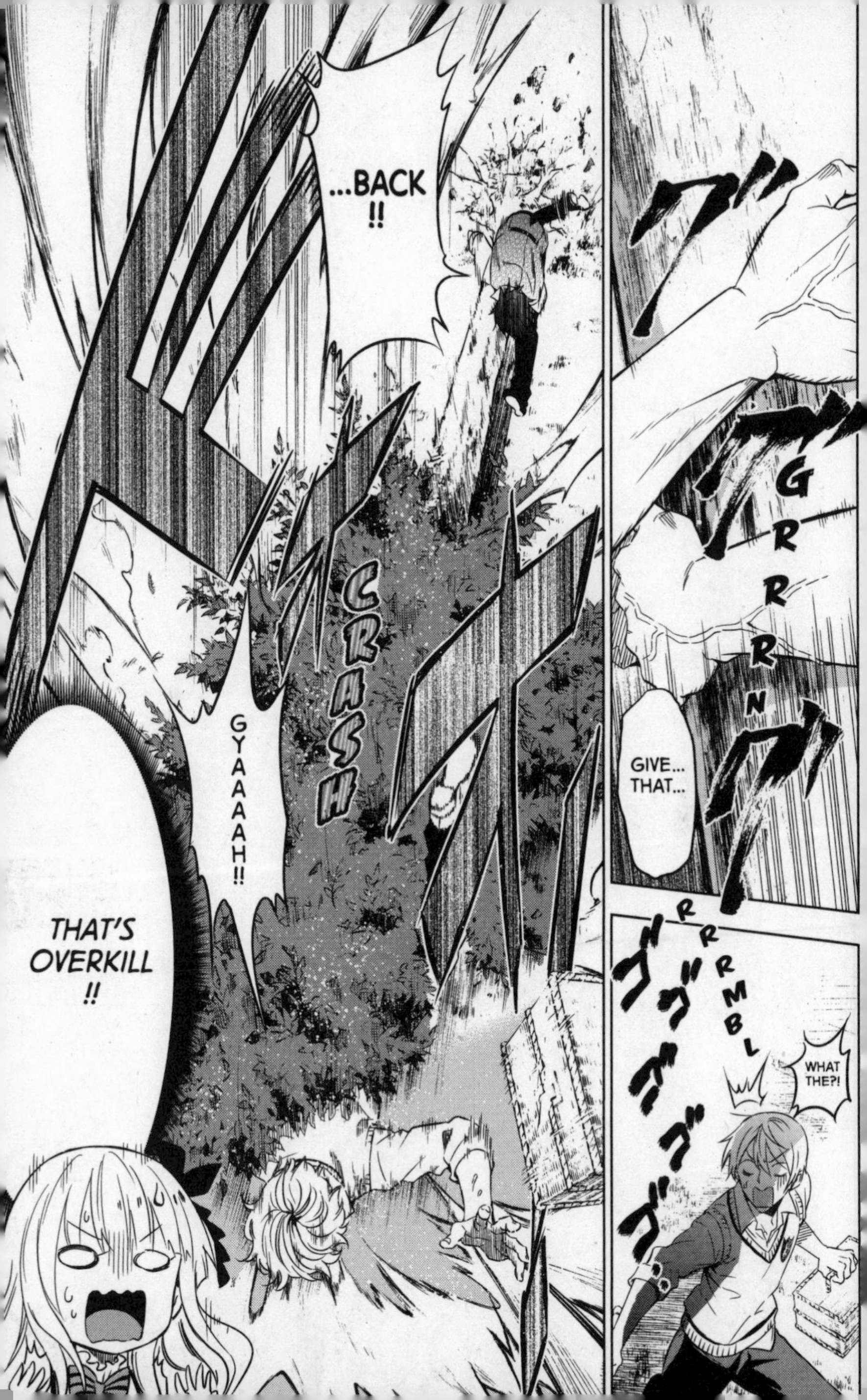
GRRRN
GIVE... THAT...
RRRRMBL
WHAT THE?!
...BACK !!
CRASH
GYAAAAAH!!
THAT'S OVERKILL !!

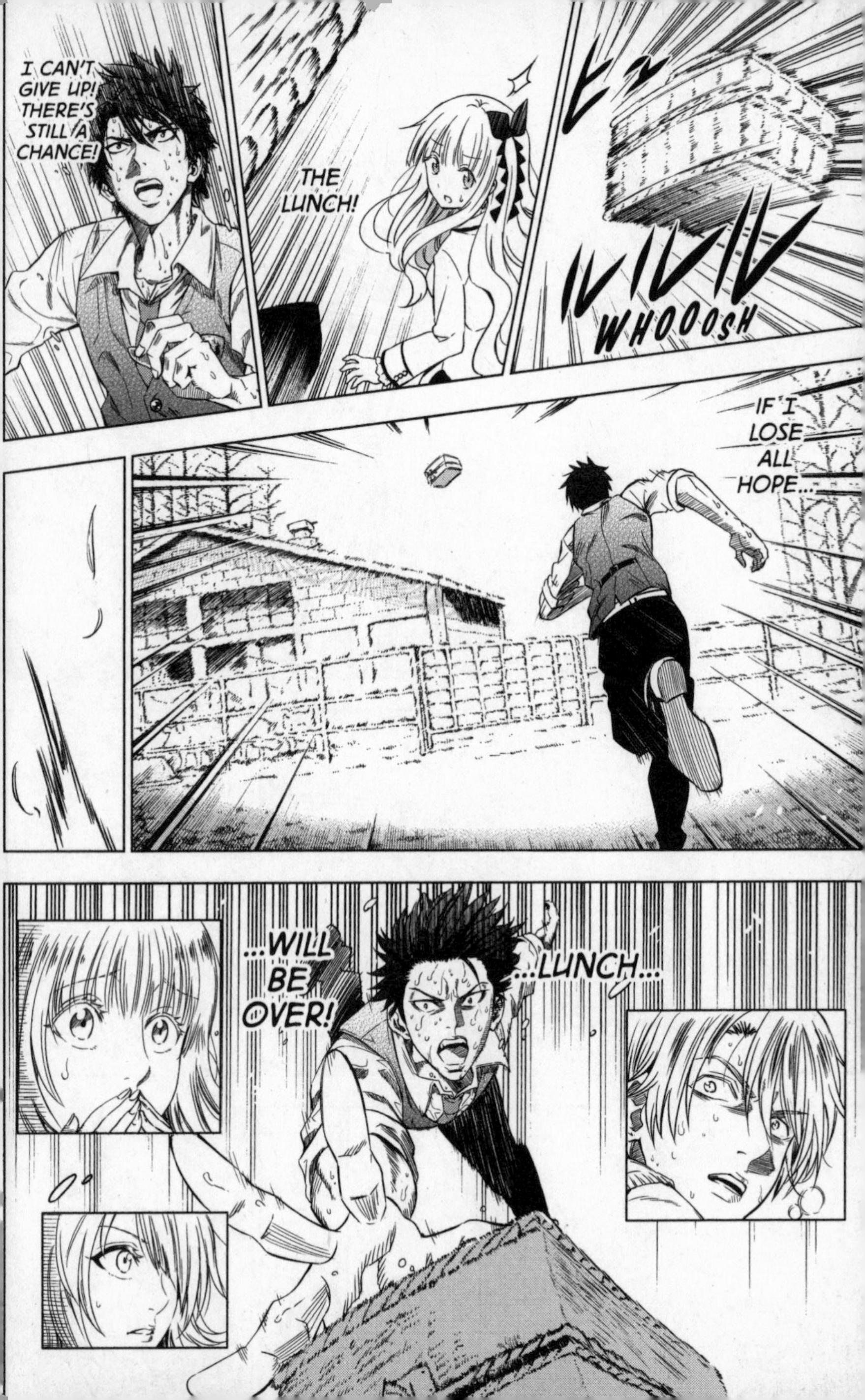
WHOOOSH
THE LUNCH!
I CAN'T GIVE UP! THERE'S STILL A CHANCE!
IF I LOSE ALL HOPE...
...LUNCH...
...WILL BE OVER!

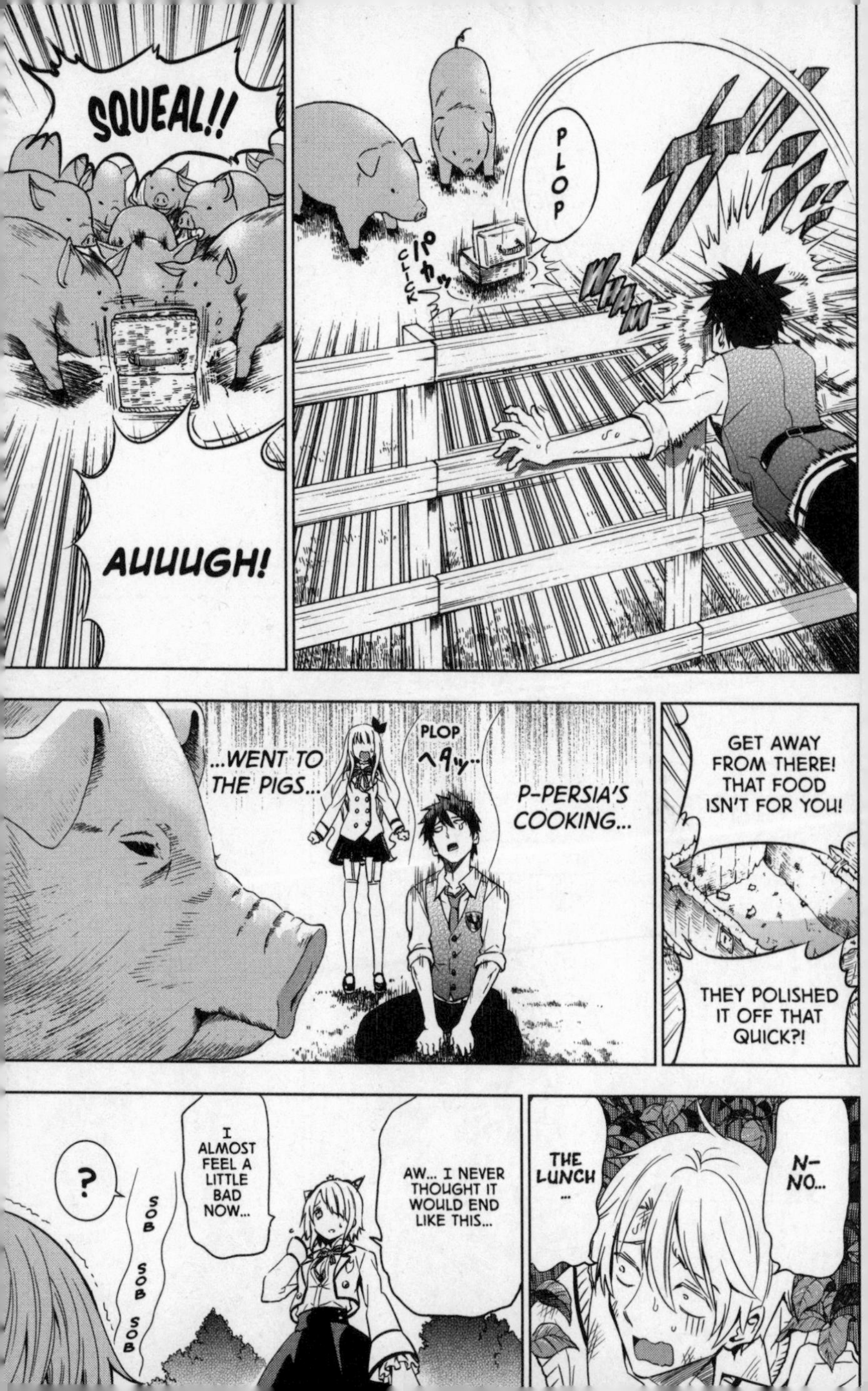
PLOP
WHAM
パカッ CLICK
SQUEAL!!
AUUUGH!
GET AWAY FROM THERE! THAT FOOD ISN'T FOR YOU!
THEY POLISHED IT OFF THAT QUICK?!
P-PERSIA'S COOKING...
PLOP へタッ...
...WENT TO THE PIGS...
N-NO...
THE LUNCH ...
AW... I NEVER THOUGHT IT WOULD END LIKE THIS...
I ALMOST FEEL A LITTLE BAD NOW...
SOB SOB SOB
?

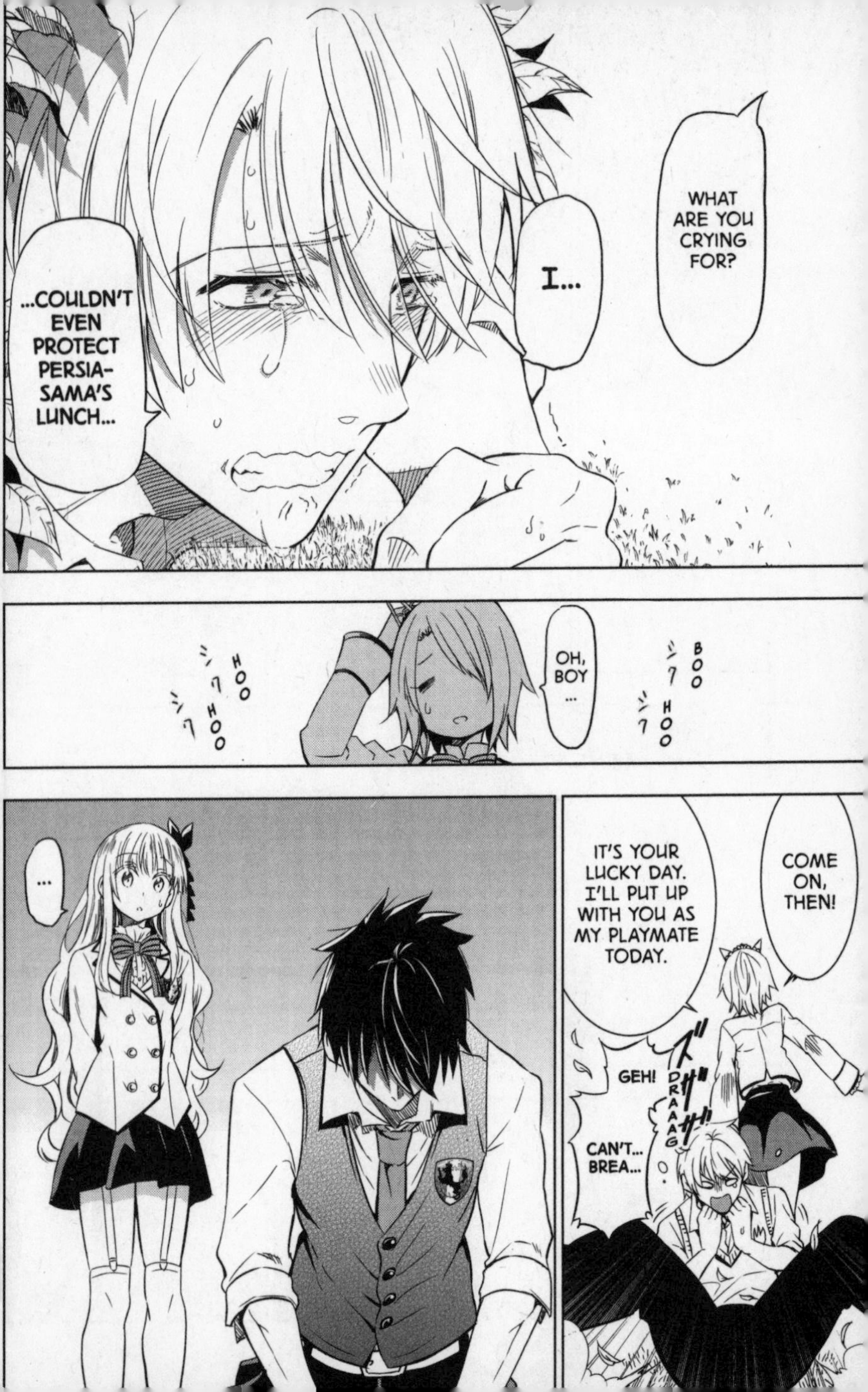
WHAT ARE YOU CRYING FOR?
I...
...COULDN'T EVEN PROTECT PERSIA-SAMA'S LUNCH...
BOO HOO
OH, BOY ...
HOO HOO
COME ON, THEN!
IT'S YOUR LUCKY DAY. I'LL PUT UP WITH YOU AS MY PLAYMATE TODAY.
GEH!
DRAAAG
CAN'T... BREA...
...

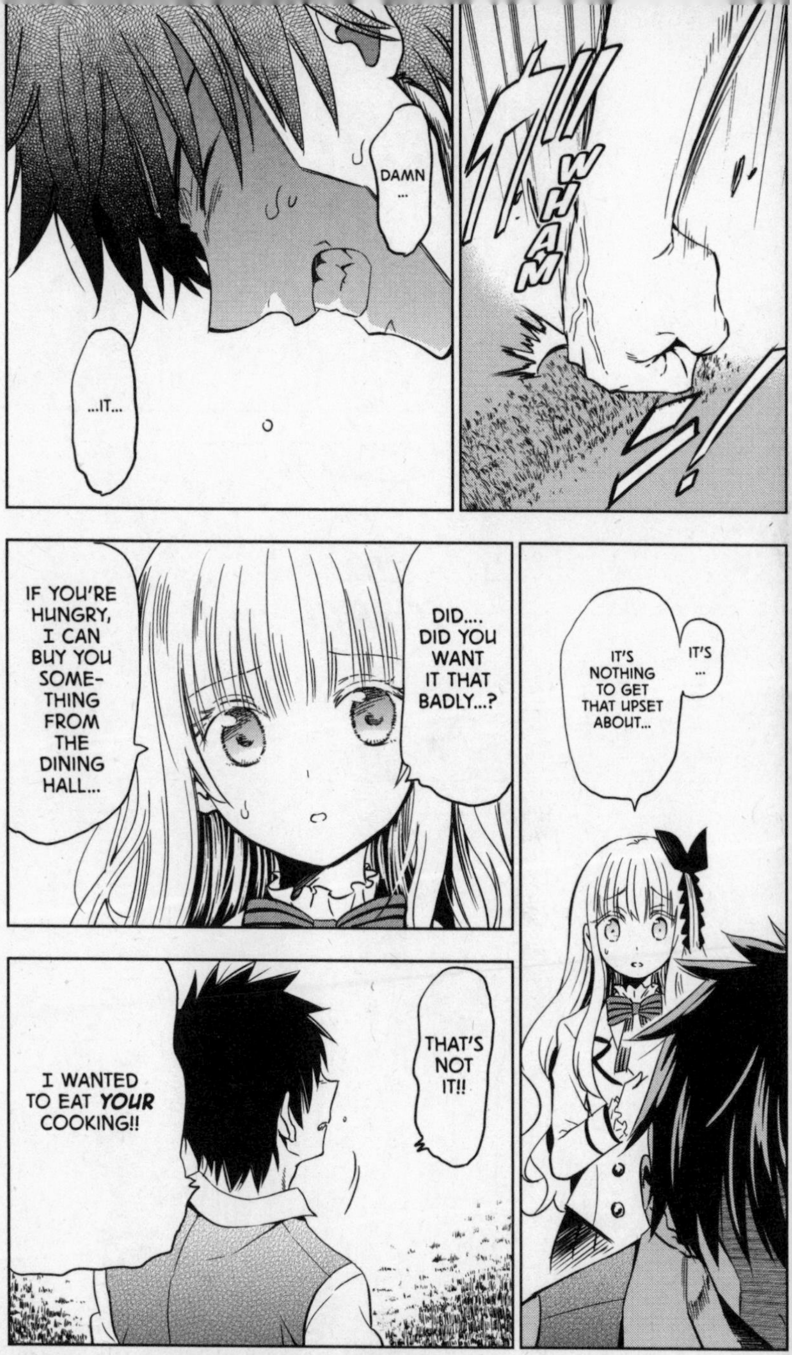
WHAM
DAMN ...
...IT...
IT'S ...
IT'S NOTHING TO GET THAT UPSET ABOUT...
DID.... DID YOU WANT IT THAT BADLY...?
IF YOU'RE HUNGRY, I CAN BUY YOU SOME-THING FROM THE DINING HALL...
THAT'S NOT IT!!
I WANTED TO EAT *YOUR* COOKING!!

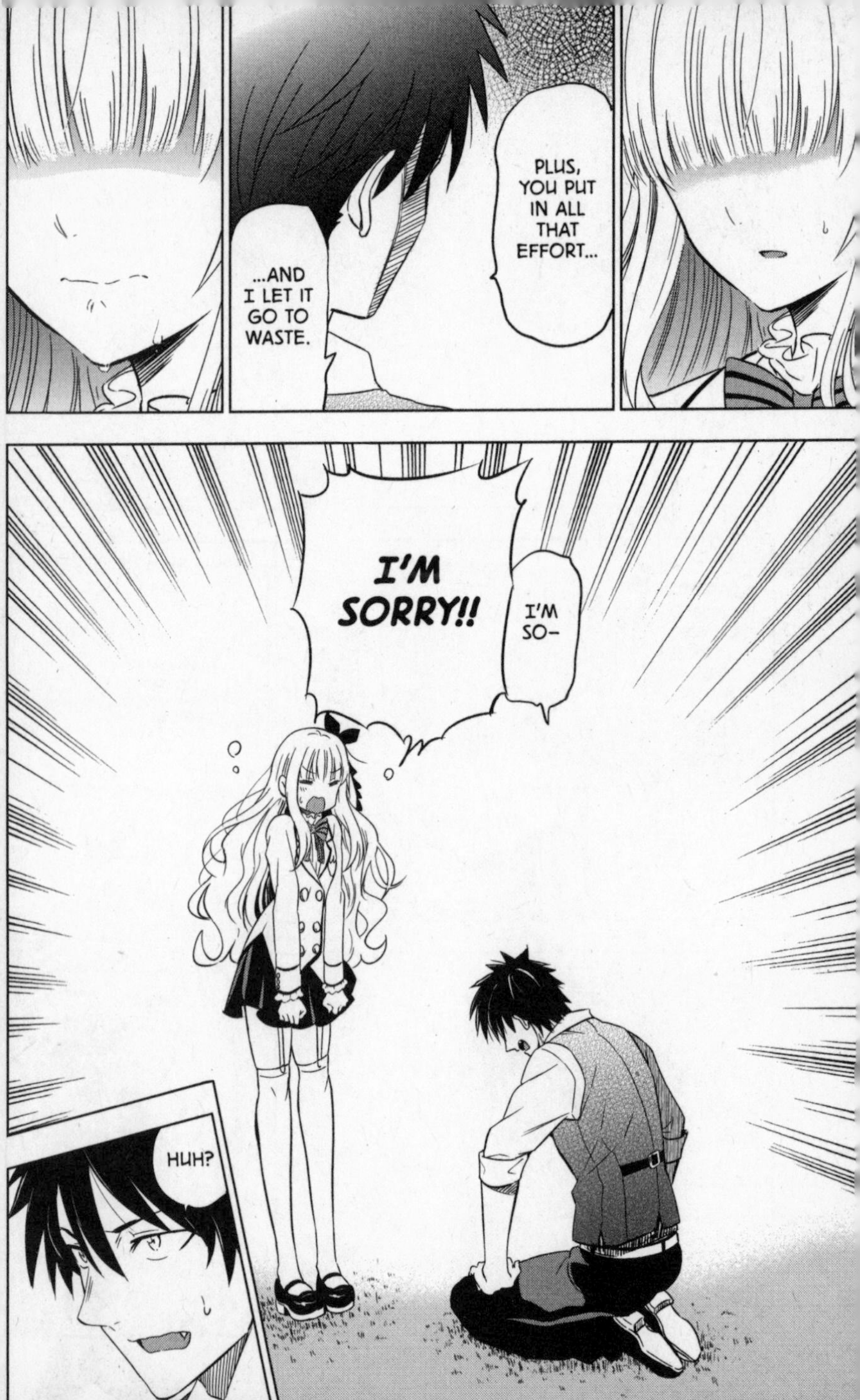
PLUS, YOU PUT IN ALL THAT EFFORT...
...AND I LET IT GO TO WASTE.
I'M SO-
I'M SORRY!!
HUH?

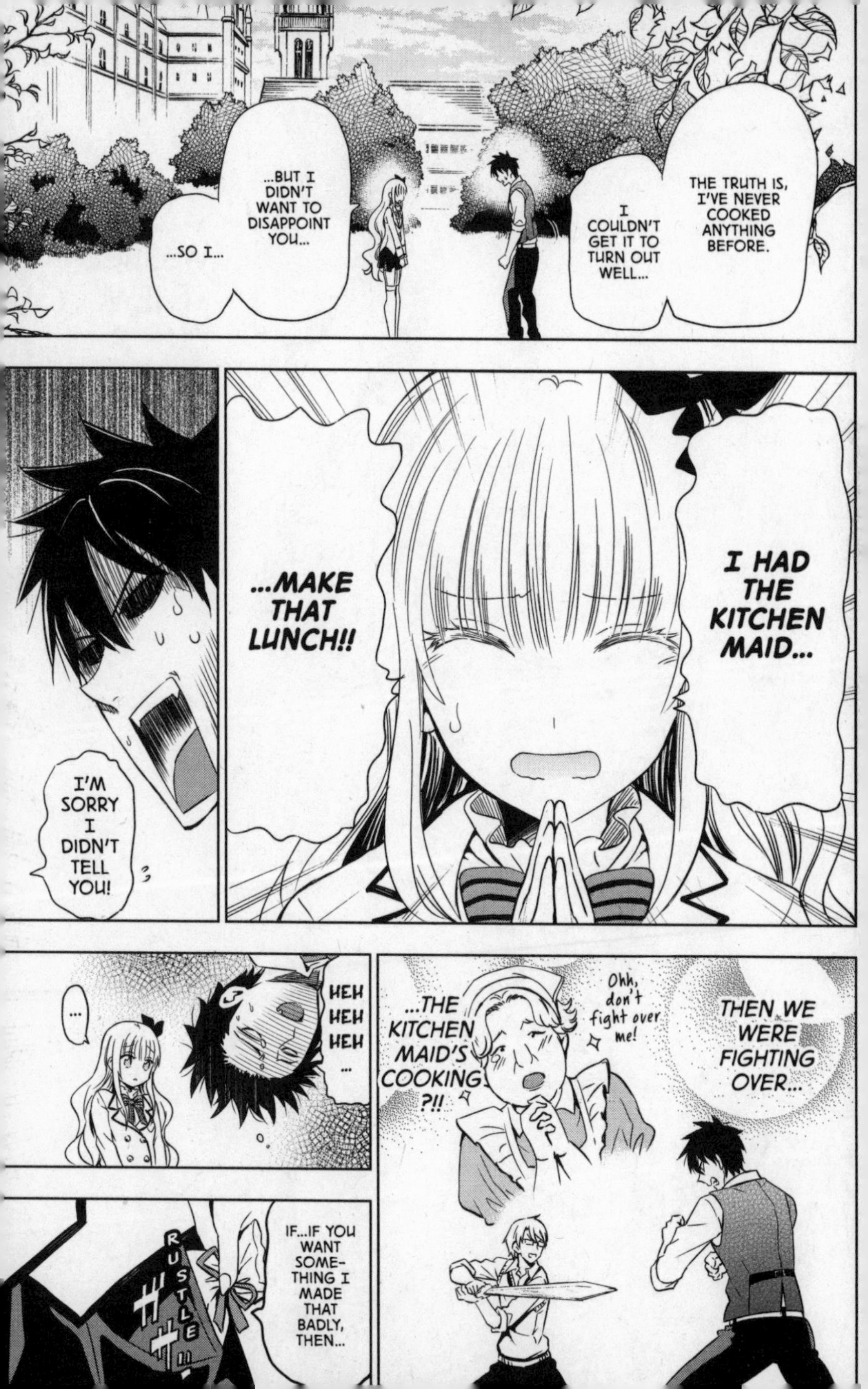
THE TRUTH IS, I'VE NEVER COOKED ANYTHING BEFORE.
I COULDN'T GET IT TO TURN OUT WELL...
...BUT I DIDN'T WANT TO DISAPPOINT YOU...
...SO I...
I HAD THE KITCHEN MAID...
...MAKE THAT LUNCH!!
I'M SORRY I DIDN'T TELL YOU!
THEN WE WERE FIGHTING OVER...
Ohh, don't fight over me!
...THE KITCHEN MAID'S COOKING?!!
HEH HEH HEH...
...
IF...IF YOU WANT SOMETHING I MADE THAT BADLY, THEN...
RUSTLE

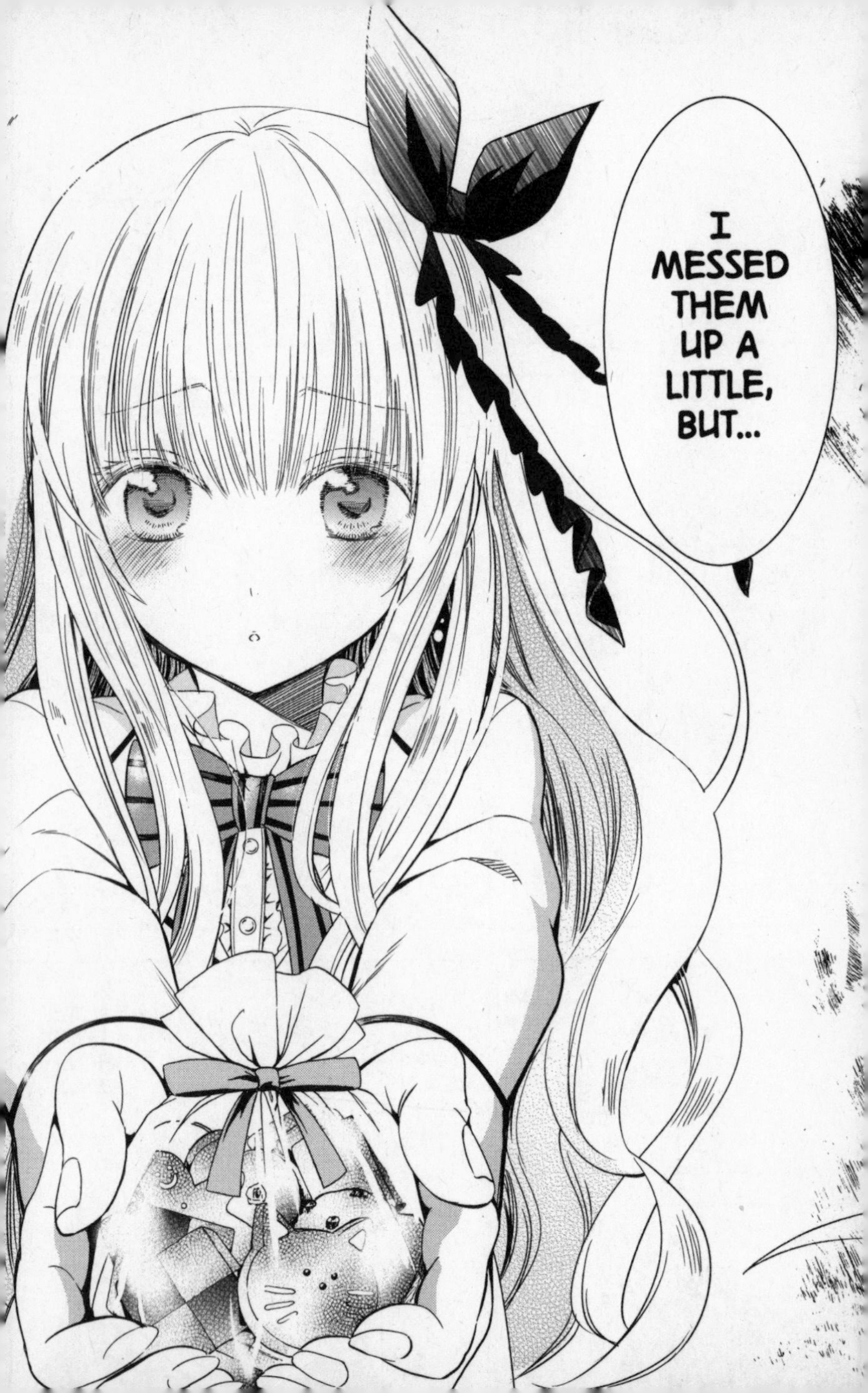
I MESSED THEM UP A LITTLE, BUT...

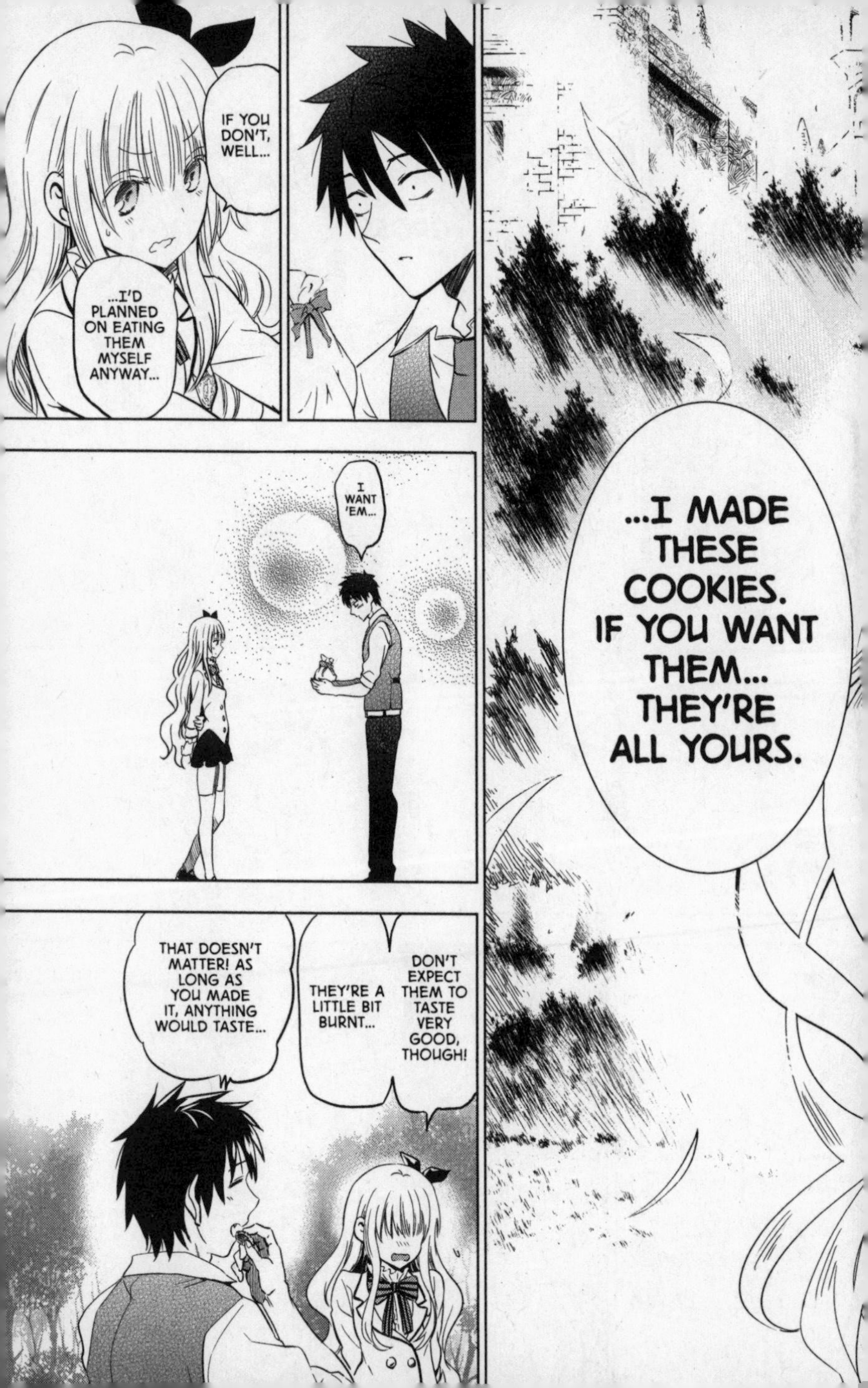
...I MADE THESE COOKIES. IF YOU WANT THEM... THEY'RE ALL YOURS.
IF YOU DON'T, WELL...
...I'D PLANNED ON EATING THEM MYSELF ANYWAY...
I WANT 'EM...
DON'T EXPECT THEM TO TASTE VERY GOOD, THOUGH!
THEY'RE A LITTLE BIT BURNT...
THAT DOESN'T MATTER! AS LONG AS YOU MADE IT, ANYTHING WOULD TASTE...

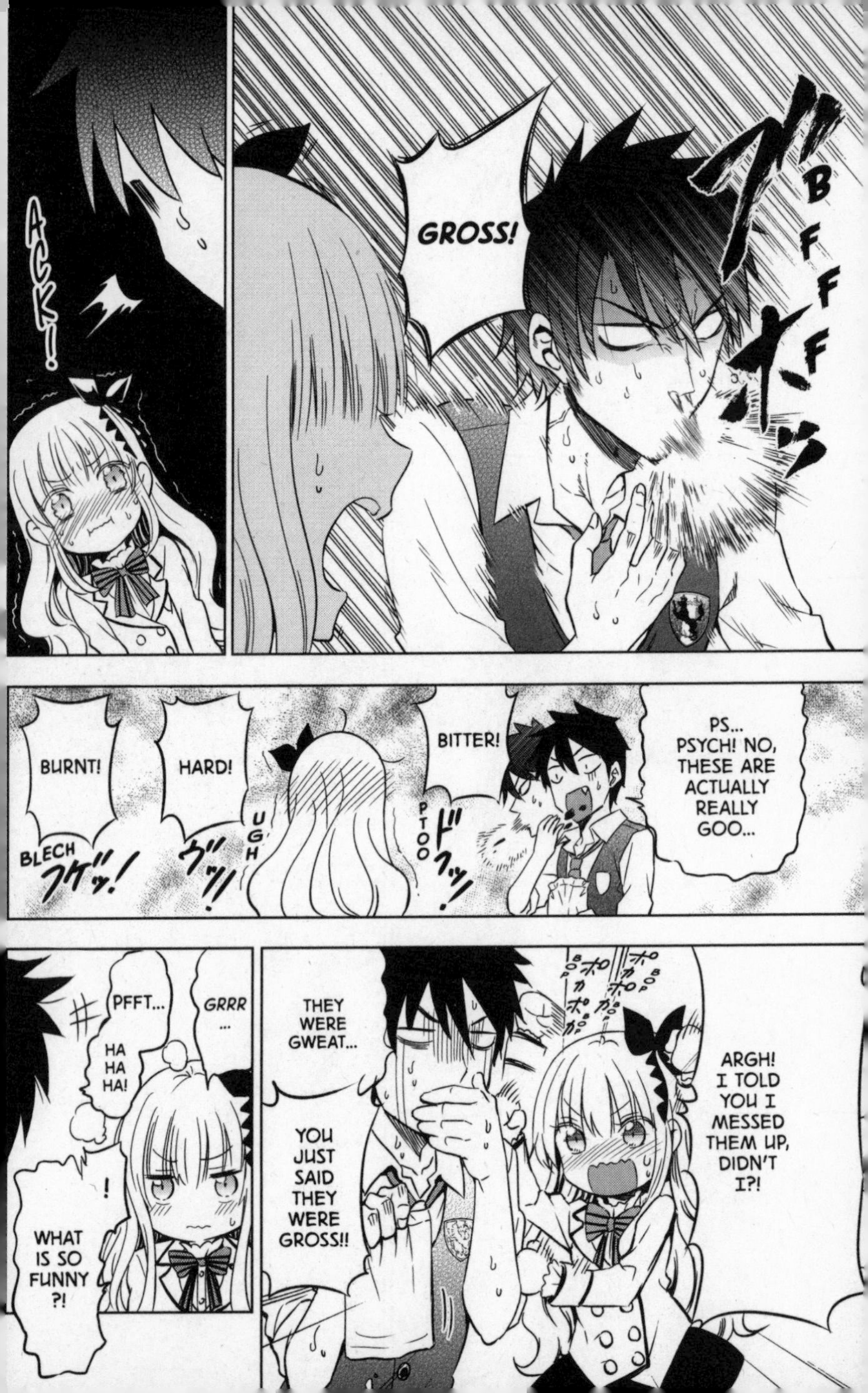
BFFFF
GROSS!
ACK!
PS... PSYCH! NO, THESE ARE ACTUALLY REALLY GOO...
BITTER!
PTOO
UGH
HARD!
BURNT!
BLECH
ARGH! I TOLD YOU I MESSED THEM UP, DIDN'T I?!
BOP BOP
THEY WERE GWEAT...
YOU JUST SAID THEY WERE GROSS!!
GRRR...
PFFT...
HA HA HA!
!
WHAT IS SO FUNNY ?!

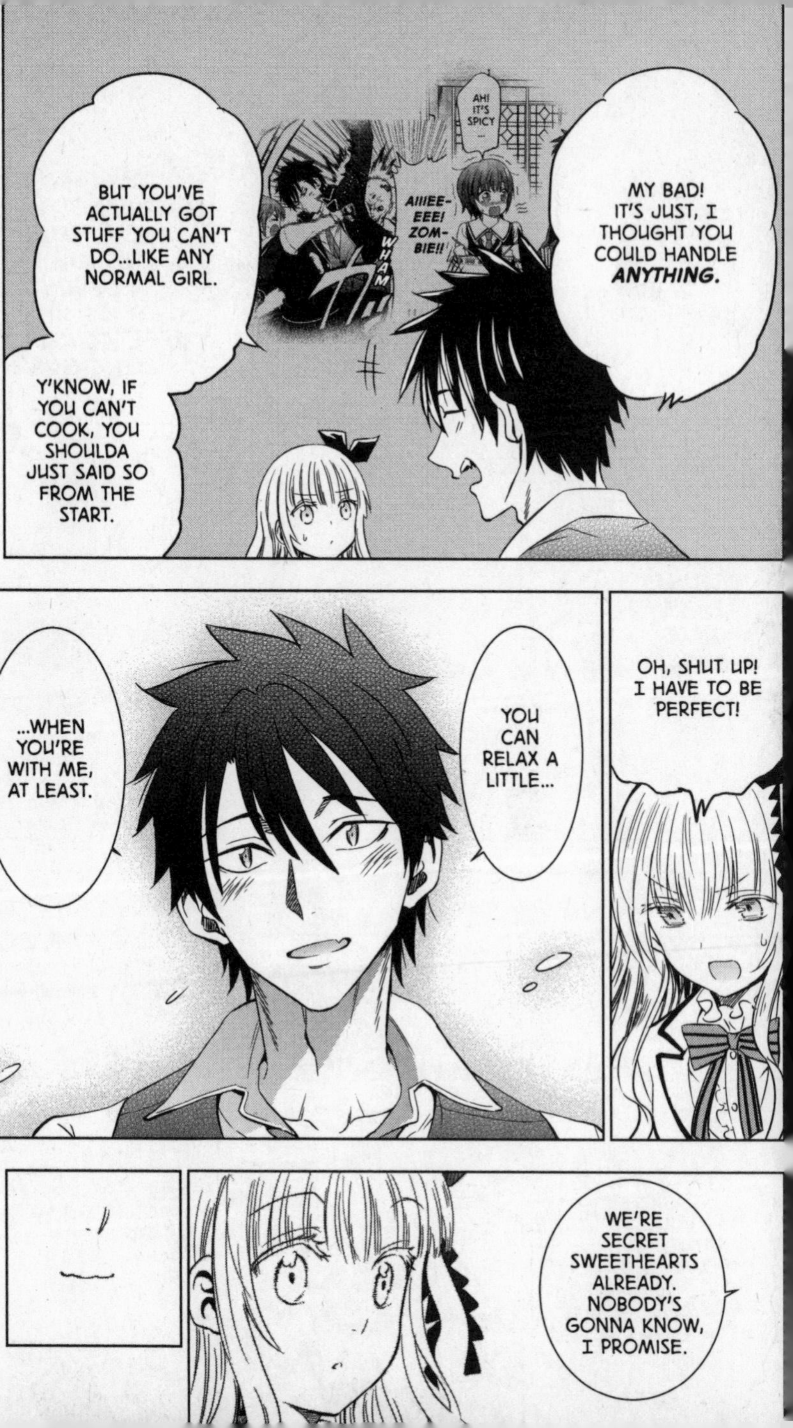
MY BAD! IT'S JUST, I THOUGHT YOU COULD HANDLE ***ANYTHING.***
AH! IT'S SPICY ...
AIIIEE-EEE! ZOMBIE!!
WHAM
BUT YOU'VE ACTUALLY GOT STUFF YOU CAN'T DO...LIKE ANY NORMAL GIRL.
Y'KNOW, IF YOU CAN'T COOK, YOU SHOULDA JUST SAID SO FROM THE START.
OH, SHUT UP! I HAVE TO BE PERFECT!
YOU CAN RELAX A LITTLE...
...WHEN YOU'RE WITH ME, AT LEAST.
WE'RE SECRET SWEETHEARTS ALREADY. NOBODY'S GONNA KNOW, I PROMISE.

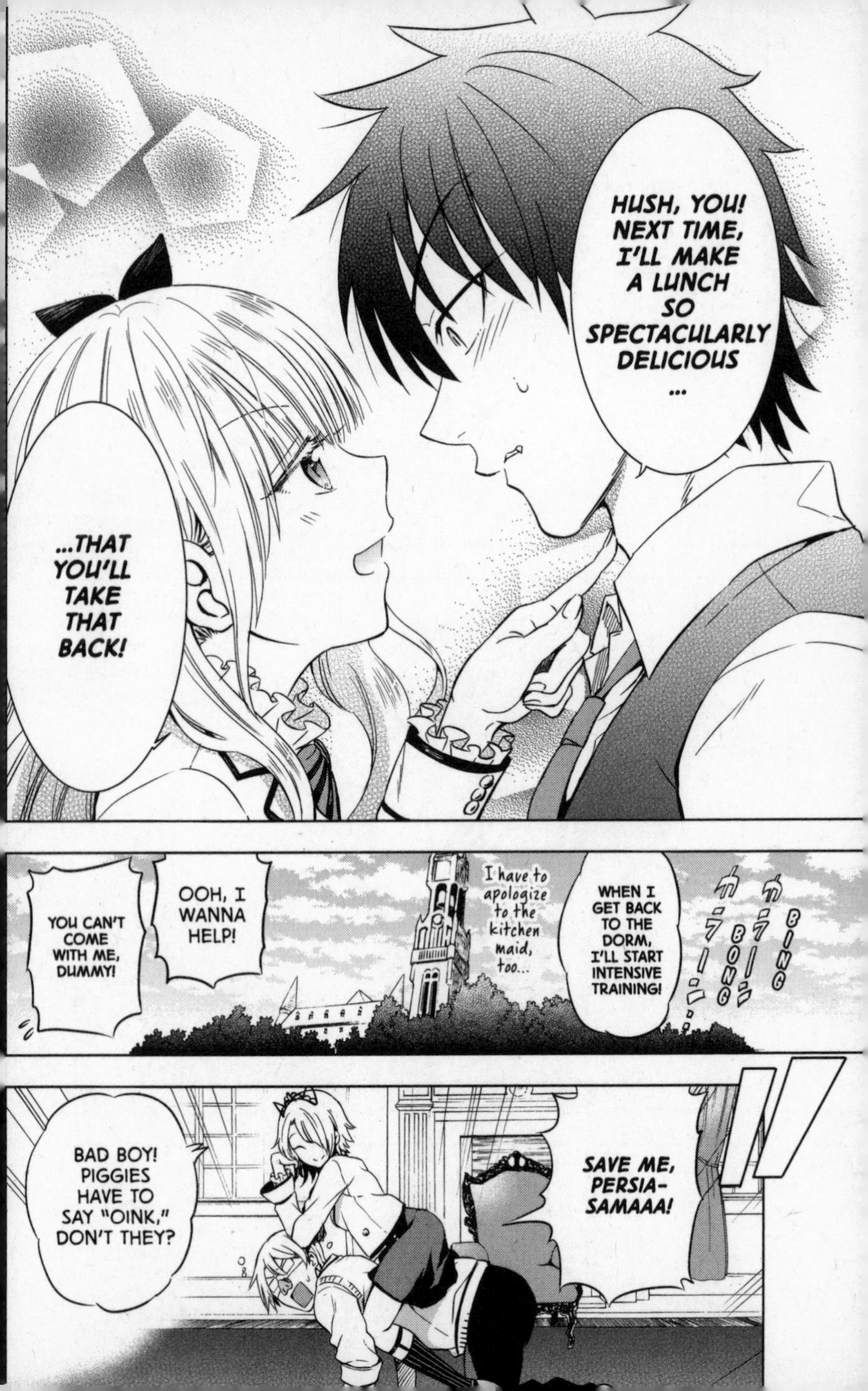
HUSH, YOU! NEXT TIME, I'LL MAKE A LUNCH SO SPECTACULARLY DELICIOUS ...
...THAT YOU'LL TAKE THAT BACK!
BING BONG
WHEN I GET BACK TO THE DORM, I'LL START INTENSIVE TRAINING!
I have to apologize to the kitchen maid, too...
OOH, I WANNA HELP!
YOU CAN'T COME WITH ME, DUMMY!
SAVE ME, PERSIA-SAMAAA!
BAD BOY! PIGGIES HAVE TO SAY "OINK," DON'T THEY?

ACT 9:

ROMIO & THE SPORTS FESTIVAL

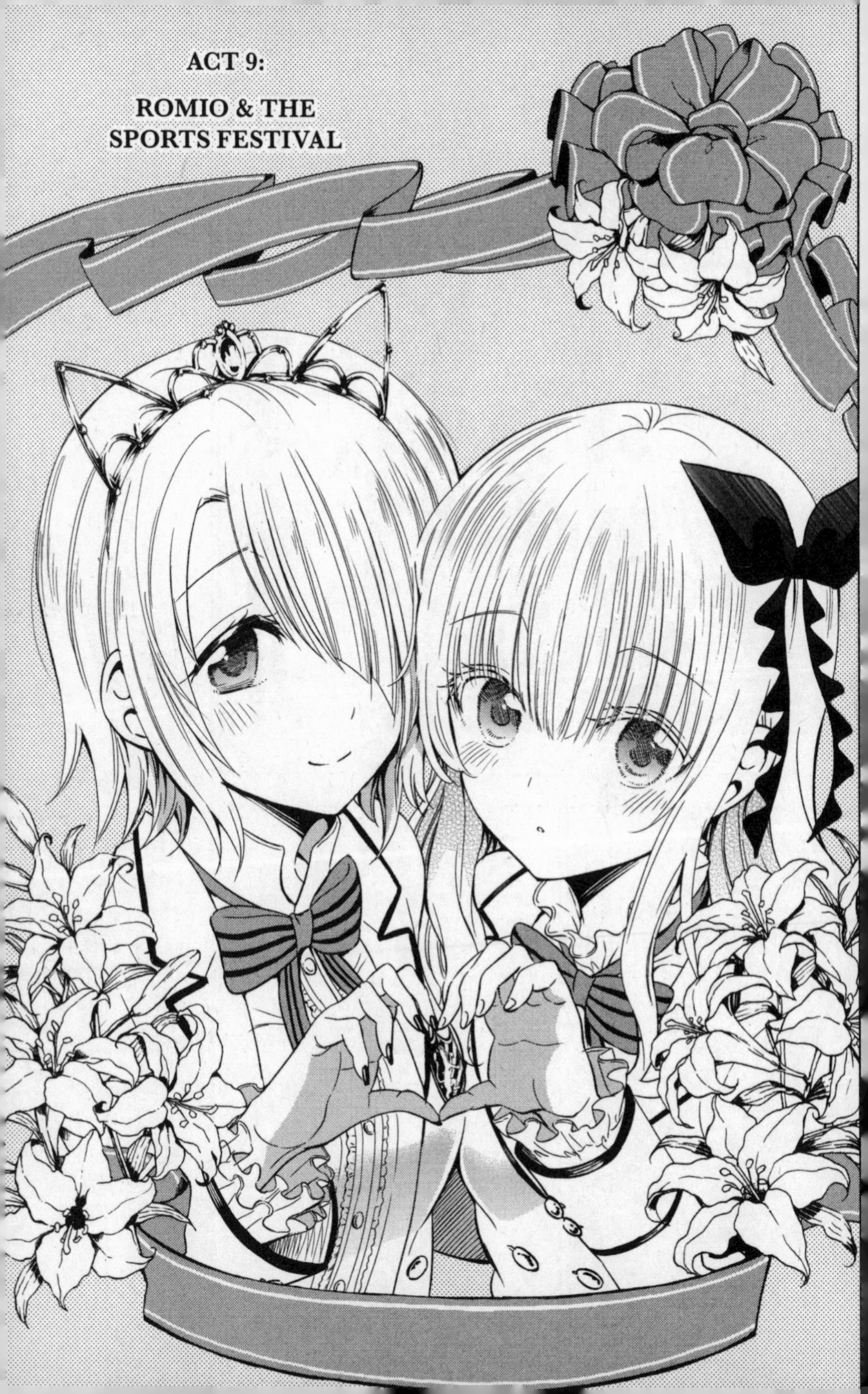

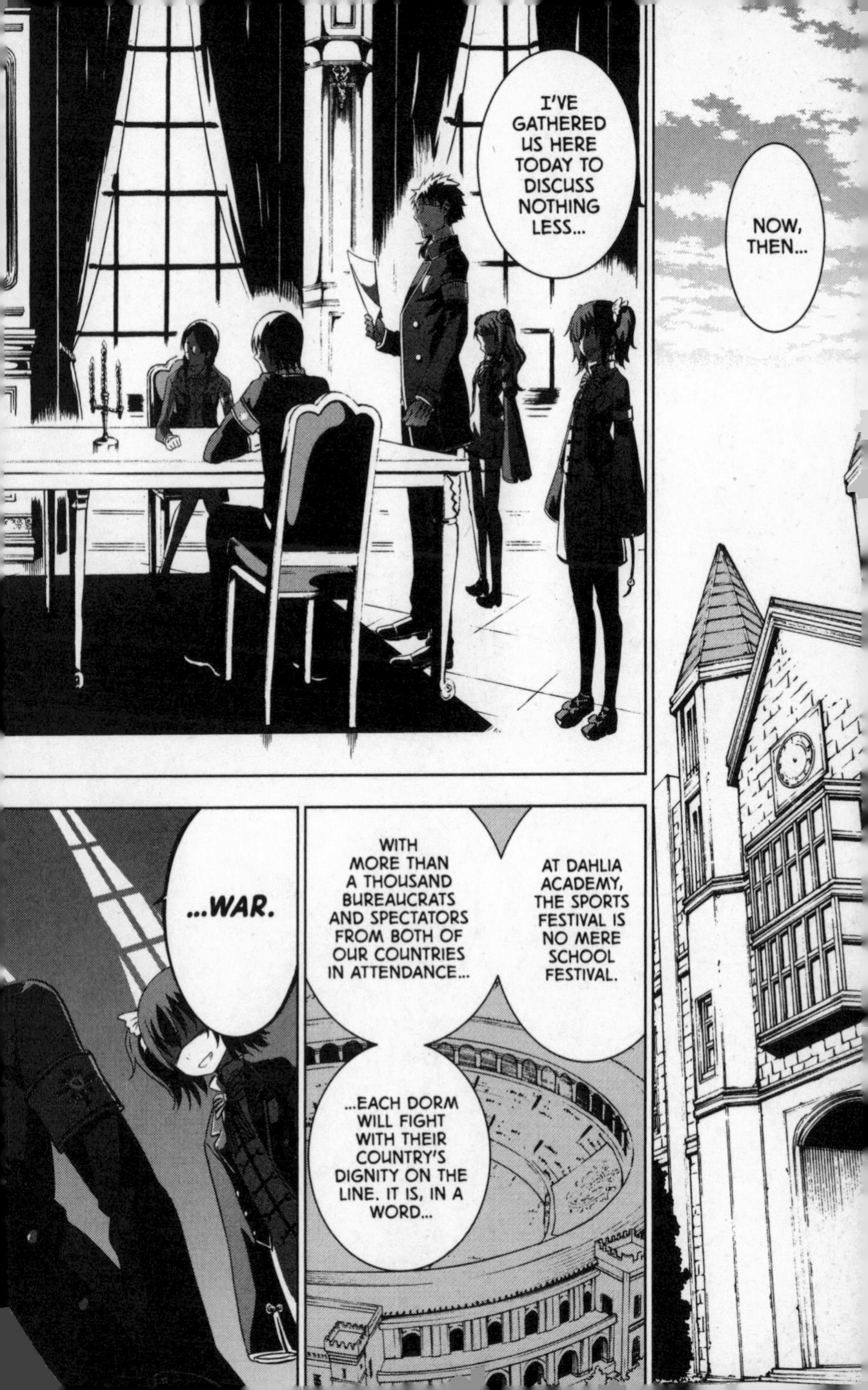
NOW, THEN...
I'VE GATHERED US HERE TODAY TO DISCUSS NOTHING LESS...
AT DAHLIA ACADEMY, THE SPORTS FESTIVAL IS NO MERE SCHOOL FESTIVAL.
WITH MORE THAN A THOUSAND BUREAUCRATS AND SPECTATORS FROM BOTH OF OUR COUNTRIES IN ATTENDANCE...
...EACH DORM WILL FIGHT WITH THEIR COUNTRY'S DIGNITY ON THE LINE. IT IS, IN A WORD...
...WAR.

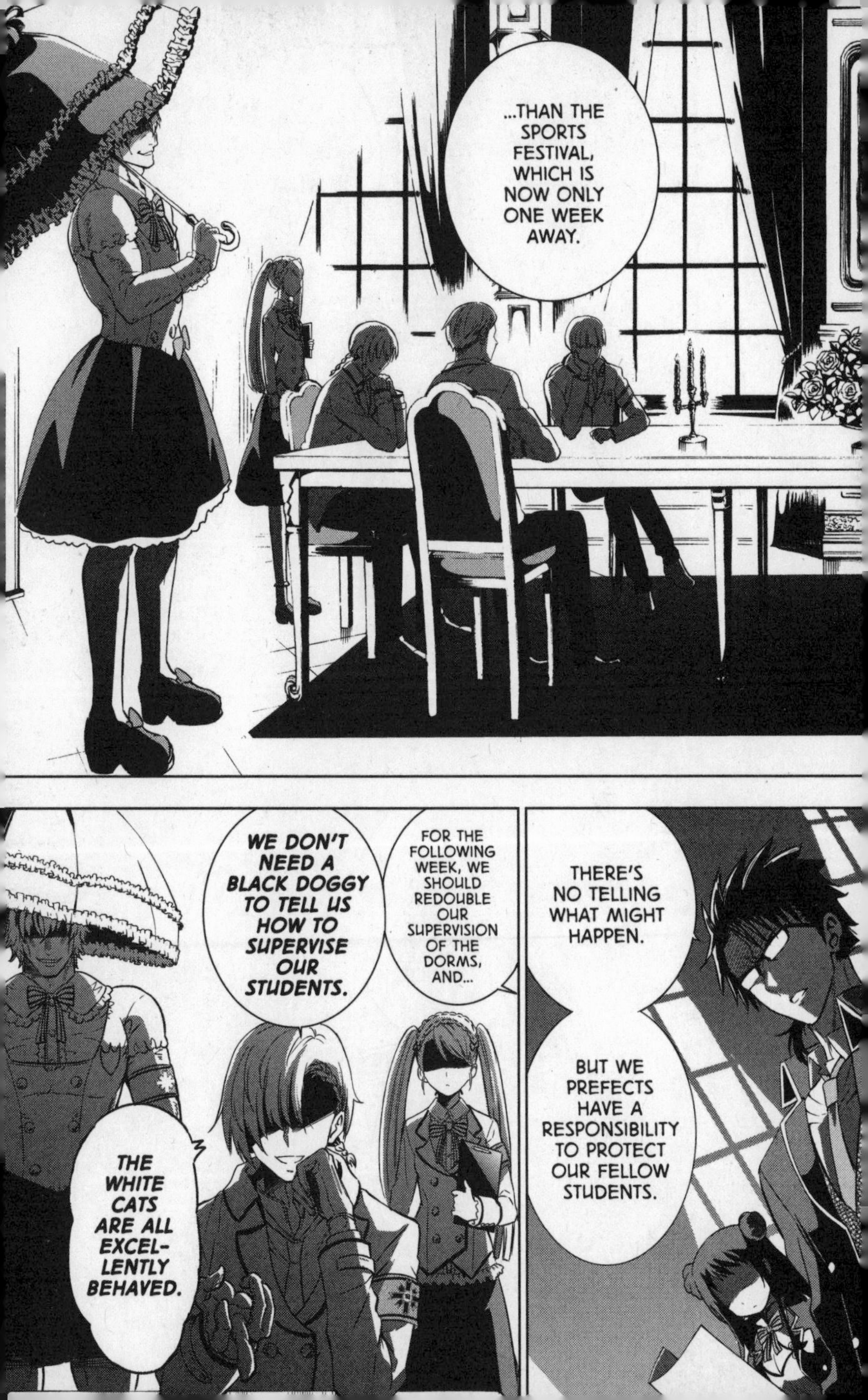
...THAN THE SPORTS FESTIVAL, WHICH IS NOW ONLY ONE WEEK AWAY.
THERE'S NO TELLING WHAT MIGHT HAPPEN.
BUT WE PREFECTS HAVE A RESPONSIBILITY TO PROTECT OUR FELLOW STUDENTS.
FOR THE FOLLOWING WEEK, WE SHOULD REDOUBLE OUR SUPERVISION OF THE DORMS, AND...
WE DON'T NEED A BLACK DOGGY TO TELL US HOW TO SUPERVISE OUR STUDENTS.
THE WHITE CATS ARE ALL EXCEL-LENTLY BEHAVED.

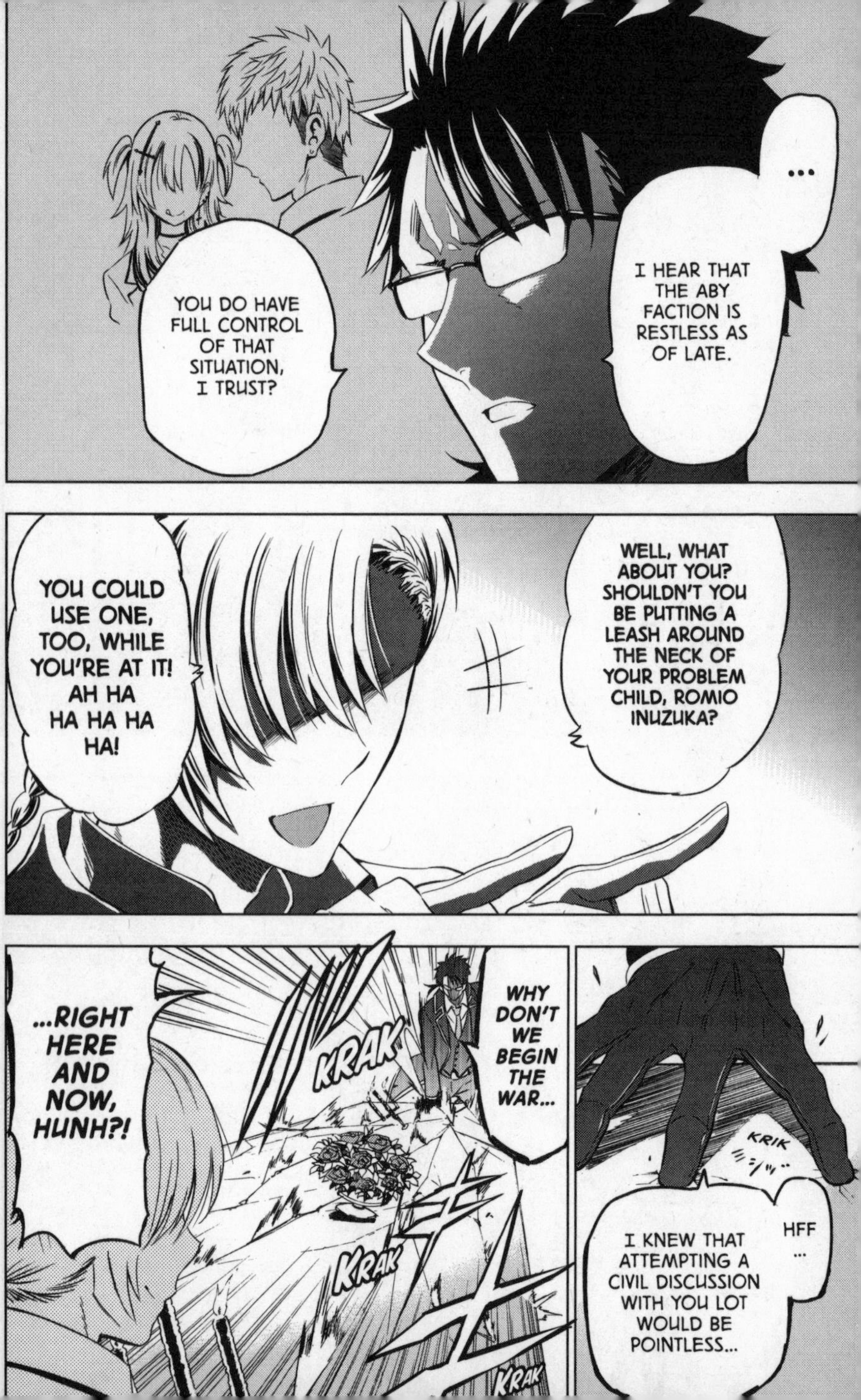
...
I HEAR THAT THE ABY FACTION IS RESTLESS AS OF LATE.
YOU DO HAVE FULL CONTROL OF THAT SITUATION, I TRUST?
WELL, WHAT ABOUT YOU? SHOULDN'T YOU BE PUTTING A LEASH AROUND THE NECK OF YOUR PROBLEM CHILD, ROMIO INUZUKA?
YOU COULD USE ONE, TOO, WHILE YOU'RE AT IT! AH HA HA HA HA HA!
KRIK
HFF ...
I KNEW THAT ATTEMPTING A CIVIL DISCUSSION WITH YOU LOT WOULD BE POINTLESS...
WHY DON'T WE BEGIN THE WAR...
KRAK
KRAK
KRAK
...RIGHT HERE AND NOW, HUNH?!

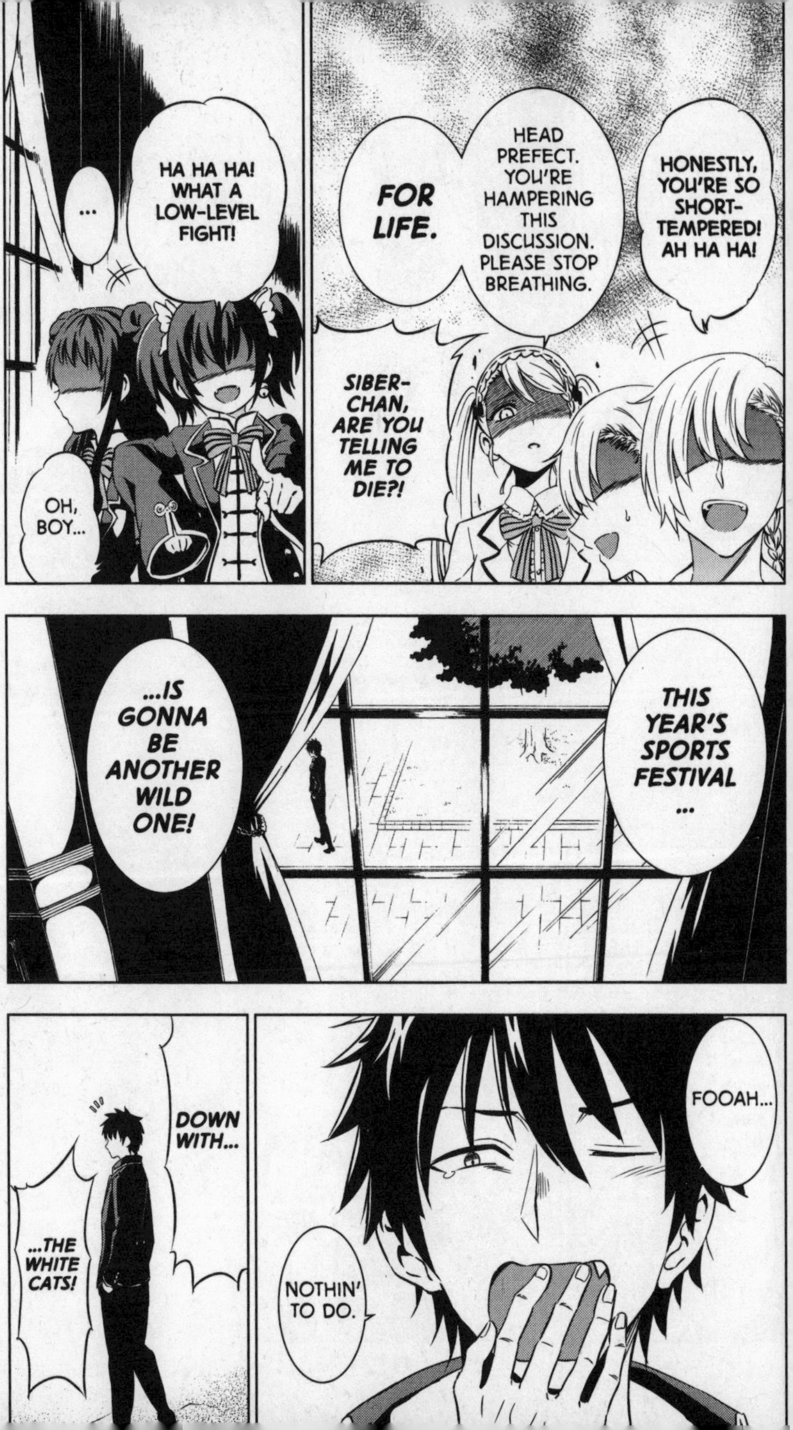
HONESTLY, YOU'RE SO SHORT-TEMPERED! AH HA HA!
HEAD PREFECT. YOU'RE HAMPERING THIS DISCUSSION. PLEASE STOP BREATHING.
FOR LIFE.
SIBER-CHAN, ARE YOU TELLING ME TO DIE?!
HA HA HA! WHAT A LOW-LEVEL FIGHT!
...
OH, BOY...
THIS YEAR'S SPORTS FESTIVAL ...
...IS GONNA BE ANOTHER WILD ONE!
FOOAH...
NOTHIN' TO DO.
DOWN WITH...
...THE WHITE CATS!

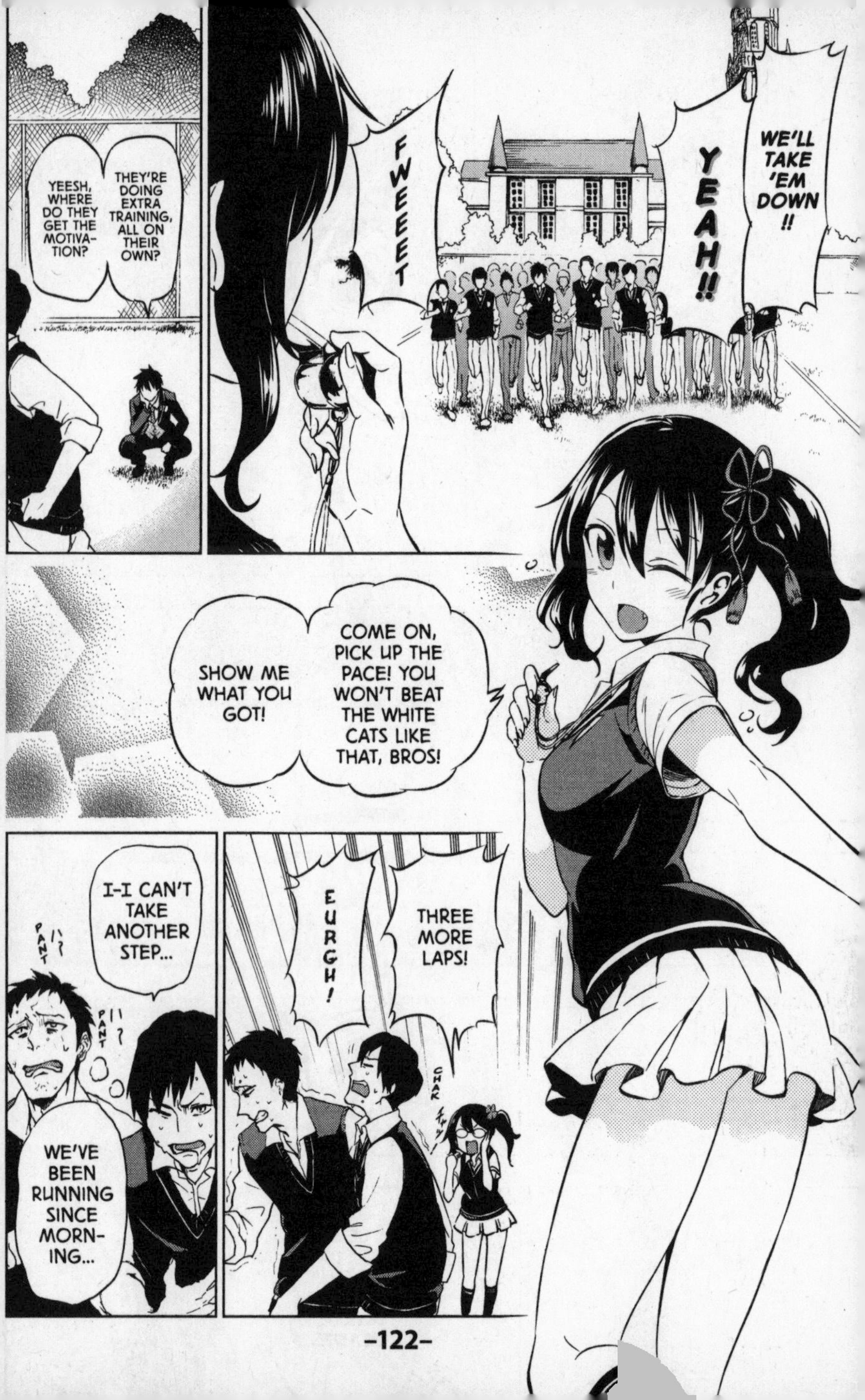
WE'LL TAKE 'EM DOWN!!
YEAH!!
FWEEET
THEY'RE DOING EXTRA TRAINING, ALL ON THEIR OWN?
YEESH, WHERE DO THEY GET THE MOTIVATION?
COME ON, PICK UP THE PACE! YOU WON'T BEAT THE WHITE CATS LIKE THAT, BROS!
SHOW ME WHAT YOU GOT!
THREE MORE LAPS!
EURGH!
CHAK
I-I CAN'T TAKE ANOTHER STEP...
PANT
PANT
WE'VE BEEN RUNNING SINCE MORNING...

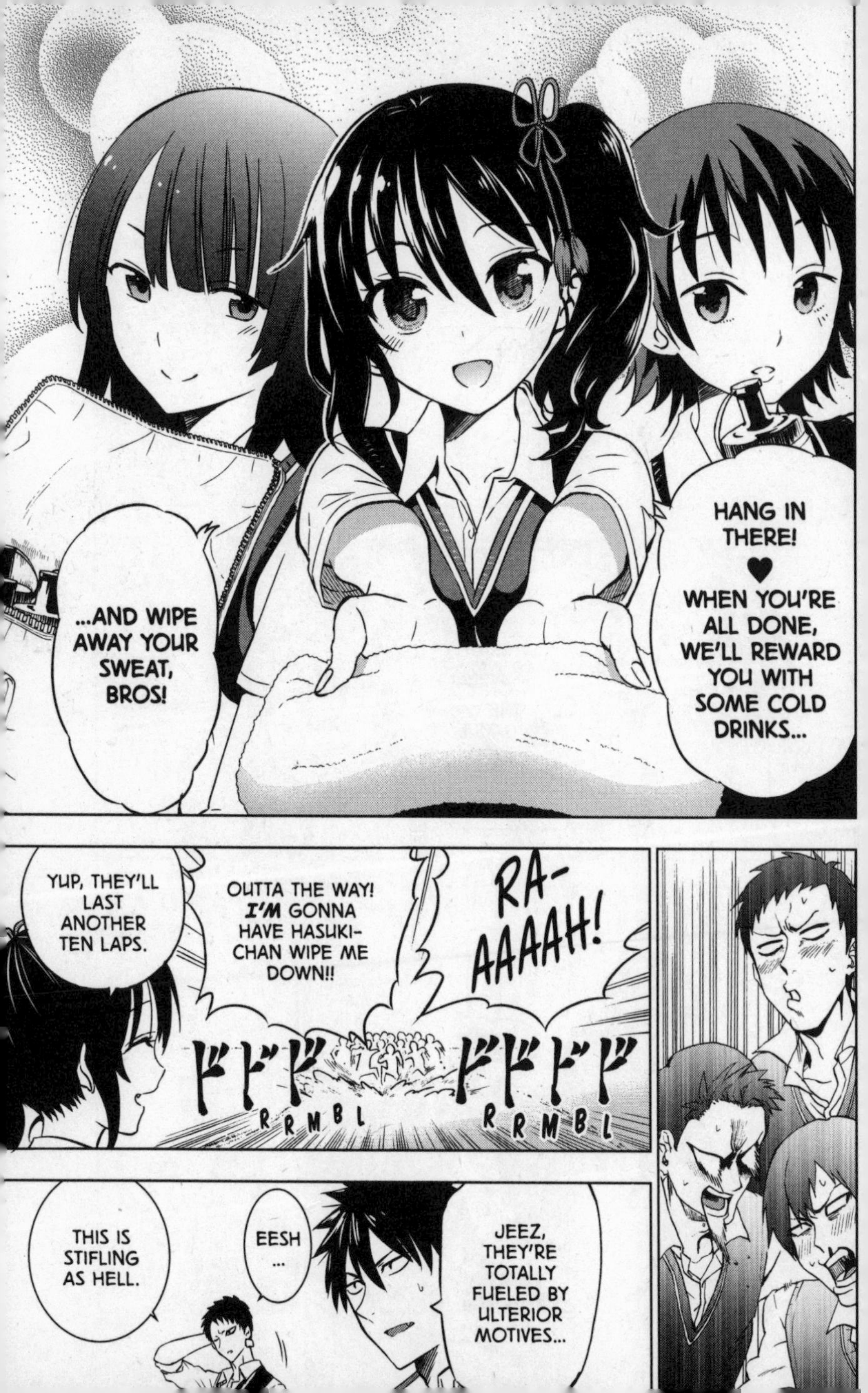
HANG IN THERE! ♥ WHEN YOU'RE ALL DONE, WE'LL REWARD YOU WITH SOME COLD DRINKS...
...AND WIPE AWAY YOUR SWEAT, BROS!
RA-AAAAH!
OUTTA THE WAY! *I'M* GONNA HAVE HASUKI-CHAN WIPE ME DOWN!!
YUP, THEY'LL LAST ANOTHER TEN LAPS.
ドドドド
RRMBL
ドドド
RRMBL
JEEZ, THEY'RE TOTALLY FUELED BY ULTERIOR MOTIVES...
EESH ...
THIS IS STIFLING AS HELL.

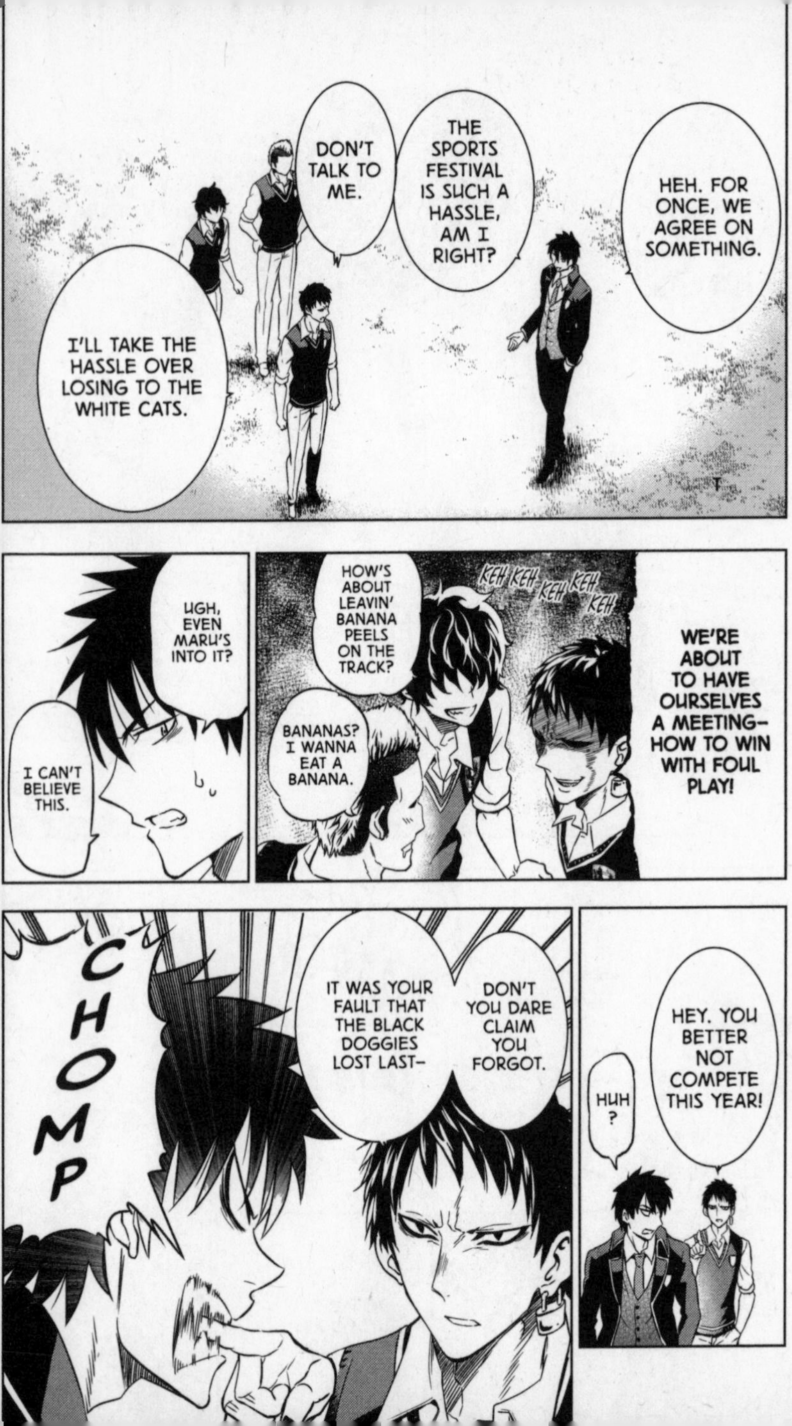
HEH. FOR ONCE, WE AGREE ON SOMETHING.
THE SPORTS FESTIVAL IS SUCH A HASSLE, AM I RIGHT?
DON'T TALK TO ME.
I'LL TAKE THE HASSLE OVER LOSING TO THE WHITE CATS.
WE'RE ABOUT TO HAVE OURSELVES A MEETING— HOW TO WIN WITH FOUL PLAY!
KEH KEH KEH KEH KEH
HOW'S ABOUT LEAVIN' BANANA PEELS ON THE TRACK?
BANANAS? I WANNA EAT A BANANA.
UGH, EVEN MARU'S INTO IT?
I CAN'T BELIEVE THIS.
HEY. YOU BETTER NOT COMPETE THIS YEAR!
HUH?
DON'T YOU DARE CLAIM YOU FORGOT.
IT WAS YOUR FAULT THAT THE BLACK DOGGIES LOST LAST—
CHOMP

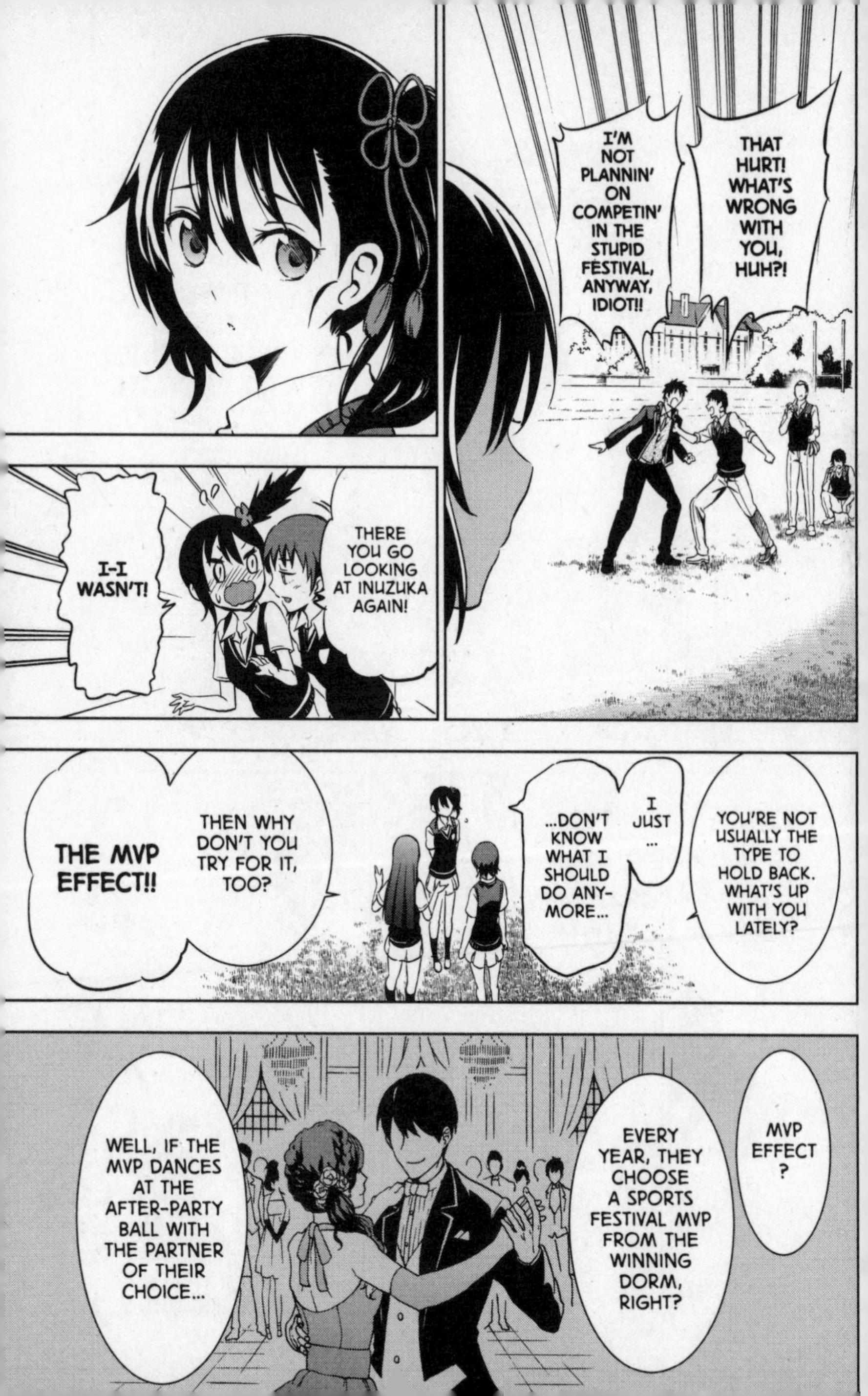
THAT HURT! WHAT'S WRONG WITH YOU, HUH?!
I'M NOT PLANNIN' ON COMPETIN' IN THE STUPID FESTIVAL, ANYWAY, IDIOT!!
THERE YOU GO LOOKING AT INUZUKA AGAIN!
I-I WASN'T!
YOU'RE NOT USUALLY THE TYPE TO HOLD BACK. WHAT'S UP WITH YOU LATELY?
I JUST ...
...DON'T KNOW WHAT I SHOULD DO ANY-MORE...
THEN WHY DON'T YOU TRY FOR IT, TOO?
THE MVP EFFECT!!
MVP EFFECT?
EVERY YEAR, THEY CHOOSE A SPORTS FESTIVAL MVP FROM THE WINNING DORM, RIGHT?
WELL, IF THE MVP DANCES AT THE AFTER-PARTY BALL WITH THE PARTNER OF THEIR CHOICE...

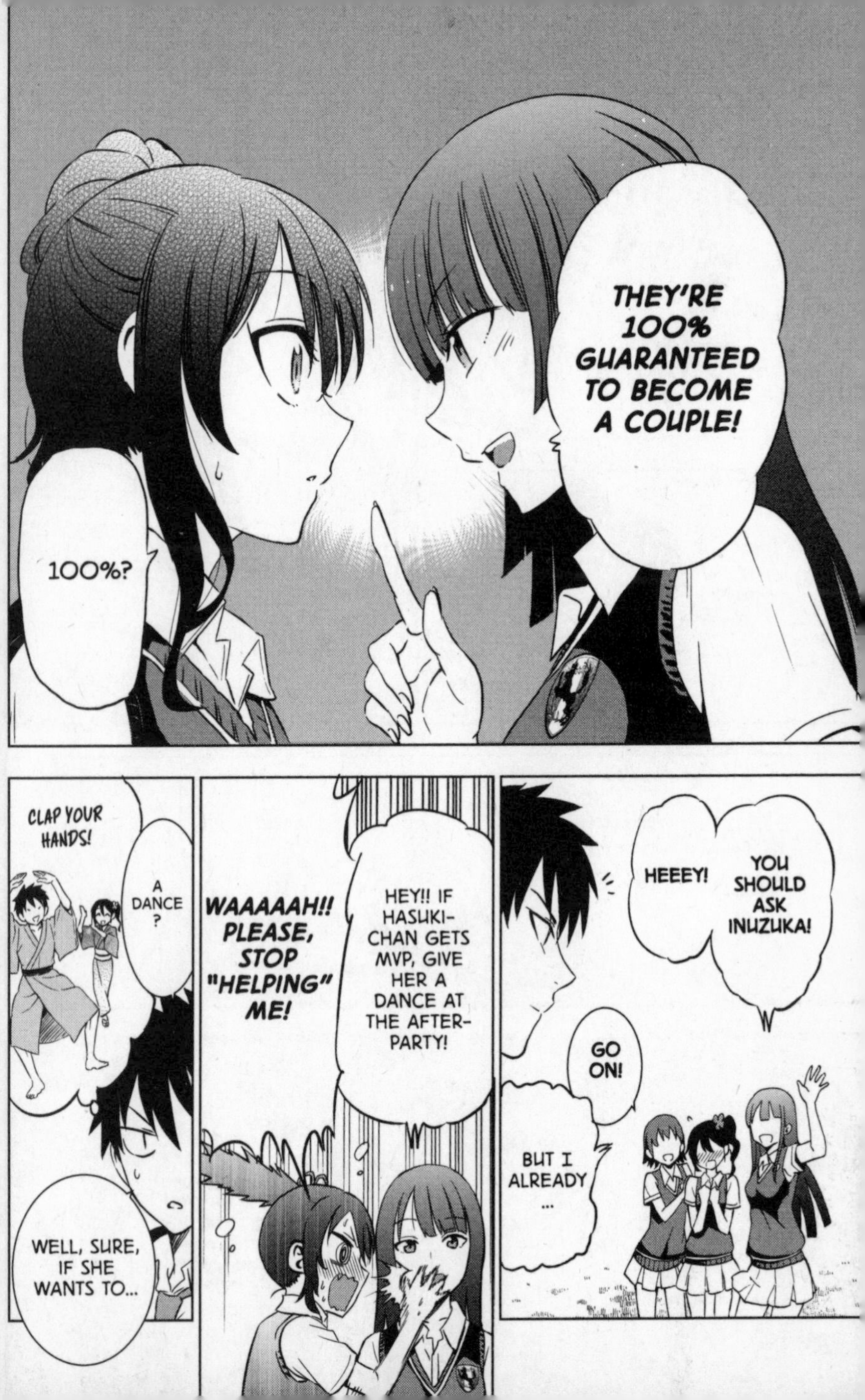
THEY'RE 100% GUARANTEED TO BECOME A COUPLE!
100%?
YOU SHOULD ASK INUZUKA!
HEEEY!
GO ON!
BUT I ALREADY ...
HEY!! IF HASUKI-CHAN GETS MVP, GIVE HER A DANCE AT THE AFTER-PARTY!
WAAAAAH!! PLEASE, STOP "HELPING" ME!
A DANCE ?
CLAP YOUR HANDS!
WELL, SURE, IF SHE WANTS TO...

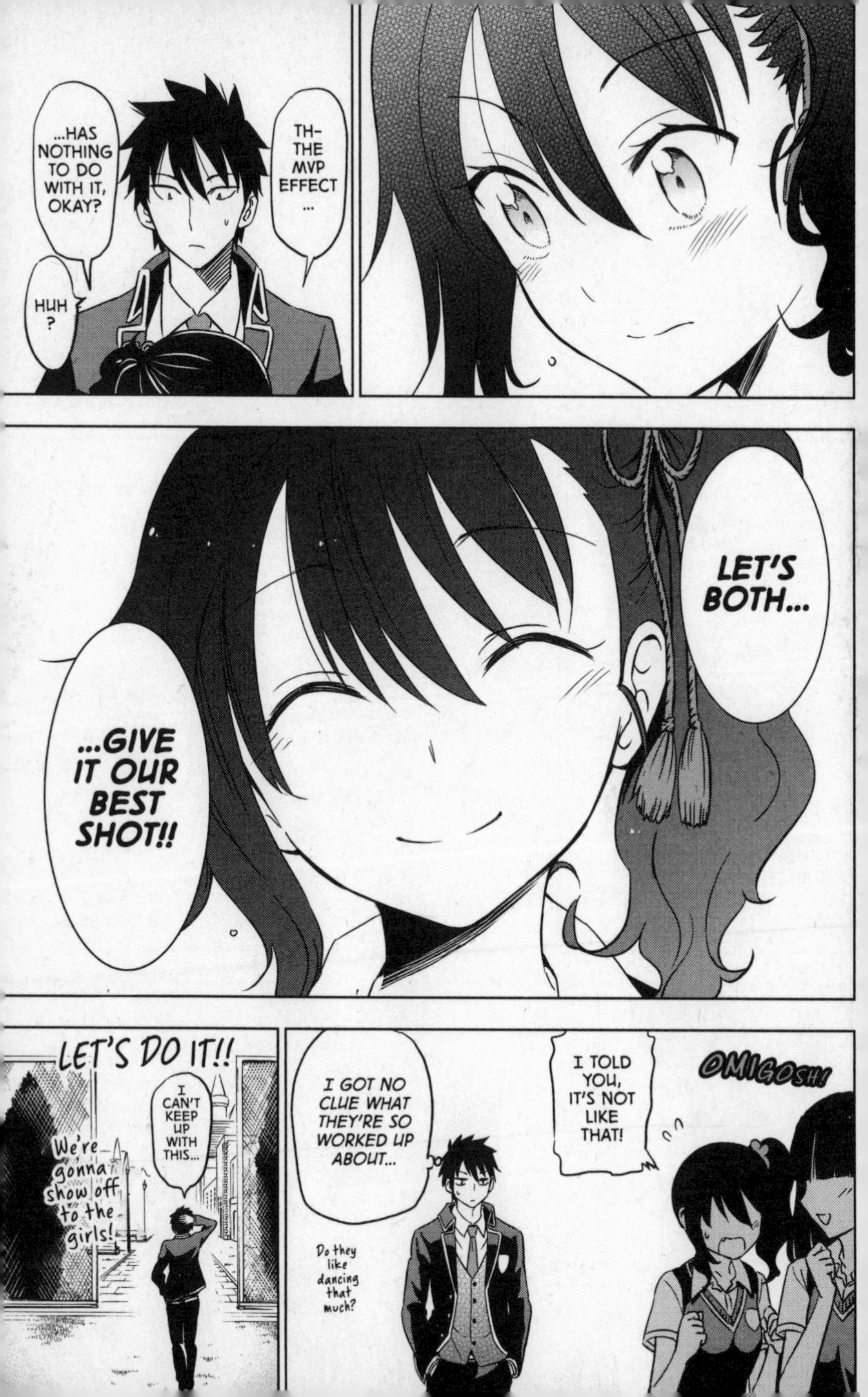
TH-THE MVP EFFECT...
...HAS NOTHING TO DO WITH IT, OKAY?
HUH?
LET'S BOTH...
...GIVE IT OUR BEST SHOT!!
OMIGOSH!
I TOLD YOU, IT'S NOT LIKE THAT!
I GOT NO CLUE WHAT THEY'RE SO WORKED UP ABOUT...
Do they like dancing that much?
LET'S DO IT!!
I CAN'T KEEP UP WITH THIS...
We're gonna show off to the girls!

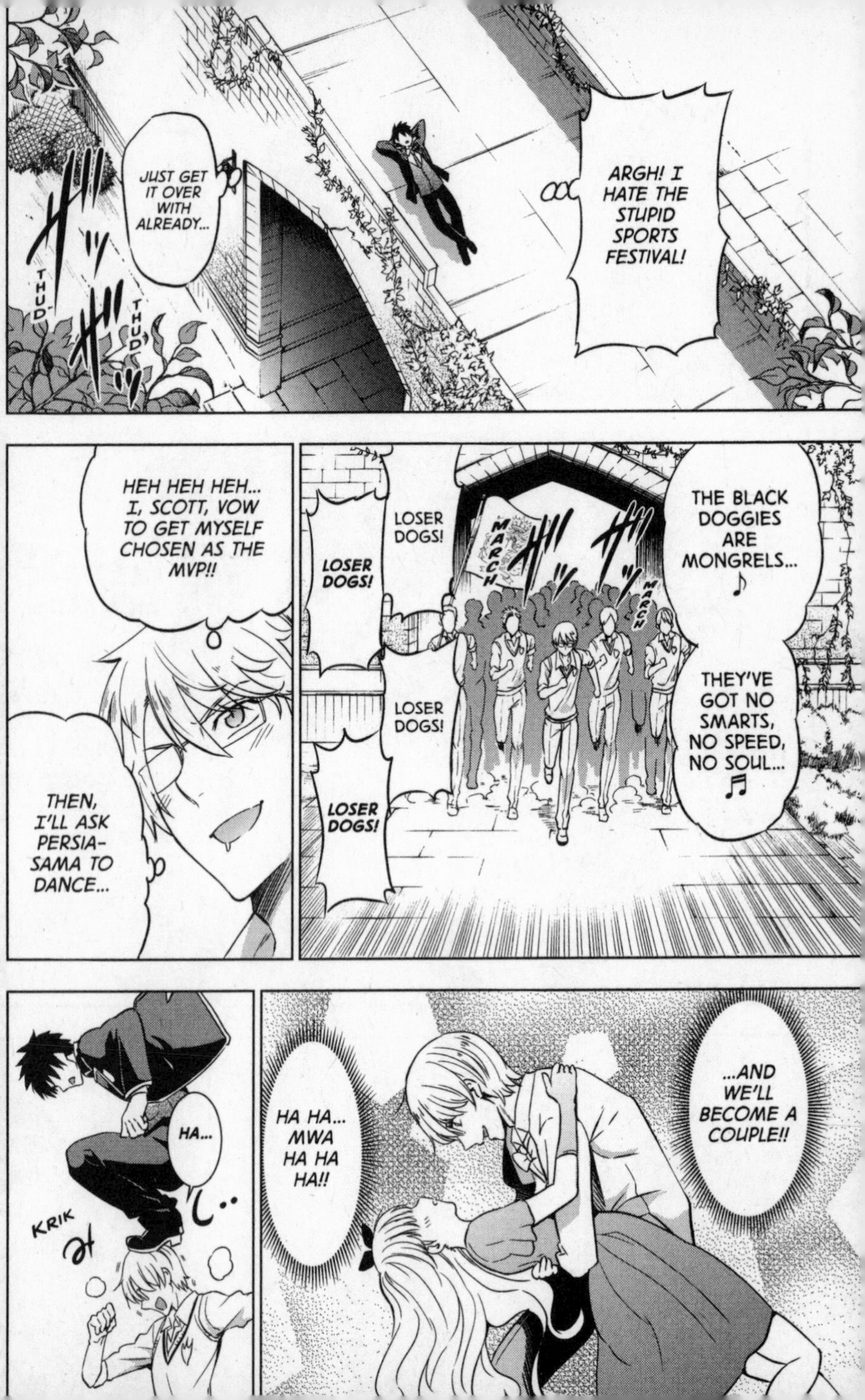
ARGH! I HATE THE STUPID SPORTS FESTIVAL!
JUST GET IT OVER WITH ALREADY...
THUD
THUD
THE BLACK DOGGIES ARE MONGRELS... ♪
THEY'VE GOT NO SMARTS, NO SPEED, NO SOUL... ♬
MARCH
MARCH
LOSER DOGS!
LOSER DOGS!
LOSER DOGS!
LOSER DOGS!
HEH HEH HEH... I, SCOTT, VOW TO GET MYSELF CHOSEN AS THE MVP!!
THEN, I'LL ASK PERSIA-SAMA TO DANCE...
...AND WE'LL BECOME A COUPLE!!
HA HA... MWA HA HA HA!!
HA...
KRIK

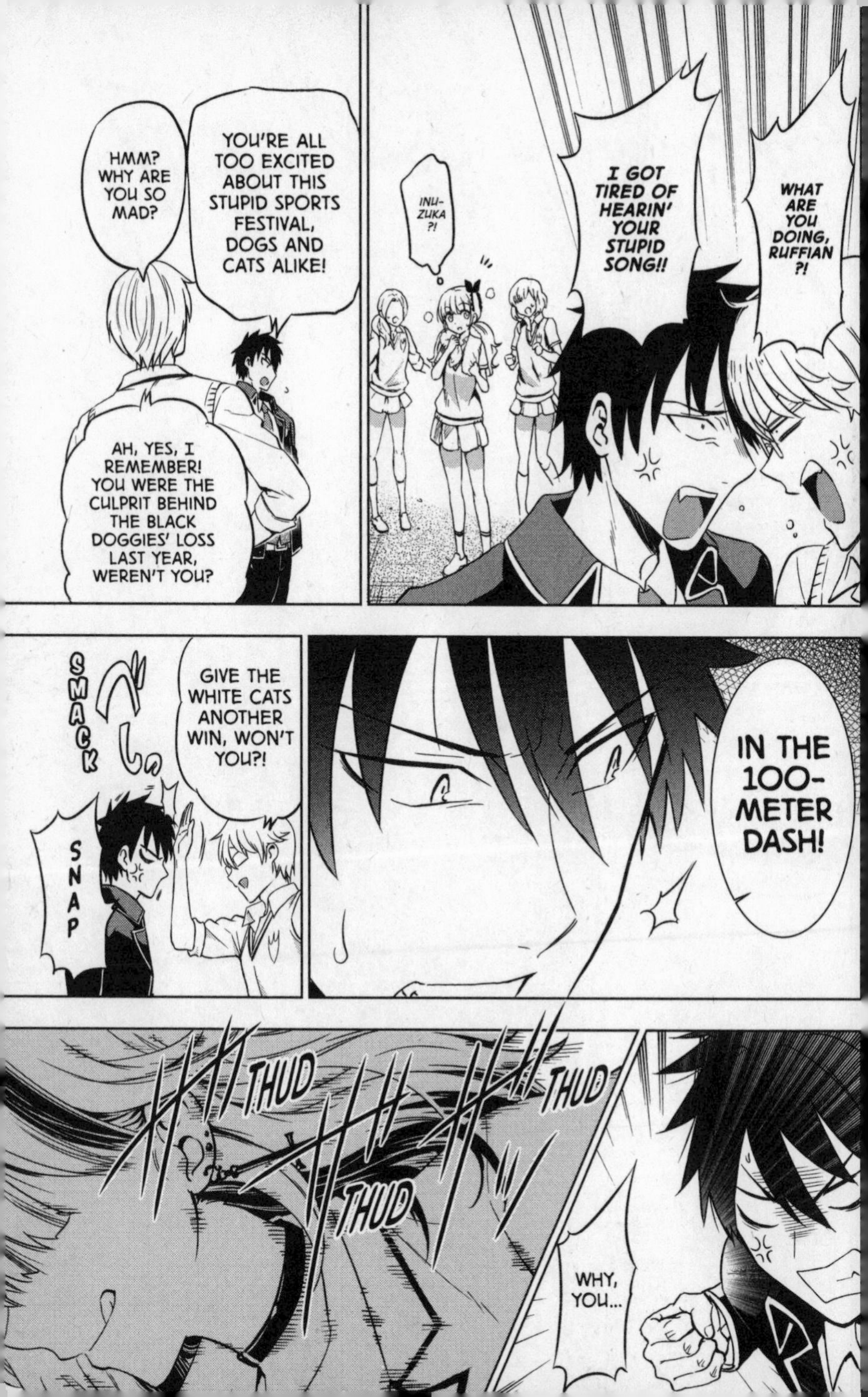
WHAT ARE YOU DOING, RUFFIAN?!
I GOT TIRED OF HEARIN' YOUR STUPID SONG!!
INU-ZUKA?!
YOU'RE ALL TOO EXCITED ABOUT THIS STUPID SPORTS FESTIVAL, DOGS AND CATS ALIKE!
HMM? WHY ARE YOU SO MAD?
AH, YES, I REMEMBER! YOU WERE THE CULPRIT BEHIND THE BLACK DOGGIES' LOSS LAST YEAR, WEREN'T YOU?
IN THE 100-METER DASH!
GIVE THE WHITE CATS ANOTHER WIN, WON'T YOU?!
SMACK
SNAP
THUD
THUD
THUD
WHY, YOU...

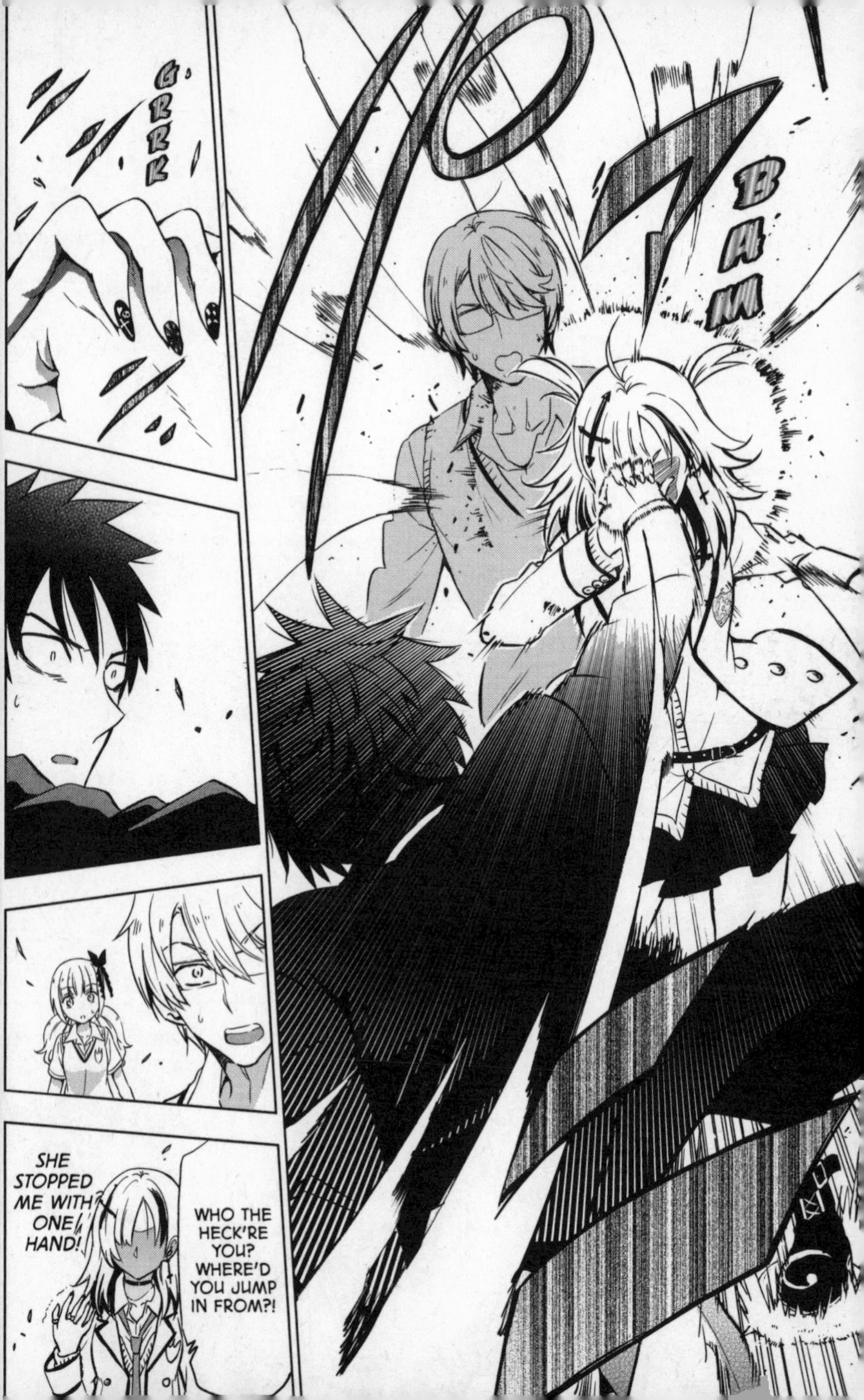
BAM
GRRK
WHO THE HECK'RE YOU? WHERE'D YOU JUMP IN FROM?!
SHE STOPPED ME WITH ONE HAND!

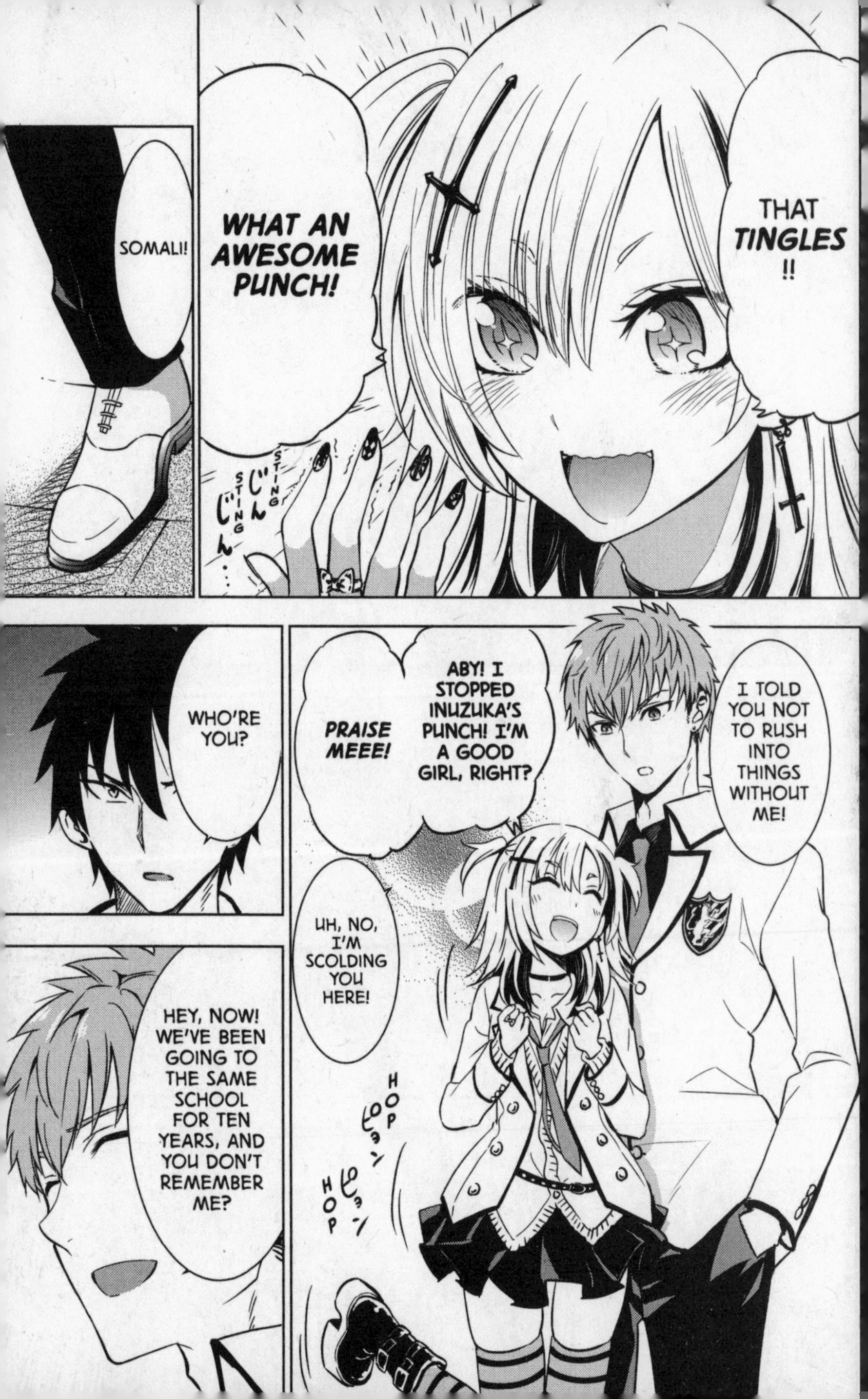
THAT TINGLES!!
WHAT AN AWESOME PUNCH!
STING
STING
SOMALI!
I TOLD YOU NOT TO RUSH INTO THINGS WITHOUT ME!
ABY! I STOPPED INUZUKA'S PUNCH! I'M A GOOD GIRL, RIGHT?
PRAISE MEEE!
UH, NO, I'M SCOLDING YOU HERE!
HOP
HOP
WHO'RE YOU?
HEY, NOW! WE'VE BEEN GOING TO THE SAME SCHOOL FOR TEN YEARS, AND YOU DON'T REMEMBER ME?

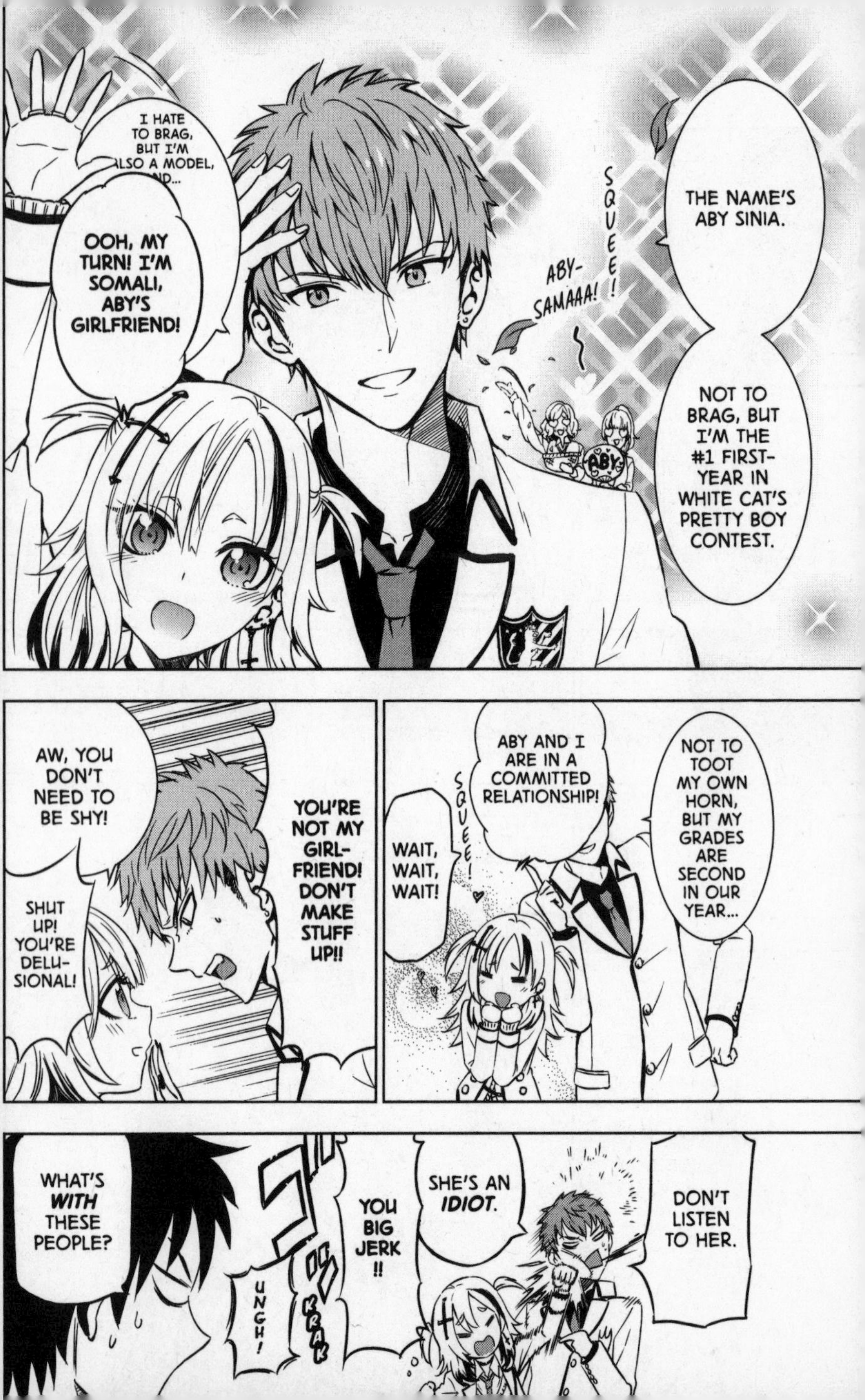
THE NAME'S ABY SINIA.
NOT TO BRAG, BUT I'M THE #1 FIRST-YEAR IN WHITE CAT'S PRETTY BOY CONTEST.
SQUEEE!
ABY-SAMAAA!
I HATE TO BRAG, BUT I'M ALSO A MODEL, AND...
OOH, MY TURN! I'M SOMALI, ABY'S GIRLFRIEND!
NOT TO TOOT MY OWN HORN, BUT MY GRADES ARE SECOND IN OUR YEAR...
ABY AND I ARE IN A COMMITTED RELATIONSHIP!
SQUEEE!
WAIT, WAIT, WAIT!
YOU'RE NOT MY GIRL-FRIEND! DON'T MAKE STUFF UP!!
AW, YOU DON'T NEED TO BE SHY!
SHUT UP! YOU'RE DELU-SIONAL!
DON'T LISTEN TO HER.
SHE'S AN *IDIOT*.
YOU BIG JERK!!
KRAK
UNGH!
WHAT'S *WITH* THESE PEOPLE?

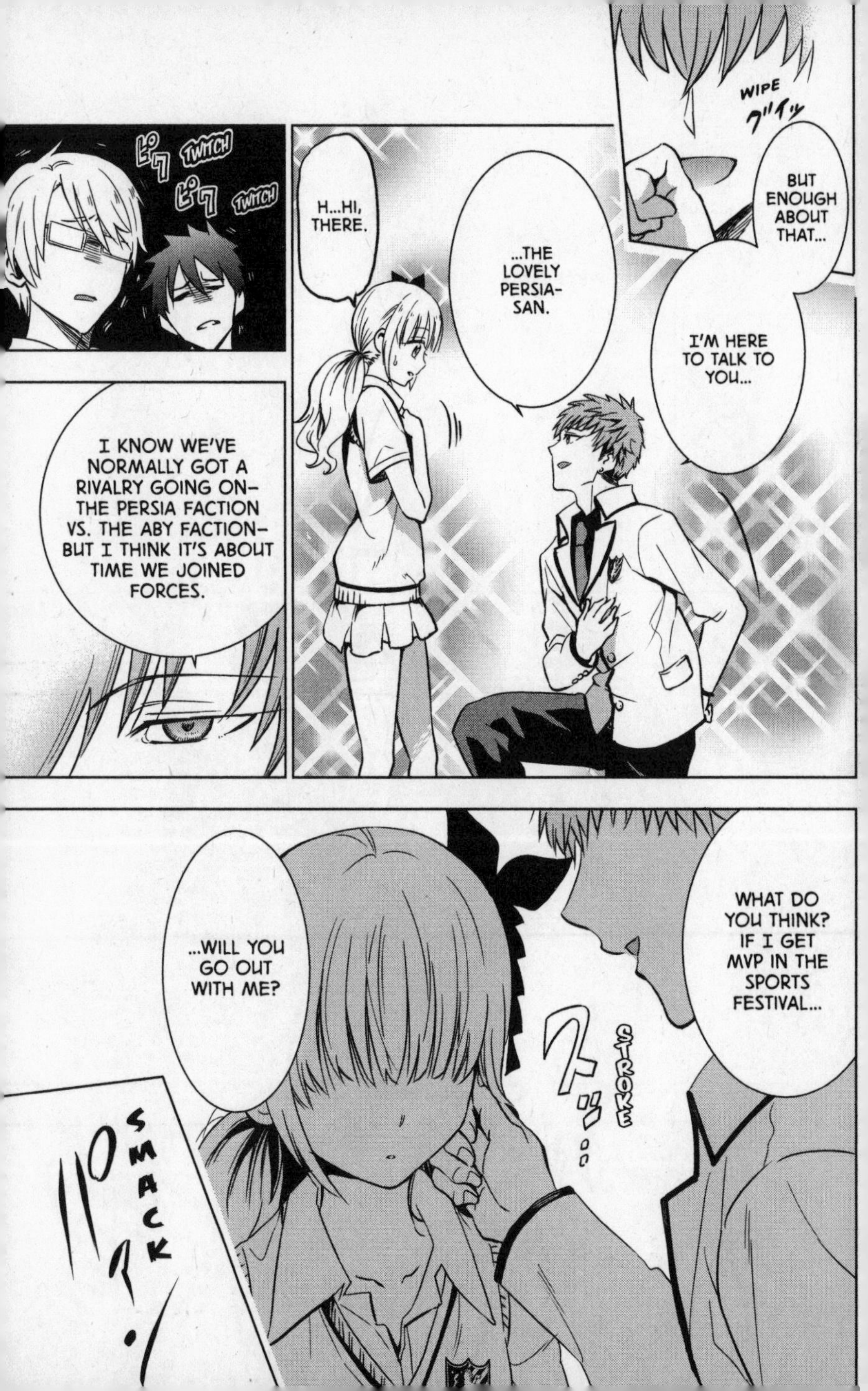
WIPE
グイッ
BUT ENOUGH ABOUT THAT...
I'M HERE TO TALK TO YOU...
...THE LOVELY PERSIA-SAN.
H...HI, THERE.
ピク TWITCH
ピク TWITCH
I KNOW WE'VE NORMALLY GOT A RIVALRY GOING ON—THE PERSIA FACTION VS. THE ABY FACTION—BUT I THINK IT'S ABOUT TIME WE JOINED FORCES.
WHAT DO YOU THINK? IF I GET MVP IN THE SPORTS FESTIVAL...
...WILL YOU GO OUT WITH ME?
STROKE
SMACK

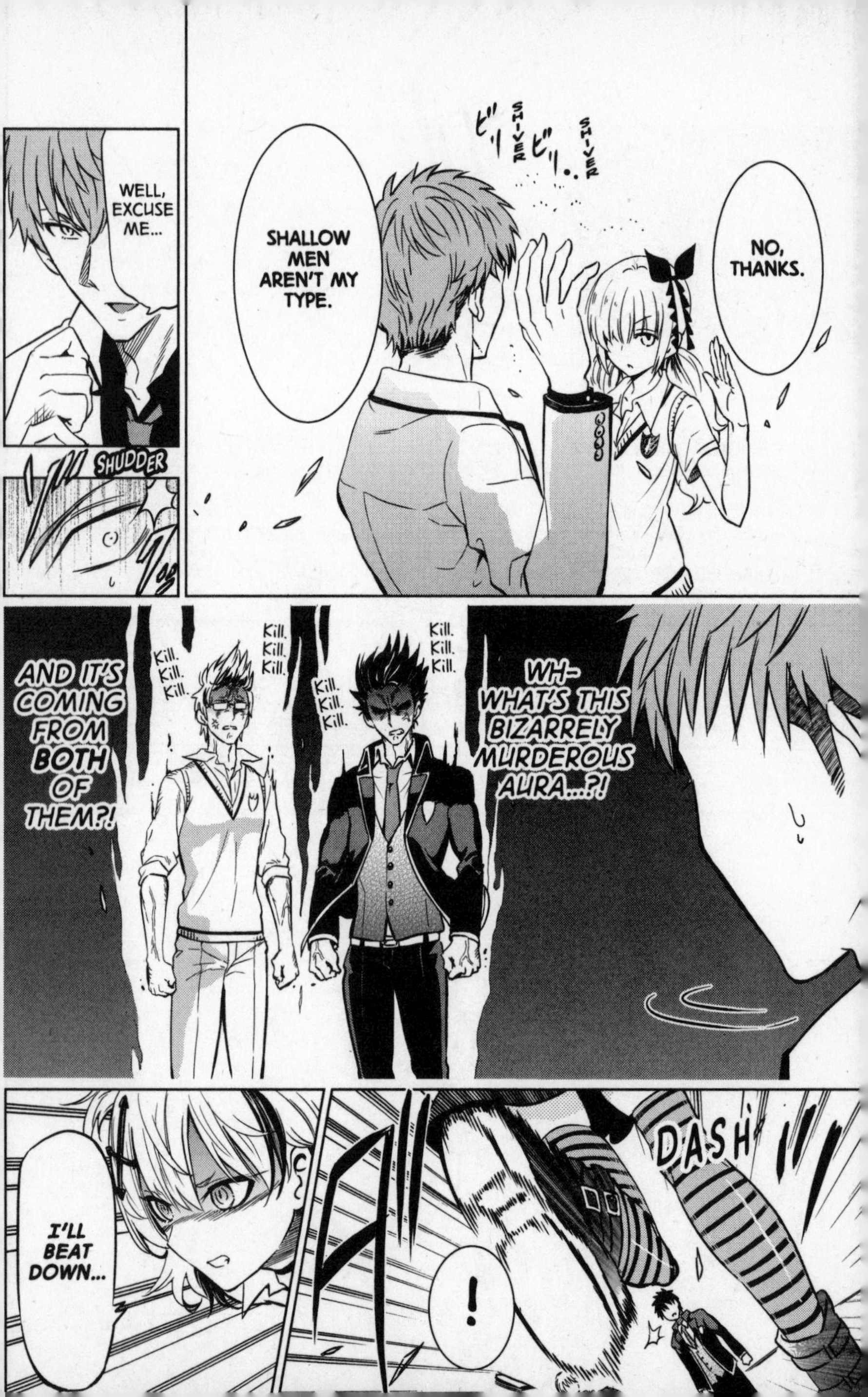
ビリ SHIVER ビリ SHIVER
NO, THANKS.
SHALLOW MEN AREN'T MY TYPE.
WELL, EXCUSE ME...
SHUDDER
WH- WHAT'S THIS BIZARRELY MURDEROUS AURA...?!
Kill. Kill. Kill.
Kill. Kill. Kill.
Kill. Kill. Kill.
Kill. Kill. Kill.
AND IT'S COMING FROM BOTH OF THEM?!
DASH
!
I'LL BEAT DOWN...

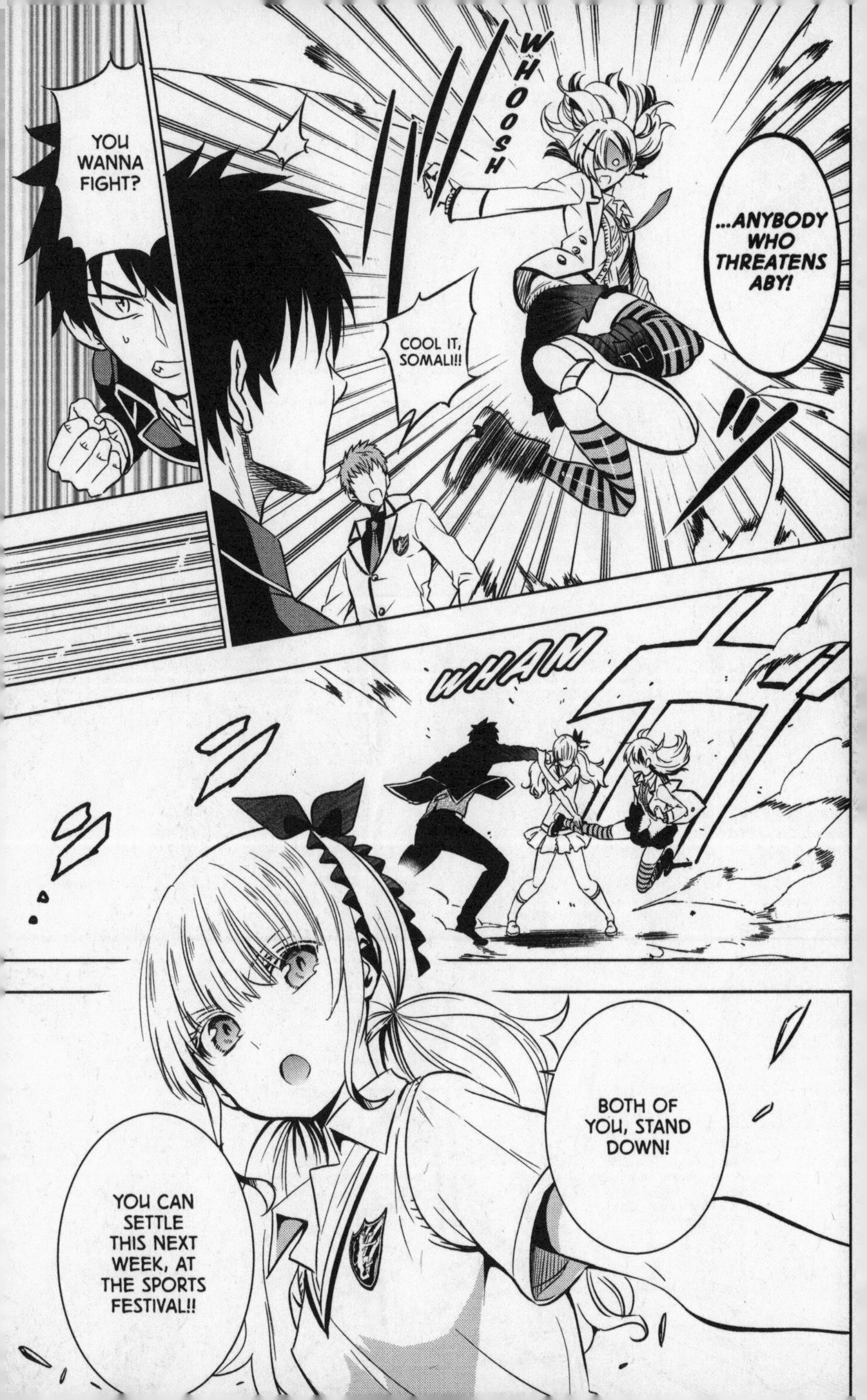
...ANYBODY WHO THREATENS ABY!
WHOOSH
COOL IT, SOMALI!!
YOU WANNA FIGHT?
WHAM
BOTH OF YOU, STAND DOWN!
YOU CAN SETTLE THIS NEXT WEEK, AT THE SPORTS FESTIVAL!!

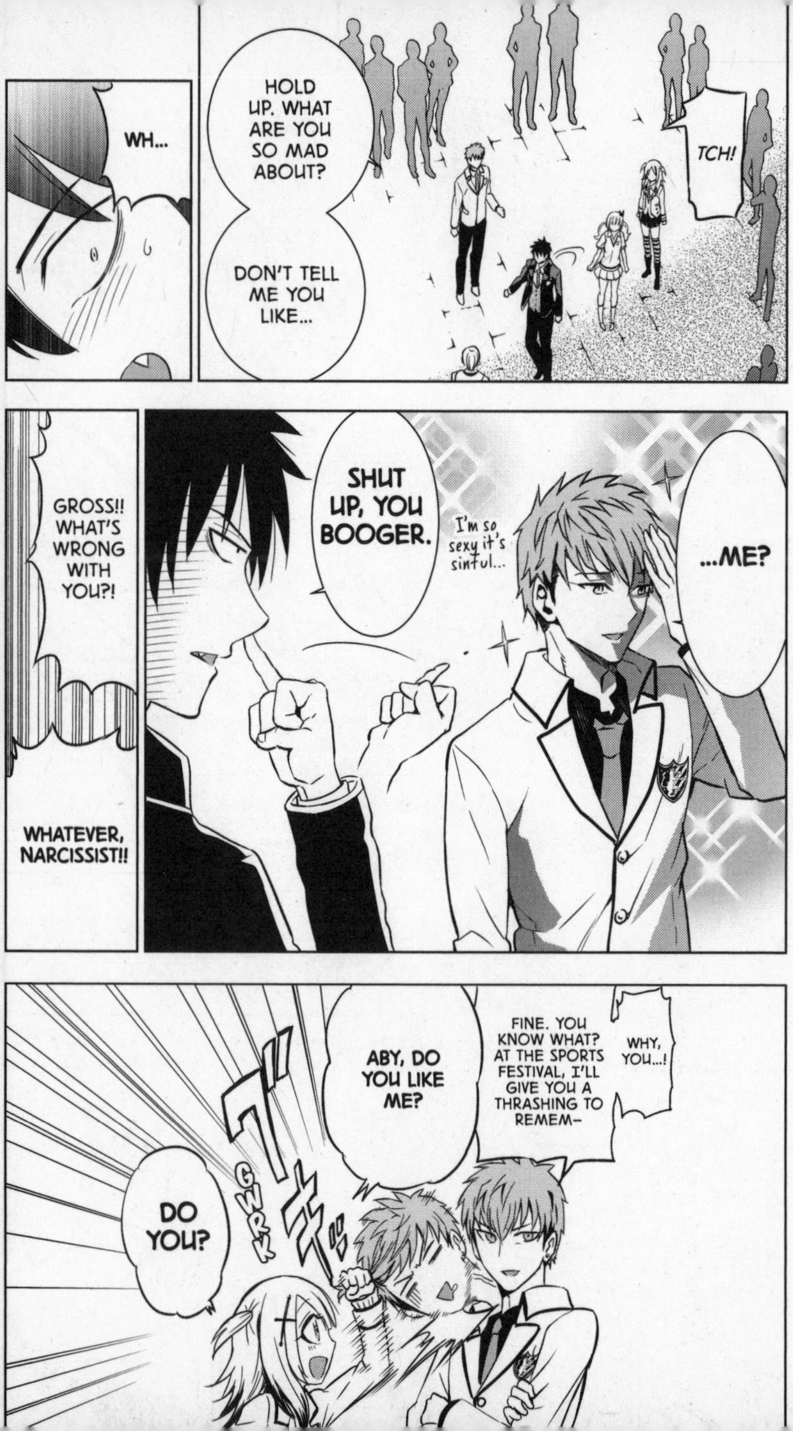
TCH!
HOLD UP. WHAT ARE YOU SO MAD ABOUT?
DON'T TELL ME YOU LIKE...
WH...
...ME?
I'm so sexy it's sinful...
SHUT UP, YOU BOOGER.
GROSS!! WHAT'S WRONG WITH YOU?!
WHATEVER, NARCISSIST!!
WHY, YOU...!
FINE. YOU KNOW WHAT? AT THE SPORTS FESTIVAL, I'LL GIVE YOU A THRASHING TO REMEM–
ABY, DO YOU LIKE ME?
GWRK
DO YOU?

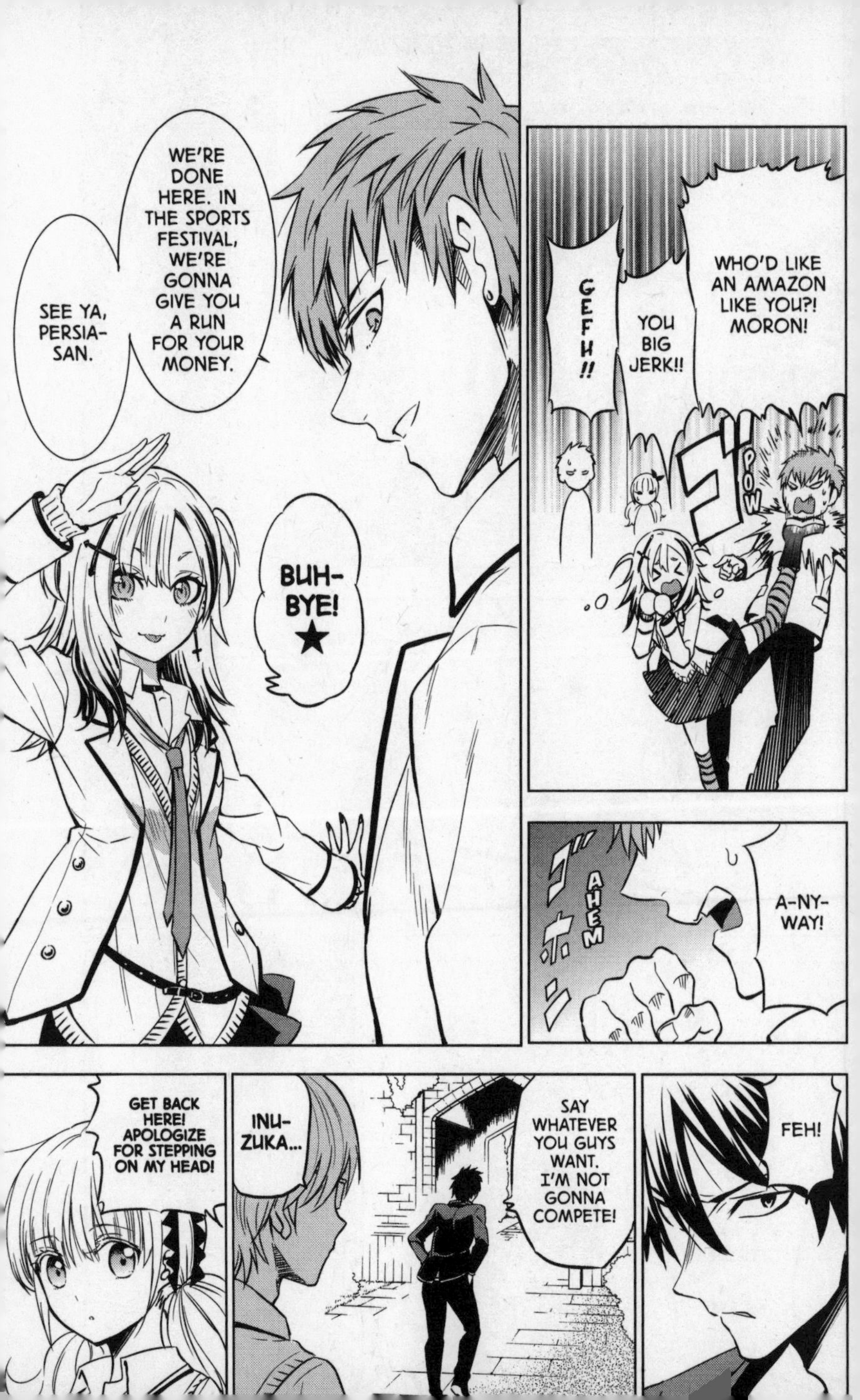
WHO'D LIKE AN AMAZON LIKE YOU?! MORON!
YOU BIG JERK!!
GEFH!!
POW
A-NY-WAY!
AHEM
WE'RE DONE HERE. IN THE SPORTS FESTIVAL, WE'RE GONNA GIVE YOU A RUN FOR YOUR MONEY.
SEE YA, PERSIA-SAN.
BUH-BYE! ★
FEH!
SAY WHATEVER YOU GUYS WANT. I'M NOT GONNA COMPETE!
INU-ZUKA...
GET BACK HERE! APOLOGIZE FOR STEPPING ON MY HEAD!

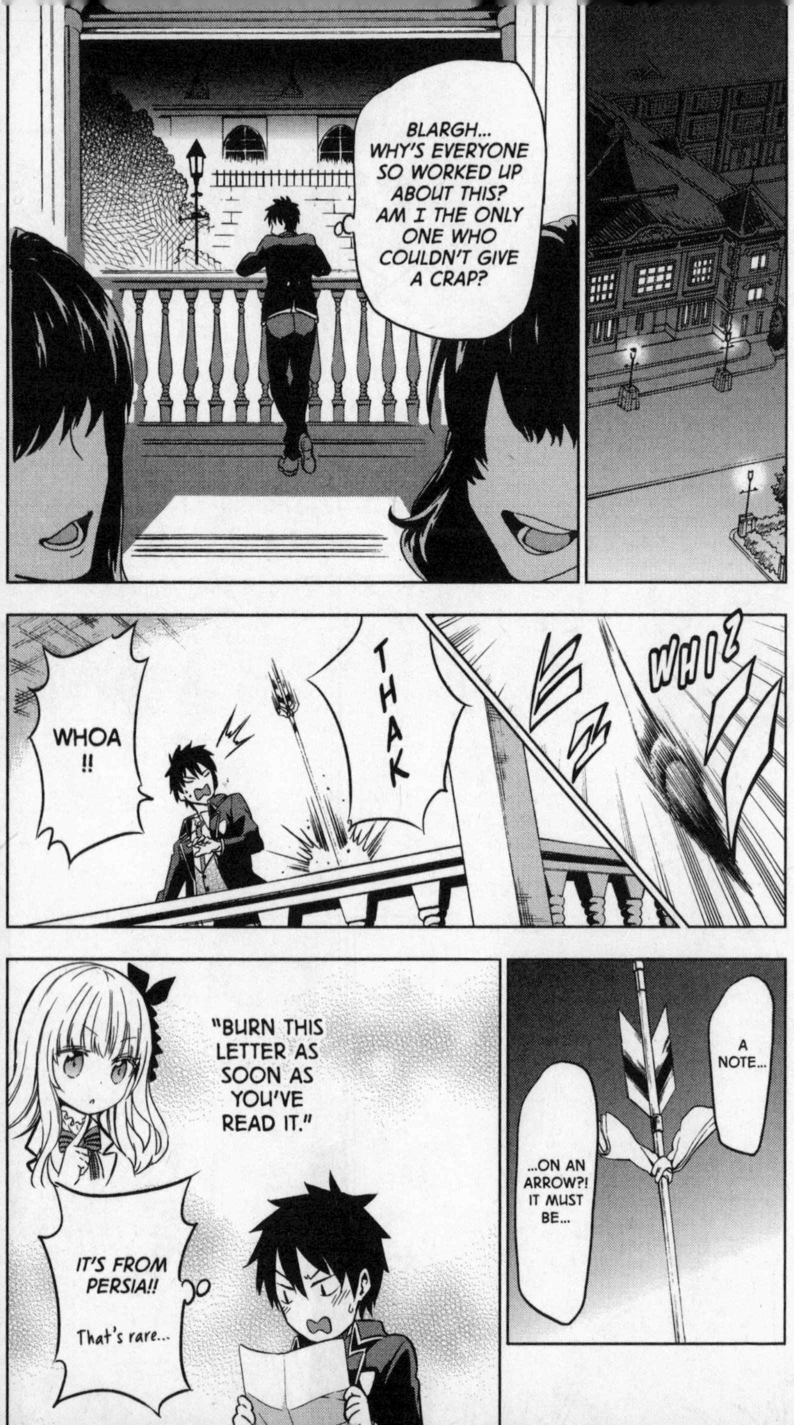
BLARGH... WHY'S EVERYONE SO WORKED UP ABOUT THIS? AM I THE ONLY ONE WHO COULDN'T GIVE A CRAP?
WHIZ
THAK
WHOA!!
A NOTE...
...ON AN ARROW?! IT MUST BE...
"BURN THIS LETTER AS SOON AS YOU'VE READ IT."
IT'S FROM PERSIA!!
That's rare...

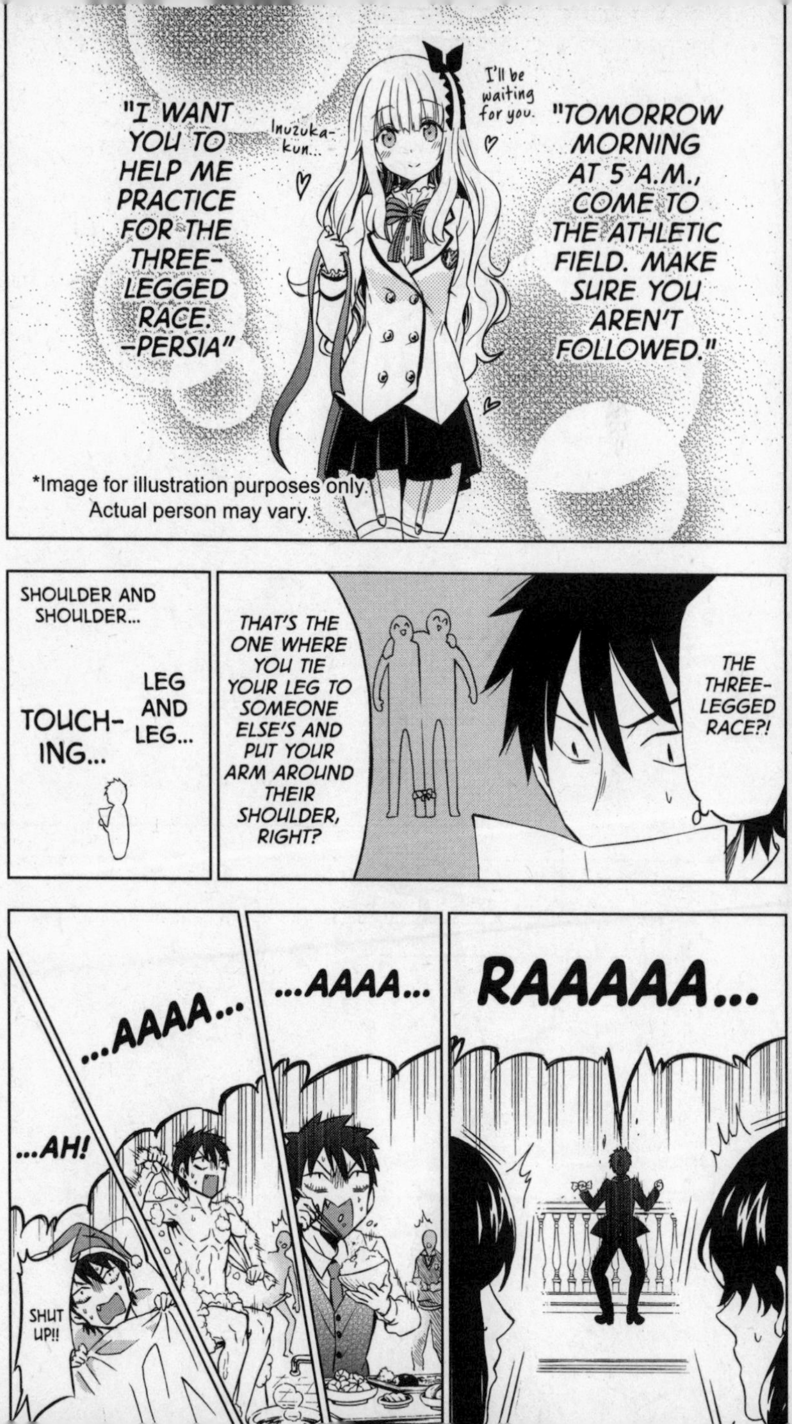
"TOMORROW MORNING AT 5 A.M., COME TO THE ATHLETIC FIELD. MAKE SURE YOU AREN'T FOLLOWED."
I'll be waiting for you.
Inuzuka-kun...
"I WANT YOU TO HELP ME PRACTICE FOR THE THREE-LEGGED RACE. -PERSIA"
*Image for illustration purposes only. Actual person may vary.
THE THREE-LEGGED RACE?!
THAT'S THE ONE WHERE YOU TIE YOUR LEG TO SOMEONE ELSE'S AND PUT YOUR ARM AROUND THEIR SHOULDER, RIGHT?
SHOULDER AND SHOULDER...
LEG AND LEG...
TOUCHING...
RAAAAA...
...AAAA...
...AAAA...
...AH!
SHUT UP!!

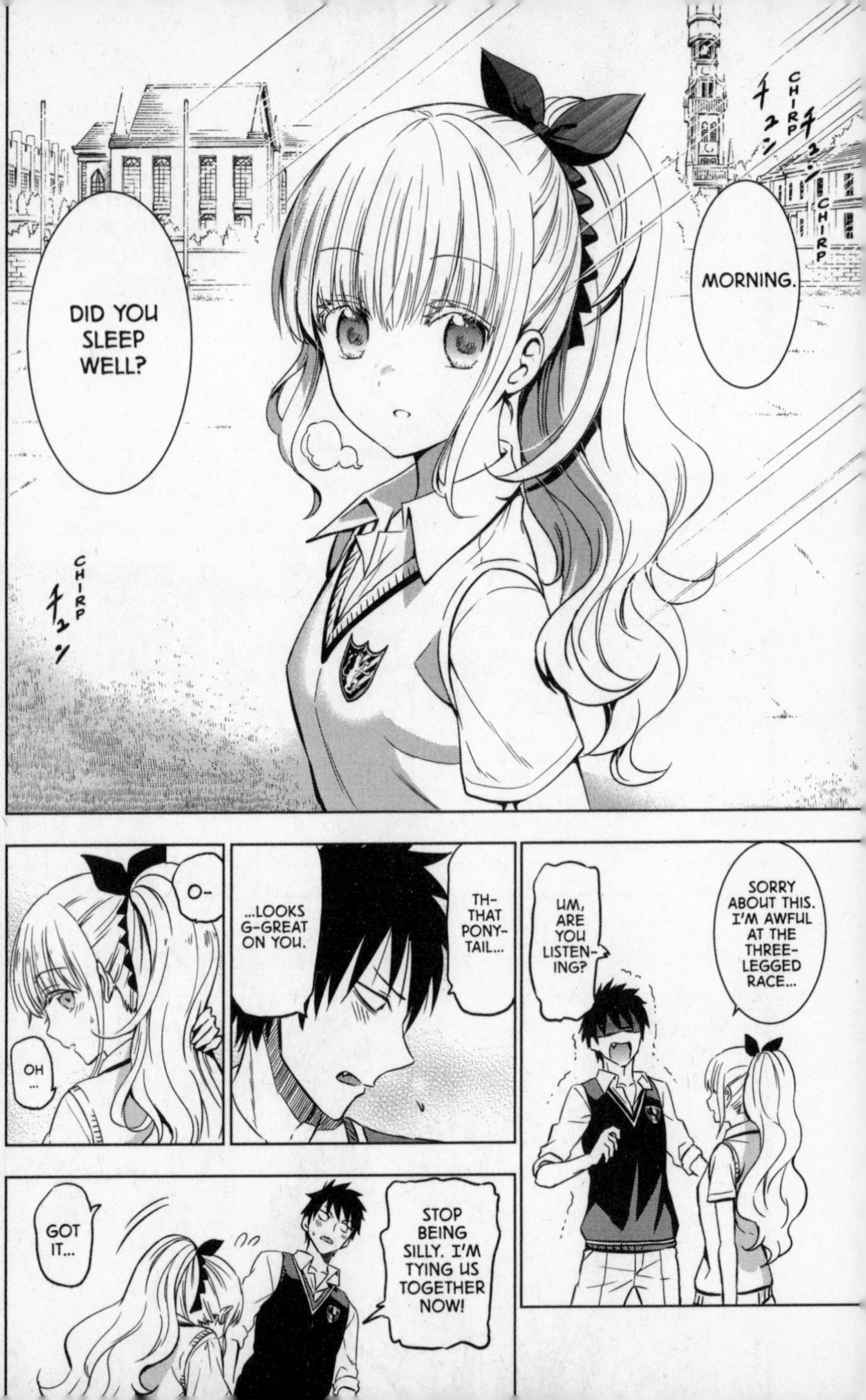

チュン CHIRP チュン CHIRP
MORNING.
DID YOU SLEEP WELL?
チュン CHIRP
SORRY ABOUT THIS. I'M AWFUL AT THE THREE-LEGGED RACE...
UM, ARE YOU LISTENING?
TH- THAT PONY-TAIL...
...LOOKS G-GREAT ON YOU.
O-
OH ...
STOP BEING SILLY. I'M TYING US TOGETHER NOW!
GOT IT...

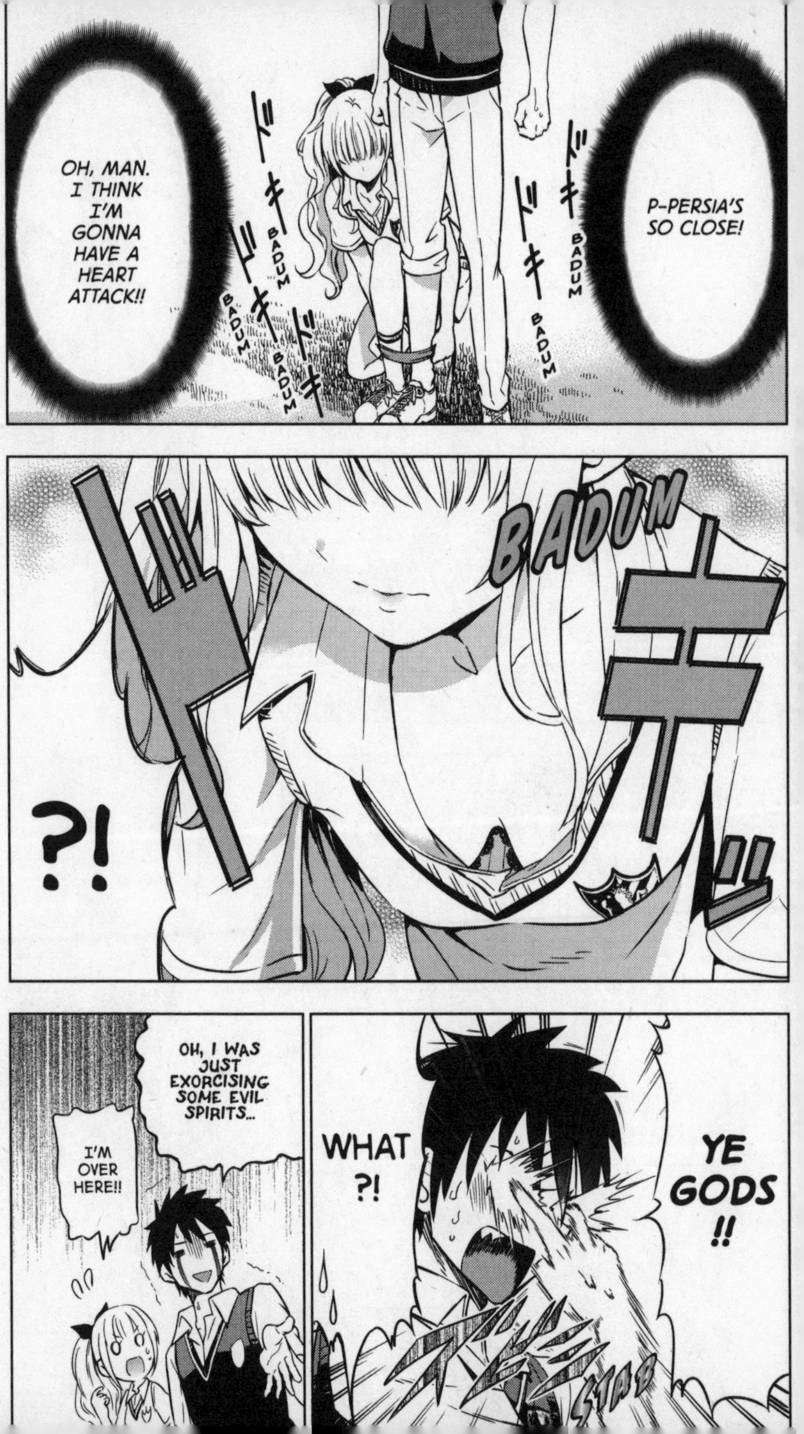
P-PERSIA'S SO CLOSE!
BADUM
BADUM
BADUM
BADUM
BADUM
OH, MAN. I THINK I'M GONNA HAVE A HEART ATTACK!!
BADUM
?!
YE GODS!!
WHAT?!
STAB
OH, I WAS JUST EXORCISING SOME EVIL SPIRITS...
I'M OVER HERE!!

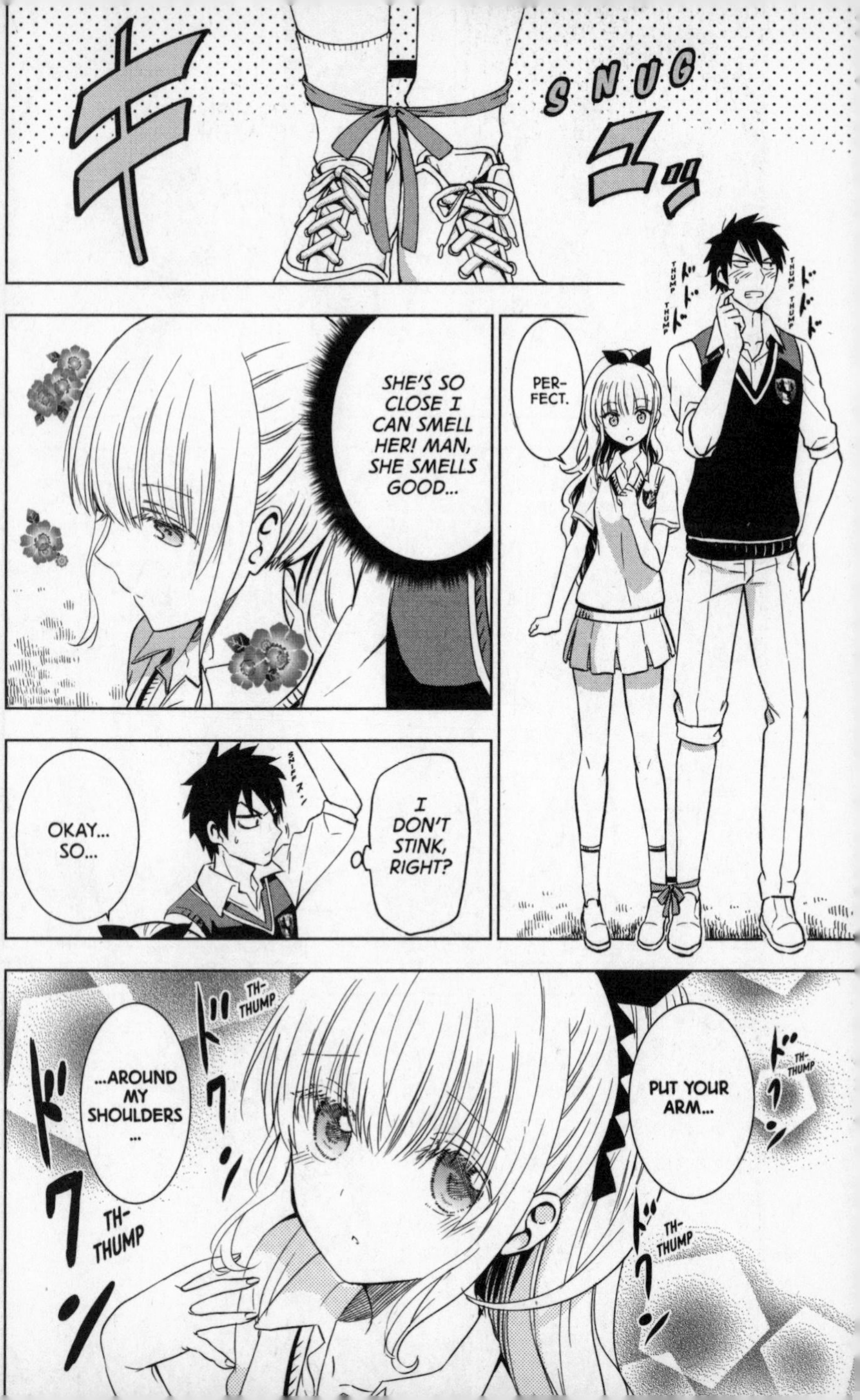
SNUG
THUMP THUMP
THUMP THUMP
PER-FECT.
SHE'S SO CLOSE I CAN SMELL HER! MAN, SHE SMELLS GOOD...
I DON'T STINK, RIGHT?
OKAY... SO...
TH-THUMP
PUT YOUR ARM...
TH-THUMP
TH-THUMP
...AROUND MY SHOULDERS ...
TH-THUMP

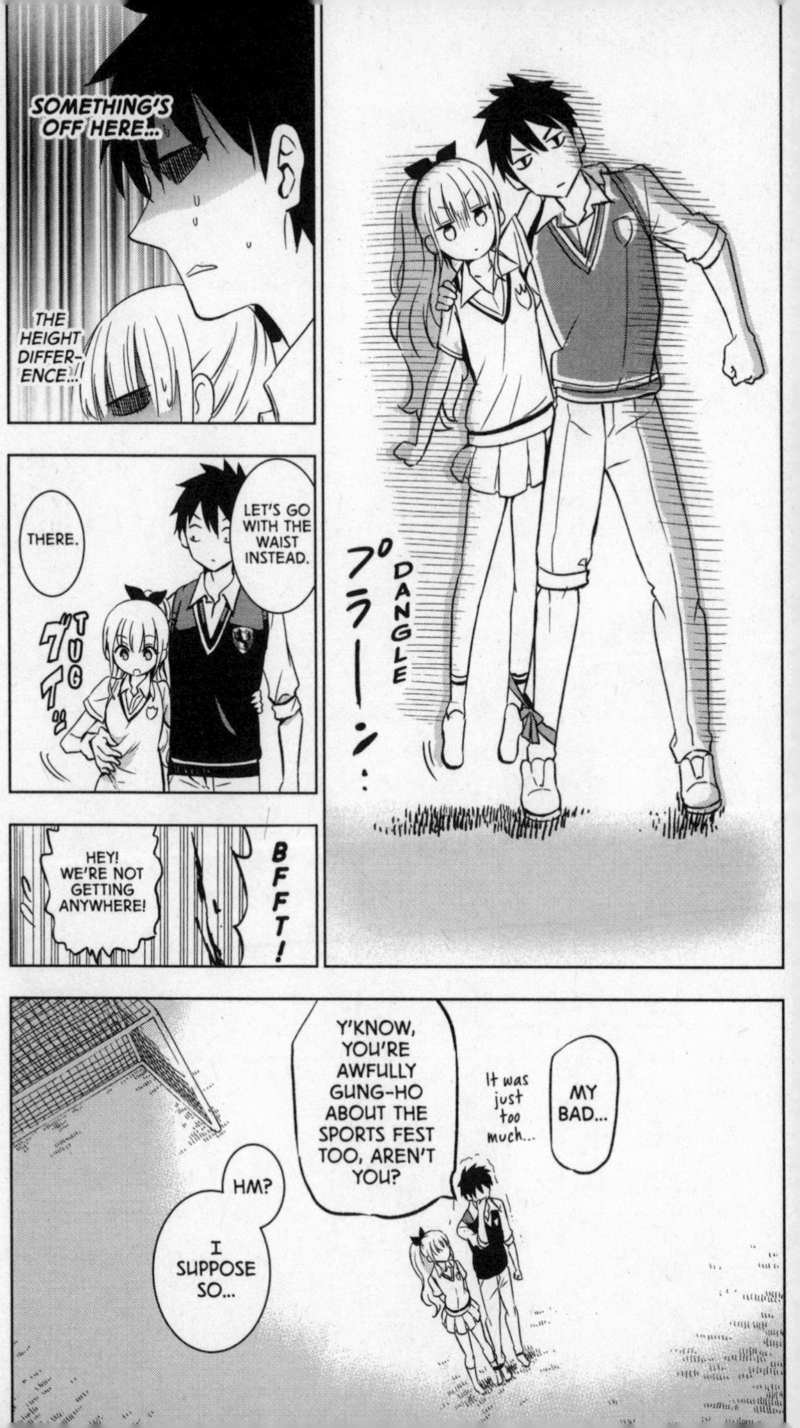
プラーン…
DANGLE
SOMETHING'S OFF HERE...
THE HEIGHT DIFFER-ENCE...!
LET'S GO WITH THE WAIST INSTEAD.
THERE.
グイッ
TUG
BFFT!
HEY! WE'RE NOT GETTING ANYWHERE!
MY BAD...
It was just too much...
Y'KNOW, YOU'RE AWFULLY GUNG-HO ABOUT THE SPORTS FEST TOO, AREN'T YOU?
HM?
I SUPPOSE SO...

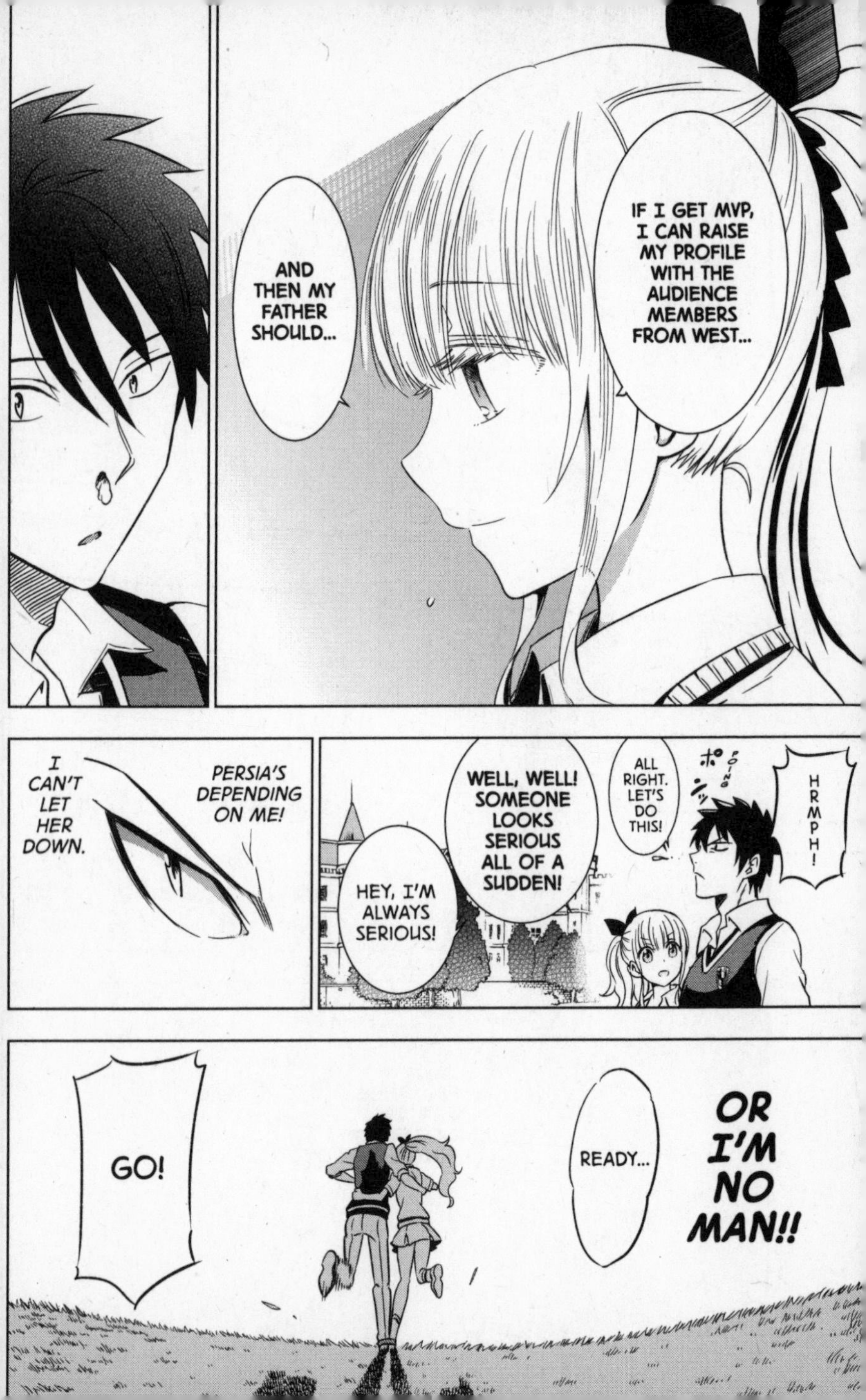
IF I GET MVP, I CAN RAISE MY PROFILE WITH THE AUDIENCE MEMBERS FROM WEST...
AND THEN MY FATHER SHOULD...
HRMPH!
POING
ALL RIGHT. LET'S DO THIS!
WELL, WELL! SOMEONE LOOKS SERIOUS ALL OF A SUDDEN!
HEY, I'M ALWAYS SERIOUS!
PERSIA'S DEPENDING ON ME!
I CAN'T LET HER DOWN.
OR I'M NO MAN!!
READY...
GO!

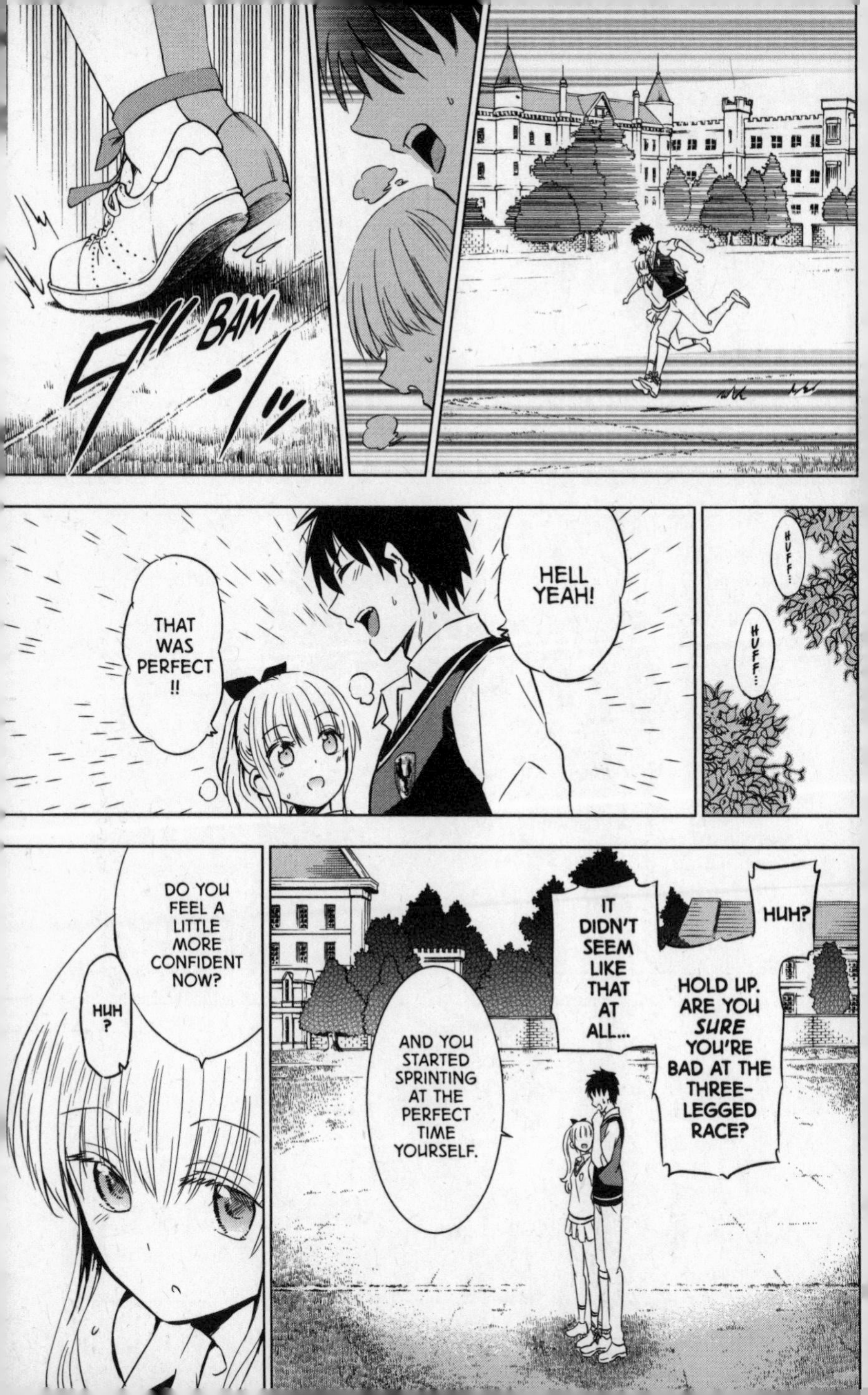
BAM
HUFF...
HUFF...
HELL YEAH!
THAT WAS PERFECT!!
HUH?
HOLD UP. ARE YOU *SURE* YOU'RE BAD AT THE THREE-LEGGED RACE?
IT DIDN'T SEEM LIKE THAT AT ALL...
AND YOU STARTED SPRINTING AT THE PERFECT TIME YOURSELF.
DO YOU FEEL A LITTLE MORE CONFIDENT NOW?
HUH?

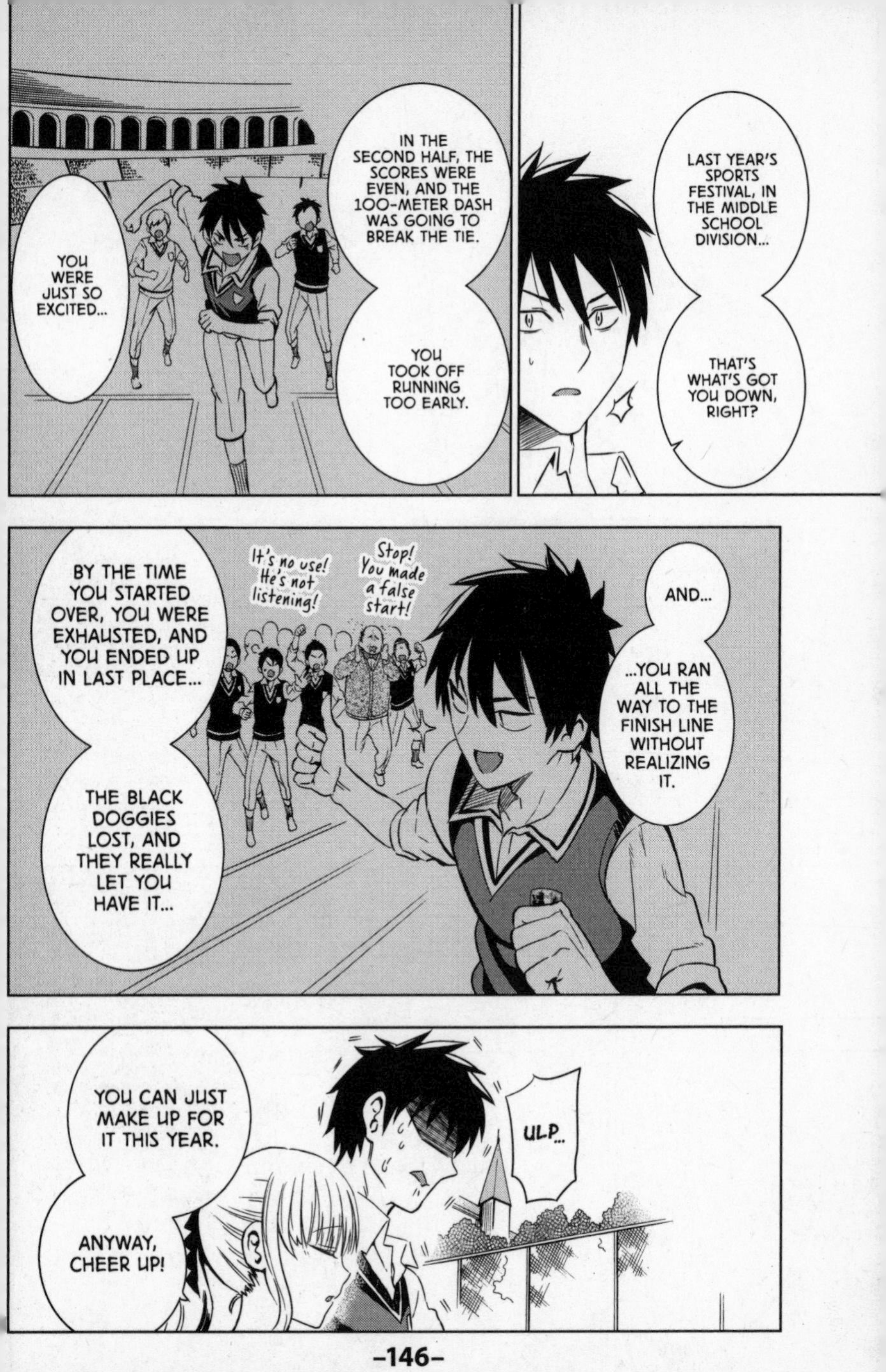
LAST YEAR'S SPORTS FESTIVAL, IN THE MIDDLE SCHOOL DIVISION...
THAT'S WHAT'S GOT YOU DOWN, RIGHT?
IN THE SECOND HALF, THE SCORES WERE EVEN, AND THE 100-METER DASH WAS GOING TO BREAK THE TIE.
YOU TOOK OFF RUNNING TOO EARLY.
YOU WERE JUST SO EXCITED...
AND...
...YOU RAN ALL THE WAY TO THE FINISH LINE WITHOUT REALIZING IT.
Stop! You made a false start!
It's no use! He's not listening!
BY THE TIME YOU STARTED OVER, YOU WERE EXHAUSTED, AND YOU ENDED UP IN LAST PLACE...
THE BLACK DOGGIES LOST, AND THEY REALLY LET YOU HAVE IT...
ULP...
YOU CAN JUST MAKE UP FOR IT THIS YEAR.
ANYWAY, CHEER UP!

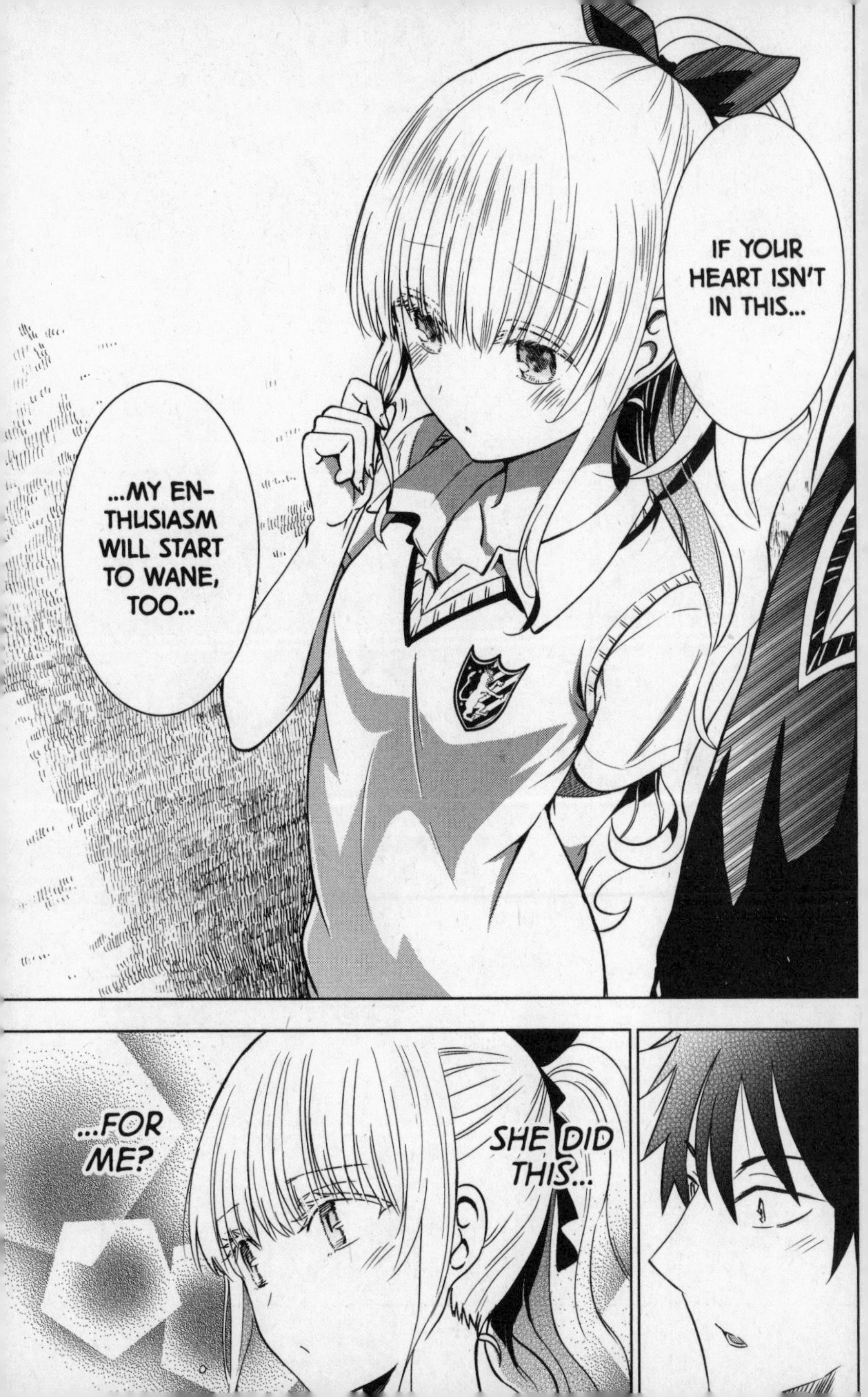
IF YOUR HEART ISN'T IN THIS...
...MY EN-THUSIASM WILL START TO WANE, TOO...
SHE DID THIS...
...FOR ME?

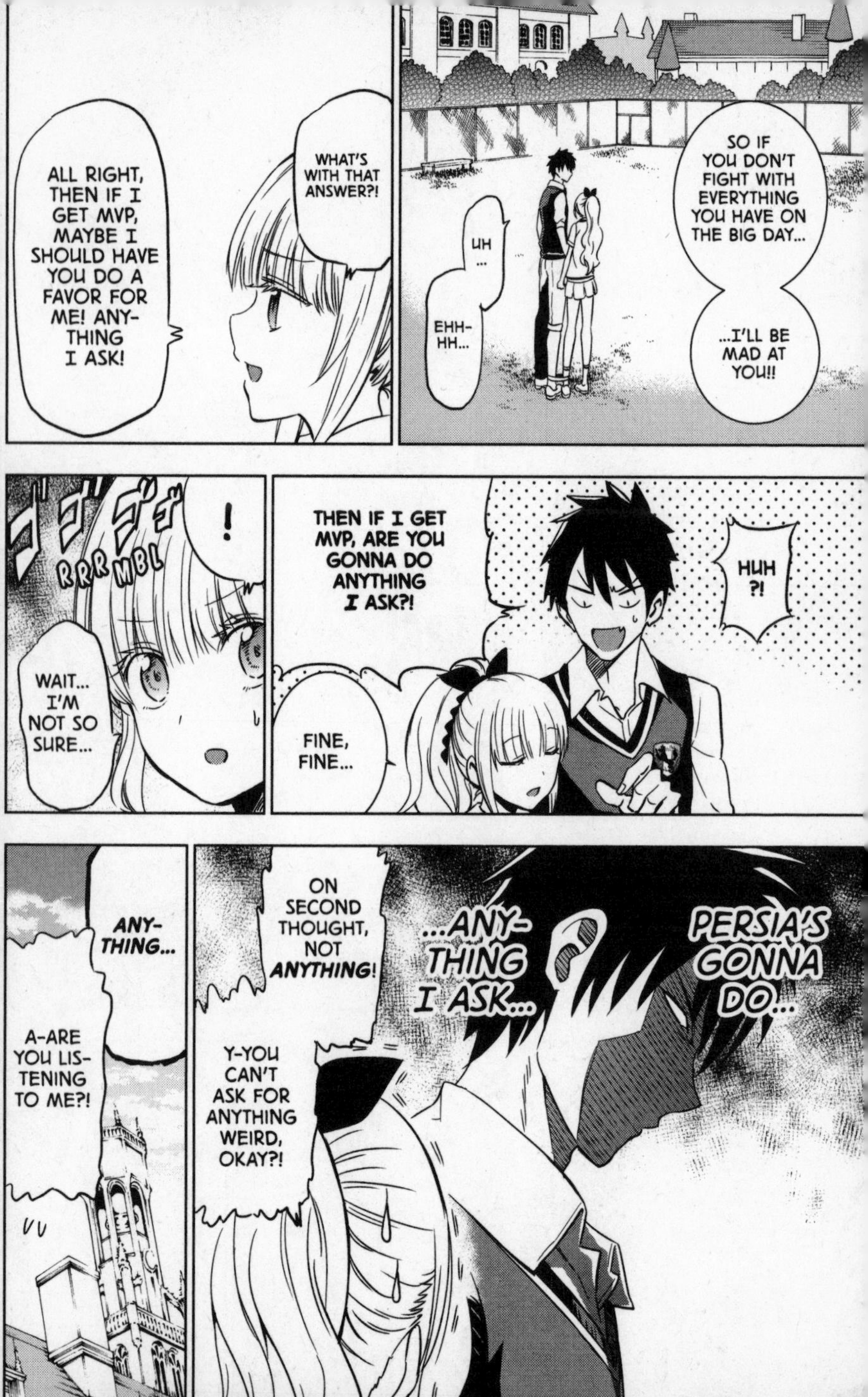
SO IF YOU DON'T FIGHT WITH EVERYTHING YOU HAVE ON THE BIG DAY...
...I'LL BE MAD AT YOU!!
UH ...
EHH-HH...
WHAT'S WITH THAT ANSWER?!
ALL RIGHT, THEN IF I GET MVP, MAYBE I SHOULD HAVE YOU DO A FAVOR FOR ME! ANY-THING I ASK!
HUH ?!
THEN IF I GET MVP, ARE YOU GONNA DO ANYTHING I ASK?!
FINE, FINE...
!
RRRMBL
WAIT... I'M NOT SO SURE...
PERSIA'S GONNA DO...
...ANY-THING I ASK...
ON SECOND THOUGHT, NOT ANYTHING!
Y-YOU CAN'T ASK FOR ANYTHING WEIRD, OKAY?!
ANY-THING...
A-ARE YOU LIS-TENING TO ME?!

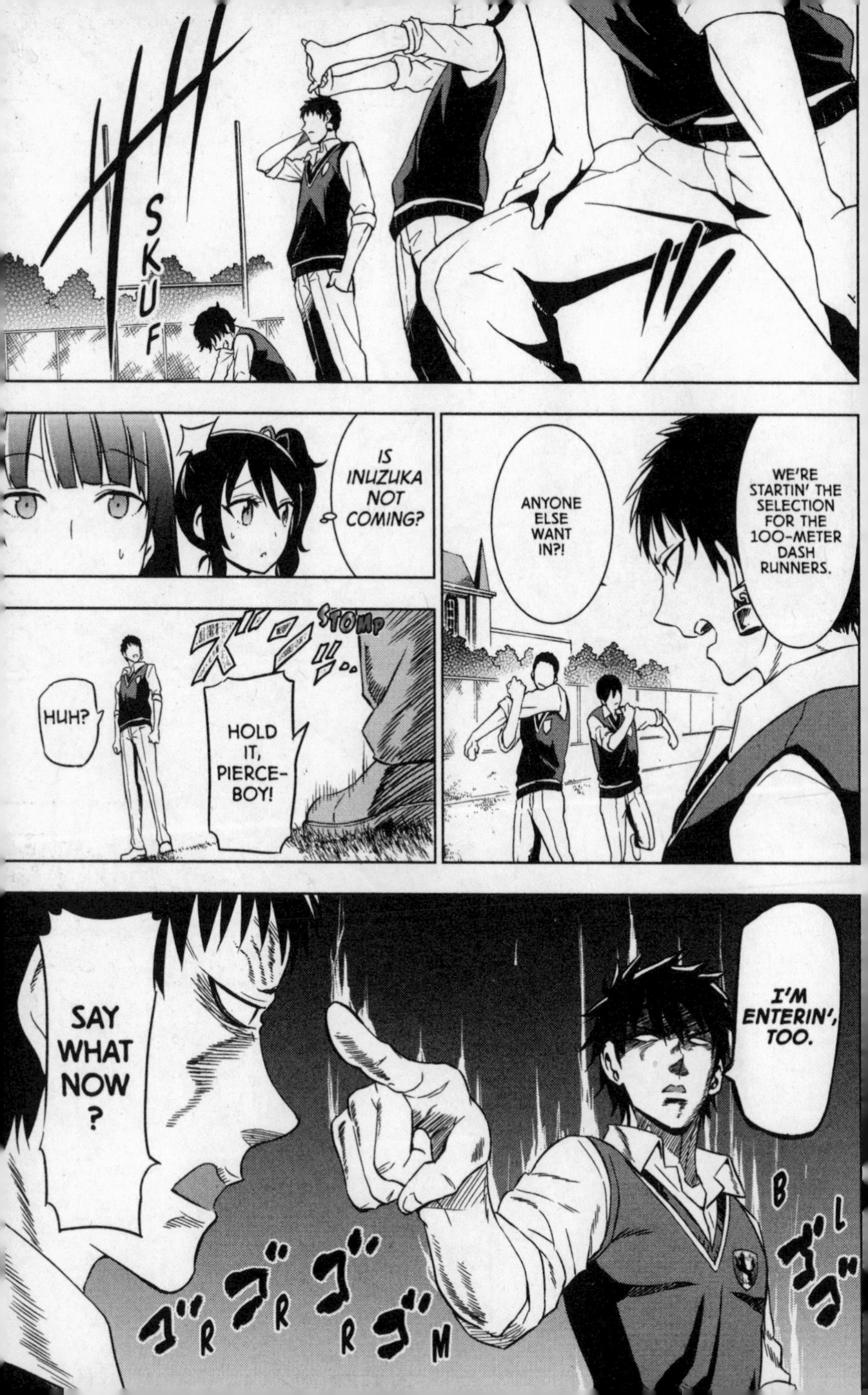
SKUF
IS INUZUKA NOT COMING?
WE'RE STARTIN' THE SELECTION FOR THE 100-METER DASH RUNNERS.
ANYONE ELSE WANT IN?!
STOMP
HOLD IT, PIERCE-BOY!
HUH?
I'M ENTERIN', TOO.
BL
SAY WHAT NOW?
RRRM

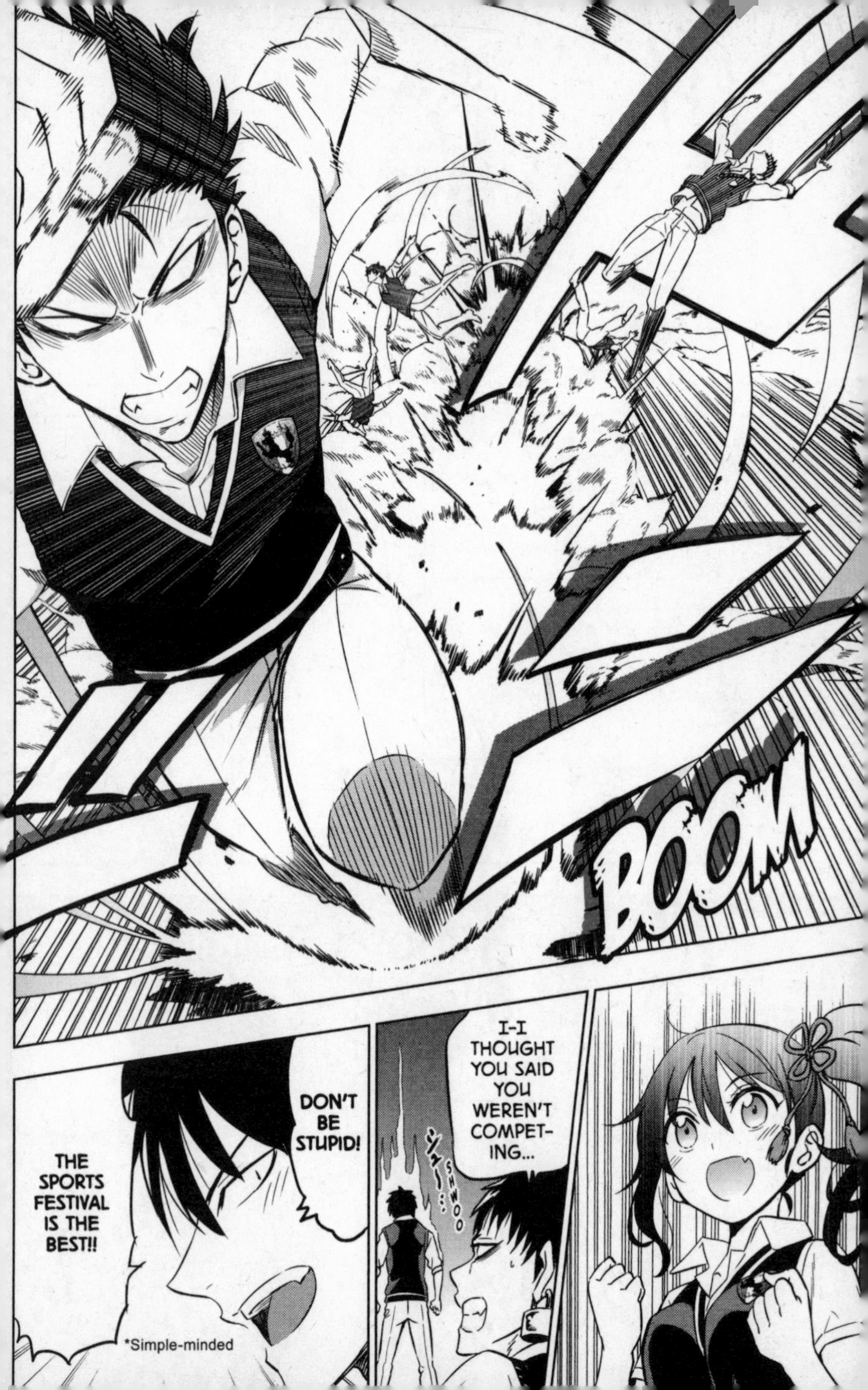
BOOM
I-I THOUGHT YOU SAID YOU WEREN'T COMPET-ING...
SHWOO
DON'T BE STUPID!
THE SPORTS FESTIVAL IS THE BEST!!
*Simple-minded

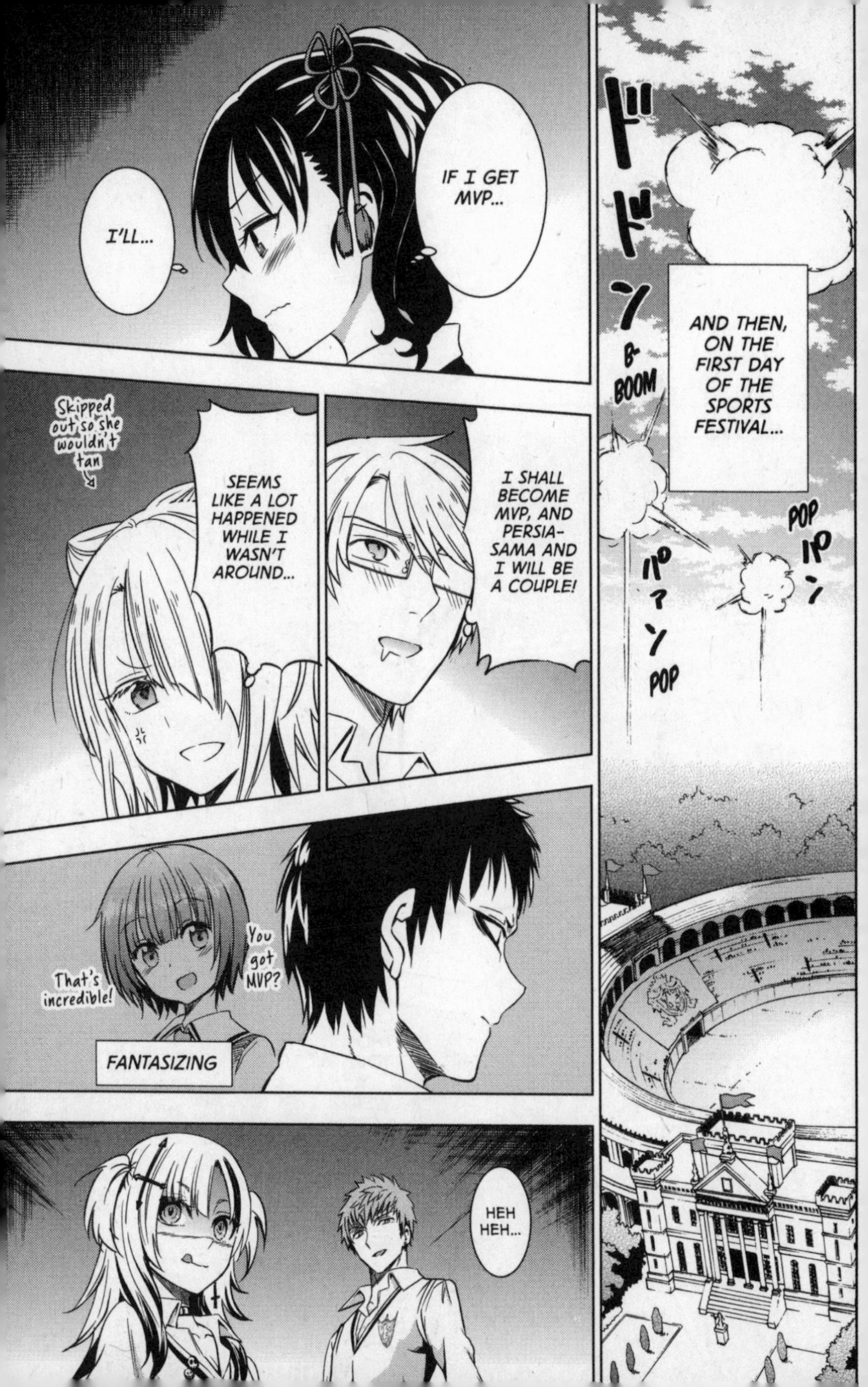
ドドン
B-BOOM
AND THEN, ON THE FIRST DAY OF THE SPORTS FESTIVAL...
POP
パン
パァン
POP
IF I GET MVP...
I'LL...
I SHALL BECOME MVP, AND PERSIA-SAMA AND I WILL BE A COUPLE!
SEEMS LIKE A LOT HAPPENED WHILE I WASN'T AROUND...
Skipped out so she wouldn't tan
You got MVP?
That's incredible!
FANTASIZING
HEH HEH...

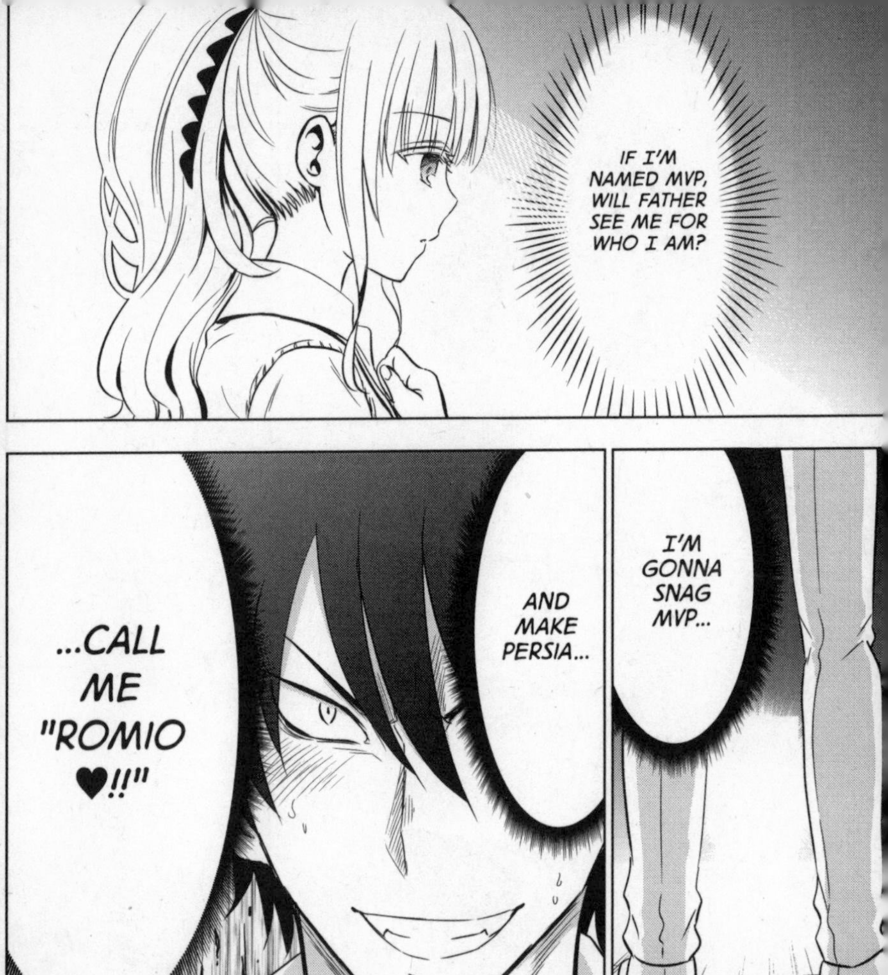
IF I'M NAMED MVP, WILL FATHER SEE ME FOR WHO I AM?
I'M GONNA SNAG MVP...
AND MAKE PERSIA...
...CALL ME "ROMIO ♥!!"

*NOTE: IN JAPANESE, CALLING SOMEONE BY THEIR GIVEN NAME WITH NO HONORIFIC ATTACHED INDICATES VERY CLOSE INTIMACY, ESSENTIALLY LIMITING IT TO FAMILY AND ROMANTIC PARTNERS.

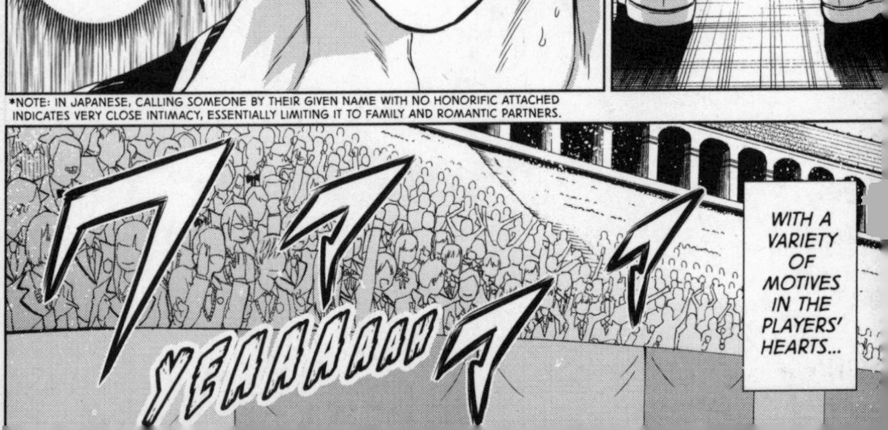
WITH A VARIETY OF MOTIVES IN THE PLAYERS' HEARTS...
YEAAAAAAH

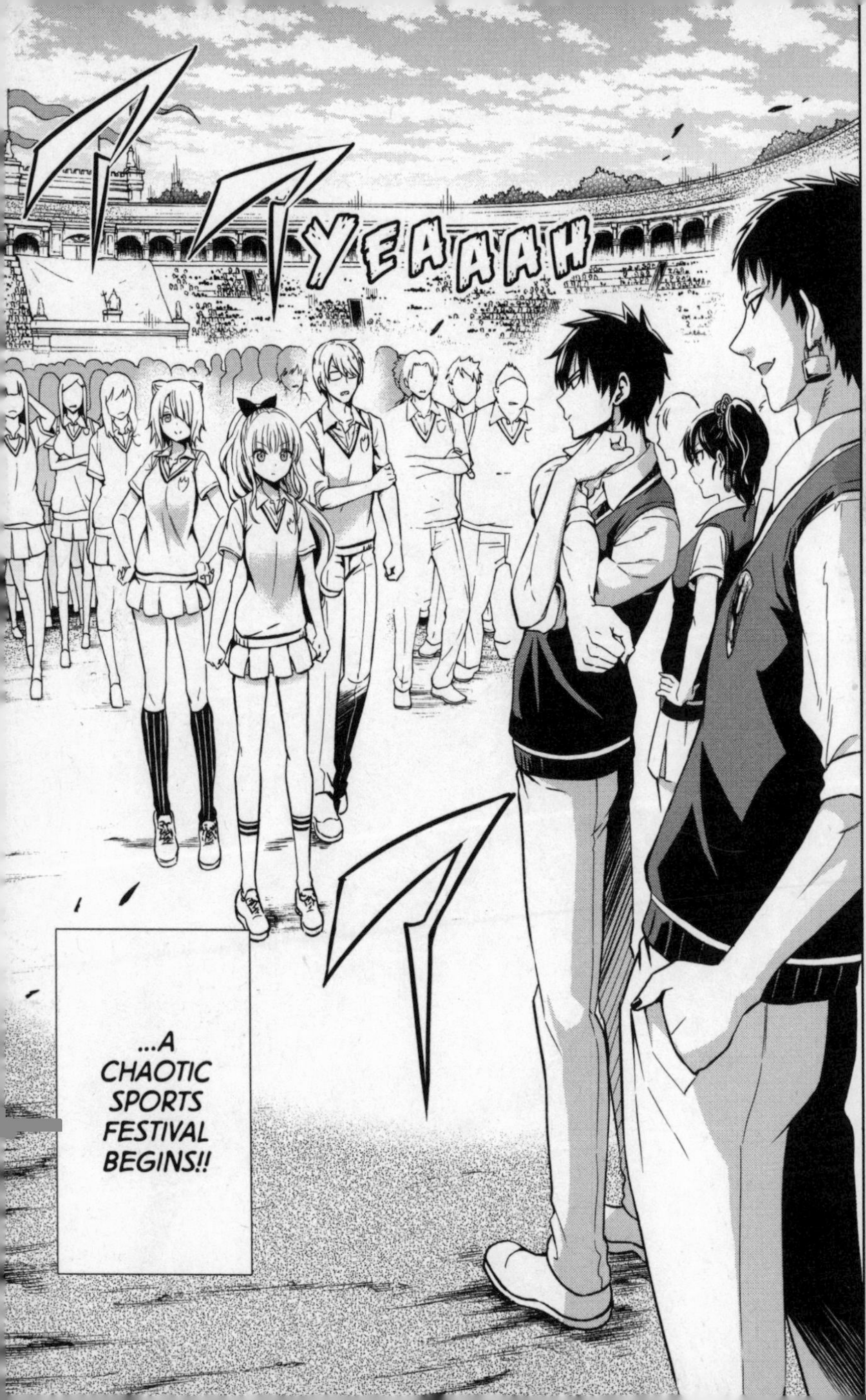
YEAAAH
...A CHAOTIC SPORTS FESTIVAL BEGINS!!

ACT 10:

THE SPORTS FESTIVAL & JULIET

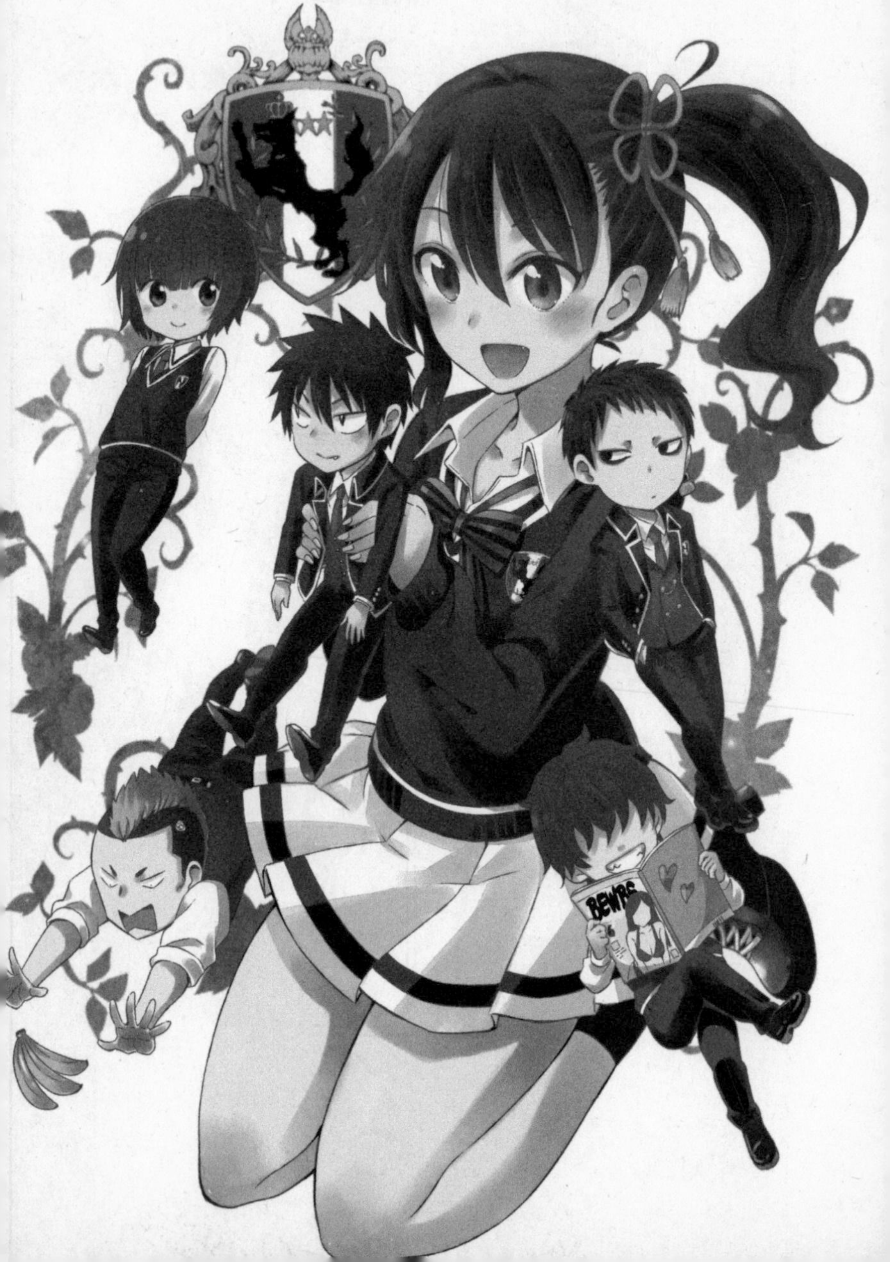

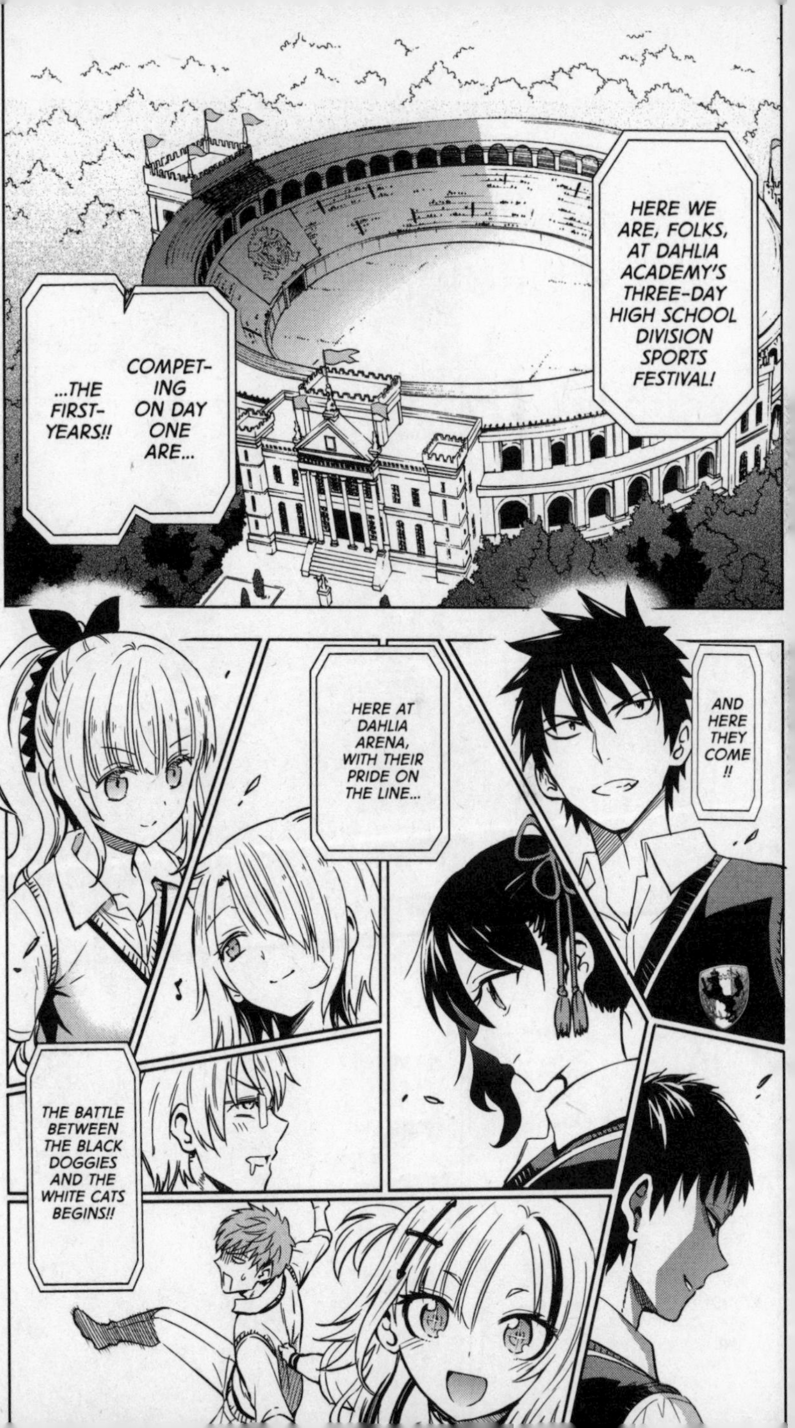
HERE WE ARE, FOLKS, AT DAHLIA ACADEMY'S THREE-DAY HIGH SCHOOL DIVISION SPORTS FESTIVAL!
COMPET-ING ON DAY ONE ARE...
...THE FIRST-YEARS!!
AND HERE THEY COME !!
HERE AT DAHLIA ARENA, WITH THEIR PRIDE ON THE LINE...
THE BATTLE BETWEEN THE BLACK DOGGIES AND THE WHITE CATS BEGINS!!

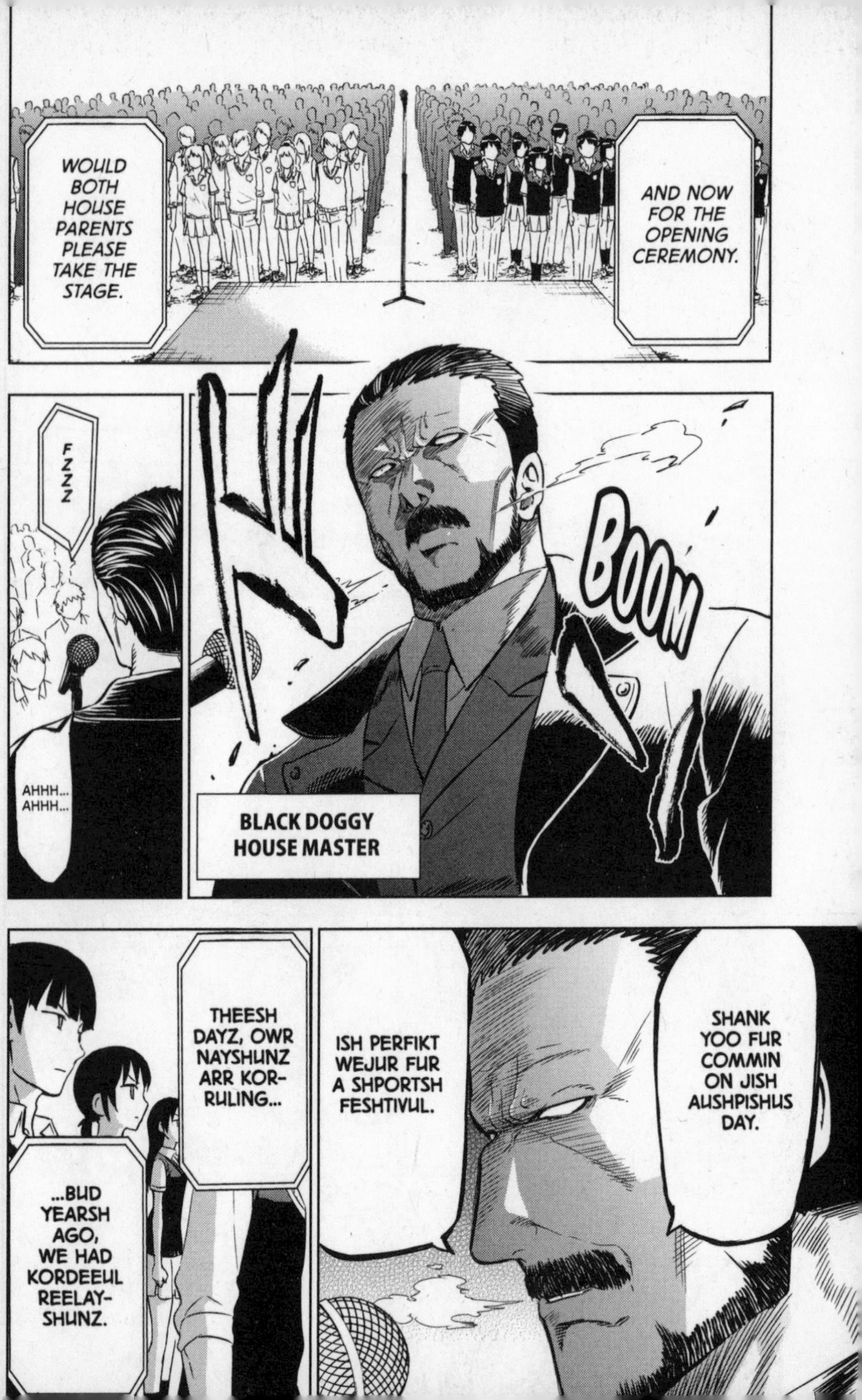
AND NOW FOR THE OPENING CEREMONY.
WOULD BOTH HOUSE PARENTS PLEASE TAKE THE STAGE.
BOOM
BLACK DOGGY HOUSE MASTER
FZZZ
AHHH... AHHH...
SHANK YOO FUR COMMIN ON JISH AUSHPISHUS DAY.
ISH PERFIKT WEJUR FUR A SHPORTSH FESHTIVUL.
THEESH DAYZ, OWR NAYSHUNZ ARR KOR-RULING...
...BUD YEARSH AGO, WE HAD KORDEEUL REELAY-SHUNZ.

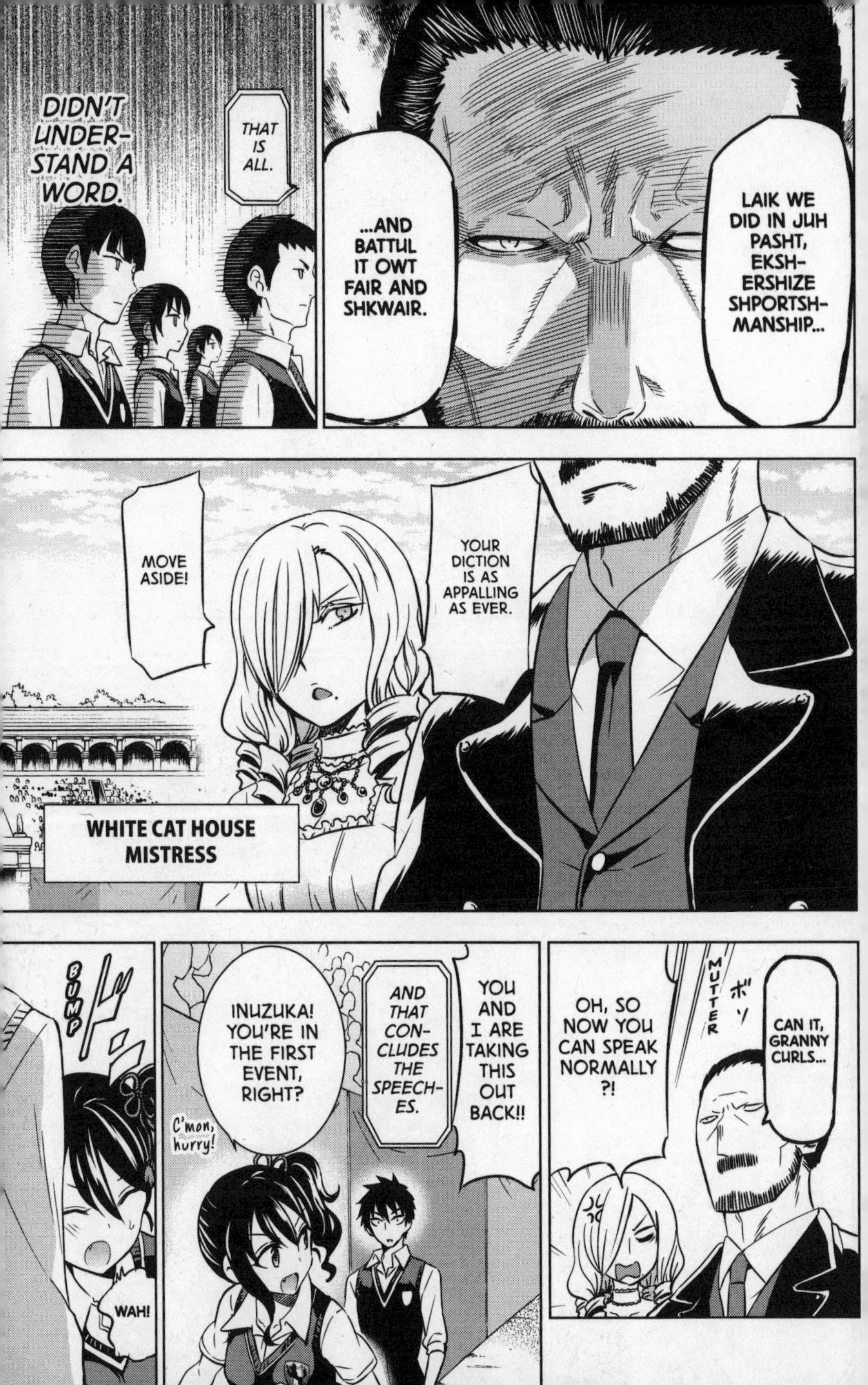
LAIK WE DID IN JUH PASHT, EKSH-ERSHIZE SHPORTSH-MANSHIP...
...AND BATTUL IT OWT FAIR AND SHKWAIR.
THAT IS ALL.
DIDN'T UNDER-STAND A WORD.
YOUR DICTION IS AS APPALLING AS EVER.
MOVE ASIDE!
WHITE CAT HOUSE MISTRESS
CAN IT, GRANNY CURLS...
ボソ
MUTTER
OH, SO NOW YOU CAN SPEAK NORMALLY?!
YOU AND I ARE TAKING THIS OUT BACK!!
AND THAT CON-CLUDES THE SPEECH-ES.
INUZUKA! YOU'RE IN THE FIRST EVENT, RIGHT?
C'mon, hurry!
BUMP
WAH!

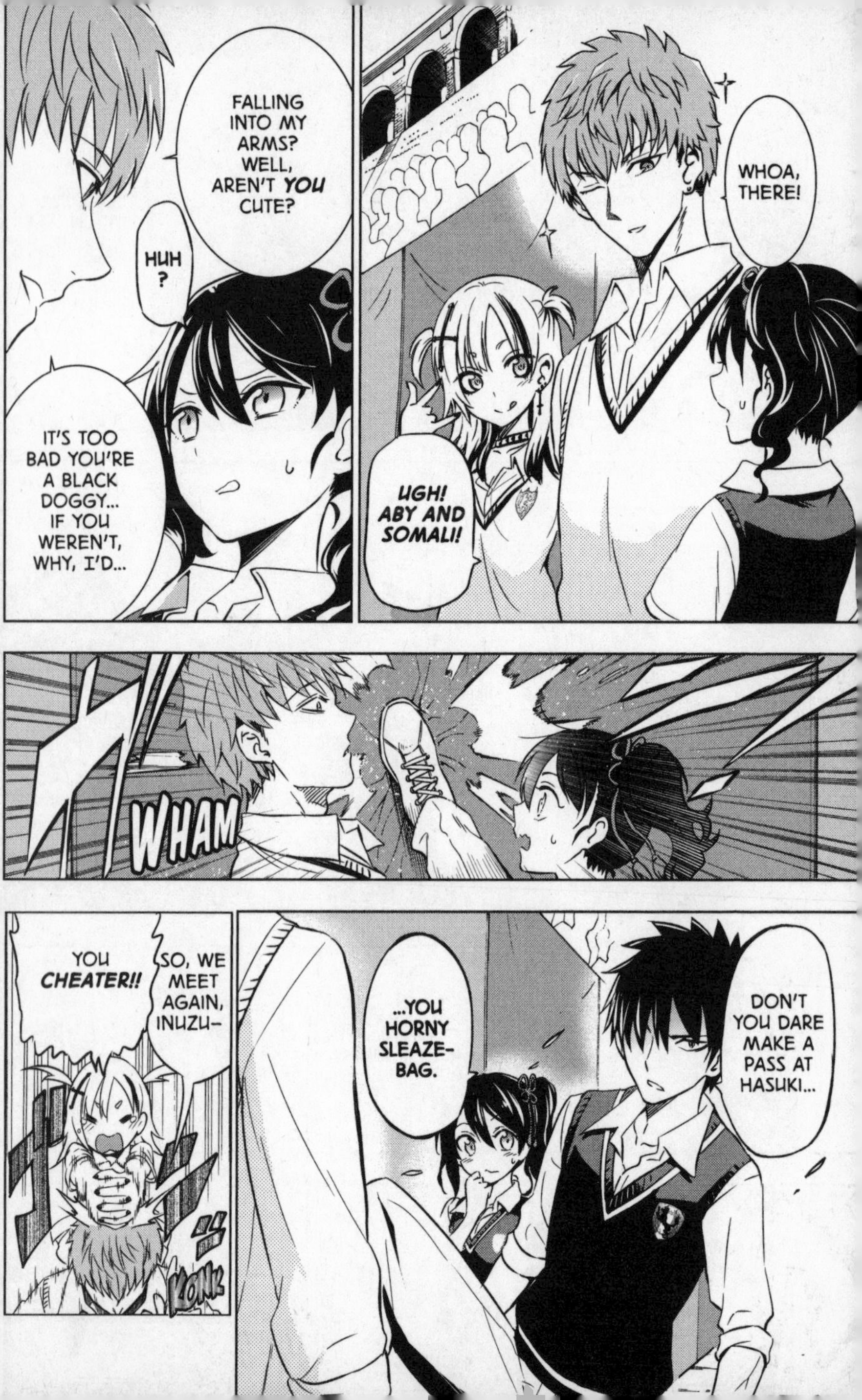
WHOA, THERE!
UGH! ABY AND SOMALI!
FALLING INTO MY ARMS? WELL, AREN'T YOU CUTE?
HUH?
IT'S TOO BAD YOU'RE A BLACK DOGGY... IF YOU WEREN'T, WHY, I'D...
WHAM
DON'T YOU DARE MAKE A PASS AT HASUKI...
...YOU HORNY SLEAZE-BAG.
SO, WE MEET AGAIN, INUZU-
YOU CHEATER!!
KONK

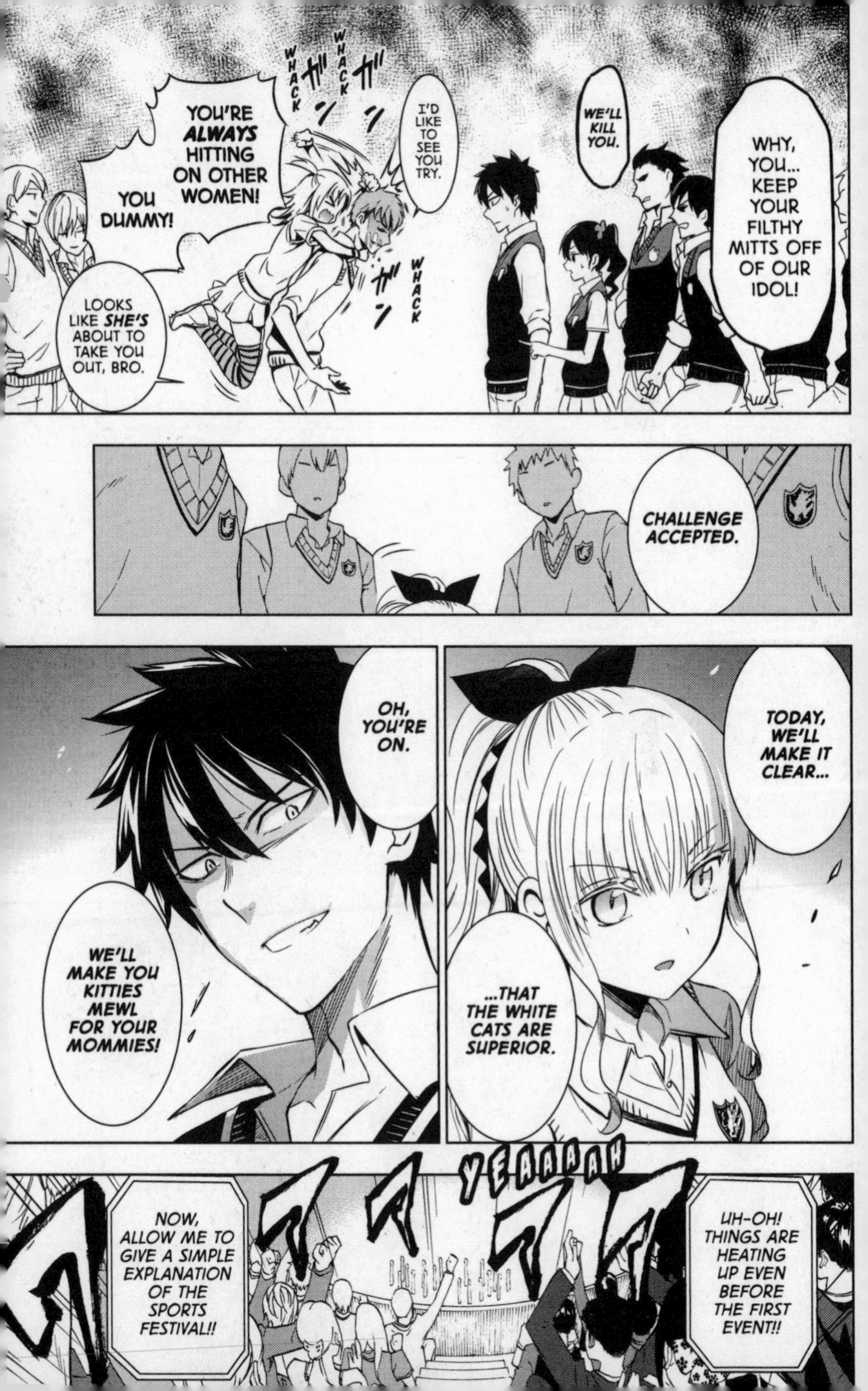
WHY, YOU... KEEP YOUR FILTHY MITTS OFF OF OUR IDOL!
WE'LL KILL YOU.
I'D LIKE TO SEE YOU TRY.
WHACK
WHACK
WHACK
YOU'RE ALWAYS HITTING ON OTHER WOMEN! YOU DUMMY!
LOOKS LIKE SHE'S ABOUT TO TAKE YOU OUT, BRO.
CHALLENGE ACCEPTED.
TODAY, WE'LL MAKE IT CLEAR...
...THAT THE WHITE CATS ARE SUPERIOR.
OH, YOU'RE ON.
WE'LL MAKE YOU KITTIES MEWL FOR YOUR MOMMIES!
UH-OH! THINGS ARE HEATING UP EVEN BEFORE THE FIRST EVENT!!
YEAAAAH
NOW, ALLOW ME TO GIVE A SIMPLE EXPLANATION OF THE SPORTS FESTIVAL!!

THERE ARE NINE EVENTS IN ALL.

DAY 3	DAY 2	DAY 1
THIRD-YEARS	SECOND-YEARS	FIRST-YEARS

AT THIS SPECIALLY PREPARED STADIUM, FOR THREE DAYS...

THE DORM THAT EARNS THE MOST TOTAL POINTS IS THE VICTOR.

...THE TWO DORMS WILL BATTLE IT OUT, BY GRADE YEAR.

WHERE YOU DANCE WITH A GUY AND THEN YOU'LL BE A COUPLE, RIGHT? MAYBE I'LL GO FOR IT, TOO!

THE MVP EFFECT IS BETTER THAN ANY AWARD!

...WILL BE GIVEN AN AWARD! GOOD LUCK TO ALL OF YOU!!

AND AN MVP SELECTED FROM THE WINNING DORM...

O-ON SECOND THOUGHT, MAYBE NOT...

...IS GONNA BE ME!! ...WILL BE ME, BRO!! ...WILL BE ME!! ...SHALL BE I!!

THE MVP...

RRMBL
RR

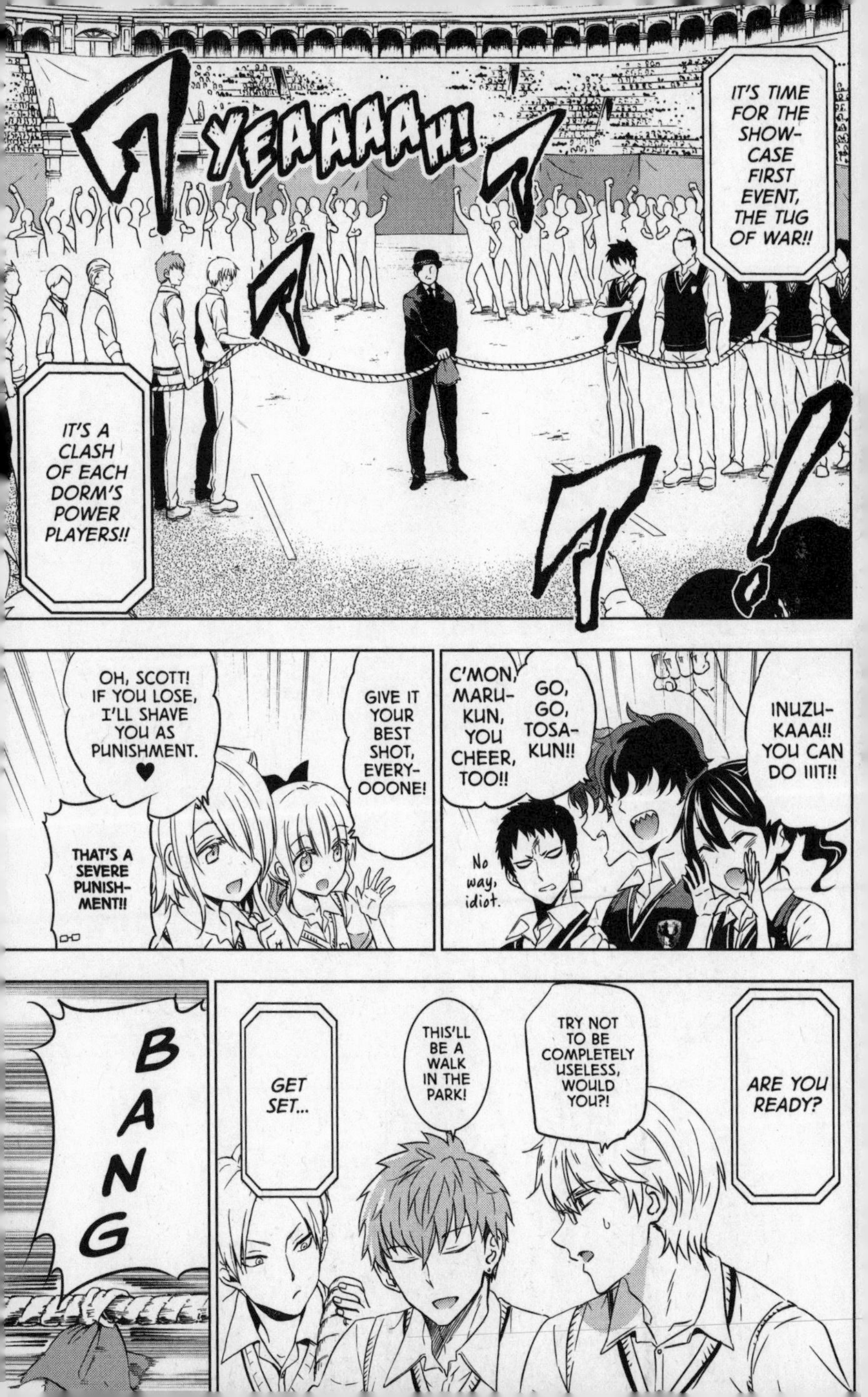
IT'S TIME FOR THE SHOWCASE FIRST EVENT, THE TUG OF WAR!!
YEAAAAH!
IT'S A CLASH OF EACH DORM'S POWER PLAYERS!!
!
INUZUKAAA!! YOU CAN DO IIIT!!
GO, GO, TOSA-KUN!!
C'MON, MARU-KUN, YOU CHEER, TOO!!
No way, idiot.
GIVE IT YOUR BEST SHOT, EVERYOOONE!
OH, SCOTT! IF YOU LOSE, I'LL SHAVE YOU AS PUNISHMENT. ♥
THAT'S A SEVERE PUNISHMENT!!
ARE YOU READY?
TRY NOT TO BE COMPLETELY USELESS, WOULD YOU?!
THIS'LL BE A WALK IN THE PARK!
GET SET...
BANG

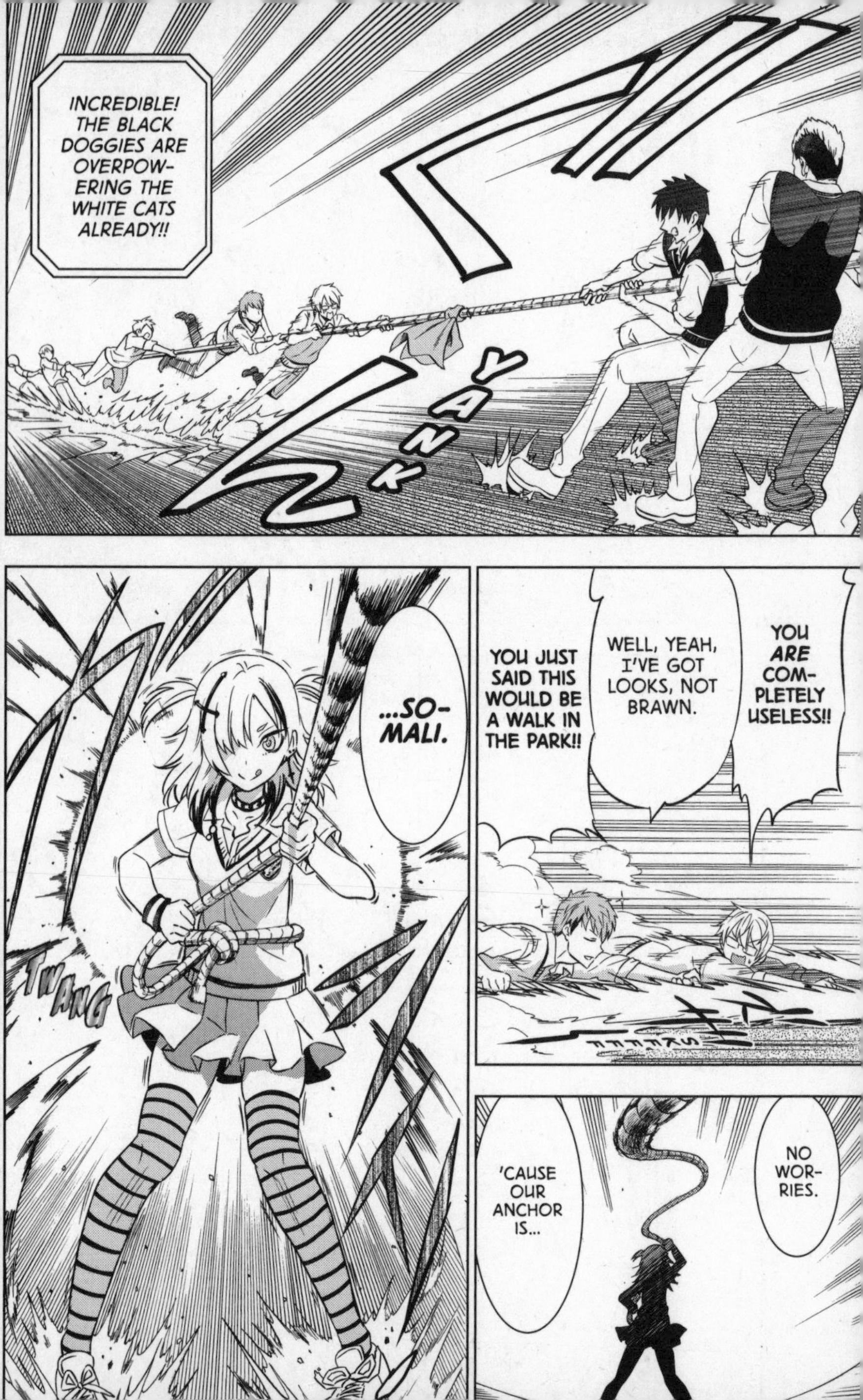
INCREDIBLE! THE BLACK DOGGIES ARE OVERPOW-ERING THE WHITE CATS ALREADY!!
YANK
YOU *ARE* COM-PLETELY USELESS!!
WELL, YEAH, I'VE GOT LOOKS, NOT BRAWN.
YOU JUST SAID THIS WOULD BE A WALK IN THE PARK!!
NO WOR-RIES.
'CAUSE OUR ANCHOR IS...
...SO-MALI.
TWANG

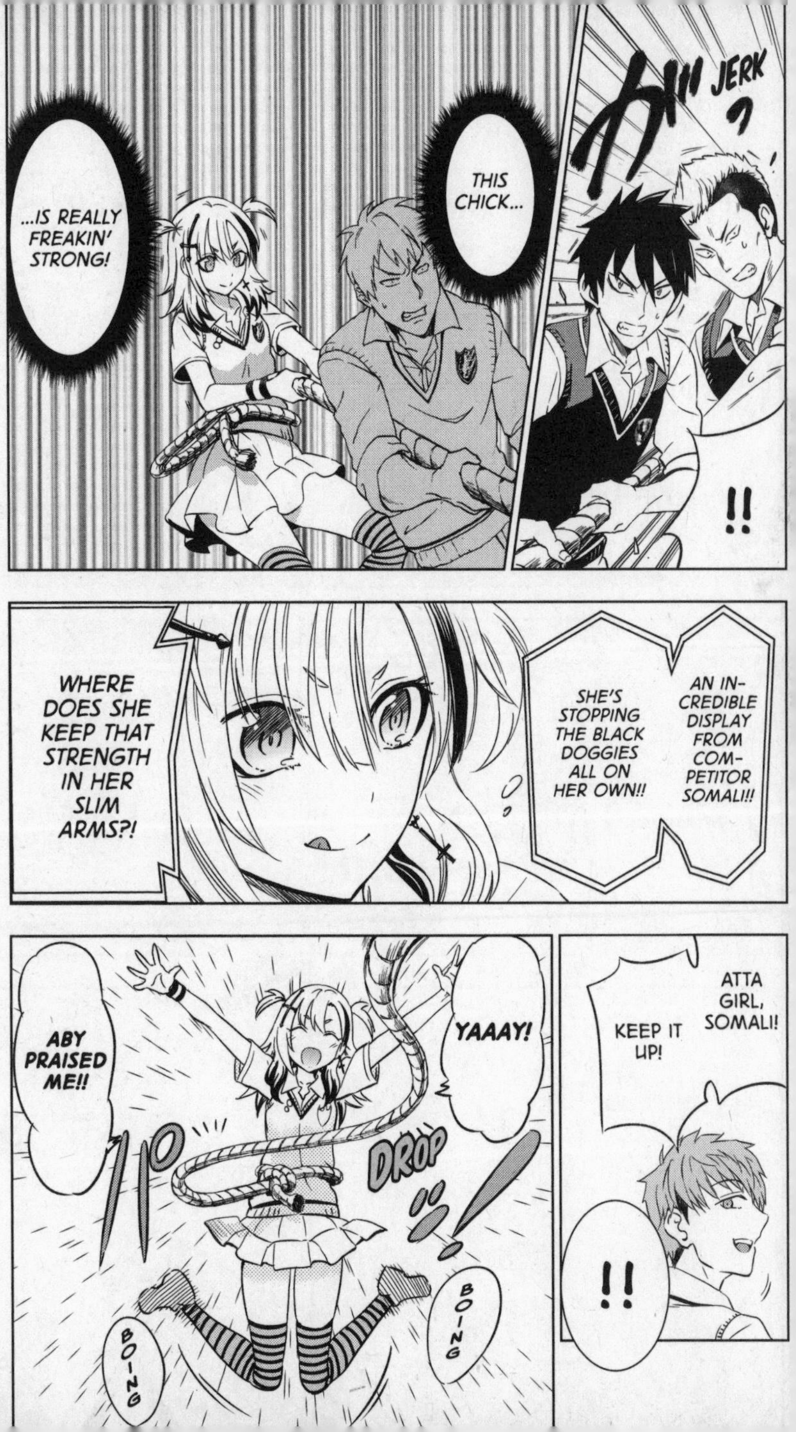
JERK
!!
THIS CHICK...
...IS REALLY FREAKIN' STRONG!
AN IN-CREDIBLE DISPLAY FROM COM-PETITOR SOMALI!!!
SHE'S STOPPING THE BLACK DOGGIES ALL ON HER OWN!!
WHERE DOES SHE KEEP THAT STRENGTH IN HER SLIM ARMS?!
ATTA GIRL, SOMALI!
KEEP IT UP!
!!
YAAAY!
ABY PRAISED ME!!
DROP
BOING
BOING

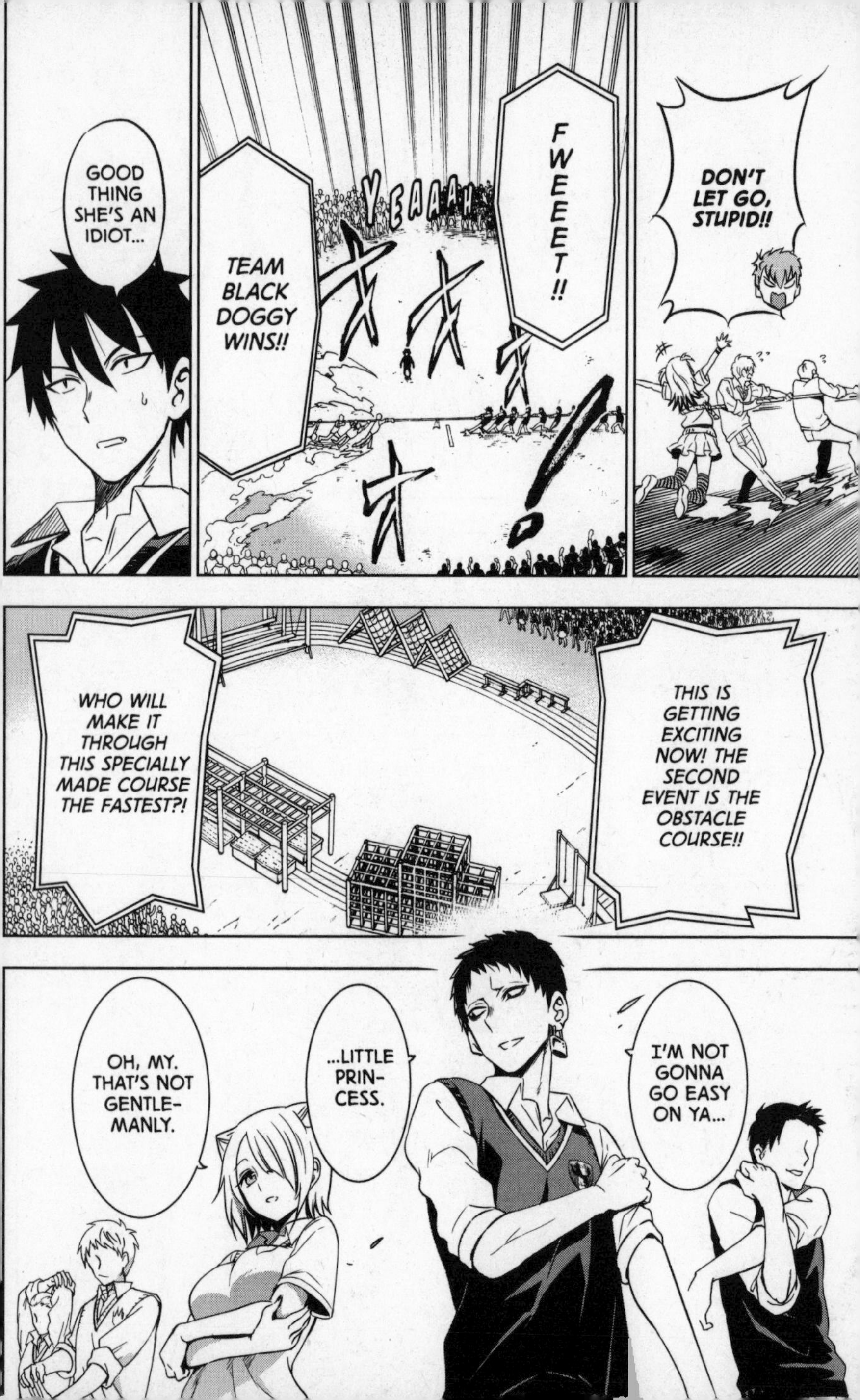
DON'T LET GO, STUPID!!
FWEEET!!
YEAAAH
TEAM BLACK DOGGY WINS!!
GOOD THING SHE'S AN IDIOT...
THIS IS GETTING EXCITING NOW! THE SECOND EVENT IS THE OBSTACLE COURSE!!
WHO WILL MAKE IT THROUGH THIS SPECIALLY MADE COURSE THE FASTEST?!
I'M NOT GONNA GO EASY ON YA...
...LITTLE PRIN-CESS.
OH, MY. THAT'S NOT GENTLE-MANLY.

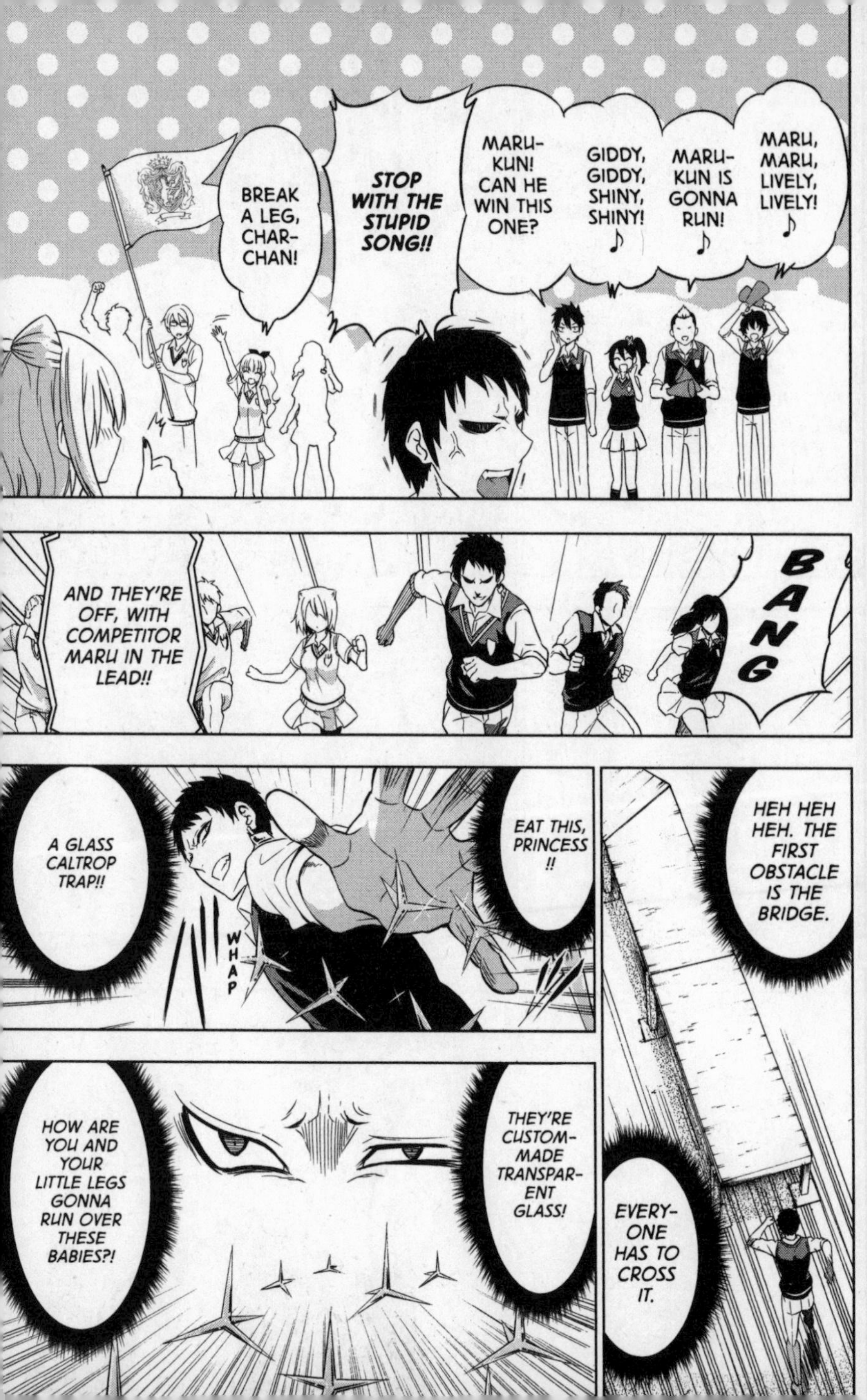
MARU, MARU, LIVELY, LIVELY! ♪
MARU-KUN IS GONNA RUN! ♪
GIDDY, GIDDY, SHINY, SHINY! ♪
MARU-KUN! CAN HE WIN THIS ONE?
STOP WITH THE STUPID SONG!!
BREAK A LEG, CHAR-CHAN!
BANG
AND THEY'RE OFF, WITH COMPETITOR MARU IN THE LEAD!!
HEH HEH HEH. THE FIRST OBSTACLE IS THE BRIDGE.
EVERYONE HAS TO CROSS IT.
EAT THIS, PRINCESS!!
A GLASS CALTROP TRAP!!
WHAP
THEY'RE CUSTOM-MADE TRANSPARENT GLASS!
HOW ARE YOU AND YOUR LITTLE LEGS GONNA RUN OVER THESE BABIES?!

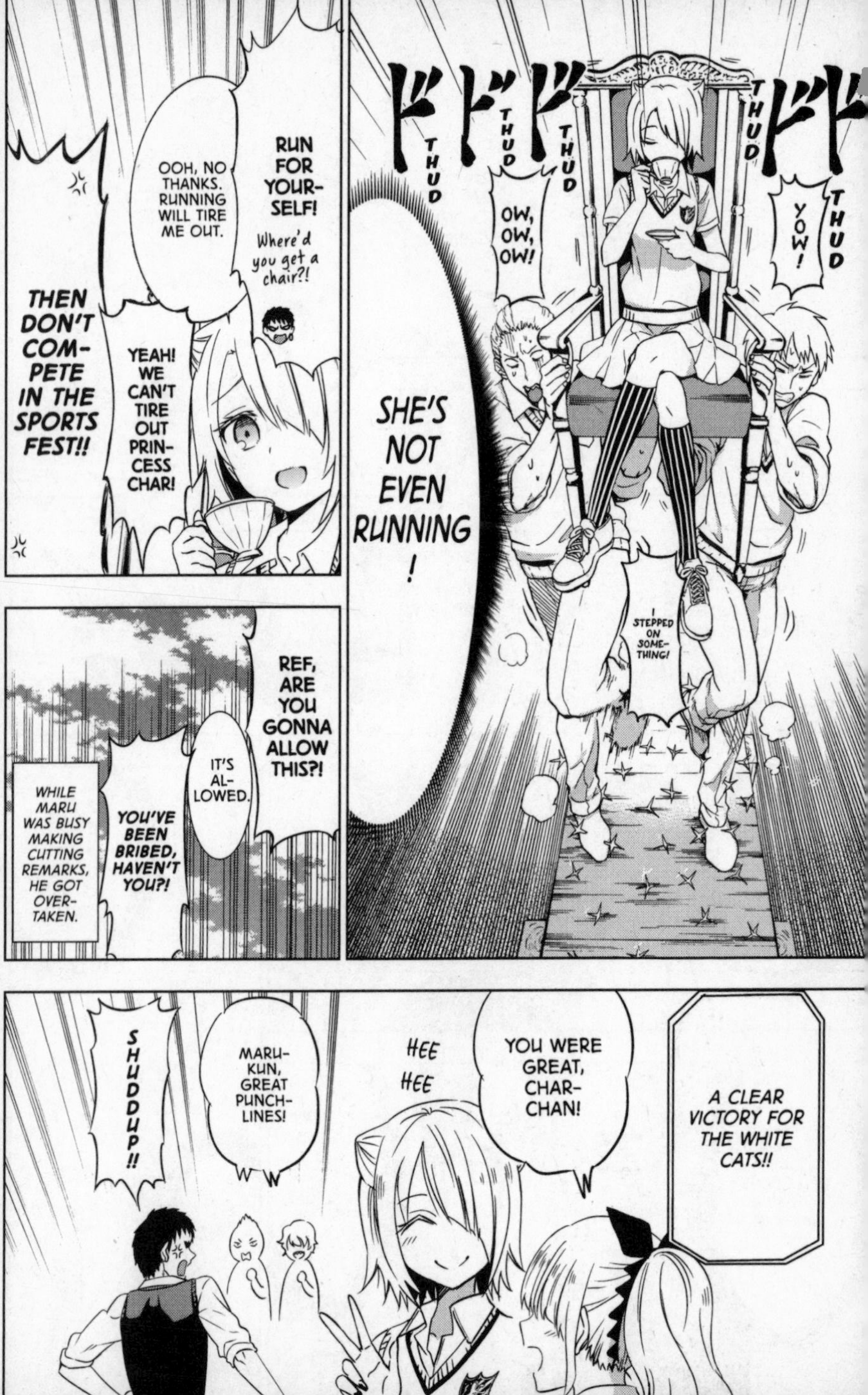
ドド
THUD
YOW!
THUD
ドドド
THUD
THUD
THUD
OW, OW, OW!
SHE'S NOT EVEN RUNNING!
I STEPPED ON SOMETHING!
RUN FOR YOURSELF!
Where'd you get a chair?!
OOH, NO THANKS. RUNNING WILL TIRE ME OUT.
YEAH! WE CAN'T TIRE OUT PRINCESS CHAR!
THEN DON'T COMPETE IN THE SPORTS FEST!!
REF, ARE YOU GONNA ALLOW THIS?!
IT'S AL-LOWED.
YOU'VE BEEN BRIBED, HAVEN'T YOU?!
WHILE MARU WAS BUSY MAKING CUTTING REMARKS, HE GOT OVER-TAKEN.
A CLEAR VICTORY FOR THE WHITE CATS!!
YOU WERE GREAT, CHAR-CHAN!
HEE HEE
MARU-KUN, GREAT PUNCH-LINES!
SHUDDUP!!

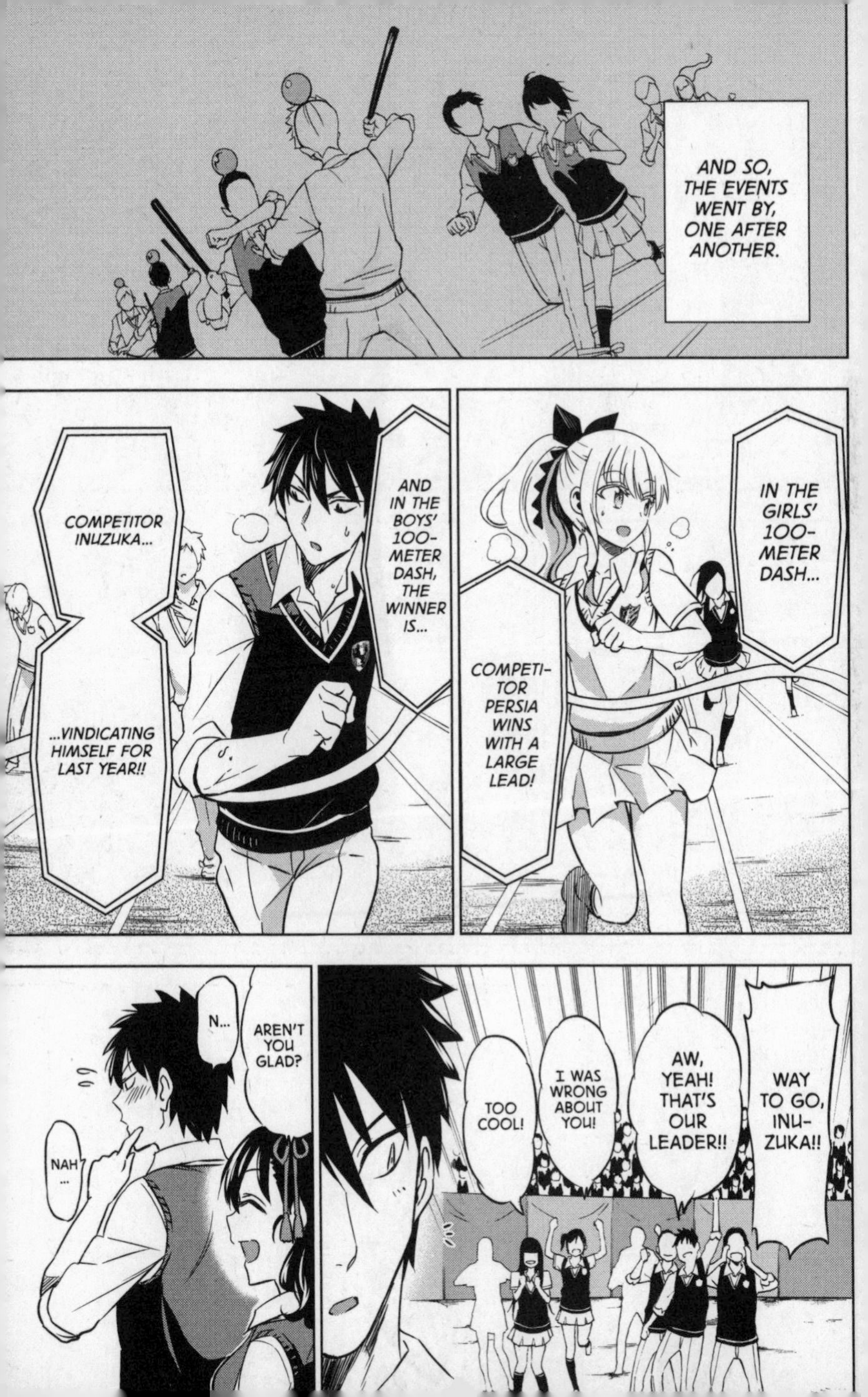

AND SO, THE EVENTS WENT BY, ONE AFTER ANOTHER.
IN THE GIRLS' 100-METER DASH...
COMPETITOR PERSIA WINS WITH A LARGE LEAD!
AND IN THE BOYS' 100-METER DASH, THE WINNER IS...
COMPETITOR INUZUKA...
...VINDICATING HIMSELF FOR LAST YEAR!!
WAY TO GO, INUZUKA!!
AW, YEAH! THAT'S OUR LEADER!!
I WAS WRONG ABOUT YOU!
TOO COOL!
...
AREN'T YOU GLAD?
N...
NAH...

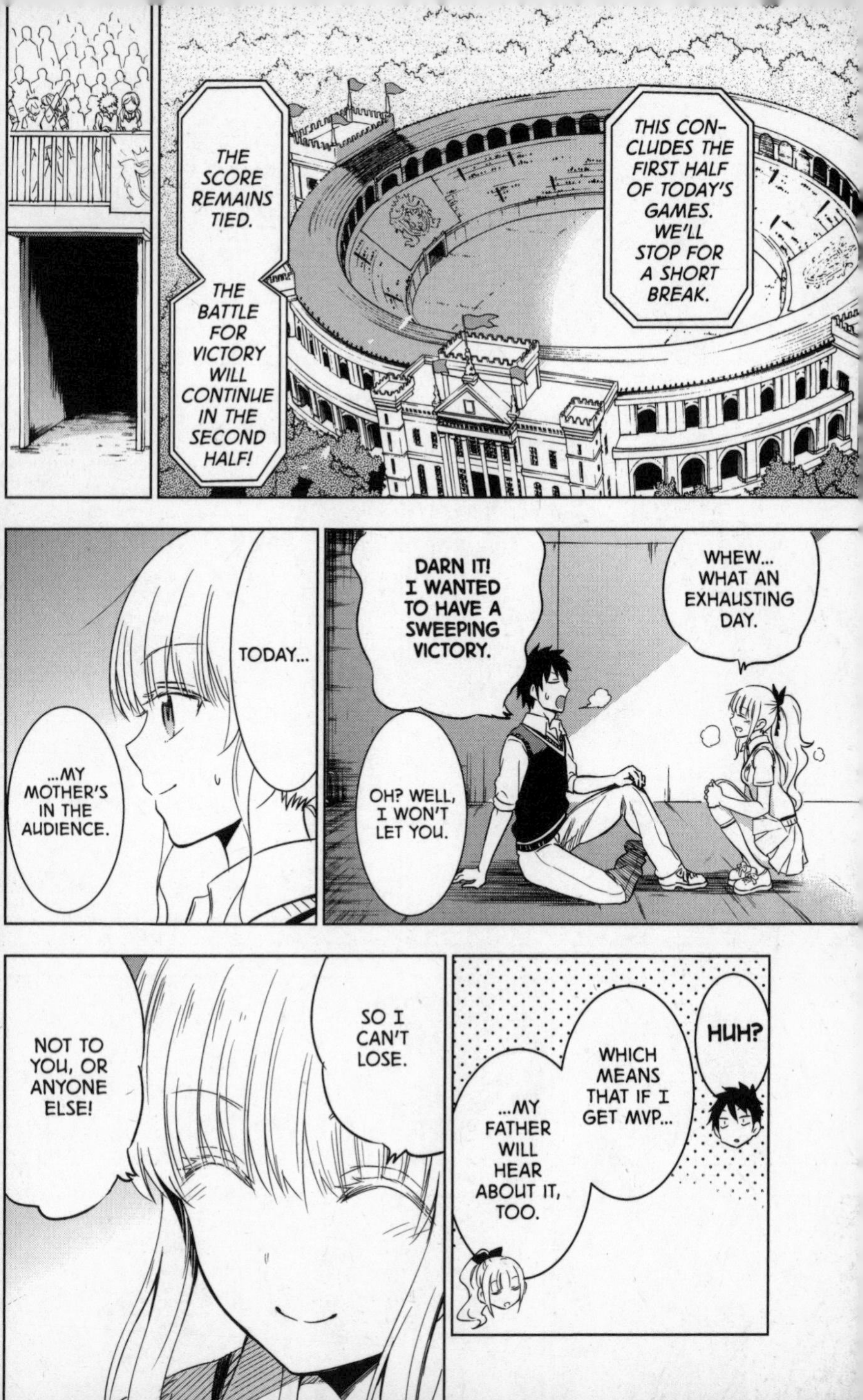
THIS CON-CLUDES THE FIRST HALF OF TODAY'S GAMES. WE'LL STOP FOR A SHORT BREAK.
THE SCORE REMAINS TIED.
THE BATTLE FOR VICTORY WILL CONTINUE IN THE SECOND HALF!
WHEW... WHAT AN EXHAUSTING DAY.
DARN IT! I WANTED TO HAVE A SWEEPING VICTORY.
OH? WELL, I WON'T LET YOU.
TODAY...
...MY MOTHER'S IN THE AUDIENCE.
HUH?
WHICH MEANS THAT IF I GET MVP...
...MY FATHER WILL HEAR ABOUT IT, TOO.
SO I CAN'T LOSE.
NOT TO YOU, OR ANYONE ELSE!

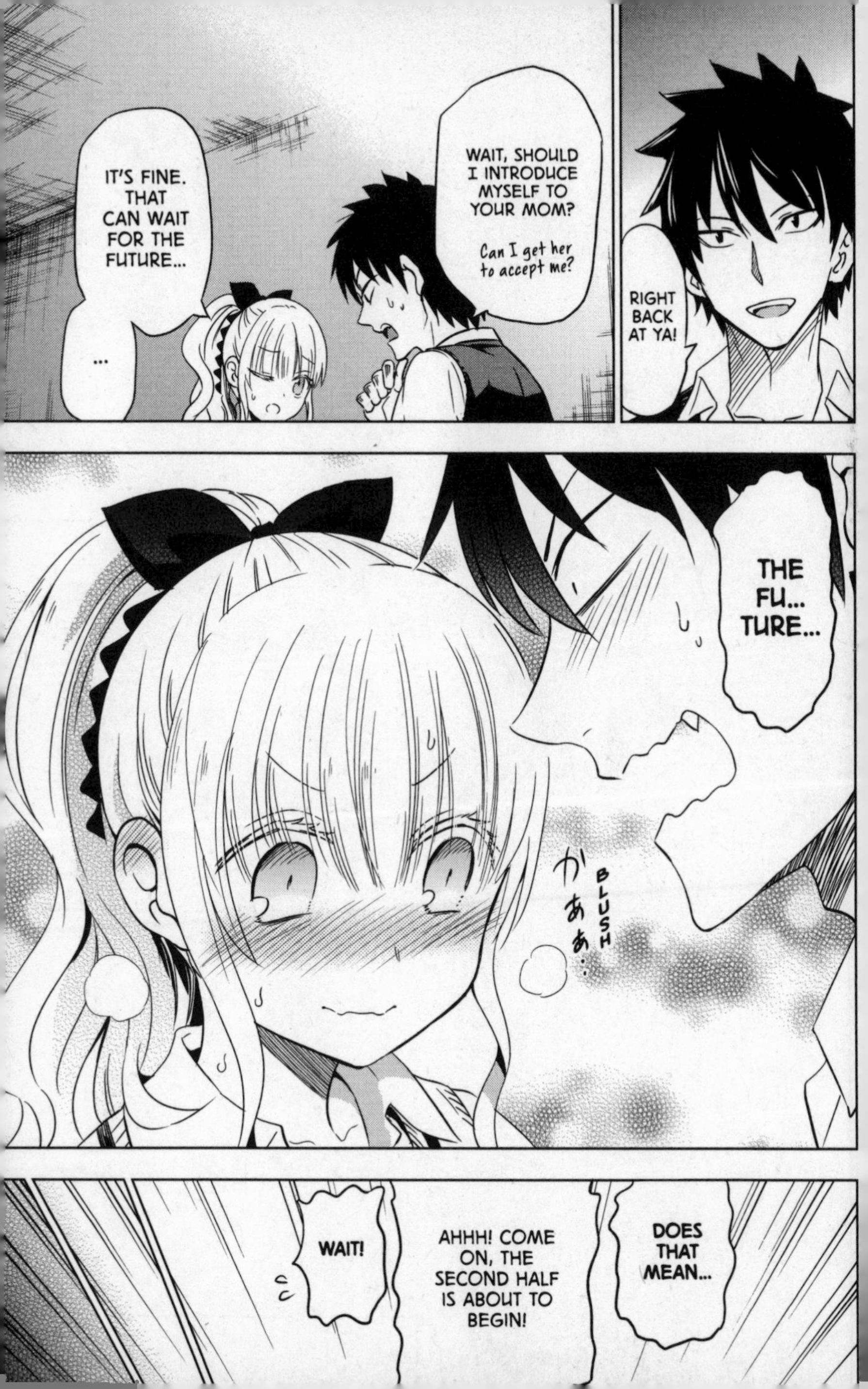
RIGHT BACK AT YA!
WAIT, SHOULD I INTRODUCE MYSELF TO YOUR MOM?
Can I get her to accept me?
IT'S FINE. THAT CAN WAIT FOR THE FUTURE...
...
THE FU... TURE...
かあぁ…
BLUSH
DOES THAT MEAN...
AHHH! COME ON, THE SECOND HALF IS ABOUT TO BEGIN!
WAIT!

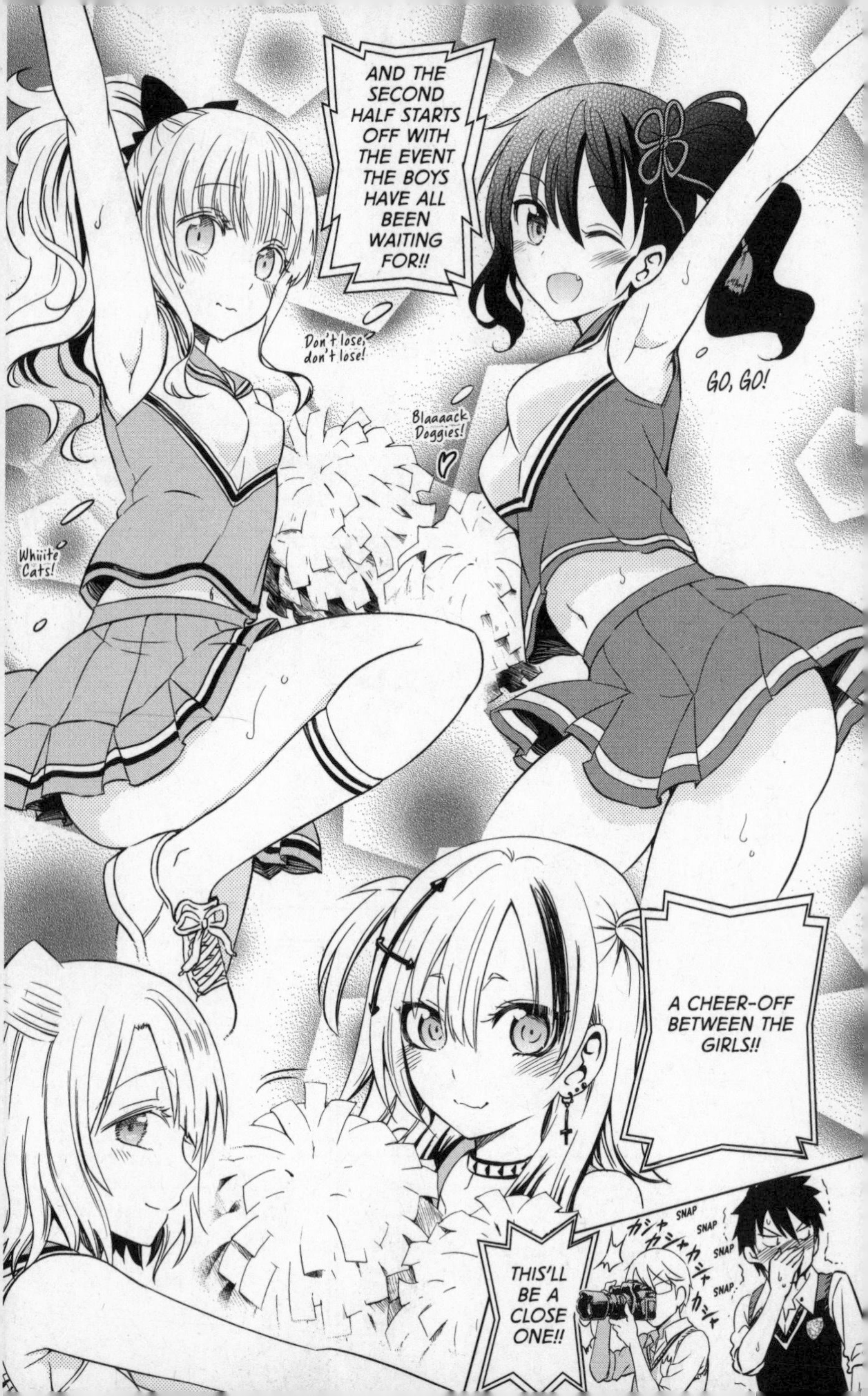
AND THE SECOND HALF STARTS OFF WITH THE EVENT THE BOYS HAVE ALL BEEN WAITING FOR!!
GO, GO!
Blaaaack Doggies!
Don't lose, don't lose!
Whiiite Cats!
A CHEER-OFF BETWEEN THE GIRLS!!
SNAP SNAP SNAP SNAP
カシャ カシャ カシャ カシャ
THIS'LL BE A CLOSE ONE!!

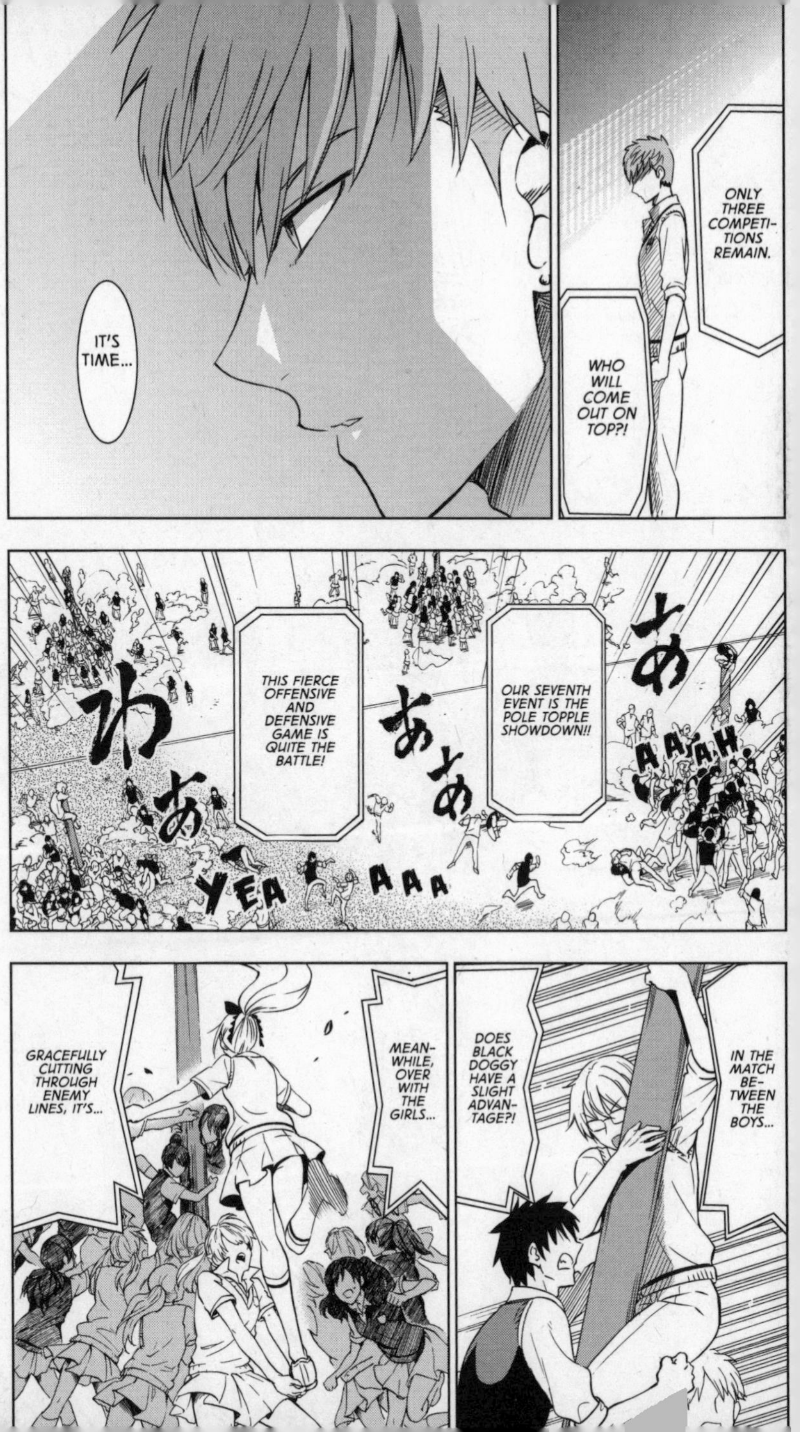
ONLY THREE COMPETITIONS REMAIN.
WHO WILL COME OUT ON TOP?!
IT'S TIME...
あ
AAAAH
OUR SEVENTH EVENT IS THE POLE TOPPLE SHOWDOWN!!
ああ
THIS FIERCE OFFENSIVE AND DEFENSIVE GAME IS QUITE THE BATTLE!
わあ
YEA AAA
IN THE MATCH BETWEEN THE BOYS...
DOES BLACK DOGGY HAVE A SLIGHT ADVANTAGE?!
MEANWHILE, OVER WITH THE GIRLS...
GRACEFULLY CUTTING THROUGH ENEMY LINES, IT'S...

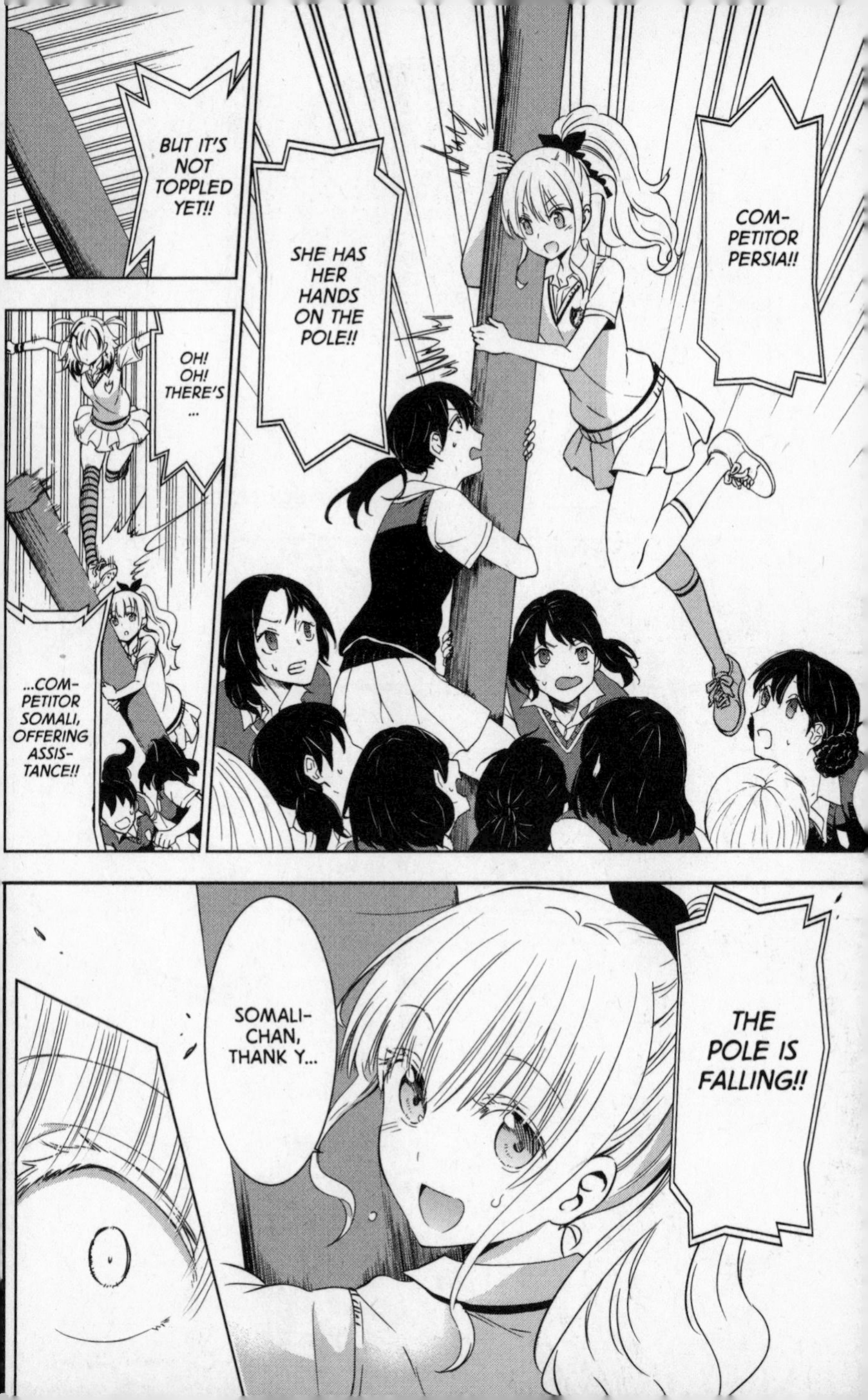
COMPETITOR PERSIA!!
SHE HAS HER HANDS ON THE POLE!!
BUT IT'S NOT TOPPLED YET!!
OH! OH! THERE'S ...
...COMPETITOR SOMALI, OFFERING ASSISTANCE!!
THE POLE IS FALLING!!
SOMALI-CHAN, THANK Y...

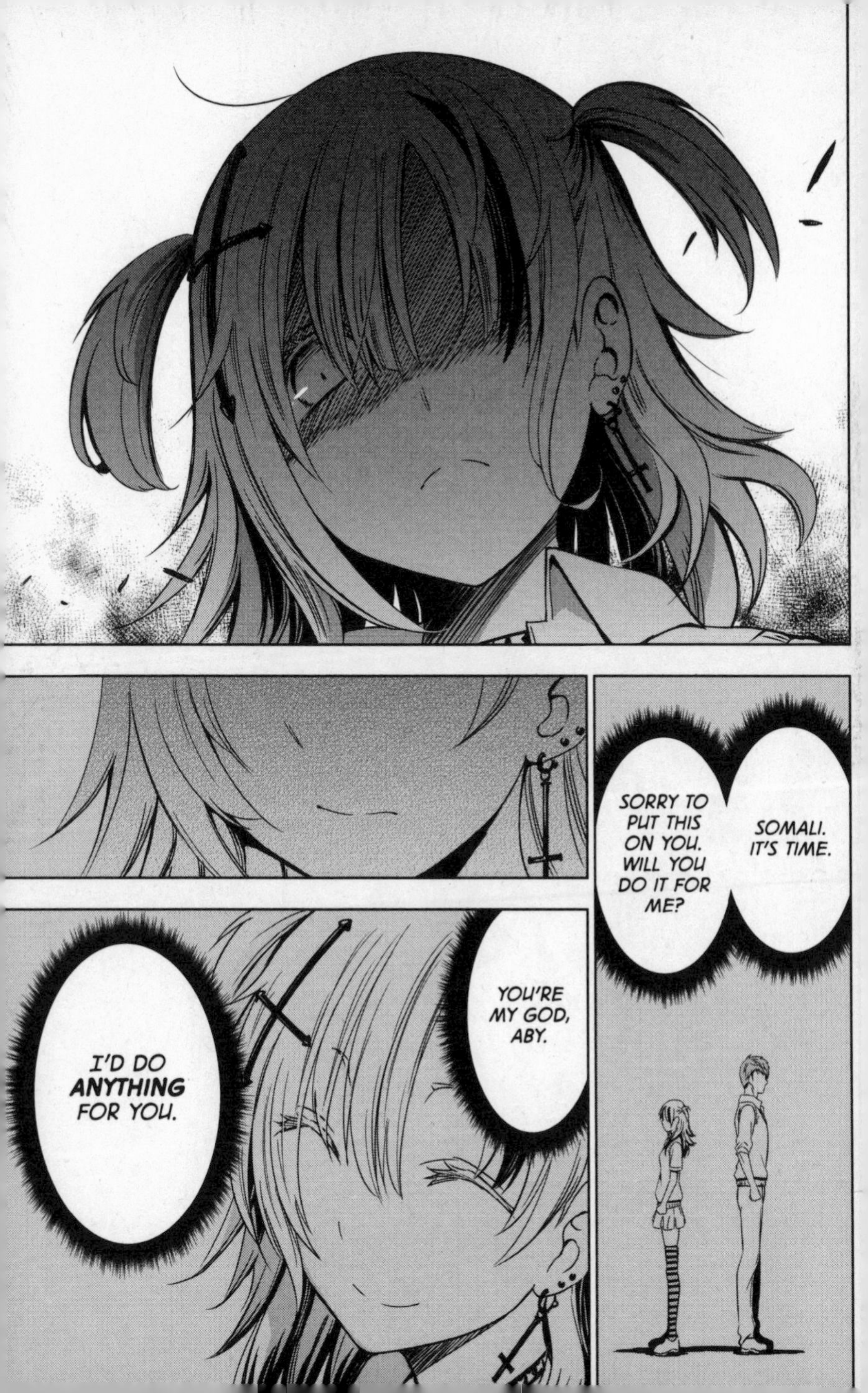
SOMALI. IT'S TIME.
SORRY TO PUT THIS ON YOU. WILL YOU DO IT FOR ME?
YOU'RE MY GOD, ABY.
I'D DO **ANYTHING** FOR YOU.

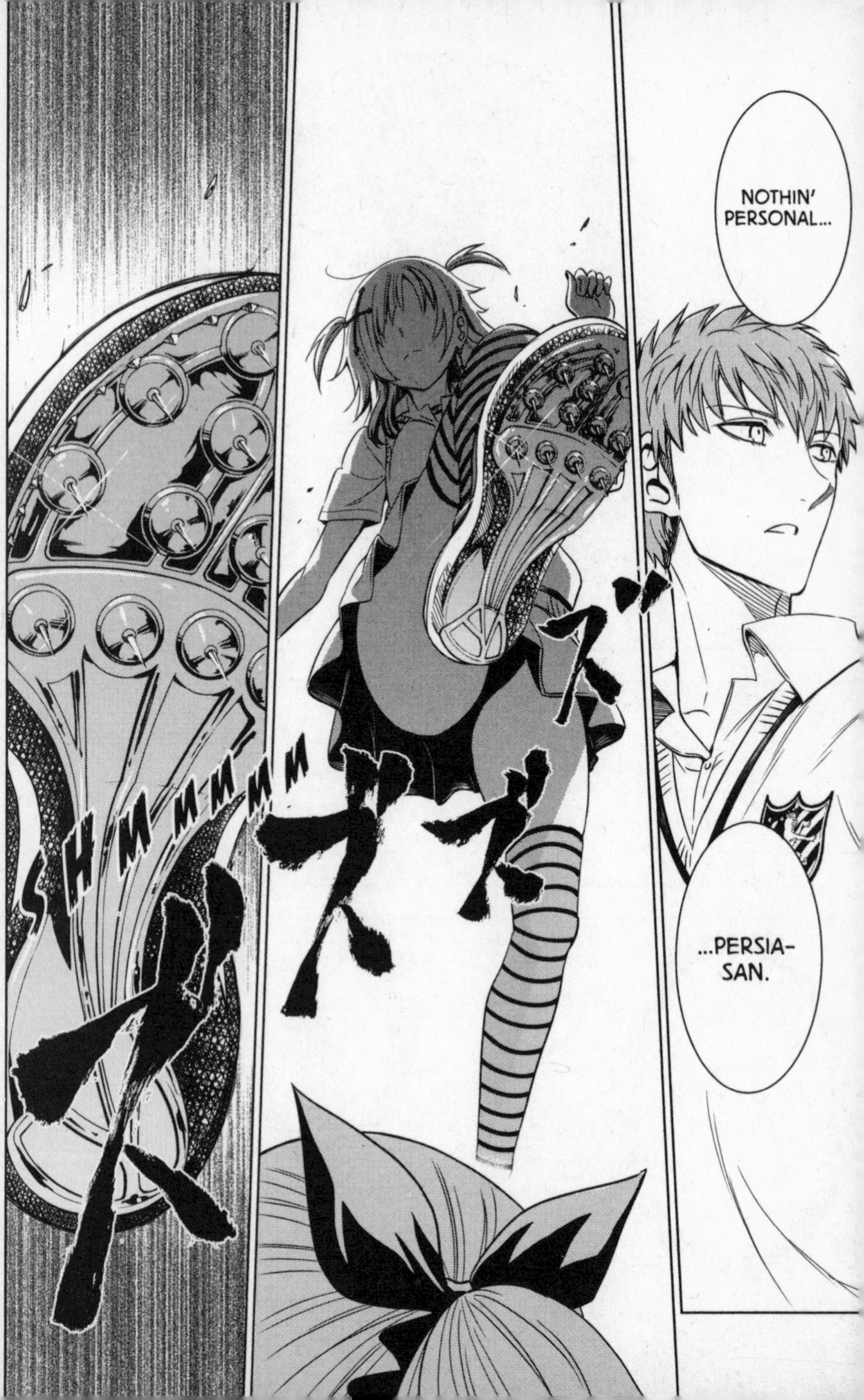
NOTHIN' PERSONAL...
...PERSIA-SAN.
SHMMMMMM

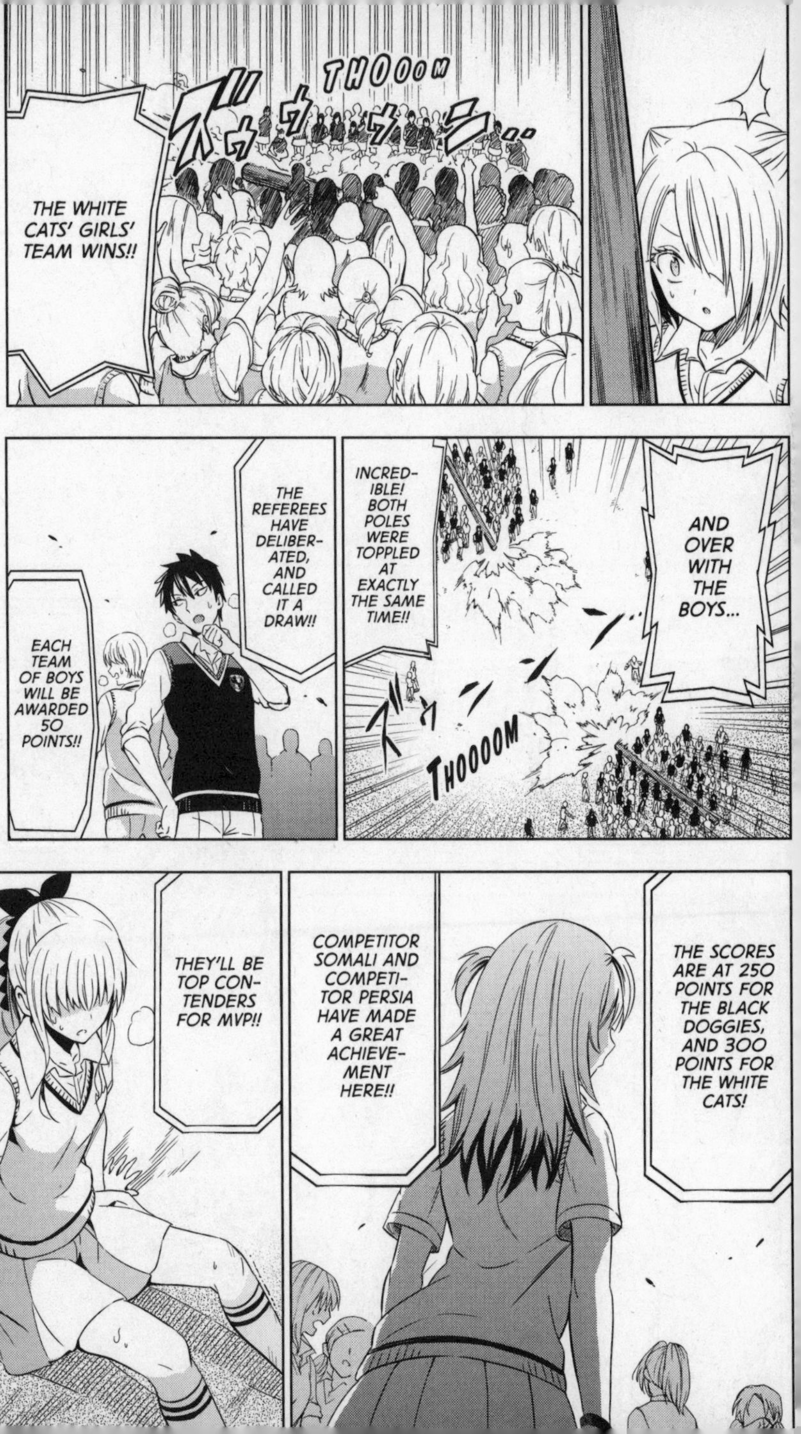
THOOOM
THE WHITE CATS' GIRLS' TEAM WINS!!
AND OVER WITH THE BOYS...
THOOOOM
INCREDIBLE! BOTH POLES WERE TOPPLED AT EXACTLY THE SAME TIME!!
THE REFEREES HAVE DELIBERATED, AND CALLED IT A DRAW!!
EACH TEAM OF BOYS WILL BE AWARDED 50 POINTS!!
THE SCORES ARE AT 250 POINTS FOR THE BLACK DOGGIES, AND 300 POINTS FOR THE WHITE CATS!
COMPETITOR SOMALI AND COMPETITOR PERSIA HAVE MADE A GREAT ACHIEVEMENT HERE!!
THEY'LL BE TOP CONTENDERS FOR MVP!!

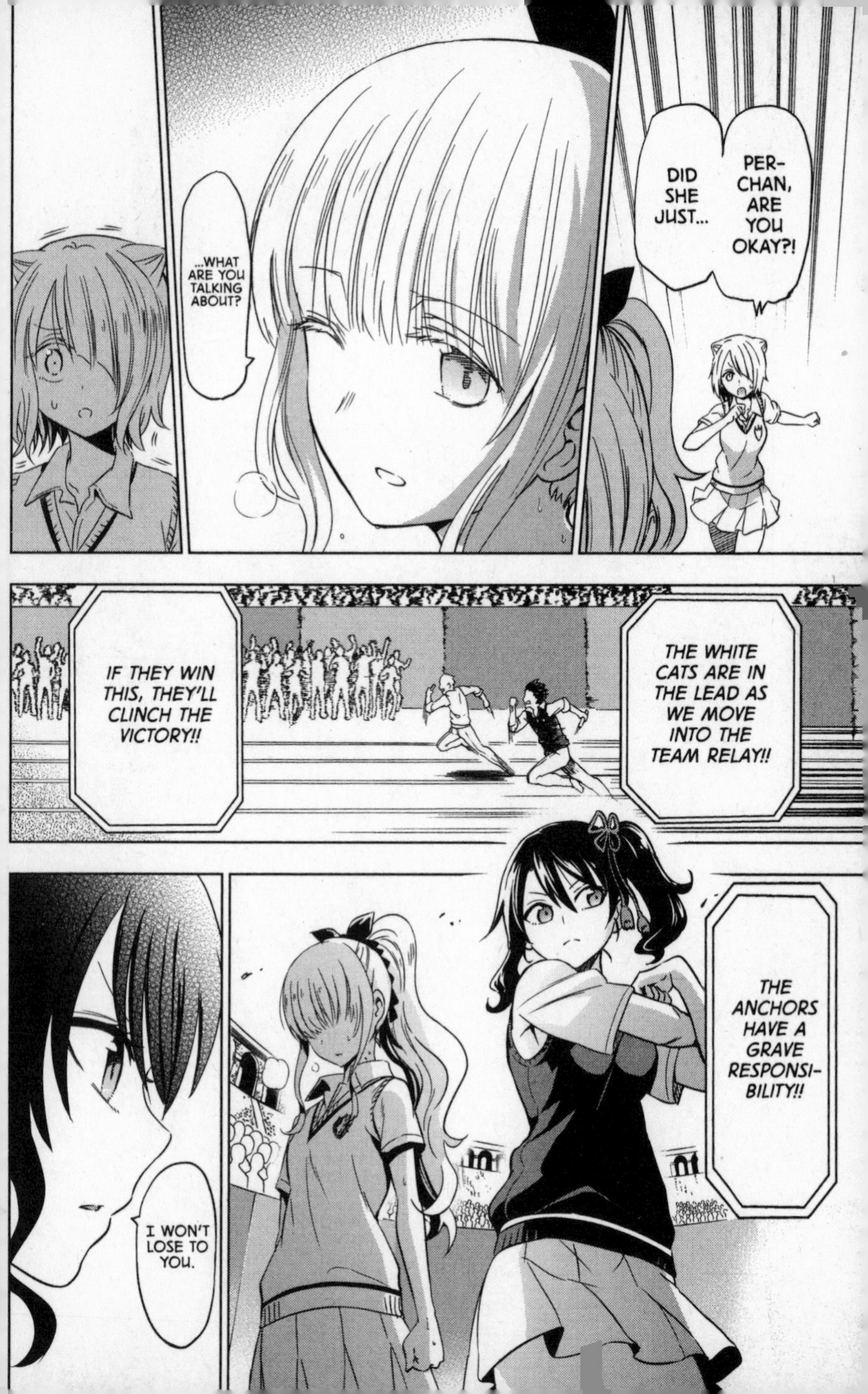
PER-CHAN, ARE YOU OKAY?!
DID SHE JUST...
...WHAT ARE YOU TALKING ABOUT?
THE WHITE CATS ARE IN THE LEAD AS WE MOVE INTO THE TEAM RELAY!!
IF THEY WIN THIS, THEY'LL CLINCH THE VICTORY!!
THE ANCHORS HAVE A GRAVE RESPONSIBILITY!!
I WON'T LOSE TO YOU.

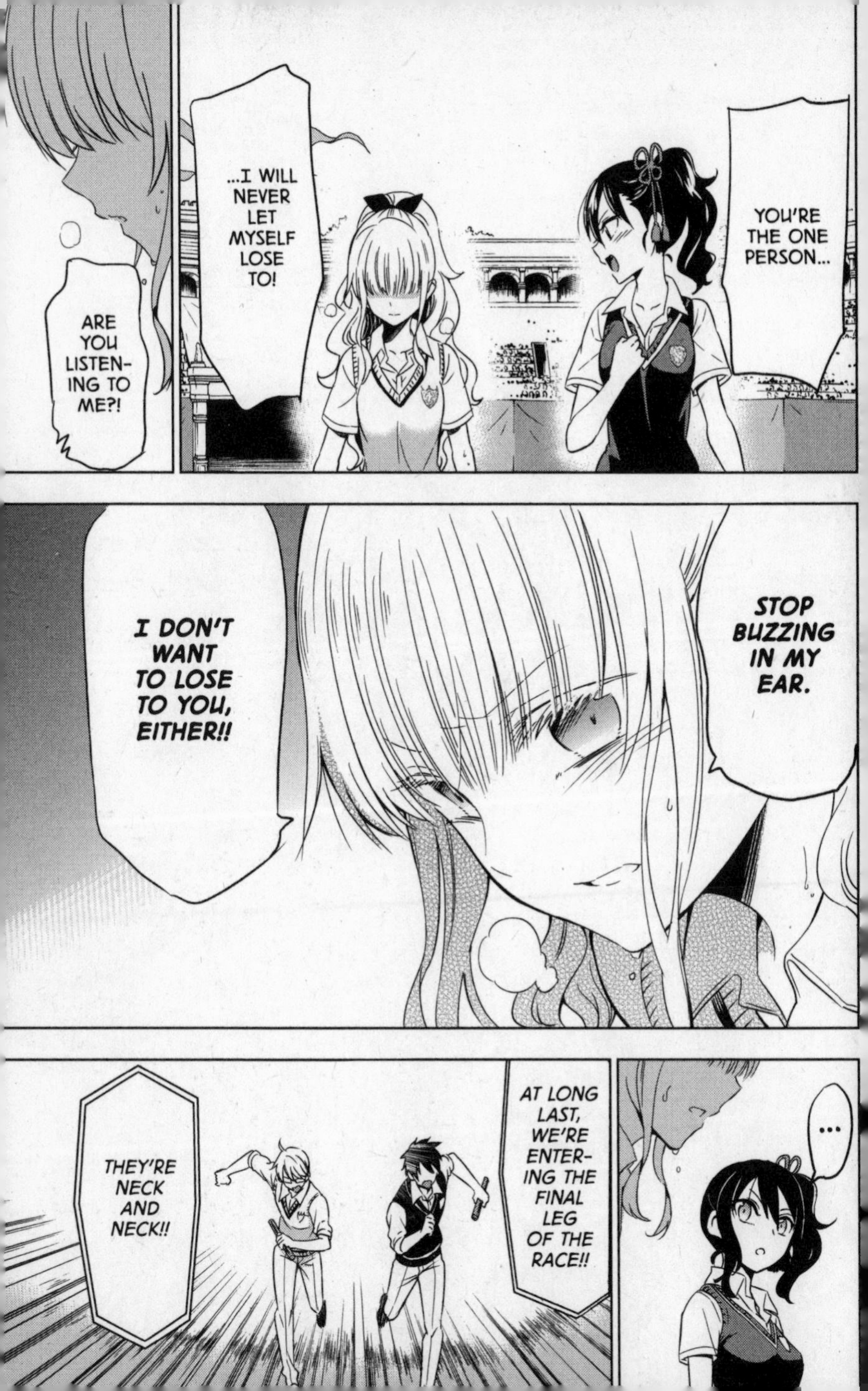
YOU'RE THE ONE PERSON...
...I WILL NEVER LET MYSELF LOSE TO!
ARE YOU LISTEN-ING TO ME?!
STOP BUZZING IN MY EAR.
I DON'T WANT TO LOSE TO YOU, EITHER!!
...
AT LONG LAST, WE'RE ENTER-ING THE FINAL LEG OF THE RACE!!
THEY'RE NECK AND NECK!!

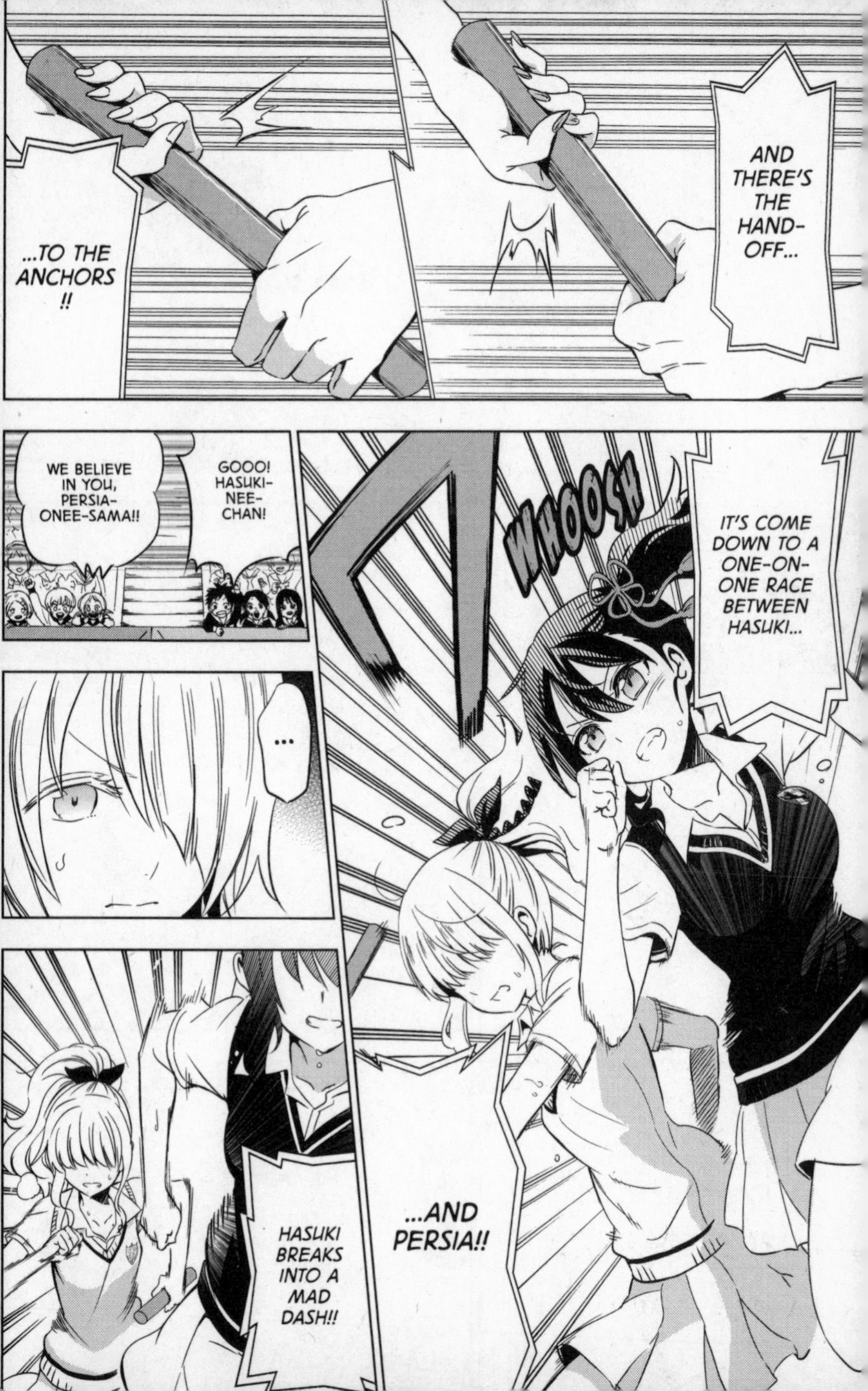
AND THERE'S THE HAND-OFF...
...TO THE ANCHORS !!
WHOOSH
IT'S COME DOWN TO A ONE-ON-ONE RACE BETWEEN HASUKI...
...AND PERSIA!!
GOOO! HASUKI-NEE-CHAN!
WE BELIEVE IN YOU, PERSIA-ONEE-SAMA!!
...
HASUKI BREAKS INTO A MAD DASH!!

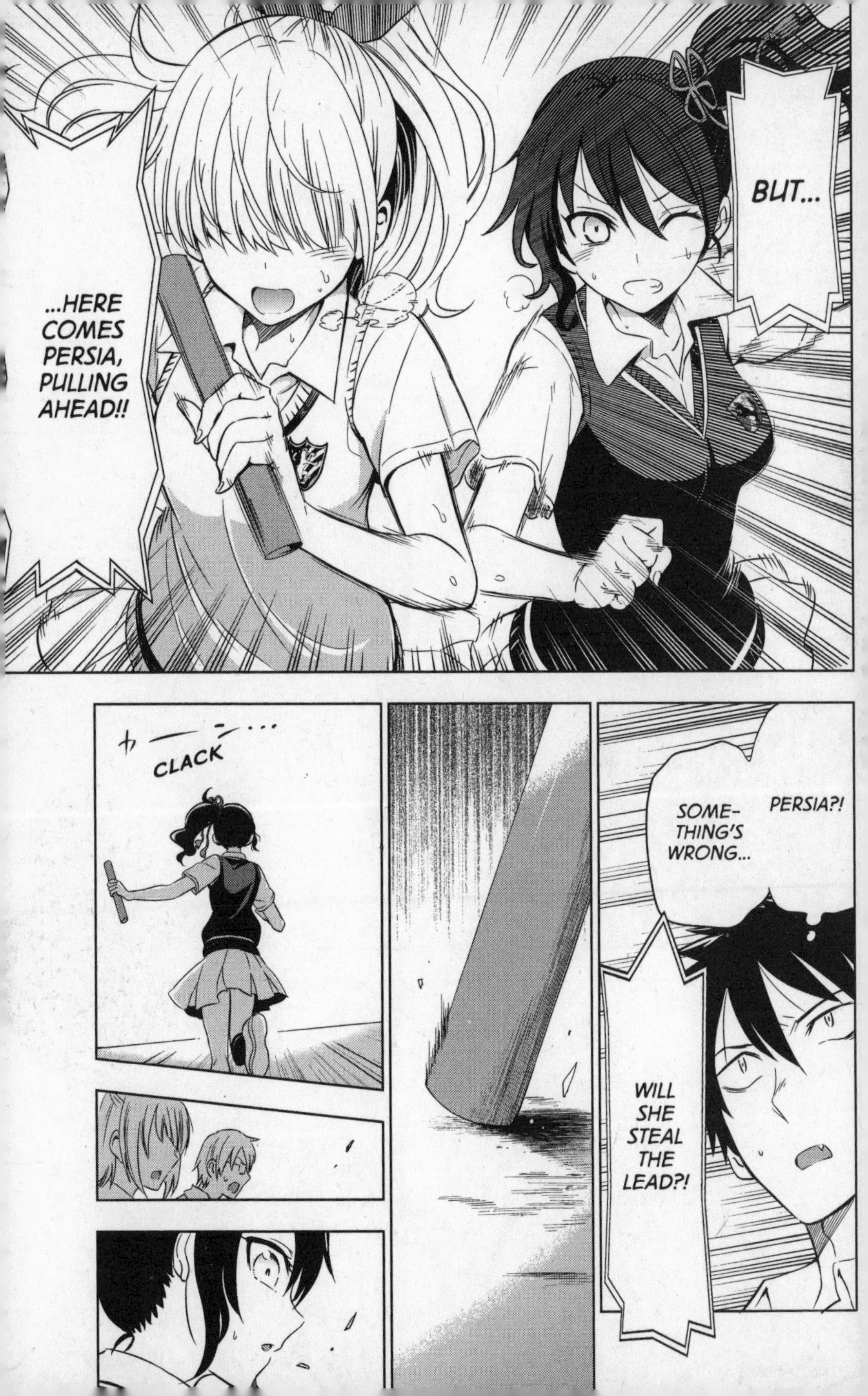
BUT...
...HERE COMES PERSIA, PULLING AHEAD!!
PERSIA?!
SOME-THING'S WRONG...
WILL SHE STEAL THE LEAD?!
CLACK

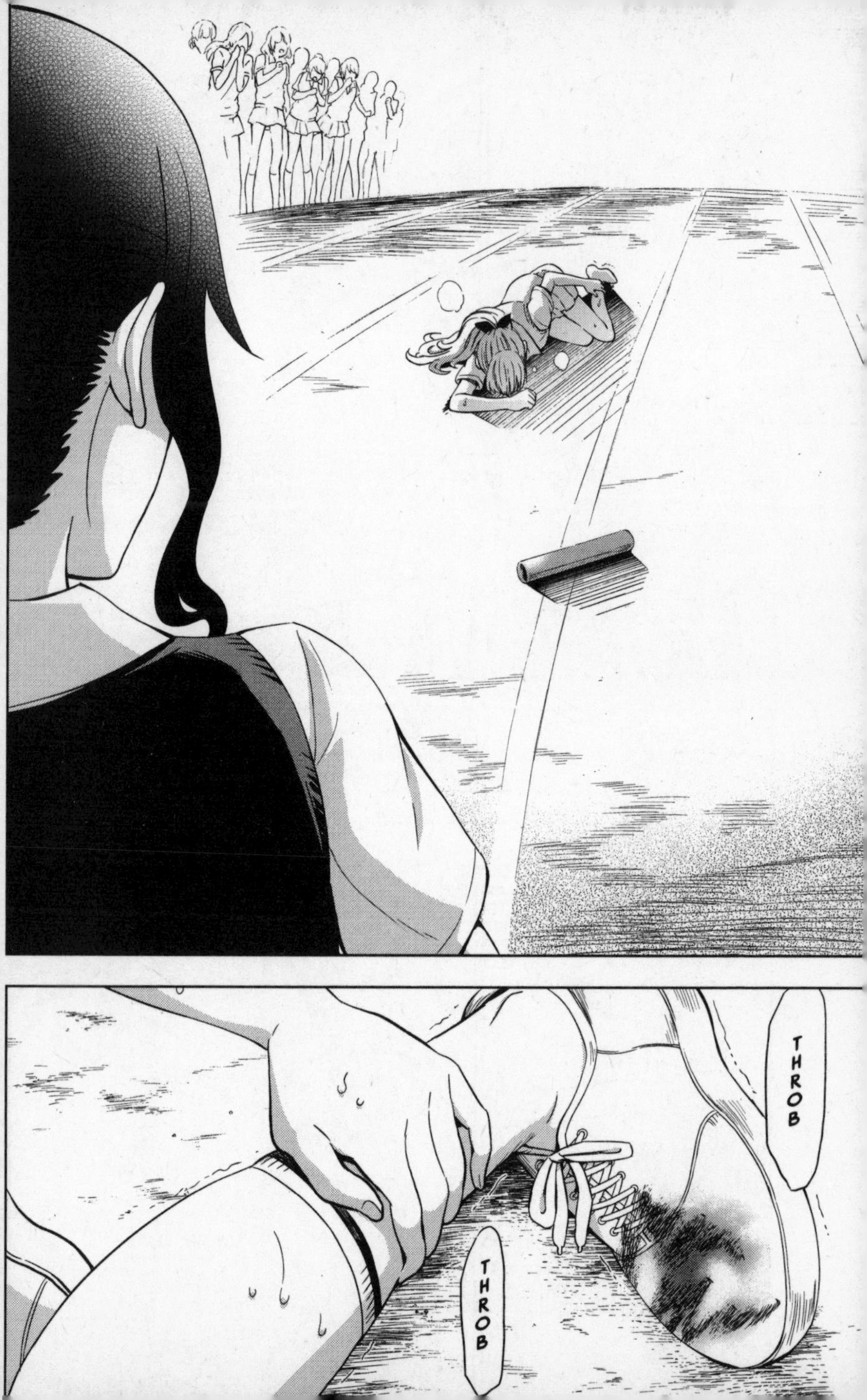
THROB
THROB

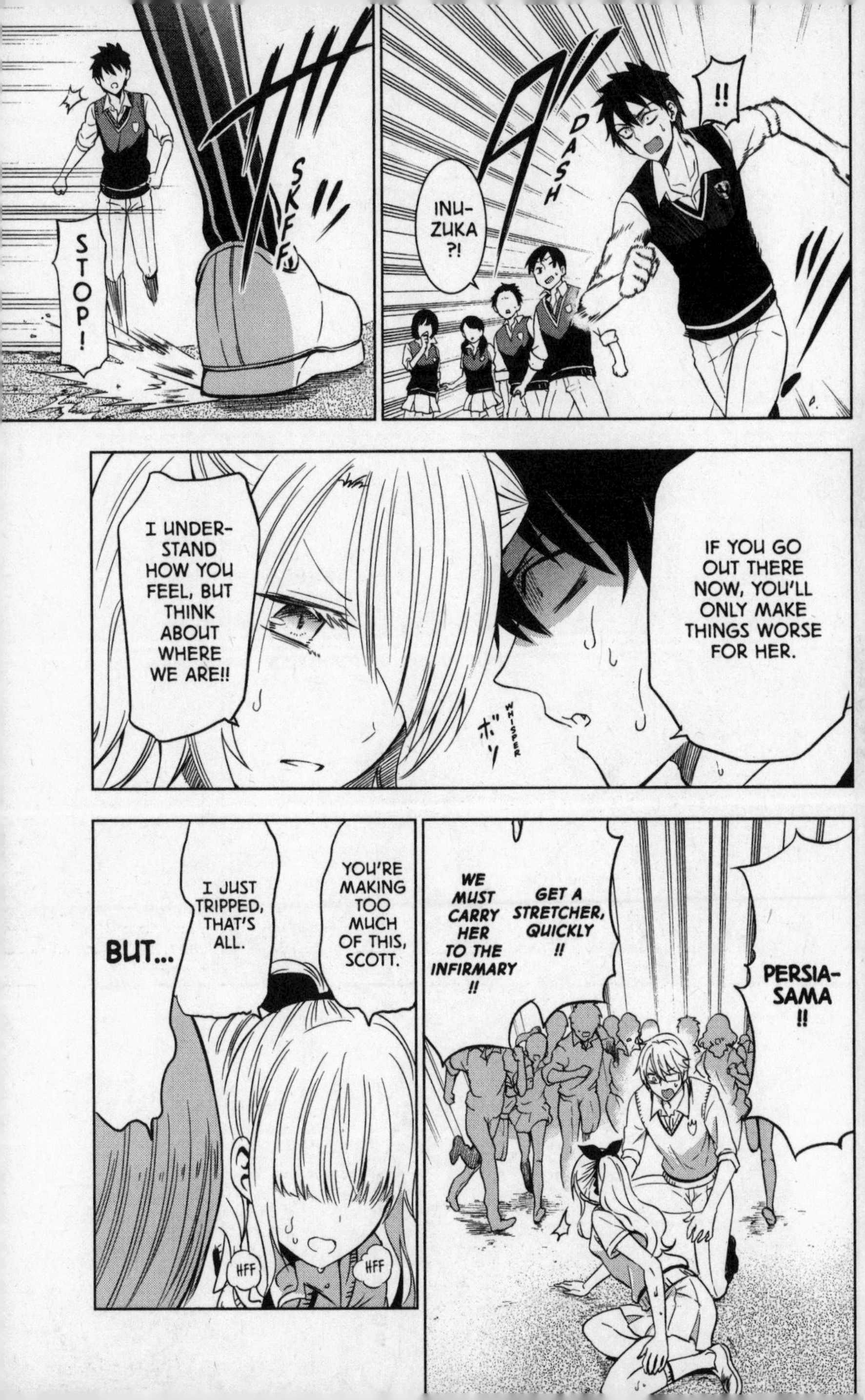
!!
DASH
INU-ZUKA ?!
SKFF
STOP!
IF YOU GO OUT THERE NOW, YOU'LL ONLY MAKE THINGS WORSE FOR HER.
WHISPER
I UNDER-STAND HOW YOU FEEL, BUT THINK ABOUT WHERE WE ARE!!
PERSIA-SAMA !!
GET A STRETCHER, QUICKLY !!
WE MUST CARRY HER TO THE INFIRMARY !!
YOU'RE MAKING TOO MUCH OF THIS, SCOTT.
I JUST TRIPPED, THAT'S ALL.
BUT...
HFF
HFF

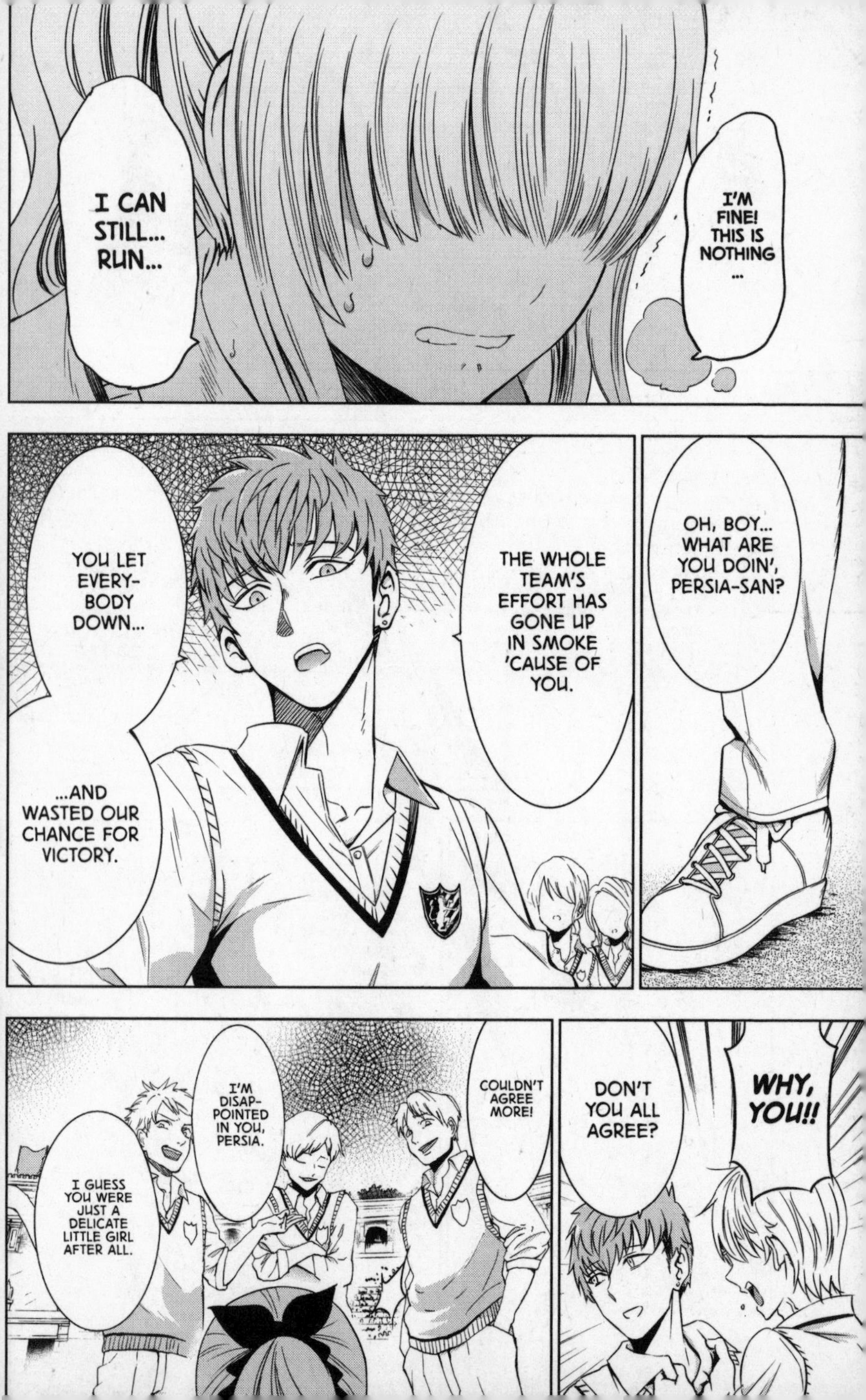
I'M FINE! THIS IS NOTHING ...
I CAN STILL... RUN...
OH, BOY... WHAT ARE YOU DOIN', PERSIA-SAN?
THE WHOLE TEAM'S EFFORT HAS GONE UP IN SMOKE 'CAUSE OF YOU.
YOU LET EVERY-BODY DOWN...
...AND WASTED OUR CHANCE FOR VICTORY.
WHY, YOU!!
DON'T YOU ALL AGREE?
COULDN'T AGREE MORE!
I'M DISAP-POINTED IN YOU, PERSIA.
I GUESS YOU WERE JUST A DELICATE LITTLE GIRL AFTER ALL.

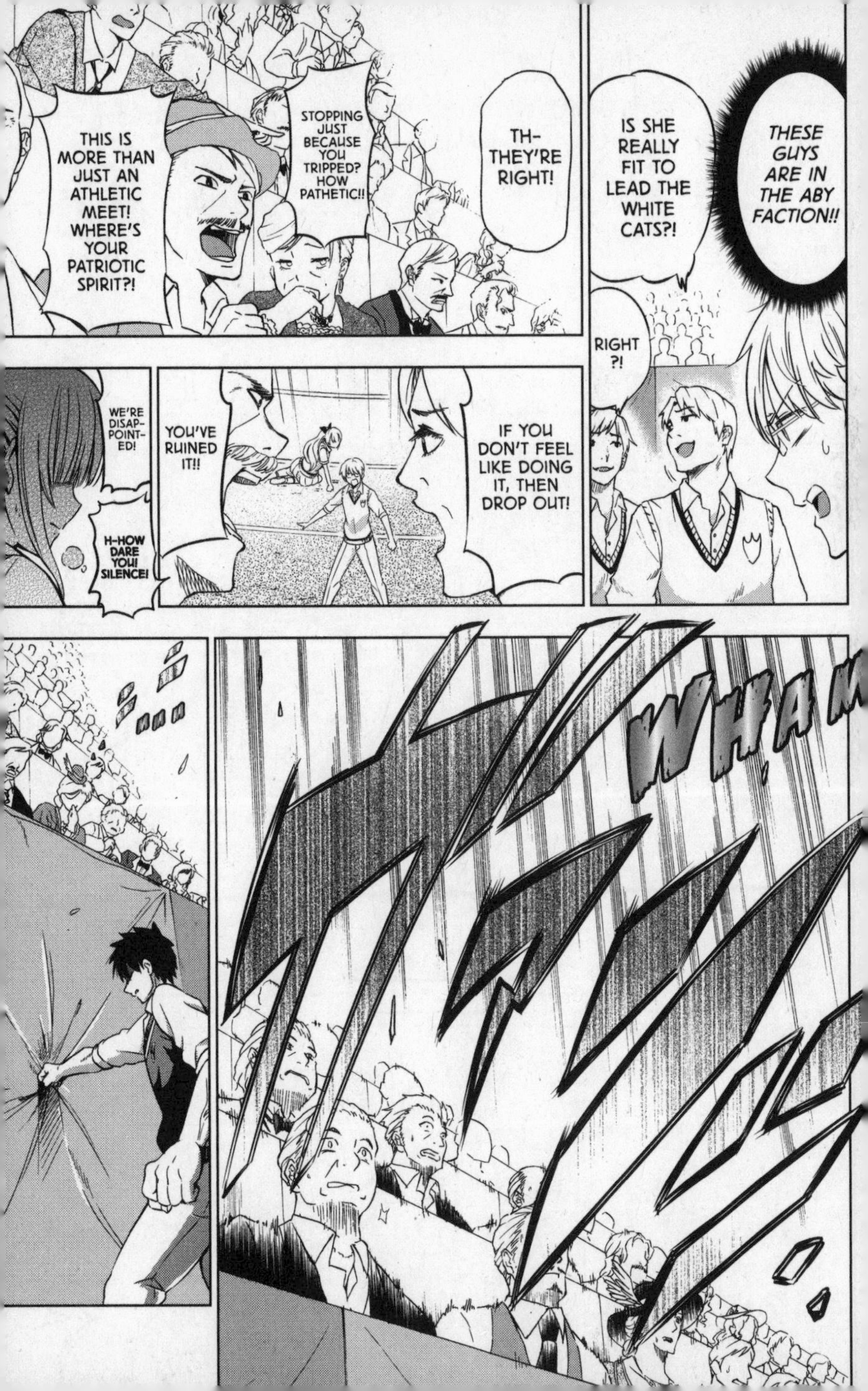
THESE GUYS ARE IN THE ABY FACTION!!
IS SHE REALLY FIT TO LEAD THE WHITE CATS?!
RIGHT?!
TH- THEY'RE RIGHT!
STOPPING JUST BECAUSE YOU TRIPPED? HOW PATHETIC!!
THIS IS MORE THAN JUST AN ATHLETIC MEET! WHERE'S YOUR PATRIOTIC SPIRIT?!
IF YOU DON'T FEEL LIKE DOING IT, THEN DROP OUT!
YOU'VE RUINED IT!!
WE'RE DISAPPOINTED!
H-HOW DARE YOU! SILENCE!
WHAM

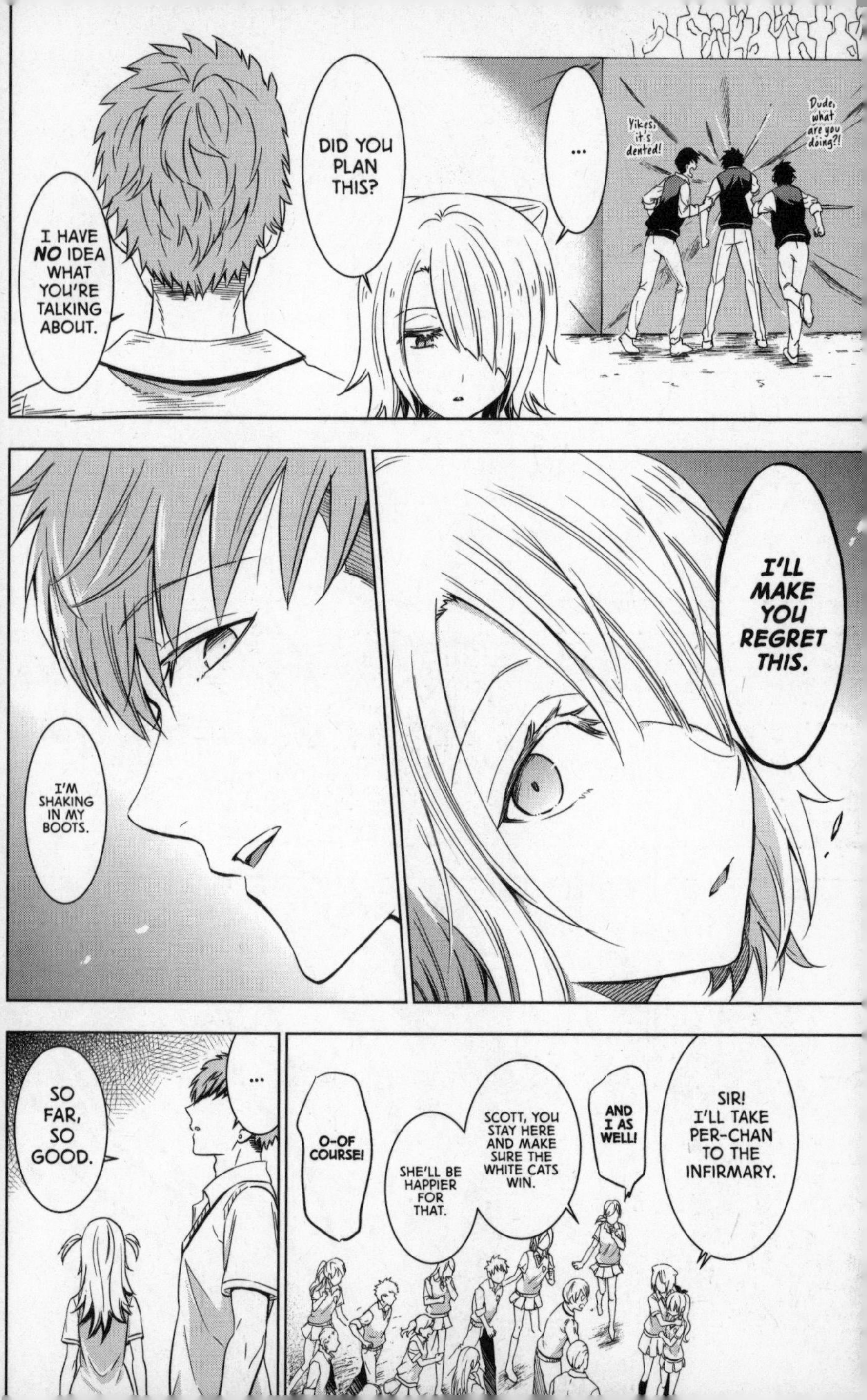
Dude, what are you doing?!
Yikes, it's dented!
...
DID YOU PLAN THIS?
I HAVE NO IDEA WHAT YOU'RE TALKING ABOUT.
I'LL MAKE YOU REGRET THIS.
I'M SHAKING IN MY BOOTS.
SIR! I'LL TAKE PER-CHAN TO THE INFIRMARY.
AND I AS WELL!
SCOTT, YOU STAY HERE AND MAKE SURE THE WHITE CATS WIN.
SHE'LL BE HAPPIER FOR THAT.
O-OF COURSE!
...
SO FAR, SO GOOD.

ALL THAT'S LEFT IS TO CRUSH INUZUKA IN THE MOCK CAVALRY BATTLE...

...AND WE'LL BE ONE STEP CLOSER TO OUR GOAL...

YEAH.

INFIRMARY

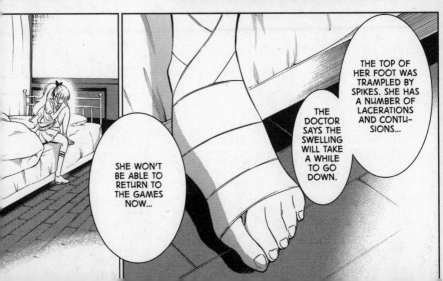

THE TOP OF HER FOOT WAS TRAMPLED BY SPIKES. SHE HAS A NUMBER OF LACERATIONS AND CONTUSIONS...

THE DOCTOR SAYS THE SWELLING WILL TAKE A WHILE TO GO DOWN.

SHE WON'T BE ABLE TO RETURN TO THE GAMES NOW...

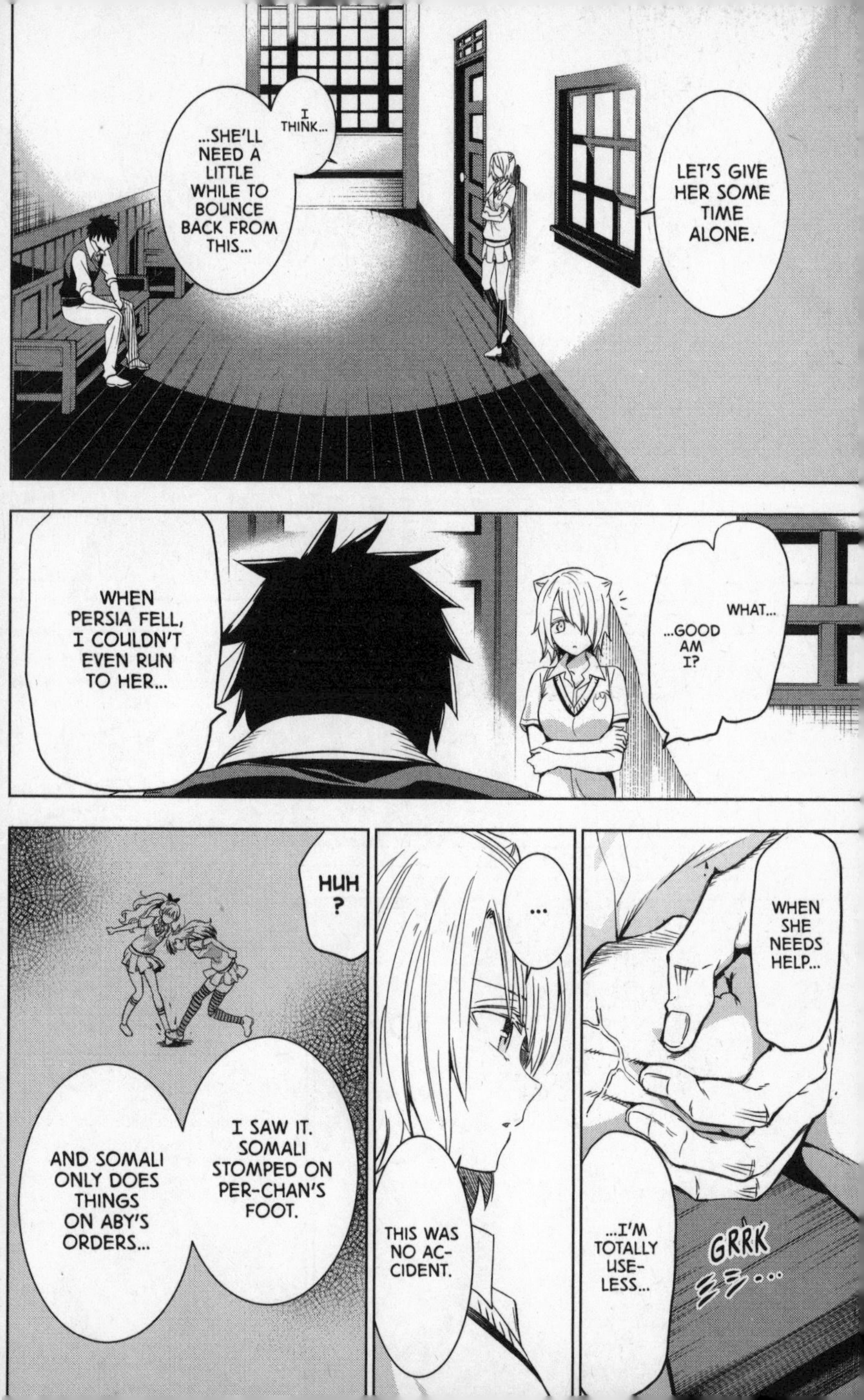
LET'S GIVE HER SOME TIME ALONE.
I THINK...
...SHE'LL NEED A LITTLE WHILE TO BOUNCE BACK FROM THIS...
WHAT...
...GOOD AM I?
WHEN PERSIA FELL, I COULDN'T EVEN RUN TO HER...
WHEN SHE NEEDS HELP...
...I'M TOTALLY USE-LESS...
GRRK
...
THIS WAS NO AC-CIDENT.
HUH?
I SAW IT. SOMALI STOMPED ON PER-CHAN'S FOOT.
AND SOMALI ONLY DOES THINGS ON ABY'S ORDERS...

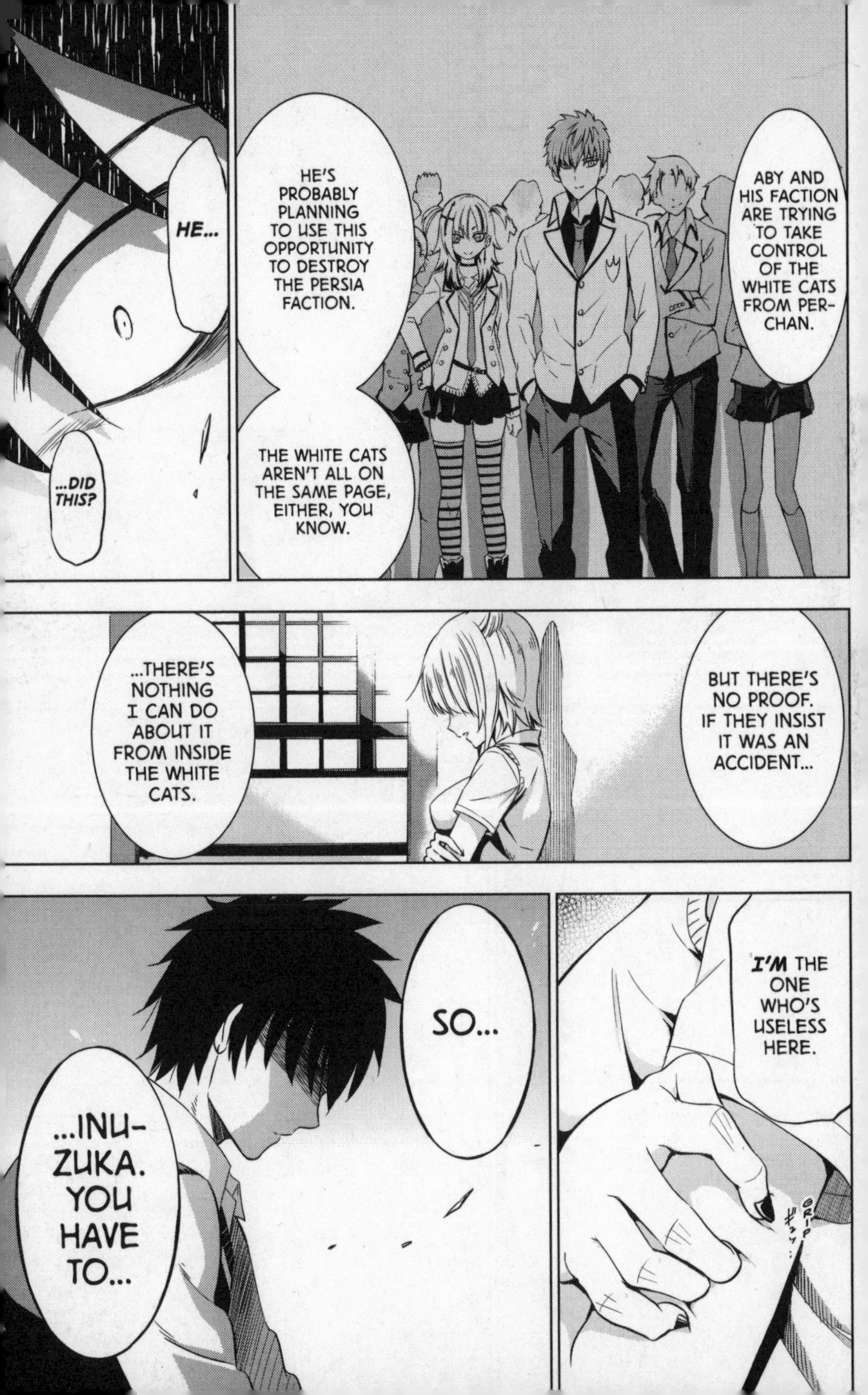
ABY AND HIS FACTION ARE TRYING TO TAKE CONTROL OF THE WHITE CATS FROM PER-CHAN.
HE'S PROBABLY PLANNING TO USE THIS OPPORTUNITY TO DESTROY THE PERSIA FACTION.
THE WHITE CATS AREN'T ALL ON THE SAME PAGE, EITHER, YOU KNOW.
HE...
...DID THIS?
BUT THERE'S NO PROOF. IF THEY INSIST IT WAS AN ACCIDENT...
...THERE'S NOTHING I CAN DO ABOUT IT FROM INSIDE THE WHITE CATS.
I'M THE ONE WHO'S USELESS HERE.
GRIP
SO...
...INU-ZUKA. YOU HAVE TO...

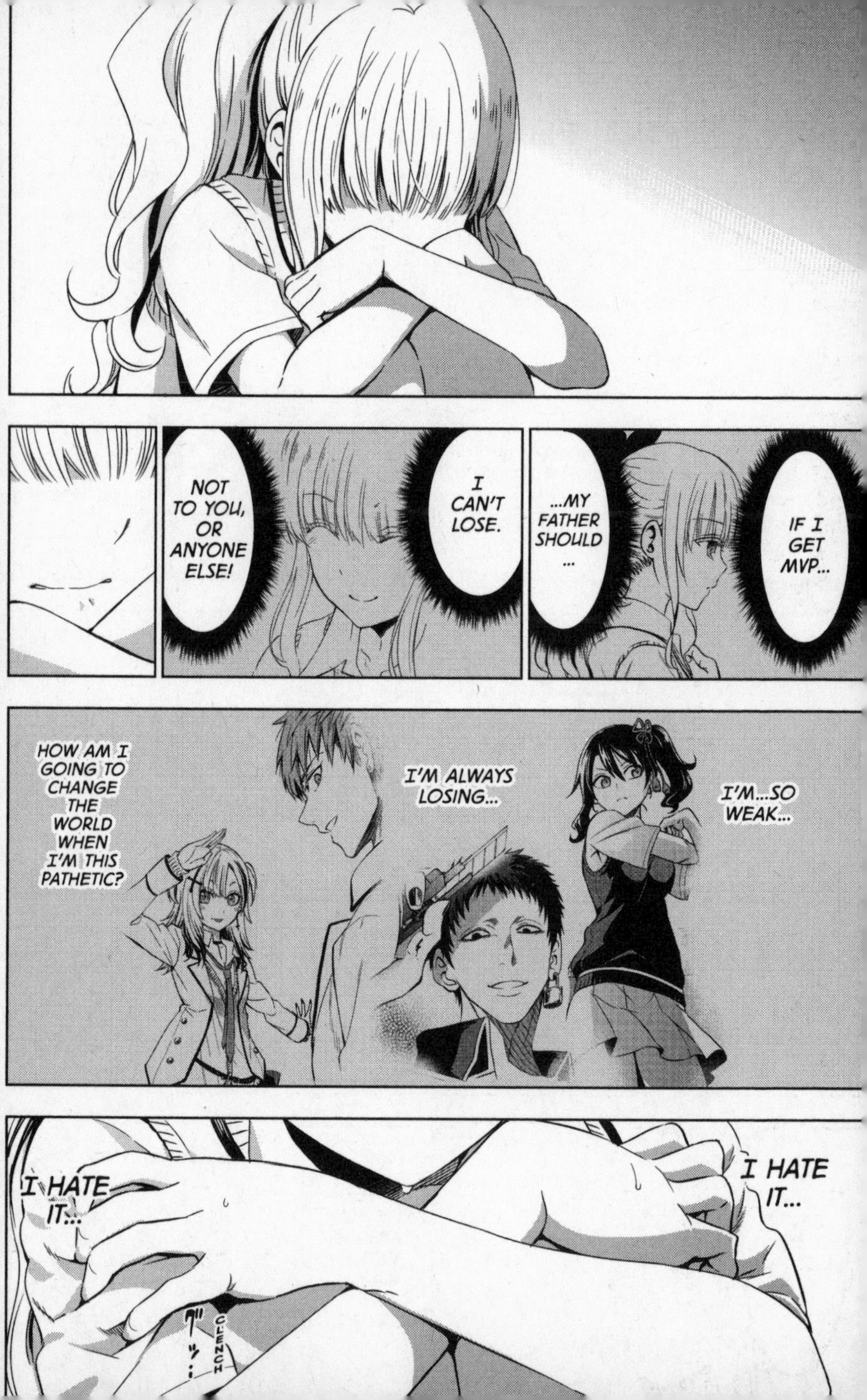
IF I GET MVP...
...MY FATHER SHOULD ...
I CAN'T LOSE.
NOT TO YOU, OR ANYONE ELSE!
I'M...SO WEAK...
I'M ALWAYS LOSING...
HOW AM I GOING TO CHANGE THE WORLD WHEN I'M THIS PATHETIC?
I HATE IT...
I HATE IT...
グッ…
CLENCH

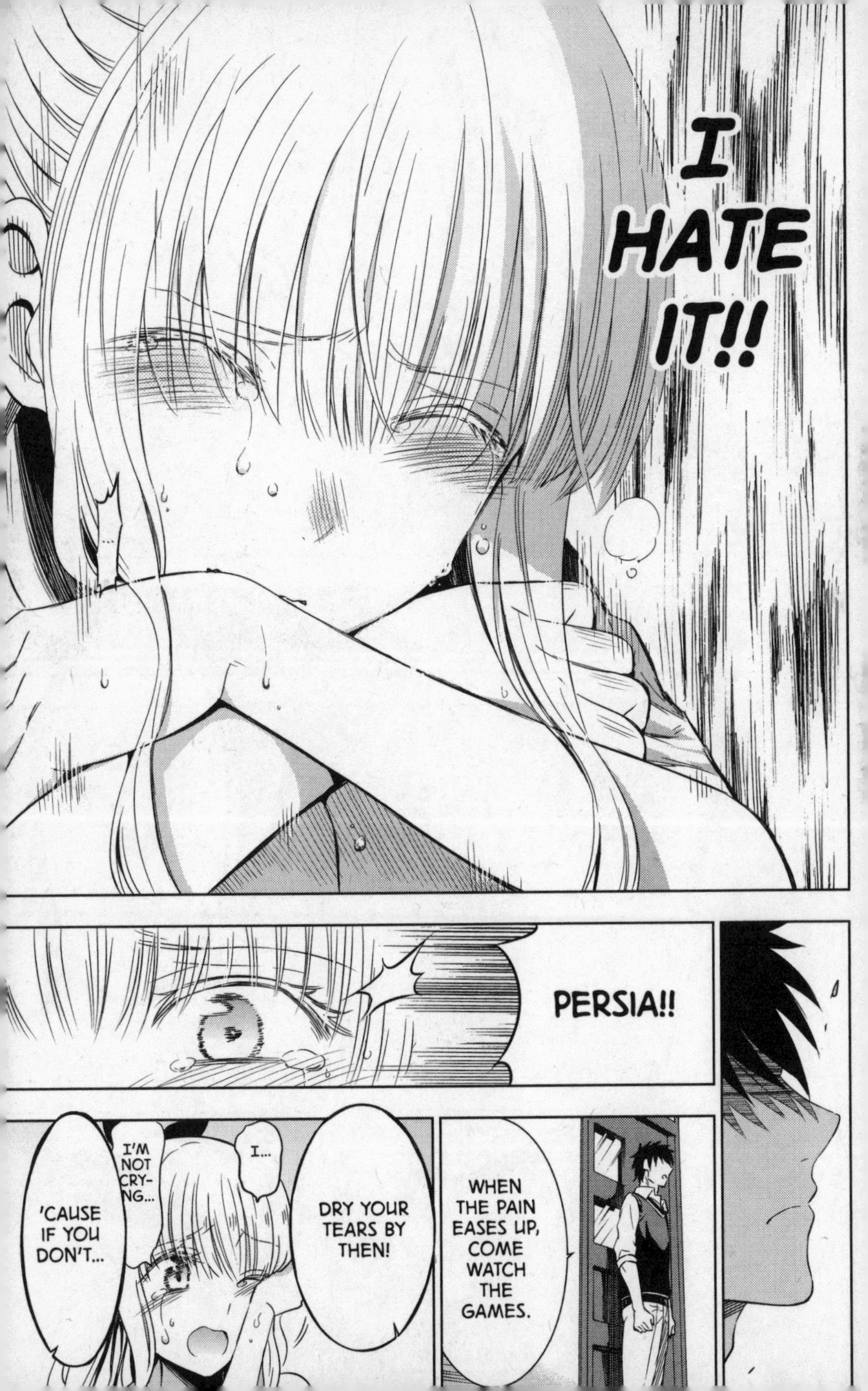
I HATE IT!!
…
PERSIA!!
WHEN THE PAIN EASES UP, COME WATCH THE GAMES.
DRY YOUR TEARS BY THEN!
I…
I'M NOT CRY-NG…
'CAUSE IF YOU DON'T…

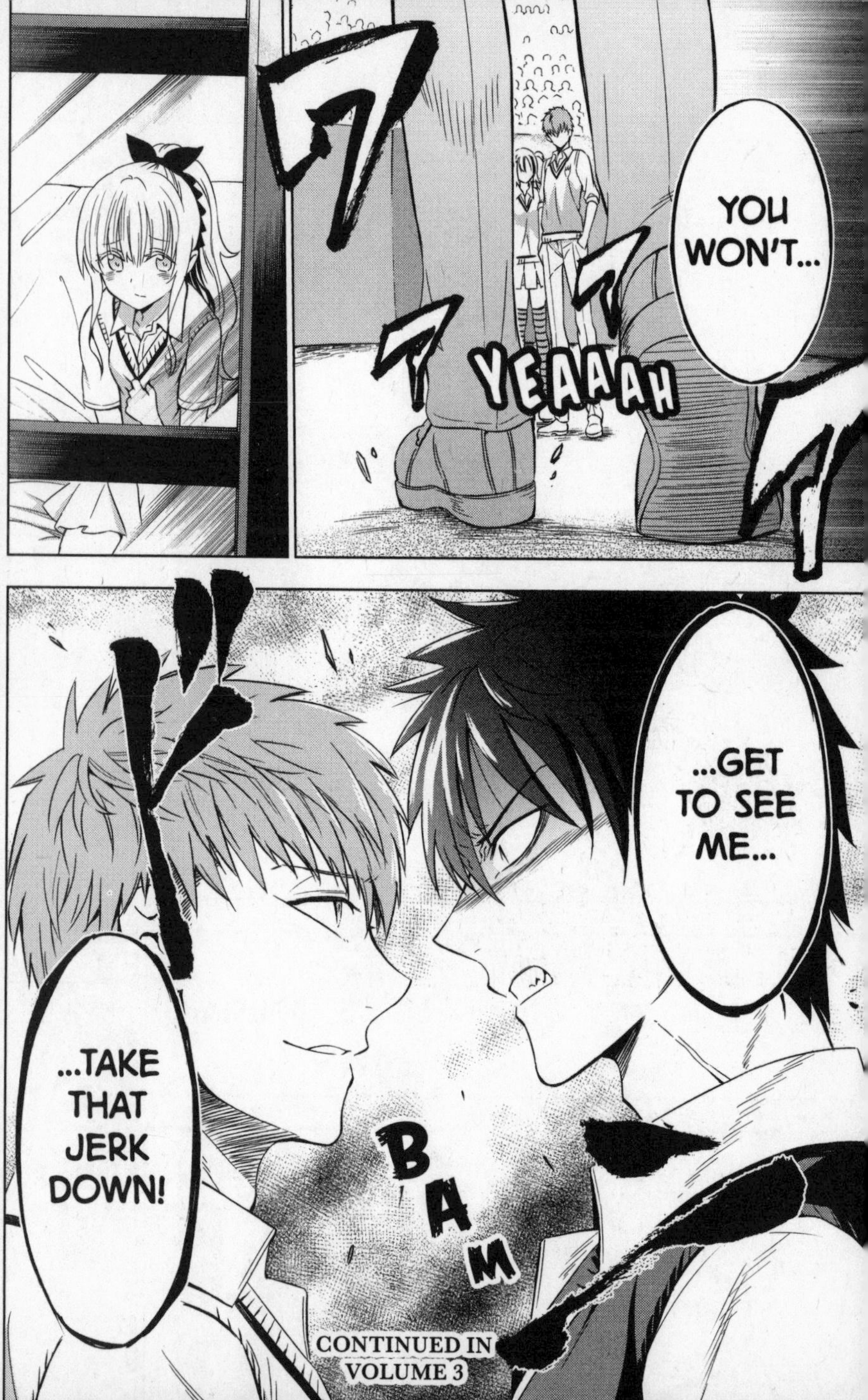
YOU WON'T...
YEAAAAH
...GET TO SEE ME...
...TAKE THAT JERK DOWN!
BAM

CONTINUED IN VOLUME 3

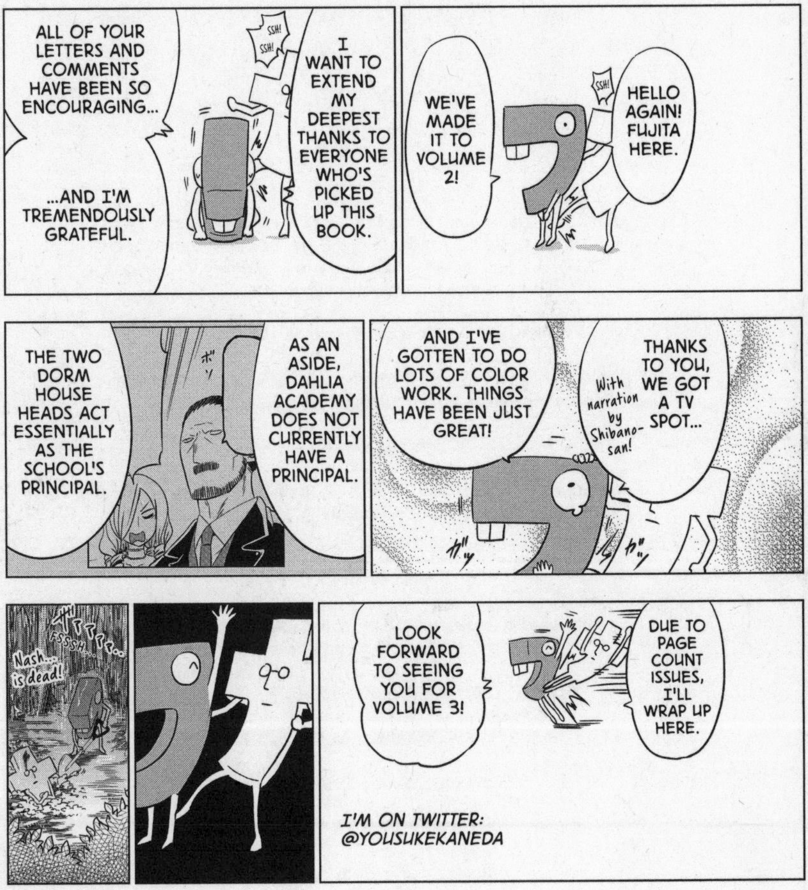
SSH!
HELLO AGAIN! FUJITA HERE.
WE'VE MADE IT TO VOLUME 2!
SSH!
SSH!
I WANT TO EXTEND MY DEEPEST THANKS TO EVERYONE WHO'S PICKED UP THIS BOOK.
ALL OF YOUR LETTERS AND COMMENTS HAVE BEEN SO ENCOURAGING...
...AND I'M TREMENDOUSLY GRATEFUL.
THANKS TO YOU, WE GOT A TV SPOT...
With narration by Shibano-san!
AND I'VE GOTTEN TO DO LOTS OF COLOR WORK. THINGS HAVE BEEN JUST GREAT!
AS AN ASIDE, DAHLIA ACADEMY DOES NOT CURRENTLY HAVE A PRINCIPAL.
THE TWO DORM HOUSE HEADS ACT ESSENTIALLY AS THE SCHOOL'S PRINCIPAL.
DUE TO PAGE COUNT ISSUES, I'LL WRAP UP HERE.
LOOK FORWARD TO SEEING YOU FOR VOLUME 3!
I'M ON TWITTER: @YOUSUKEKANEDA
FSSSH...
Nash... is dead!

Boarding School Juliet

VOLUME 3 COMING SOON!

A Kodansha Comics Trade Paperback Original.

Boarding School Juliet volume 2 copyright © 2016 Yousuke Kaneda
English translation copyright © 2018 Yousuke Kaneda

Published in the United States by Kodansha Comics,
an imprint of Kodansha USA Publishing, LLC, New York.

Publication rights for this English edition arranged through
Kodansha Ltd., Tokyo.

First published in Japan in 2016 by Kodansha Ltd., Tokyo, as
Kishuku Gakkou no Jurietto volume 2.

ISBN 978-1-63236-752-5

Printed in the United States of America.

www.kodanshacomics.com

9 8 7 6 5 4 3 2 1

Translation: Amanda Haley
Lettering: James Dashiell
Editing: Erin Subramanian and Paul Starr
Kodansha Comics edition cover design: Phil Balsman